The Locksmith Craft
in Early Modern Edinburgh

The Locksmith Craft in Early Modern Edinburgh

A. M. Allen

Edinburgh 2007
SOCIETY OF ANTIQUARIES OF SCOTLAND

Cover images: Jost Amman & Hans Sachs, 'Der Schlosser' and 'Der Uhrmacher', in *Ständebuch* (Frankfurt am Main, 1568); 'Schlosser' (1528) in *Hausbuch der Mendelschen Zwölfbrüderstiftung* (Nürnberg, 1388 – 1799); NMS locks and keys: MJ 69, MJ 49, MJ 8, K 2002.432 (courtesy of the Trustees of the National Museum of Scotland)
End papers: James Gordon, *Edinodunensis Tabulam…*1647 [NLS shelfmark: EMS.s.52] (courtesy of the Trustees of the National Library of Scotland)

Published in 2007 by Society of Antiquaries of Scotland

Society of Antiquaries of Scotland, Royal Museum of Scotland,
Chambers Street, Edinburgh EH1 1JF
Tel 0131 247 4115
Fax 0131 247 4163
Email admin@socantscot.org
Website www.soctantscot.org

British Library Cataloguing-in-Publication Data
A catalogue record for this book is available from the British Library.

ISBN 10: 0 903903 44 X
ISBN 13: 978 0 903903 44 8

Copyright © Aaron M Allen, 2007

All rights reserved. No part of this publication may be reproduced, stored in or introduced into a retrieval system, or transmitted, in any form, or by any means (electronic, mechanical, photocopying, recording or otherwise) without the prior written permission of the publisher. Any person who does any unauthorised act in relation to this publication may be liable to criminal prosecution and civil claims for damages.

The Society gratefully acknowledges grant-aid towards the publication of this volume from the Incorporation of Hammermen of Edinburgh.

Typeset in Bembo by Waverley Typesetters, Fakenham
Designed by Lawrie Law and Alison Rae
Manufactured in Spain

Contents

List of figures	vii
List of tables and charts	ix
Conventions	xi
Introduction	1
By Hammer in Hand: The Edinburgh Incorporation of Hammermen	5
The Crafts and Craftsmen	24
The Locksmith Craft	61
The Locksmiths' Workplace	90
The Locksmiths' Work	107
Summary	162
Appendix: 1483 Seal of Cause	166
Glossary	168
Bibliography	169
Index	174

List of figures

3.1	Guild board from 1595 showing the relationship in Ulm, Germany, of the locksmiths, gunsmiths and clockmakers	62
3.2	A Parisian gunsmith's shop, *c.* 1660	72
3.3	*Der Uhrmacher*, 1568	77
3.4	Stocking knitters, 1698	79
4.1	Detail of stonework above North doorway to Heriot's Hospital, showing a goldsmith's booth, *c.* 1630	92
4.2	Floor plan of Mossman's Land (John Knox House) in 1600 showing four booths	93
4.3	A locksmith's shop in 1528 – Nürnberg, Germany	94
4.4	A locksmith's booth in 1568 – Nürnberg, Germany	94
4.5	A locksmith's booth in 1698 – Nürnberg, Germany	95
4.6	Moxon's illustration of a smith's forge from 1678	97
4.7	Diderot's picture of a hand lathe for boring pipe keys	100
5.1	Sprent band for a chest lock dated 1664. England.	110
5.2	Boss lock – *serrure à bosse*. France – *c.* 1751	110
5.3	Wall anchors shown in cutaway illustration)	114
5.4	Moxon's illustration of a spring lock from 1678	116
5.5	Large iron door lock	123
5.6	Back of large iron door lock	123
5.7	Plate from Monceau's *Art Du Serrurier*, 1767	126
5.8	X-rays of padlocks	128
5.9	X-rays of padlock 'MJ 19', front view with key in four different positions	130–1
5.10	Front of chest lock. Seventeenth century?	133
5.11	Door jamb with original sneckhead. From Mylne's Court, Lawnmarket, Edinburgh	135
5.12	Keys	137
5.13	Keys	137
5.14	Keys	137
5.15	Lock and keys	138
5.16	Key	138
5.17	Keys	138
5.18	Keys	139
5.19	Keys	139
5.20	Keys	140
5.21	Keys	140
5.22	Datable keys – 1627, *c.* 1660, *c.* 1810	140
5.23	Belt loop and keys	141
5.24	Belt loops	141
5.25	Key	141
5.26	Deacon Brodie's picks	142
5.27	Deacon Brodie's picks	142
5.28	Deacon Brodie's picks	142
5.29	Deacon Brodie's picks – detail showing thread wrapped around tops of bits	143

5.30	Key	143
5.31	Keys	143
5.32	Keys	144
5.33	Keys	144
5.34	Keys. 1812	144
5.35	Keys	145
5.36	Keys	145
5.37	Keys	145
5.38	Group of keys	146
5.39	Door lock (front and back)	146
5.40	Door lock and plate stock lock	147
5.41	Door lock and plate stock lock	147
5.42	Plate stock lock	147
5.43	Stock lock	148
5.44	Stock lock	148
5.45	Stock lock	148
5.46	Stock lock	149
5.47	Stock lock	149
5.48	Stock lock	149
5.49	Stock lock	150
5.50	Stock lock	150
5.51	Stock-lock keys	150
5.52	Stock-lock keys	151
5.53	Stock lock and stock-lock keys	151
5.54	One pipe and two stock-lock keys	152
5.55	Padlocks	152
5.56	Barrel padlocks	153
5.57	Padlocks	153
5.58	Padlocks	154
5.59	Boss padlocks	154
5.60	Padlocks	154
5.61	Padlock	155
5.62	Padlock	155
5.63	Padlocks	155
5.64	Padlock	156
5.65	Padlocks	156
5.66	Padlocks	157
5.67	Chest or kist locks	157
5.68	Chest or kist lock	157
5.69	Chest or kist locks	158
5.70	Chest or kist locks	158
5.71	Cabinet lock	159
5.72	Cabinet lock	159

List of tables and charts

List of tables

1.0	Dates of seals of cause	7
1.1	Original crafts	7
1.2	Later crafts	8
1.3	Examples of wares made by hammermen trades in 1483	9
1.4	Hammermen attaining burgess-ship	15
1.5	Smith group attaining burgess-ship	15
1.6	Percentage of overall incorporation of hammermen	16
1.7	Hammermen in suburbs	17
1.8	Hammermen trades in suburbs	17
1.9	Tax of every hundred pounds	18
1.10	Numbers of Edinburgh hammermen masters	20
2.0	Hammermen lists stating trade: numbers of masters	26
2.1	Number of apprenticeships booked	31
2.2	Apprentices' place of origin	31
2.3	Comparison of incoming masters (shown by burgess-ship) and apprentices	32
2.4	Method of attaining guildry	41
2.5	Cost of guildry	44
2.6	Hammermen attaining guildry	45
2.7	Percentage of freeman hammermen attaining guildry	46
2.8	Rank of hammermen crafts attaining guildry	47
2.9	Hammermen groupings and guildry	49
2.10	Deacons of the Edinburgh Incorporation of Hammermen	50–5
2.11	Number of times elected deacon 1494–1750	56
2.12	Number of times elected boxmaster 1600–1750	56
3.0	Edinburgh locksmiths	64
3.1	Edinburgh locksmiths and trades joined with them	64
3.2	Whitelaw's four types of gunlocks	69
3.3	General typology of gunlocks used in Edinburgh	69
3.4	Approximate number of parts of gunlocks	71
3.5	Edinburgh freeman locksmiths list (partial)	81–4
3.6	Edinburgh knockmakers/watchmakers list (partial)	85–6
3.7	Edinburgh freeman dagmakers/gunsmith list (partial)	87
5.0	Locksmiths' essay	108–9
5.1	Sample of prices for locksmiths' products	112
5.2	Sample of prices for locksmiths' services	112
5.3	Daily wages in shillings	113
5.4	Price of wheatbread	113
5.5	NMS locks and keys	119

5.6	NMS locks and keys percentages	119
5.7	NMS keys percentages	119
5.8	NMS padlock types percentages	119
5.9	NMS keys	120
5.10	NMS door locks	122
5.11	NMS padlocks	125
5.12	NMS barrel padlocks	125

List of charts

1.0	Hammermen attaining burgess-ship	19
1.1	Freemen population	21
3.0	Growth rates – burgess rolls	63
3.1	Edinburgh locksmiths and trades joined with them	65
3.2	Populations of the locksmiths and those trades joined with them	66
3.3	Number of gunlock parts	71
5.0	NMS Scottish sample	134
5.1	NMS foreign sample	134

Conventions

The spelling has been modernized where appropriate. The British style is used, except for citations of North American book titles. The occasional Scots word is left where it emphasizes the text, or is not found in the *Concise Scots Dictionary*.[1] The crafts had their own jargon, which is not always decipherable. The dates have been given as stated in the original sources. Prior to 1 January 1600, the new year started on 25 March. In the text, the years will all be deemed to start on 1 January for clarity. Henceforth, 24 February 1567–8 will be simply given as 24 February 1568. The Scots monetary system for accounts consists mainly of pence (d), shillings (s) and pounds (£).

Prices are given in Scots, unless otherwise stated. The Scots pound was a money of account only; no physical pound coin existed in early modern Scotland. One English pound sterling was equal to about £4 10s Scots in 1560. The French crown was equal to £1 6s 8d Scots. In 1601 the English pound was worth £12 Scots and the French crown was worth £3 6s 8d Scots.[2] The actual coin conversions in Scots for the seventeenth century are as follows:[3]

$$
\begin{aligned}
2d &= 1 \text{ bodle} \\
2 \text{ bodles} &= 1 \text{ plack} \\
3 \text{ bodles} &= 1 \text{ bawbee} \\
2 \text{ bawbees} &= 12d = 1s \\
13s\ 4d &= 1 \text{ merk} \\
20s &= £1 \\
3 \text{ merks} &= £2 \\
1s \text{ Scots} &= 1d \text{ sterling}
\end{aligned}
$$

NOTES

[1] Robinson 1992.
[2] Goodare 1999, Conventions and Abbreviations. See also, Gilbert 1977.
[3] This is based on Robinson 1992, 817.

Introduction

While there were several studies of Scottish craft guilds or publications of their records around the first half of the twentieth century, research in more recent times has been exceedingly limited. Lately, there has been much analysis done on the merchant communities in Scotland, but it has been claimed that 'there has been only one recent study of a craft occupation but this, because it deals with one of the smallest and humblest of the guilds [in Edinburgh], has little light to shed on general occupational patterns'.[1] This refers to Dr Bennett's 1981 PhD thesis on the Edinburgh Incorporation of Bonnetmakers.[2] While other studies have been made since, notably two excellent books on the surgeons[3] and goldsmiths,[4] the majority of recent craft research has been more general in topic, dealing mainly with occupational structure or demography.[5] Detailed work on specific crafts has been severely underdeveloped.

In 1906, John Smith published a book on the Incorporation of Hammermen of Edinburgh which printed the records of this guild, the largest of the fourteen crafts, up to c. 1560.[6] The following study was based on a MSc and PhD which were meant to continue Smith's research. In the process, the field was narrowed down to one specific branch of the Incorporation of Hammermen: the locksmiths. Locksmiths were found in most towns and all cities across early modern Europe. The period considered is from 1483, when the metalworkers were incorporated, to 1750, which is an arbitrarily chosen point, before which Edinburgh was an increasingly demanding consumer society, but which predates the new technology prompted by the Industrial Revolution. In this period, locks were still being made using the medieval technology of warding. Edinburgh was not wholly typical of Scottish burghs;[7] if any generalizations can be made from this survey, they are more applicable to the European urban experience, as no other Scottish burghs came close to Edinburgh's size. While Edinburgh had fourteen incorporated trades, no other Scottish burgh had more than nine.[8] The intent is to get a better understanding of what was a fundamental trade in the European urban environment before industrialization changed the structure of craft-production.

So why the locksmiths? There were many trades in early modern Edinburgh that warrant studying, fourteen of which were incorporated. There are minute books for several of the incorporated trades held by either the Edinburgh City Archives, the National Archives of Scotland, or the Trades Maiden Hospital.[9] There are numerous foreign sources on other trades that would give much insight into the processes involved for baxters baking bread, or skinners processing hides. The impetus for doing research on the locksmith craft was the combination of complete minute books from 1494 to present and the remarkable surviving material culture in the collections of the National Museum of Scotland.

The Incorporation of Hammermen was an important craft. Tax rolls and demographics show that they were one of the larger and wealthier of Edinburgh's crafts.[10] The research in this study shows that the locksmiths were in the higher echelon of the hammermen. Locks and keys were an important part of the early-modern metalwares market. In 1580, when England was kitting out a ship to be sent to Japan, various items were included to impress upon the Japanese magnates how sophisticated England's products were. Included were, 'locks and keys, hinges, bolts, hasps, &c., great and small, of excellent workmanship'.[11]

The significance of keys was not lost on governmental officials in the early modern period. As Gerald Strauss pointed out in his book, *Nuremberg in the 16th Century*, the 'two Losunger exercise the highest honour and dignity, for to them are entrusted the keys to Nuremberg's treasury'.[12] Keys were a way of granting access, and therefore a symbol of prominence.

It should not be assumed that because Scotland was not a rich country by European standards, that the metalwork done here was inferior. For example, Scottish pistols were often given to foreign dignitaries; Louis XIII of France owned a pair of Scottish pistols.[13] Scotland's craftsmen were not primitive, and the locksmiths were among the most skilled.

The research for this book on the locksmiths included several disciplines. The crafts fall under both social and urban history. Because this is a study of a single town, it is also local history. As one of the most important types of evidence is the surviving objects, material culture is also heavily relied on. By using several approaches, a clearer picture of the everyday life of a locksmith in a European capital is pieced together.

The main primary sources were the records of the Incorporation of Hammermen and the surviving material culture in museums. The Incorporation of Hammermen's minute books are in the Edinburgh City Archives.[14] They consist of fourteen volumes, and are extant from 1494 to the twentieth century. The minute books from 1494 to c. 1560 have been partially transcribed for us by John Smith, and can be found in his book, *The Hammermen of Edinburgh and their Altar in St. Giles Church*.[15] There are a few areas in Smith's transcription that may not be exactly as written in the original, but they are meant only to be excerpts. The National Museum of Scotland have in their archives Charles Whitelaw's notes on arms and armour. Included is a partial transcription of the minute books from c. 1500 to 1662.[16] These also are only excerpts, and not always in chronological order.

A drawback to the original minute books is that they can be quite vague. The person who wrote them knew the minor details that connected the words he wrote with the real-life happenings of the Incorporation. As a result, some entries consist only of a few names with little description. Others go into great detail. They are very much the random notes of meetings based on knowledge in the clerk's head. Some of the pages are numbered; others are not. Where possible, the page number is given in the citations.

This does not mean that the minute books are without merit; they are filled with interesting social details. One example is a reference to a payment for ale provided to builders who were working on a property owned by the Incorporation. Beer was seen as a food source in the early modern period, even on the job.[17] Other interesting social details include the emphasis on religion, which was key to the formation of many of the craft guilds in the pre-Reformation minutes. The first volume of the minute books deals almost completely with the religious aspects of a craftsman's life. As was noted of Aberdeen's pre-Reformation church, 'ecclesiastical institutions ... formed part of the rich pattern of foundation, endowment and patronage which linked each constituent part of local society ...'[18] Many pre-Reformation entries in the hammermen's minutes deal with Saint Eloi's Day, the production of banners, and the saying of mass. There are often entries of candles being purchased for St Eloi's altar in the St Giles' Kirk. In the first part of the first volume, no essays were delineated. After the Reformation this changed. More technical detail was added. One example is an entry from 1586 in the second minute book, which gives a locksmith's essay to become a freeman of the Incorporation: 'ane kist lock'.[19] After the Reformation, business matters dominate the minutes of the meetings. Religion was always present though, as can be seen by pre-meeting prayers and the craftsmen's oaths before God; the pre-Reformation sense of a corpus christianum was replaced by a godly body which called itself 'the house'.

There are also other documents relating to the hammermen in the Edinburgh City Archives. There are sasines, charters and instruments.[20] There are treasurer's accounts and ledgers.[21] There are various kinds of correspondences, memorials, vouchers[22] and 'miscellaneous volumes' from 1566 to 1865.[23] Unfortunately, not all of the documents survived up to the modern day. The minute book for 1749 makes a reference to a separate book for listing the names of the journeymen.[24] Today its whereabouts are unknown.

Other than the records of the Incorporation of Hammermen, the most important primary source for this study was the surviving material culture. The three best sources for this were the National Museum of Scotland's collection of locks and keys,[25] Joseph Moxon's *Mechanick Excercises* (1678), and Ivor Noël Hume's indispensable book, *A Guide to Artifacts of Colonial America*.

Moxon's book was published in 1678 – the same year as his election to be a fellow of the Royal Society of London for Improving Natural Knowledge. His book set out to record the mechanic arts. In the process he left one of the best accounts of seventeenth-century locksmithing techniques in English.[26]

Hume, a twentieth-century archaeologist, wrote what is arguably still the best resource for British/ North American material culture. Of particular interest was his in-depth section on locks and keys based on his personal experience with excavations of colonial sites.[27] There is an emphasis on stock locks and padlocks – two of the more prevalent objects in the NMS sample.

Where possible, correlations were drawn with European locksmiths, based on a wide variety of primary and secondary sources, including museum displays and collections in Germany, Sweden, the

INTRODUCTION

Czech Republic, England, Norway and several other countries. They are cited in the text and bibliography.

NOTES

[1] Lynch 1987, 3.
[2] Bennett 1981 (thesis).
[3] Dingwall 1995.
[4] Dalgleish & Maxwell 1987.
[5] Such as McMillan 1984 (thesis), Makey 1987, Whyte 1987 and Dingwall 1994.
[6] There is a little material from later than 1560, though it is not comprehensive. There are also a few inaccuracies. Smith 1906, 181.
[7] Torrie 1988.
[8] Lynch 1987, 9.
[9] For example, the Edinburgh City Archives hold the minute books for the hammermen, skinners and baxters, while there are several volumes at the Trades Maiden Hospital, including the minute books for the bonnetmakers.
[10] Lynch 1988, 274 and 276 and Dingwall 1994, 77.
[11] Milton 2002, 44.
[12] Strauss 1966, 62.
[13] Kelvin 1996, 110.
[14] ECA ED008/1.
[15] Smith 1906.
[16] NMS Whitelaw EHMB.
[17] ECA ED008/1/5.
[18] White 1987, 89.
[19] Smith 1906 and ECA ED008/1/2, 44.
[20] ECA ED008/2.
[21] Ibid., ED008/3.
[22] Ibid., ED008/5.
[23] Ibid., ED008/4.
[24] Ibid., ED008/1/8, 6 May 1749.
[25] NMS MJ, MK, K2002, L.
[26] Moxon 1989.
[27] Hume 1969, 243–52.

Chapter 1

By Hammer in Hand:
The Edinburgh Incorporation of Hammermen

The locksmith craft was not an independent entity in the burgh structure, but instead a branch of a hierarchical group of metalworkers known as the Incorporation of Hammermen, which was itself part of a greater urban framework. To appreciate where the Edinburgh locksmiths fit into early modern society, we must first look at the structures that governed the social and business aspects of burgh life. After looking at the origins of the incorporated trades and in particular the Incorporation of Hammermen, it will be beneficial to review the burgh hierarchy to which the hammermen subscribed. With this general background, it will be easier to understand the hammermen's and in turn, the locksmiths' roles in the early modern capital of Scotland. How influential were the hammermen? What patterns of growth and decline are visible in the surviving records for the hammermen as a whole?

RISE OF THE INCORPORATED TRADES

The incorporated trades have their origins in the older Edinburgh guild system. The word 'guild' is an Anglo-Saxon word which means payment or contribution to a common fund. This early guild was a fraternal body which was given a monopoly in a particular town for the buying of raw materials and regulation of trade. It was set up to protect the guild brethren from receiving too little money for goods and services, while at the same time protecting the consumers against fraudulent dealers.[1] They minimized external competition by controlling who had the right to sell or produce goods in the town and prevented internal competition amongst guild members.[2] It is generally accepted that the 'Statuta Guilde' of Berwick, which dates from 1249 to 1295, acted as the model for the guilds of the other Scottish burghs,[3] but the guild seems to have been in the burghs before this. Marwick points out that their existence in Edinburgh is mentioned in an enactment of the 'Laws of the Four Burghs', basically stating that dyers, fleshers, shoemakers and fishers should not be in the merchant guild unless they abstained from the practice of their trade with their own hands and conducted it exclusively by servants. As the 'Laws of the Four Burghs' predate the 'Statuta Guilde', it would appear that Berwick's guild statutes served as a guide for revamping an older guild structure.[4] Guilds were known in England as early as 688 AD.[5] It is hard to be sure when guilds first appeared in Scotland, but many burghs had a merchant guild by the fifteenth century.

It would appear that there was also some organization of craftsmen. In 1469 James III (1460–88) passed a statute to regulate the election of burgh officers, empowering each craft to 'choose a person of the same craft, that shall have voice in the said election of the officers for that time, in likewise year by year'.[6] Each individual craft was a separate group, with limited voice in burgh affairs.

It was not until the fourteenth century that Edinburgh achieved the importance we now associate with it. Before Edinburgh's ascendancy, Berwick was Scotland's most important town due to its lucrative cloth and wool industries.[7] When Berwick became a permanent English possession, trade shifted north to Edinburgh, which became the economic and political centre of Scotland.[8]

As Edinburgh grew and prospered, the merchant guild became more powerful, which caused friction with the craftsmen. Wages were fixed and craftsmen were required to have their work inspected. The craftsmen were expected to share in burgh duties, but were deprived of certain guild privileges. Guild brethren were not allowed to dirty their hands by working; they could only be employers.[9] This barred the majority of craftsmen from joining the guild. Some merchants abused their guild privileges by bringing in cheaply produced wares from craftsmen outside the burgh, which hurt Edinburgh craftsmen's business. They started to feel resentment towards the guild. While there is some contention over the extent to which the burghs polarized into merchants versus craftsmen, by the fifteenth century there was strong enough feeling that the craftsmen started banding together to protect their interests. Many of these interests were economic in nature. For example, when the Incorporation of Hammermen received their 1483 seal of cause, it listed several complaints: the 'down coming of the black money', walking and warding, payment of yields and extents, and 'that they were havely hurt be the daily market made through the high street in crames and on the backside the town in bachling of hammermen's work'.[10]

The 'down coming of black money' referred to a copper coinage which was introduced in the 1460s. Copper coins were a revolutionary step at the time and severely unpopular with the Scots. Due to public outcry in 1482, the currency was 'cried down', meaning that it was either demonetised or devalued to the value of a farthing. This 'down coming' probably would not have hurt the affluent of Edinburgh as much as it did the craftsmen. It clearly touched the metalworkers.[11]

Walking and warding, or town watch duties, took valuable time from the hammermen, while the payment of taxes has never been popular. The reference to crames, which were stalls where goods were sold, indicates the hammermen's desire for a monopoly on metalwares. Small merchants were selling types of wares that the craftsmen were trying to make their living from.

The craftsmen formed themselves into craft guilds, by incorporating all like crafts into one 'incorporated trade'. In the case of the Edinburgh Incorporation of Hammermen, the blacksmiths, goldsmiths, lorimers, saddlers, cutlers, buckler makers and armourers banded together.[12] These trades all dealt with an aspect of metalware production or hammered work. The woodwork and building trades, such as the coopers, wrights and masons, formed themselves into the Incorporation of Mary's Chapel.[13] Other burghs also formed such incorporated trades. This process, which happened in cities across Europe in the later medieval period, has been labelled 'corporatism' by modern historians.

Corporatism was a new approach to the theory and organization of work. One recent description of corporatism states that it

> laid out organizing principles which shaped social, political, as well as economic, organization, embracing the principles of paternalism, hierarchy, and discipline in the social and political realm, and the economic principle of containing competition to preserve the livelihood of artisans and channel quality goods to the consuming public at a fair price.[14]

Whether in the form of *corps*, *handwerken*, companies, or incorporations, by the beginning of the early modern period craft guilds had gone through subtle but significant changes. They were more politicized and more hierarchical than the previous guilds.[15]

Incorporation, which was Scotland's label for the corporate structure, served both the craftsmen and the burgh officials. Craftsmen were given a degree of autonomy to regulate prices and quality of their products. They were given the privilege of electing their deacon, or kirkmaster, who was the head of the craft for that year. By 1551 they had two seats on the town council and, with the 1583 decreet arbitral, six seats and theoretical equality to the merchants.[16] As Lynch points out, the town council in return got a deacon and political system to use as a means of controlling the craftsmen and ensuring burgh peace.[17] Stereotypically being young and restless, journeymen and apprentices were often a cause for concern in early modern urban society.[18] With the incorporations in place, the council could depend on the craft deacons to make them behave through economic pressure. If they misbehaved, they could be fined or barred from work. The burgh also got quality control standards for the wares produced by the crafts.

The crafts were also allowed to hold meetings. The focal point of the Incorporation of Hammermen was its meeting house in the Cowgate, the Magdalen Chapel. Before this, the incorporation met at either St Leonards or Blackfriars.[19] In 1553 the chapel's patron Janet Rynd passed away. By 1563 the Magdalen Chapel was bequeathed to the Incorporation of Hammermen and became their centre of administration.[20] Groups of people congregating could be seen as dangerous by the council, but the incorporations had meeting houses where they held meetings under the supervision of the deacon and masters. In this manner the meetings were in a semi-controlled, structured environment.

Other benefits came with incorporation, such as the extensive charity network. Before the Reformation, one aspect of this charity was the care of altars set up in St Giles' Kirk, along with chaplains, for prayers to patron saints. Saint Eloi was the patron saint of hammermen. Once a week, their chaplain would collect a penny from each craftsman for the upkeep of the altar. Around 1500, this was changed to a quarterly contribution, with the Sunday collection becoming a free-will donation.[21] This money was a form of charity, as it provided daily access for the craftsmen and their kin to an altar for the worship of God through St Eloi. They could pray for the souls of loved ones and in this way attain comfort in times of grief.[22]

Another aspect of the incorporations' charity was the aid given to craftsmen's families, widows and orphans. In the seventeenth and eighteenth centuries, the incorporations would give quarterly pensions and extended charities to decrepit craftsmen, or their widows and orphans.[23] At times, the crafts would reaffirm their charity publicly, as in March 1580 when all the crafts of Edinburgh promised to 'take and sufficiently sustain and uphold from begging their own poor, sic as are failed craftsmen, with their wives, bairns and servants'.[24] Sometimes this was in payments to widows for living expenses and other times it was in the usage of a tenement. Often it was aid in funeral costs. Sometimes there was no specific destination for the charity. In 1740 the house appointed and ordained 'the deacon and treasurer to buy two more deals of coals and two more pecks of meal to be distributed to such persons and by such proportions as the deacon in his discretion [thought] proper'.[25] Obligation to the brethren of the craft seems to have parallels with the kinship system of more rural areas of Scotland.

In order for the craftsmen to gain incorporated status, they sought support and recognition from the burgh officials. This support was granted in the form of seals of cause. The seal of cause was a charter given to the body of craftsmen stating that they had certain rights dealing with the regulation of their specific trade. The first trade in Edinburgh to receive a seal of cause was the Incorporation of Hatmakers in 1473.[26] They were followed by the skinners in 1474, Mary's Chapel and the websters, or weavers, in 1475 and the cordwainers in 1479.[27]

TABLE 1.0
Dates of seals of cause (From Marwick, Colston and Smith)

Incorporation	Date of seal of cause
Hatmakers	1473
Skinners	1474
Mary's Chapel	1475
Websters (weavers)	1475
Cordwainers	1479
Hammermen	1483
Fleshers	1490
Waulkers	1500
Tailors	1500
Chirurgeons/Barbers	1505
Candlemakers	1517
Baxters (bakers)	1522–3
Bonnet-makers	1530
Goldsmiths	1581

Over the early modern period other crafts would be incorporated, as can be seen in the table above. These incorporations were not static entities; crafts broke away from their incorporations, as was the case of the goldsmiths leaving the Incorporation of Hammermen and receiving their own seal of cause in 1581.[28] The bonnetmakers departed from the waulkers in 1520. Other trades joined, such as the Incorporation of Hatters, which incorporated with

TABLE 1.1
Original crafts (Marwick 1909, Colston 1891 and Smith 1906)

Incorporation	Crafts incorporated at date of seal of cause
Baxters (bakers)	Baxters
Hatmakers	Hatmakers
Skinners	Skinners
Mary's Chapel	Wrights, Masons
Websters (weavers)	Websters
Cordwainers	Cordwainers
Hammermen	Blacksmiths, Goldsmiths, Lorimers, Saddlers, Cutlers, Buckler Makers, Armourers
Fleshers	Fleshers
Waulkers	Waulkers
Tailors	Tailors
Chirurgeons/Barbers	Chirurgeons, Barbers
Candlemakers	Candlemakers
Bonnet-makers	Bonnet-makers
Goldsmiths	Goldsmiths

TABLE 1.2
Later crafts (Marwick 1909, Colston 1891 and Smith 1906)

Incorporation	Crafts Incorporated Later
Baxters (bakers)	
Hatmakers	
Skinners	Furriers, Glovers
Mary's Chapel	
Websters (weavers)	
Cordwainers	
Hammermen	Locksmiths, Gunsmiths, Knockmakers, Pewterers, White-ironmen, Founders, etc.
Fleshers	Fishmongers, Poulterers
Waulkers	Shearmen, Hatmakers, Bonnet-makers (separated in 1530)
Tailors	
Chirurgeons/Barbers	
Candlemakers	
Bonnet-makers	Litsters, Dyers
Goldsmiths	Jewellers

the waulkers in 1672. From 1473 to 1523, more than twenty-one different craft occupations existed in the incorporated trades of Edinburgh. As the urban economy expanded and diversified, new occupations were absorbed into the older structures, in respect to work-types. Watchmakers, pewterers, gunsmiths and white-ironsmiths joined the hammermen. Poulterers and fishmongers were under the Incorporation of Fleshers. Furriers and glovers joined the skinners. To the wrights and masons were added the coopers, bowers, glaziers, plumbers, upholsterers, painters, slaters and sievewrights.[29] Incorporations were dynamic entities, formed of common trades banding together out of common interest to protect trade privileges, though in smaller burghs the links between crafts in a particular incorporation were not always as straight forward as those in Edinburgh. Aberdeen's Incorporation of Hammermen included skinners and glovers.[30] They were probably too few to support their own incorporation.

THE INCORPORATION OF HAMMERMEN

The Incorporation of Hammermen was the sixth group of crafts in Edinburgh to receive a seal of cause. On 2 May 1483, the bailies of Edinburgh, with the consent and advice of the council, granted a seal of cause to the 'headsmen and masters of the Hammermen craft, both blacksmiths, goldsmiths, lorimers, saddlers, cutlers, buckler makers, armourers and all others, within the said burgh of Edinburgh'.[31] The seal was ratified by the crown in 1496, but the first seal of cause was by the authority of the town council.

It should also be noted that the seal of cause only applied to the 'headsmen and masters'. This illuminates the hierarchical nature of the incorporation, as apprentices, servants and journeymen were not included. The crafts that were originally incorporated into the hammermen are listed in table 1.3.

The seal of cause also stated that there were 'others', but the trades listed in the above table would have been the mainstay of the Incorporation of Hammermen in the late fifteenth century. If the others were not worth mentioning, it is safe to assume that they were not of great size at the time. By the second seal of cause in 1496, it was stated that pewterers were one of the trades;[32] they were probably included with the 'others' in the 1483 seal of cause, indicating the small size of this trade in the late fifteenth century. The locksmiths also seem to have been overlooked in 1483, though we know they existed in Edinburgh much earlier.

Several crucial items which indicate the importance of a seal of cause and what it achieved in relation to craftsmen's rights are detailed. The first item of the 1483 seal of cause was that no hammerman was allowed to '... exercise or use any more crafts but alanerly ane and to live thereupon, so that his other brother and craftsmen of the said crafts [were] not hurt through his large exertion and exceeding bounds'.[33] The seal of cause

TABLE 1.3
Examples of wares made by hammermen trades in 1483

Trades (1483)	Medium	Examples of Wares
Blacksmith	Iron	Nails, horseshoes, architectural hardware, agricultural implements
Goldsmith	Silver and Gold	Jewellery, communion plate, fine table wares
Lorimer	Iron	Horse accoutrements, buckles, spurs, sword guards
Saddler	Leather	Saddles
Cutler	Iron	Knives, razors
Buckler maker	Leather	Bucklers (shields), targets (shields), sheaths
Armourer	Iron	Armour, swords

was not a licence for craftsmen to do as they pleased; it was a set of rules. The hammermen were given much freedom in their particular trade, but were barred from other mediums. Sometimes special agreements were made in which permission was granted by one trade for a craftsman of a different trade to cross over in types of work, but this was technically forbidden. A cutler could make any sort of knife he wished, but was barred from making jewellery. Blacksmiths were not allowed to work in gold or silver and armourers were not to make cutlery. This is not to say that crossing of work never happened, but actions were taken by the incorporations to preserve the privileges of working in certain mediums.

Several items in the seal of cause dealt with markets.[34] These made for regulated competition by limiting the selling of metalwares to the market, in order to protect the Incorporation's privilege. If individuals wanted to sell metalwork, they had to either pay stallenger's fees for the market, or purchase freedom of the Incorporation.

One item stated that each Saturday afternoon 'two or three of the worthiest masters [with] most of knowledge of the said crafts',[35] were to take an officer and search the craftsmen's work. If they found faulty products they were to forbid their sale. This set up a quality control for the craftsmen to ensure that the public received quality metalwares, showing again how the incorporations were used by the council as a social control.[36]

The seal of cause also stated that all unfree hammermen, meaning those that had not yet joined the Incorporation, had to be examined and made freemen of the Incorporation.[37] This clause forced the craftsmen working in the burgh into the corporate structure of freemen, servants, journeymen or apprentices; if a metalworker wanted to work in Edinburgh, he had to join the Incorporation. To do this, they had to produce a worthy essay.[38] Otherwise, they had to work for a master as an apprentice, a journeyman, or a servant doing unskilled labour. Stallengers were individuals who were not guild brethren or members of an incorporation and did not have freedom to work in the town, but instead bought the privilege of selling wares in stalls during fairs.[39] They were limited to one year's selling privileges in the burgh. This section of the seal of cause brought all metalwork made or sold in the burgh, under the jurisdiction of the Incorporation of Hammermen, ensuring protection of privilege and quality metalwares.

One last item from the 1483 seal of cause was that '... no common cramers in the town use to sell or tap any hammerman's work, nor regrate it again to other men's use ...'[40] This clause was to keep the non-craftsmen cramers from selling metalwork, whether it was from Edinburgh hammermen, or hammermen from other towns or countries. It protected the hammermen from encroachment by the merchants and ensured that people bought metalwork from their local producers.

The rest of the 1483 seal of cause dealt with meeting times, fines and other details of administration. At different times other legislation was added or taken away to refine the system of privilege and government for the craftsmen. The seals of cause for the other crafts were similar in many respects, but not identical. Most of them included compulsory admission to freedom before a craftsman could work in the town and clauses about quality control. Aside from the provision of searchers in the markets, there were also standards for raw materials, such as the quality of flour for the baxters[41] or the freshness of the meat for the fleshers.[42] The seal of cause for the wrights and masons stated that two masons and two wrights were sworn in and sent to look over all works being erected.[43] Apprentices were often mentioned; the goldsmiths were not allowed to admit craftsmen with less than seven years' apprenticeship.[44] The cordiners' seal of cause demanded five years', with three years' service with a freeman for 'meat and fee' after.[45] Most seals of cause explicitly stated that it was illegal to harbour or employ another man's apprentice. Seals of cause also included clauses particular to the crafts which were incorporating. The Surgeons' seal of cause demanded a decent knowledge of anatomy.[46] The wobsters were not to receive nor work another man's yarn.[47] There were many similarities in the seals of cause, but also many unique items.

GOVERNING THE CRAFTSMEN

Incorporation was the Scottish solution to the problem of governing craftsmen. While many towns and cities in Europe used a similar system, not all urban areas had craft guilds or corporations. Nürnberg craftsmen, for example, were not allowed to form craft guilds.[48] In the 1300s there were craft riots across the German areas of the Holy Roman Empire. Nürnberg's council smarted from this and therefore denied the town's crafts any degree of autonomy. Every aspect of craft production was regulated directly by the local government while the craftsmen had no say whatsoever.[49] However, the incorporations which Edinburgh started in the 1400s did not represent a rebellious craftsman sub-culture taking power and autonomy from a weak town council; incorporation was very much a convenient mechanism for ordering and controlling the craftsmen. The council gave the craftsmen privileges, but they could also take them away. While there was the occasional craft riot in Edinburgh, incorporation was on the whole a functional system; it lasted for nearly 400 years.

As burgh status was itself a privilege granted by the crown, burgh politics were often tampered with by the king or queen, or one of the various factions of nobles. This was most readily seen with the office of provost. The provost was the head of the burgh as well as chairman and chief magistrate of the town council.[50] Although he was supposed to be elected, he was often imposed on the council by the crown or some faction of nobles,[51] as was the case for all twenty-five years from 1553 to 1578. Mary of Guise even imposed bailies on the council in 1559.[52] Though it had a more immediate effect on the town council, crown intervention was also felt by the incorporated trades.

The main power over the incorporated trades was the town council, which concerned itself with many of the details of the everyday lives of craftsmen. The council regulated admissions to the guarded freedoms of burgess-ship and guild brethrenship.[53] With too many practitioners of any occupation, business would have been poor. Hence forth, the council watched this carefully. With the assistance of an alderman of the crafts, they fixed the prices of materials, the cost of labour and the prices of made work.[54] The seals of cause detail how the council expected the crafts to run their businesses, so that the burgh would run smoothly and the craftsmen would lead quiet, productive lives.

The town council consisted of seven office bearers, ten non-craft councillors and two craft councillors.[55] The first of the office bearers was the provost, who from 1482 also exercised the office of sheriff. When absent from a council meeting, the provost's job was taken over by 'presidents'.[56]

The next of the seven office bearers were the four bailies. Each quarter of Edinburgh had a bailie.[57] The bailies were responsible for many things, such as calling meetings of the Guild,[58] having burgh suits tried before them[59] and being present at the exchange of sasines.[60] Sasines were documents attesting to property ownership.[61]

After the bailies came the dean of guild. Through this officer, the council controlled the entrance of burgess-ship and guild brethrenship[62] and accepted entrance fees.[63] He also presided over the Neighbourhood Court, which controlled building regulations,[64] was responsible for the upkeep of St Giles'[65] and, after the Reformation, took care of the revenues from the old ecclesiastical foundations.[66] It was the dean of guild who paid John Knox's salary from the council.

The seventh office bearer was the treasurer. The treasurer's role seems to have been purely monetary. For example, in 1555 it was declared that the treasurer had no right to appoint a person to burgess-ship.[67] This was the business of other magistrates.

Along with the seven office bearers were twelve councillors. The first ten of these were non-craftsmen. As Michael Lynch has pointed out, in the 1500s, merchants controlled burgh politics. In 1565 a quarter of the 357 merchants listed in a tax roll sat on the council at some point.[68] Merchant power was a common theme throughout Edinburgh's early modern political history.

Craftsmen did vie for political representation. In 1469, before incorporation, each craft had been allowed to 'choose a person of the same craft that shall have voice in the said election of the officers for that time, in likewise year by year'.[69] This indicates a substantial amount of craftsmen involved in the election process, though it is not clear if their 'voice' was actually listened to. In 1508 six or eight seats in the town council had been demanded by the crafts, but they only got two.[70] While two seats on the council was better than none, it was still far less than the ten of the non-craft councillors. With fourteen incorporated trades, craft representation was still very limited. All fourteen deacons were consulted by council only when certain matters regarding the common good became an issue. For the most part, representation was restricted to the four or five most prestigious of the fourteen crafts, such as the skinners, hammermen and tailors. Sixty-six per cent of the tax levied on the fourteen incorporated trades was paid by the top five incorporations, the skinners and furriers, the baxters, the fleshers, the tailors and the hammermen.[71] Between 1551 and 1570 there were eleven hammermen councillors; more than any other craft.[72] The poorest trades, the weavers, waulkers and bonnetmakers, paid less than 3 per cent of craft taxation and had to rely on the wealthier incorporated trades to represent them in the council. Many of these trades, at least in theory, were in the process of migrating out of the city to avoid taxation anyway.[73]

Prior to 1469 the council was elected by the burgesses. Parliament then transferred control of elections to the council itself.[74] Elections, which were held at Michaelmas, came to be influenced by only two craftsmen's votes. As Lynch points out in *Edinburgh and the Reformation*, town growth brought about a more oligarchic government, but unfortunately for the craftsmen, they played only a small part in that oligarchy.[75] Town councils did intend to control the workings of the towns, but it has been argued that this was not necessarily due to a lust for power, or for greed, so much as an idealistic view that it was the council's Christian duty to lead their town in all aspects of life.[76] As such, the Edinburgh council did set out to regulate the town's craftsmen. They wanted to keep the younger craftsmen out of trouble and the elderly craftsmen and widows in shelter and food, while at the same time providing the burgesses with access to quality products at affordable prices. They wanted the town to prosper.

The main vehicle of the council's control over the incorporations was the office of deacon.[77] Deacons were not an invention that sprang up with incorporation; they were utilized by the council for some time before that. In 1424 an act of parliament was passed stating: 'In all towns each craft, with the town-officers, to choose a deacon to assay and govern the works of that craft.'[78] After the seal of cause of 1483, there was one deacon for all the hammermen; not one for every craft therein.

The deacon's job was to preside over the craftsmen, making sure that they produced quality merchandise while representing them before the town. In the early days, he was to have no connection with the craft or its craftsmen except once every fifteen days to check up on the craftsmen's work.[79] Later in the early modern period, the role of deacons became more intensive, dealing with the many aspects of running the incorporations and interceding with other groups on their behalves. In 1738, for example, the Incorporation of Hammermen asked the deacon to apply to the town magistrates in order to get a stop put to the hawkers and unfreemen buying and selling old iron, brass and other metalwares.[80] Deacons were a public face to the incorporations, as well as their elected leaders. When the deacon was sick or away from the town, a deacon from previous years filled in for him.[81] When one died, a new one was elected for the remainder of the deceased deacon's year-long term. The fourteen deacons were effectively 'presidents' of the incorporations.[82]

Although, as Lynch points out, the deacons were not always as easy to control as craft councillors,[83] they were in fact still tools of the council. In 1555, the office of deacon itself was suspended, due to '… their election having conduced to the making of leagues within burgh and betwixt burgh and burgh'.[84] The council replaced the deacons with 'visitors' from each craft, who checked the quality of the work of the craftsmen. The visitors also voted on officers, but had no power to convene the craft. The suspension did not last long and the deacons were reinstated by 1556.[85] When a Protestant council was trying to push through the Reformation and Catholic deacons were not cooperating, they were simply removed and replaced by deacons of the new faith.[86] In 1568, Deacon Wilson declared he was a man of no faith. This seems to modern sensibilities to be a politic answer to the heated issues of the day, but the council thought that atheism was even more of a threat to the town than the old faith. He too was removed from office,[87] though later he was re-elected as deacon. By 1584, parliament set out that a deacon had to have been a master of his craft for at least two years and that he could not hold the office for more than two years. These limitations, when coupled with the earlier suspension of the office, further illustrate the measures taken by the council for control.

It was a working relationship though; the deacons had a voice in the election of the provost and bailies, the management of the town property and patronage and the granting of extents and contributions.[88] The deacons also had the position of deacon convener to give them representation. When situations arose in the burgh which compelled the council to seek the opinion of the fourteen incorporated trades, the deacon convener would convene them and preside over the meeting.[89] It was one more position given to represent the voice of the craftsmen.

The incorporated trades had a sophisticated system of other offices to aid the deacons in the running of affairs. The deacon and office bearers were referred to collectively, as the 'house'.[90] Each September, immediately after the election of the deacon, the incorporation elected the boxmaster, who controlled the box where money and important papers were kept. There were three keys to open the box, which were held by other masters in the incorporation. Prior to 1600, the deacon was the boxmaster; after, a separate master was chosen. By the 1700s, the position was simply entitled 'treasurer'.[91]

There were several duties for the boxmaster. One was taking care of the monetary side of incorporation affairs. When craftsmen needed charity, it was paid out by the boxmaster. The minute books have many entries illustrating the duties of this post: 'The house ordains the boxmaster to give to Adam Grinlaw, locksmith, six pounds Scots to help him in his present straights,'[92] and 'the house ordains the treasurer to lend to Edward Ramsay, locksmith, one pound Sterling and take his bill therefore payable against Martinmas next,'[93] being just two examples. In the days before the Bank of Scotland, money was kept in coffers or chests and the boxmaster literally had control of the box. The introduction of banks might account for the change of terminology to treasurer in the 1700s.

Other duties of the boxmaster included going along with the craft masters to search the markets[94] and paying the tradesmen that took care of incorporation-owned properties, such as their meeting house, the Magdalen Chapel: 'The house appoints their treasurer to mend and gilt the weather cock and globe that was upon the top of the steeple of their Chapel … thrown down by the wind and to replace the same as formerly.'[95] That particular treasurer happened to be a skilled blacksmith, so he did not need to look far when contracting out the job. Other times, the boxmaster was given secretarial type work:

> The house likewise ordains that all the members should be warned to the meetings of the house by printed schedules in regard some members complain of their servants neglecting to tell them when they are verbally warned and exceedingly desire the boxmaster to cause print these schedules for that purpose.[96]

The boxmaster was not only the treasurer, but also the equivalent of a 'vice-president' to the deacon. It was an important and influential office, which highlights the variety of incorporation business.

Another section of the incorporation government was the panel of craft masters chosen each year to help the deacon in governing the crafts. There were eight main craft groups: blacksmiths, cutlers, saddlers, locksmiths, lorimers, armourers, pewterers and shearsmiths.[97] Each of these eight 'crafts' would present the names of their youngest and oldest master to the new deacon after September elections. For the year they represented their craft in incorporation business. The Magdalen Chapel has a half-circle of seats with the shields of the eight crafts painted on the backboards. The two masters of each craft would sit at their respective seats during meetings of the house.

In 1652 another craftsman from each craft was included with the masters to act as a searcher in the markets.[98] This was originally the job of the deacons, but the work was allocated out. The searchers would go through the markets checking the quality of the products being sold by the hammermen. The searchers were still in use in 1661. Eventually, they went back to just the two craft masters and by 1733 it was their job to check the sufficiency of the hammermen's work in the markets.[99] If work was found to be insufficient, it was seized and auctioned at the Magdalen Chapel to other craftsmen. The craftsman who bought the seized work could then fix it and resell it. In 1734 there was discussion in an incorporation meeting as to whether or not masters of one art could judge the sufficiency of the work of a craftsman from a different art.[100]

They did not check only for quality. On 9 August 1740 '… work seized from Chalmers in Potterrow for not razing his stall in the market when two of the clock in the afternoon struck … [was] returned to him in respect it was but just over the market, he always paying to the officer one shilling Stirling'.[101] The rules were enforced to ensure trade privileges were guarded.

The craft masters were an integral part of the system of social control under the deacons.

Another aide to the deacons in running the incorporations was the use of committees. There were two types of committees: general committees and craft committees. General committees were simply a group of masters gathered together to help the deacon and boxmaster take care of various bits of business and make decisions too delicate for one man to decide. They were appointed 'for the ensuing year nine to be a quorum and to meet at the deacon's call'.[102] As an example, there was a general committee appointed 'for assisting the deacon and treasurer in the concerns of the Incorporation', in September 1749. It consisted of all of the old deacons, all of the old treasurers, excepting William Armstrong who was excused by reason of 'indisposition', all the eldest masters and Patrick Crichton, Alexander Fairbairn and James Clarkson.[103] The committees would examine the accounts and oversee annual justification of expenditures and money issues. They would oversee the boxmaster's payments to various tradesmen and charities:

> the house having heard the report of the general committee anent taking under consideration the present state of their poor in this hard season, they unanimously approve of the conduct of their said committee and return them thanks therefore and ordain the persons underwritten to have the particular quantities of coals and meal after specified ...[104]

They gave coal and meal to a list of twenty-nine individuals and then extended 'the same to seven thousand four hundred weight of coals and three bolls fifteen pecks of meal'. The general committees helped to disperse representation through the craftsmen and helped the deacon deal with the work load. They also helped when the deacon or treasurer wanted public witness for the monetary issues of the year's business.

The other type of committee was more specialized. The craft committees were organized for a specific purpose pertaining to a particular craft. In May 1745, two locksmiths were appointed to a general committee of the blacksmith and locksmith arts to decide if a coachmaker could keep a blacksmith in his shop to work on his coaches only.[105]

> The deacon represented that the occasion of calling this meeting was to inform the arts that he had received a letter from Thomas Ainslie, smith in Calton of Edinburgh ... proposing that he would take it an honour done to receive him as freeman of this incorporation ... and if found qualified he would pay to the house twenty-five guineas and the deacon desired the arts their resolution thereon and what answer in return should be made to the said proposals.[106]

As this only applied to the blacksmiths and locksmiths, it was a committee made up of their arts present at the Magdalen Chapel to hear the details of the letter.

> The committee ... reported that they had met ... with Thomas Ainslie ... and had brought him up to offer five hundred merks Scots in name of upset money and dues for the Trades Maiden Hospital and that he seemed ... a proper person to be admitted a freeman locksmith among the incorporation. The locksmith art reported that they had agreed to admit the said Thomas Ainslie to ane essay and to appoint him essay masters, with a land lord, in manner and will the usual requisites, required of ordinary entrants. But a letter was produced ... importing that unless the blacksmith art would allow [Ainslie] to make his own essay and in his own shop he withdrew his proposals. Which being argued upon among the locksmiths they refused to alter the piece of work usually appointed for the essay to all entrants, or dispersing with essays being made otherways than in the shop and under the eye and custody of some freeman. Whereupon ... Ainslie's proposals were withdrawn.[107]

If the deacon had decided the case by himself, the blacksmiths and locksmiths might have protested and caused him more trouble. By forming a committee of their crafts, his life was made simpler and they had a say in the fine details.

Arguably the most important and possibly the most readily overlooked position in the Incorporation of Hammermen was the clerk. Clerks were the secretaries of the incorporations. They kept the minutes in the minute books.[108] They were educated men, capable of reading, writing and arithmetic. They played a crucial role during the meetings of the incorporations, taking down the minutes and recording all details of incorporation business. At the beginning of each meeting, the clerk read the prayer,[109] called the roll of members and read off the minutes of the last sedurunt, signing the book appropriately as he went.[110]

Clerks recorded all the day-to-day business of the Incorporation of Hammermen. The minute books have entries divided up into quarters, with election results in September and quarter compts throughout. Records of charities given, acts passed or simply read before the house, details of property management, settlements of internal craft disputes, legal matters, auction results from insufficient products found in the markets and punishments for various offences were all handwritten in various shades of black ink on the handmade paper which was bound into the minute books. Without the clerks, the incorporation would not have run smoothly and we would know very little about the craftsmen of the early modern period.

ELECTION PROCESS

The term of a deacon lasted for one year, with elections taking place annually in September. When incorporations first started, the deacon was elected directly by the council,[111] but this changed over time. The last alteration to the election process prior to 1750 happened in 1686. On 10 September there was a warrant in the Incorporation of Hammermen's minutes for booking an act of the fourteen deacons of the Edinburgh incorporations.[112] It seems that it was not until 14 September 1695, nine years later, that the new election process was finally implemented.[113] In the new system, the Incorporation would prepare a long leet of six suitable candidates for deacon. After a vote of approval by the freeman masters of the incorporation,[114] the leet would be submitted into the town council, which picked three of the deacon candidates. The next day the Incorporation would meet again to receive the short leet from the council and vote. The man who had the majority of the votes won. After he accepted, he gave an oath 'for faithful aministration'.[115] With the deacon elected, they would then proceed to elect the other officials, such as the boxmaster. This position was chosen from a leet of three and also gave an oath upon election.[116] After the boxmaster was elected, the incorporation then asked the eight crafts to give their youngest and oldest masters to act as the 'masters for the year'.[117]

After 1737, actions were taken to curb mob violence by instituting an act to be read annually after every September election. The act delineated places for the merchants and craftsment to assemble in the case of any 'mob or disorder'.[118] The council made use of the elections to remind the craftsmen of their duties to the town; in practice, this was a kind of 'fire drill' for social unrest.

Edinburgh's Incorporation of Hammermen was not unique in its election process. Glasgow's hammermen also elected deacons in either September or early October. The leeting process which was apparently introduced to Edinburgh's hammermen in 1686, had been in use in the Glasgow incorporation since at least 1618.[119]

CONQUERING THE SUBURBS

The craftsmen were under the control of several burgh institutions, but *where* was that control? What was the burgh jurisdiction? The Edinburgh of the early modern period was far more compact than the sprawling city of today. The burgh boundaries were very important, as living inside them was a prerequisite for burgess-ship, guildry and freedom of an incorporation. Burghs in early modern Scotland used to have an annual event where the town council and people would walk or ride around the boundaries of the burgh, in order to demarcate and reaffirm what exactly was under their control. In the same way as the council had a specific area of control, so did the Incorporation of Hammermen.

Originally, the extent of Incorporation jurisdiction was basically the burgh wall. Edinburgh had been given permission by James II (1437–60) in 1450 to fortify the town.[120] After the defeat at Flodden in 1513, the burgh wanted a modern, defendable wall, which was started around 17 March 1514,[121] and was still being worked on in 1560.[122] The wall was eventually built around the town, encompassing most of Edinburgh. Not only was it a defensive structure, but also a reminder of what belonged to the burgh. To get a share of the privileges of trade in Edinburgh, one had to be inside the town. Canongate, outside the walls, was a separate burgh completely.[123] Leith was not in Edinburgh. Anything outside the walls, with the exception of the south-west section of Canongate, was outside Edinburgh. The majority of Edinburgh's buildings were piled into the cramped confines of the walls, though they probably would have been cramped before the wall was built. Despite the conditions, the people needed to live inside the burgh boundaries due to financial interests and trade rights.

In the 1500s Europe saw a huge increase in population. The population of Edinburgh was also experiencing a dramatic rise.[124] As the population expanded, housing became more cramped and difficult to find. With taxation being a burden, people started taking up residence outside the burgh walls forming suburbs. In Edinburgh in 1558, there were sixty-six master hammermen paying taxes. In 1583, there were only fifty-two hammermen listed in a tax roll. By 1634 there were only forty-two master hammermen paying taxes in Edinburgh.[125] As we can see from the burgess rolls (see table 1.4), the hammermen were not decreasing, but increasing. Lynch attributes this decrease in taxpaying hammermen to an 'unchecked

TABLE 1.4
Hammermen attaining burgess-ship (*Edinburgh Burgesses* 1929)

Trade	1550–1600	1600–50	1650–1700	1700–50	Total of Craft
Pewterer	14	30	53	46	143
Saddler	32	28	31	35	126
Smith	22	30	34	34	120
Locksmith	13	23	34	29	99
Armourer	12	26	23	10	71
Cutler	26	8	9	11	54
Lorimer	22	12	11	3	48
Coppersmith/Brazier	1	5	13	24	43
Watch/Knockmaker	0	3	7	26	36
Gunsmith	6	6	7	3	22
White-ironmen	0	0	3	13	16
Shearsmith	2	6	8	0	16
Beltmaker	1	6	7	1	15
Bell Founder/Founder	1	1	3	9	14
Farrier	0	1	1	4	6
Sheathmaker	1	4	0	0	5
Engraver	0	0	1	3	4
Button-mould Maker	1	1	0	1	3
Swordslipper	3	0	0	0	3
Pinmaker	0	0	2	0	2
Stocking Frame Maker	0	0	1	0	1
Damasker	1	0	0	0	1
Total Hammermen	158	190	248	252	848

flight to the suburbs', and notes that it was especially popular with the textile and clothing trades in Edinburgh. There are thirteen different trades shown by Lynch that appear to be declining.[126] If a craftsman lived outside the walls, they could not be forced to pay burgh taxes or contribute valuable time to burgh duties. If he maintained his freedom in an incorporated trade, he could still make money from the burgh markets and fairs, without paying out money in taxes and lost time. This set the majority of the tax burdens on the craftsmen which followed the law and resided in the burgh.

The town council made much effort to curb the abuse, with various acts demanding that their prodigal sons return.[127] There were even acts of parliament set up to stop this, such as in 1592 when crafts were

TABLE 1.5
Smith group attaining burgess-ship (*Edinburgh Burgesses* 1929)

Trade	1550–1600	1600–50	1650–1700	1700–50
Smith	22	30	34	34
Locksmith	13	23	34	29
Gunsmith	6	6	7	3
Watch/Knockmaker	0	3	7	26
Total Hammermen	158	190	248	252

TABLE 1.6
Percentage of overall incorporation of hammermen (*Edinburgh Burgesses* 1929)

Trade	1550–1600	1600–50	1650–1700	1700–50
Smith	14%	16%	14%	13%
Locksmith	8%	12%	14%	11%
Gunsmith	4%	3%	3%	1%
Watch/Knockmaker	0%	2%	3%	10%

forbidden from being exercised in the suburbs of the burghs,[128] but in 1669 the Court of Session decided that this did not apply to the residents of any burgh of barony.[129] In 1671 legislation was also passed saying that there could not be any suburbs within a mile of a royal burgh, though this did not rid Scotland's towns of suburbs.[130]

Edinburgh eventually got around the problem by first gaining superiority over the suburbs and then organizing the suburb crafts under their own incorporations. In 1567 Edinburgh purchased the burgh of barony of South Leith. In 1636 part of North Leith was aquired,[131] when superiority over Canongate was purchased.[132] Canongate had been granted to the Abbots of Holyrood by King David I (1124–53). Until 1636 it was a separate burgh of barony.[133]

The suburb of Portsburgh included the area from Bristo to Tollcross and Bruntsfield, which had belonged to the Touris family of Inverleith. They sold their superiority to Sir Adam Hepburn of Humbie in 1648 and he in turn sold the superiority to the magistrates and council of Edinburgh. The king turned Portsburgh into a free burgh of barony and it was absorbed into its larger neighbour.[134]

The road which ran through Bristo, known as 'Potterrow', accumulated houses as Edinburgh spilled out of the walls at the Kirk o' Field port. Apparently there were potters working in the area at one time, henceforth the name. In 1649 it became part of the newly formed barony of Portsburgh and was sometimes called 'Easter Portsburgh'.[135] This union seems to have been nominal, as their craftsmen were still separate in the early eighteenth century.

With Edinburgh's superiority over these areas, there was some contention over the rights to craft production in them. At first, even with superiority over these areas, it did not make it possible to live in them and still be a burgess of Edinburgh. In 1659 one David Hastie, a weaver in the Canongate, was admitted burgess in Edinburgh providing he move: '… the said David obliging himself to take up his residence within the town, otherwise to lose the benefit of his burgess-ship.'[136] Eventually the rules were relaxed. If Edinburgh was going to have competitors who refused to live inside the town walls, they wanted at least to have control over them. For example, in Leith in 1619, twelve coopers were allowed to join the Edinburgh coopers and continue working in Leith as long as they did not reside there.[137] Whether the craftsmen in the suburbs in the later 1600s and 1700s had to live in Edinburgh, is uncertain. The crafts were allowed to form into societies. These societies were not full incorporations; they were subordinate to the Edinburgh incorporations. They were only allowed to bring their work into Edinburgh on certain market days and were prosecuted if they did otherwise.[138] The hammermen of Leith, Portsburgh and Potterrow had to meet at the Magdalen Chapel. They were not permitted deacons; they each had an elected 'overman'.[139] Just like deacons, the elections were for a one-year term. By 1739 there were only two hammermen societies in the suburbs of Edinburgh, as the Potterrow and Portsburgh hammermen finally joined into one society.[140] The Leith hammermen formed the second society. Some hammermen trades were not permitted in some suburban areas. On 20 September 1707, the Leith hammermen were given a stiff warning and threat of future fines if they worked the gunsmith or armourer trades.[141]

Table 1.7 shows the population of the suburban hammermen compared to the Edinburgh hammermen in 1717. There are also tallies of lists for 1663, 1681 and 1683, though they are not all complete.[142] The suburbs usually had about twenty hammermen, to Edinburgh's 114 in 1717. Table 1.8 shows that Portsburgh, Leith and Potterrow all had blacksmiths and locksmiths.

TABLE 1.7
Hammermen in suburbs (ECA ED008/1/4 & 5)

Town	1663	1681	1683	1717
Portsburgh	19		14	20
Leith	23	21		16
Potterrow	10		15	23
Edinburgh				114

Portsburgh had the widest range of hammermen, with founders, beltmakers, a lorimer, a gunsmith, a saddler and an armourer. Leith had a saddler and a cardmaker, who made 'cards' for wool combing. All three had hammermen with no specific trade listed.

Canongate, though Edinburgh held superiority over it, managed to retain its own Incorporation of Hammermen. In 1856 there was still debate about Canongate craftsmen becoming burgesses in Edinburgh.[143] Superiority over the Canongate did give Edinburgh's council some say in the running of their affairs, which could put pressure on the Canongate craftsmen, but otherwise they were independent incorporations.

GROWTH OF THE INCORPORATION OF HAMMERMEN

The 'flight to the suburbs' and the eventual inclusion of these areas under Edinburgh's control, is not the only way in which Edinburgh grew. The population of Edinburgh in 1560 was around 12,500. By 1635 it had grown to about 20,000.[144] By 1650 it had tripled from what it had been one hundred years earlier.[145] The expanding population represents a numerically expanding consumer society. Not only did this mean an expanding market for metalwares, but also an expanding pool of labour to make them. In the seventeenth century, the hammermen grew to be the third largest incorporated trade in Edinburgh, with only the tailors and wrights being larger.[146] According to Friedrich's study on work and status, textile, clothing and apparel were the most important facets of urban production in early modern Europe.[147]

TABLE 1.8
Hammermen trades in suburbs (ECA ED008/1/4 & 5)

1663	Black-smith	Lock-smith	Founder	Belt-maker	Lorimer	Gunsmith	Saddler	Armourer	Card-maker	No trade given
Portsburgh	0	0	0	0	0	0	1	1	0	17
Leith	4	1	0	0	0	0	1	0	1	16
Potterrow	0	0	0	0	0	0	0	0	0	10

1683	Black-smith	Lock-smith	Founder	Belt-maker	Lorimer	Gunsmith	Saddler	Armourer	Card-maker	No trade given
Portsburgh	1	4	1	1	0	0	1	0	0	6
Leith (1681)	7	3	0	0	0	0	0	0	0	11
Potterrow	2	6	0	0	0	0	0	0	0	7

1717	Black-smith	Lock-smith	Founder	Belt-maker	Lorimer	Gunsmith	Saddler	Armourer	Card-maker	No trade given
Portsburgh	4	8	2	3	1	1	0	0	0	1
Leith										
Potterrow										

TABLE 1.9
Tax of every hundred pounds (Marwick 1909, 110)

Pre-1574	**Amount paid of every 100 lb**		
Skinners Furriors	18 lb		
Baxters	17 lb	12s	6d
Tailors	14 lb	5s	4d
Hammermen	13 lb	5s	6d
Fleshers	13 lb	2s	4d
Mary's Chapel	7 lb	2s	9d
Cordiners	6 lb	13s	4d
Goldsmiths	4 lb	11s	3d
Barbers	3 lb	1s	3d
Wobsters, Walkers, Bonnetmakers	2 lb	13s	4d
Total	100 lb	7s	7d

After 1574	**Amount paid of every 100 lb**		
Skinners Furriors	20 lb	1s	6d
Tailors	18 lb	1s	6d
Hammermen	13 lb	5s	6d
Baxters	13 lb	0s	4d
Fleshers	9 lb		
Mary's Chapel	8 lb	3s	4d
Cordiners	6 lb	13s	4d
Goldsmiths	6 lb		
Barbers	3 lb	1s	3d
Wobsters, Walkers, Bonnetmakers	2 lb	13s	4d
Total	100 lb	0s	1d

Ian D. Whyte's table of manufacturing in his study of occupational structure in Scottish burghs shows that Edinburgh was likewise dominated by clothing and textile production.[148] It appears that clothing, buildings and metalwares held an important place in the upper ranks in Edinburgh's domestic economy.

Tax is another indicator of the rise of importance of the Incorporation of Hammermen. Table 1.9 shows that prior to 1574, the hammermen had been paying the fourth largest amount of tax out of the incorporated trades of Edinburgh.

The deacon of the fleshers was forced to ask for a decrease in the taxation paid by his craft, as they were 'so depauperat that they were not able to pay taxations according to the auld rolls'.[149] The council, bailies and deacons considered the crafts that were having problems meeting the taxes and changed the rates accordingly, with the rich crafts taking up the deducted tax of the poorer crafts. The new roll was fixed on 15 September 1574. While the hammermen were not rich enough to pay more tax than the £13 5s 6d they had already been paying, the new roll made their taxes the third highest out of the incorporated trades. They were not richer, but they were not poorer either. They were stable in a difficult economic period.

The Roll of Edinburgh Burgesses and Guild Brethren is an interesting source for examining the growth of the incorporated trades. Whenever a person purchased burgess-ship or guildry, his name was entered in the burgess and guild rolls. Focusing on the Incorporation of Hammermen, the burgess rolls show a marked growth. The number of hammermen who were listed

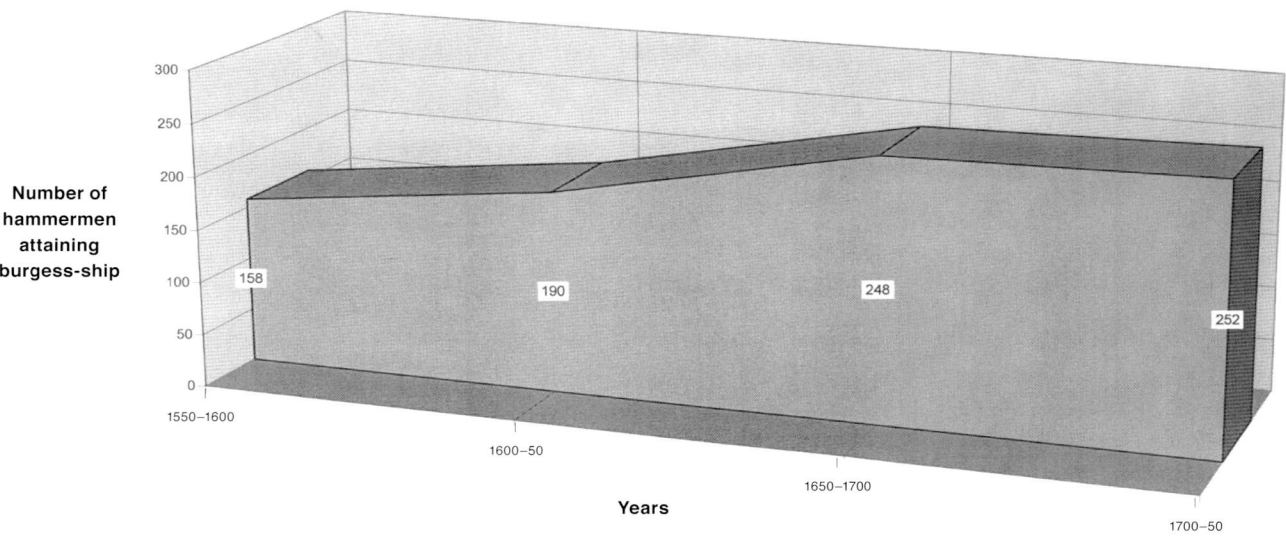

CHART 1.0
Hammermen attaining burgess-ship

is given in table 1.4, with each burgess hammerman being given a tally-mark for the fifty-year period in which they were entered. The data does not represent a time-span of their working life; it merely indicates the number of entrants in a particular fifty-year period. As we can see in table 1.4, from 1550 to 1600 there were 158 hammermen who attained burgess-ship. In the 1600 to 1650 period, the number increased to 190 hammermen. In the 1650 to 1700 period, the number reached 248 craftsmen. The 1700 to 1750 period shows the rate of growth dropped off sharply, with only 252 craftsmen attaining burgess-ship. Considering that the time-span covered by these four periods is only two-hundred years (see chart 1.0), we see that the Edinburgh Incorporation of Hammermen experienced dramatic growth from 1550 to 1650 followed by a levelling off between 1650 and 1750.[150]

The problem with the burgess rolls, however, is that they are not complete. Servants, apprentices, journeymen and unfreemen are not included. They list only the masters or freemen and even some of these are missing.[151] The burgess rolls can still be used as a rough estimate of the fluctuations in the hammermen population, but they should not be taken at face value. This said, chart 1.0, which is based on the data from table 1.4, shows a dogged increase of hammermen from 1550 to 1600 and then from 1600 to 1650, with an even sharper period of growth from 1600 to 1650 and 1650 to 1700. There is a plateau from 1650 to 1700 and 1700 to 1750.[152] The actual number of craftsmen went from 158 to 252, indicating a trend of growth, but the rate of growth increased sharply and then fell off even more sharply, indicating that the growth was not sustainable.

Another source for looking at growth of the overall Incorporation of Hammermen is the minute books held in the Edinburgh City Archives. The burgess rolls would have been made by a town clerk who might not have necessarily known the craftsmen he was listing. Some known burgesses went unmentioned in the rolls. In contrast, the lists in the minute books were recorded by the Incorporation's own clerk. He most likely knew each man on the meticulous lists. When a hammerman was absent from a meeting or funeral, it was recorded in the minute books. The lists are also more frequent than the single entry in the burgess rolls. While a burgess was only listed on the day he attained burgess-ship, a master in the incorporation was listed any time the clerk took a count of the masters; it was a tally of numbers, not a list of new members. While the burgess rolls are best viewed in fifty-year segments, the minute book lists can be viewed singly or in succession, giving a far more accurate view of the population of the Incorporation of Hammermen for a particular year or over a period of years. In table 1.10 the numbers reflect a count of names of Edinburgh hammermen masters on the lists for the corresponding year. It should be noted that the list does not include the hammermen in the suburbs, only Edinburgh proper. It also does not include servants, journeymen or apprentices; only

TABLE 1.10
Numbers of Edinburgh hammermen masters

Year	Number of hammermen masters	Source
1494	21	Smith 1906, 1–2
1496	23	Smith 1906, 10–11
1500	64	Smith 1906, 20 (and servants?)
1503	69	Smith 1906, 28–9
1546	62	Smith 1906, 130–1
1550	69	Smith 1906, 148–9
1558	66	1558 Muster Roll
1560	72	Smith 1906, 173–4
1565	66	Stent Roll
1576	91	NMS Whitelaw EHMB, 38
1592	98	ECA ED008/1/2
1596	104	
1600	115	
1606	106	
1612	62	
1614	76	
1619	87	
1629	104	ECA ED008/1/3
1640	78	
1644	66	
1646	59	
1648	69	
1654	75	
1656	79	
1660	88	
1663	90	ECA ED008/1/4
1668	83	
1670	90	
1671?	79	
1674	129	
1682	143	
1693	160	
1705	155	ECA ED008/1/5
1707	145	
1717	93	
1729–31	94	ECA ED008/5/14
1739–45	115	ECA ED008/1/7
1749	161	ECA ED008/1/8

the Edinburgh masters are listed. Chart 1.1 gives a graphic presentation of the data for the period of 1494 to 1749. The overall trend of the data is growth. In the first years in which the Incorporation was recording minutes, their numbers were small. There were about twenty master craftsmen to supply the town with metalwares. Even with their servants, journeymen and apprentices who worked in their shops and all the imported goods which could be had from the merchants, twenty masters would not have been able to provide for a town the size of Edinburgh in 1650. In order to avoid a burgh dependency on foreign goods, the skilled craftsmen had to allow and encourage growth of the incorporated trades. As we can see in chart 1.1, the growth did indeed happen.

The data in table 1.10 and chart 1.1 also illuminate that it was not a consistent rate of growth between 1494 and 1749. The time frame is spotted with six episodes of conspicuous growth and four episodes of marked decline, interspersed with three periods of relative continuity. The episodes of decline were from 1600 to 1612, 1629 to 1646 and 1693 to 1729. The first major decline took place just after the 1603 Union of Crowns. New opportunities were sought after by Scots in London. The 1612 list in the hammermen minute books states after several craftsmen's names that they were away in London or England.[153] By 1629 the Incorporation's number of masters was back up to 104, but by 1640 it had plummeted to seventy-eight. In the 1640 list is a note in the margin which was added after 1644, stating that Adam Steil, a master of the pewterer craft, was killed at Marston Moor near York.[154] The Incorporation contributed to the Covenanting war effort; it is not apparent how much support was given to the Royalist side. With the outbreak of plague and the continuation of the war, the number of freemen dropped from 104 in 1629 to fifty-nine in 1646. It is not clear how many of these were deaths by natural causes or mere absenteeism. At least one hammerman, James Boog, Younger, was killed by the plague in May 1645.[155] The third episode of decline was just after 1693. Darien was not kind to the Scottish economy and combined with famine and extremely cold winters, Scotland was under much strain. While the Incorporation's numbers undoubtedly dropped, going from 160 in 1693 to 145 in 1707, this area of the decline is not as striking as the period following the Union of 1707. The number of freemen masters in the Incorporation of Hammermen dropped from the already low 145 down to ninety-three by 1717, less than two thirds of the number at the Union.[156] With the Union came even more business opportunities. The areas of decline might reflect this.

Growth, the dominant trend, started within two years of the Incorporation's first minutes being recorded. From 1496 to 1503 the number of

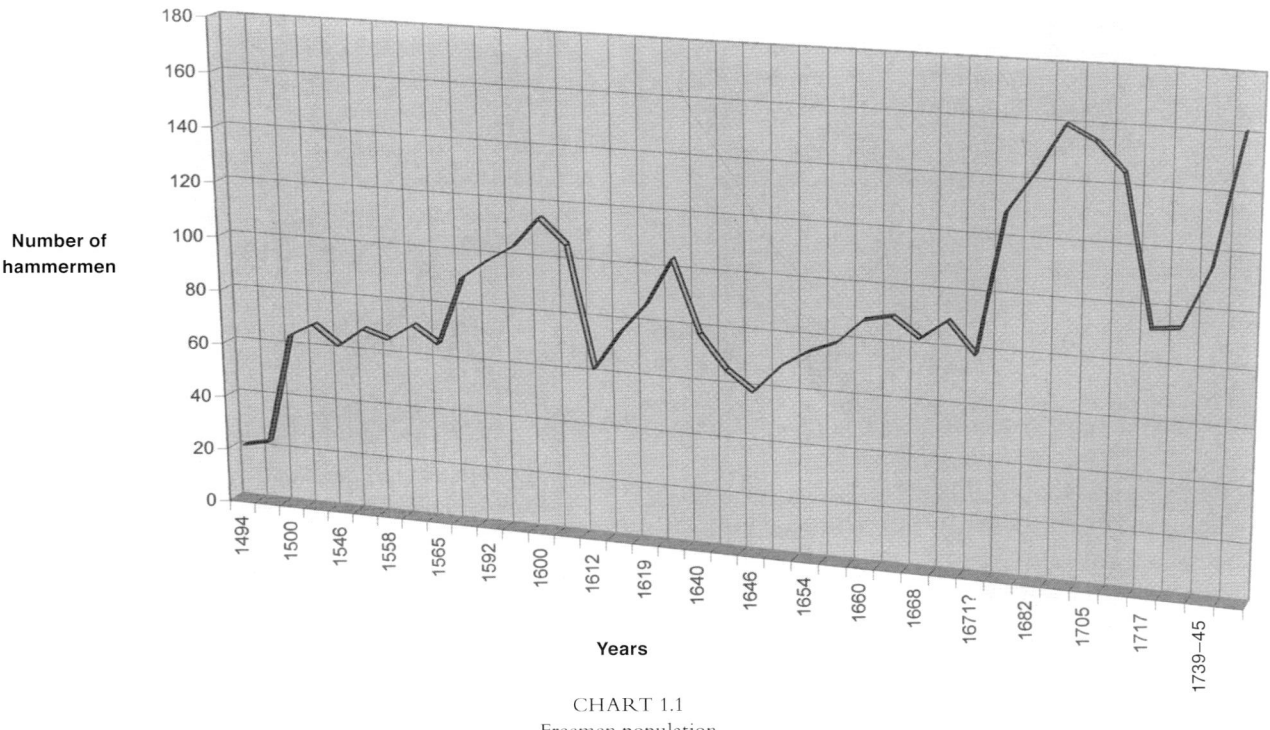

CHART 1.1
Freemen population

hammermen masters tripled. The hammermen had only been incorporated for twenty years, so it is possible that not all craftsmen had come under their jurisdiction yet. The sudden growth might also be explained by journeymen, servants and apprentices being accepted into the fold and given freedom as a conscious step by the Incorporation towards meeting the economic demand for metalwares. As masters they would then have had the opportunity to take apprentices, servants and journeymen on, some of whom would then have also attained freedom as masters. The cycle thus perpetuated, growth occurred until the ruling aristocracy did something to curb the amount of incoming freemen making use of burgh privileges and creating competition in the market.

The numbers show a period of continuity from 1503 to 1565, with a slight increase to seventy-two masters in the year 1560. Considering the upheaval of the Reformation, it is interesting that the continuity lasted as long as 1565.

From 1565 to 1600 the number of masters increased from sixty-six to 115. From 1565 to 1576 there was a sharp jump from sixty-six freemen to ninety-one, but there is no data given for the period of the 1571–3 siege of Edinburgh. The number of masters might have dropped farther before climbing up to ninety-one. By 1592, almost a decade after the 1583 decreet arbitral theoretically increased the equality between the merchants and craftsmen, the number of hammermen masters had risen by only seven freemen. The craft aristocracy benefited from the decreet, while journeymen and other unfreemen barely felt a change. Still, by 1600 the numbers were considerably higher than they had been in 1560.

From 1612 to 1629 the number of hammermen went from sixty-two to 104. Without war with England, Edinburgh seems to have prospered. The hammermen experienced dramatic growth.

After the decline around the time of the Bishops' Wars and Wars of the Covenant, there was another recovery, interestingly, starting in 1646 before the 'troubles' were over. There was steady growth up to the Restoration, going from fifty-nine hammermen in 1646 up to ninety in 1663. While still not as numerous as in 1600, there was a period of continuity from 1663 to 1671. The numbers in this period fluctuated between eighty and ninety, before a dramatic increase to 129 hammermen in 1674. By 1693 there were 160 hammermen; 101 craftsmen more than in 1646.

While there was a severe decline after the Union of 1707, by 1739 the numbers were rising again, culminating in 161 hammermen in 1749. While there were undoubted periods of severe decline, the overall trend is growth; the numbers of hammermen in 1749 were almost eight times as many as in 1494.

At the beginning of the early modern period, ideas about how work should be organized were changing in European society. As what we now call 'corporatism' took hold, cities across Europe gave new legal statuses to craft groups.[157] Edinburgh, like many other European towns, gave special rights and privileges to crafts or craft groups through seals of cause. Scotland, starting with its capital, experienced corporatism through the institution of incorporation. Inside corporatism was a hierarchy of society, and while the crafts were not as high in that hierarchy as the merchants, there was still a craft hierarchy. The Incorporation of Hammermen, who experienced marked growth and considerable political involvement over the early modern period, were part of this craft aristocracy. As the next chapter shall show, however, not all of the individual hammermen trades were as fortunate as others.

NOTES

[1] Clune 1943, 14.
[2] Friedrichs 2003, 155, 157.
[3] Marwick 1909, 30, Mackenzie 1949, 100, and Warden 1872, 88.
[4] Marwick 1909, 25–6.
[5] Ibid., 25.
[6] Ibid., 45.
[7] Lynch 2000, 62.
[8] Swanson 1999, 21.
[9] To what extent this was enforced, is unknown. Marwick 1909, 25–6.
[10] Smith 1906, 181.
[11] Holmes 1998, 22–3, 27.
[12] Marwick 1909, 34.
[13] Colston 1891, 162–3.
[14] Farr 2000, 20–1.
[15] Ibid., 24–5.
[16] Lynch 1981, 16–17.
[17] Ibid., 55.
[18] Friedrichs 2003, 233–4.
[19] Smith 1906, 47–8.
[20] As stated on a plaque found on the church which still stands west of George IV Bridge. Magdalen Chapel, 41 Cowgate, Edinburgh.
[21] Smith 1906, xxxviii.
[22] While the altars to saints in Edinburgh were removed after the Reformation, similar customs continued in Catholic countries. For example, Dijon's locksmiths held masses in 1651 to pray for not only their whole craft, but also the salvation of the souls of the dead locksmiths and their families. Farr 2000, 230.
[23] ECA ED008/1.
[24] Mackenzie 1949, 104.
[25] ECA ED008/1/7, 19.
[26] Smith 1906, xii.
[27] Colston 1891, 79, 65, 119, 93 respectively.
[28] Marwick 1909, 34.
[29] Colston 1891, xiii.
[30] Bain 1887, 197, 208.
[31] Smith 1906, 181. Other burghs also granted seals of cause to their hammermen. Aberdeen's Incorporation of Hammermen received a seal of cause in 1519. Bain 1887, 198. Glasgow's hammermen received theirs in 1536. Lumsden & Aitken 1912, 36.
[32] Smith 1906, 184.
[33] Ibid., 182.
[34] Ibid., 182.
[35] Ibid., 182–3.
[36] Lynch 1981, 55.
[37] Smith 1906, 183.
[38] A 'masterpiece'.
[39] Robinson 1992, 661.
[40] Smith 1906, 183.
[41] Colston 1891, 45.
[42] Ibid., 56.
[43] Ibid., 67.
[44] Ibid., 29.
[45] Ibid., 100.
[46] Ibid., 2.
[47] Ibid., 120.
[48] Strauss 1966, 97.
[49] This did not last forever. In 1565 the clockmakers formed a guild. Bruton 2000, 61.
[50] Robinson 1992, 524.
[51] Lynch 1981, 15.
[52] Ibid., 6.
[53] Marwick 1909, 144, 187–9, 191–2, 197.
[54] *APS* 1875, 382.
[55] Lynch 1998 (unpublished Utrecht paper), 3.
[56] Ibid., 9.
[57] Marwick 1909, 31.
[58] Ibid., 33.
[59] Ibid., 12.
[60] Ibid., 16.
[61] Robinson 1992, 581.
[62] Lynch 1981, 10.
[63] Marwick 1909, 191.
[64] Lynch 1981, 14.
[65] Ibid., 22.
[66] Ibid., 32.
[67] Marwick 1909, 83.
[68] Lynch 1981, 15.
[69] Marwick 1909, 45.
[70] Ibid., 61. This changed to six in 1583. Lynch 1981, 16–7.
[71] Lynch 1998 (unpublished Utrecht paper), 4.
[72] Lynch 1981, 24.
[73] Lynch 1998 (unpublished Utrecht paper), 4–5.
[74] Ibid., 2 and Dennison 1998a, 118.

75. Lynch 1981, 5.
76. Strauss 1966, 107.
77. Lynch 1981, 62.
78. *APS* 1875, 382.
79. Ibid., 382.
80. ECA ED008/1/6, 22 April 1738.
81. Ibid., ED008/1/8, 23 February 1749.
82. Robinson 1992, 136.
83. Lynch 1981, 59.
84. *APS* 1875, 382.
85. ECA ED008/1 and *APS* 1875, 382.
86. Lynch 1981, 57.
87. Ibid., 58.
88. *APS* 1875, 382.
89. Robinson 1992, 136.
90. ECA ED008/1.
91. Ibid., ED008/1.
92. Ibid., ED008/1/5, 21.
93. Ibid., ED008/1/7, 68.
94. Ibid., ED008/1/6, 3 August 1734.
95. Ibid., ED008/1/6, 3 February 1739.
96. Ibid., ED008/1/6, 7 August 1736.
97. Sheathmakers prior to 1615, shearsmiths from 1615, although there were no shearsmith masters in the mid-1700s. Ibid., ED008/1. For more information on craft groupings, see chapter 3.
98. Ibid., ED008/1/3, September 1652.
99. Ibid., ED008/1/6, 10 November 1733.
100. Ibid., ED008/1/6, 3 August 1734.
101. Ibid., ED008/1/7, 43.
102. Ibid., ED008/1/6, 22 September 1733 Though not called a 'committee', there is an earlier reference from 1546 stating that deacons chose four men to take care of incorporation business: 'To quhen all ye deacons chosit iiij men to gang at ye provestis bak our part of ye expensis …' Smith 1906, 127.
103. ECA ED008/1/8, 16 September 1749.
104. Ibid., ED008/1/7, 18.
105. Ibid., ED008/1/7, 14 May 1745.
106. Ibid., ED008/1/7, 30 May 1745.
107. Ibid., ED008/1/7, 15 June 1745.
108. Ibid., ED008/1/7. In the earlier days of the incorporation, notaries were paid to keep the minutes. Ibid., ED008/1/1.
109. Ibid., ED008/1/4, 1682.
110. Ibid., ED008/1/8, 16 September 1748.
111. Smith 1906, lxxix.
112. ECA ED008/1/4, 10 September 1686. Other incorporations had been using the leet system for some time.
113. Ibid., ED008/1/4, 14 September 1695.
114. Ibid., ED008/1/6, 14 September 1733.
115. Ibid., ED008/1/6, 15 September 1733.
116. Ibid., ED008/1/6, 15 September 1733.
117. Ibid., ED008/1/5, 1701 election.
118. Ibid., ED008/1/7, 51.
119. Lumsden & Aitken 1912, 37.
120. Harris 2002, 254.
121. *Edin Recs* 1869, 146.
122. Ibid., 67.
123. Yet Edinburgh's north-east quarter claimed a small part of the Canongate. One third of this quarter was outside the walls. Lynch 1981, 27.
124. Lynch 1988, 279.
125. Ibid., 274.
126. Ibid., 274–6.
127. Marwick 1909, 168.
128. *APS* 1875, 382.
129. Mackenzie 1949, 83.
130. Ibid., 74. Scotland was not the only country that wrestled with suburban growth; London is just one example of the many European cities in which the craft guilds had to deal with suburban craftsmen. Ward 1997, 27–8.
131. Harris 2002, 360.
132. Ibid., 142.
133. Mackenzie gives the date as 1639. Mackenzie 1949, 84.
134. Ibid., 84.
135. Harris 2002, 463–4.
136. Marwick 1909, 175.
137. Mowat 1994, 151.
138. ECA ED008/1/5, 19 June 1713.
139. Ibid., ED008/1/4.
140. Ibid., ED008/1/7, 1739 This was despite the fact that the two suburbs joined in 1649. Harris 2002, 463–4.
141. ECA ED008/1/5, 20 September 1707.
142. Ibid., ED008/1/4, 5.
143. Marwick 1909, 234.
144. Lynch 1988, 279.
145. Lynch 2000, 171.
146. Dingwall 1994, 136.
147. Friedrichs 2003, 153.
148. Whyte 1987, 230.
149. Marwick 1909, 109–10.
150. *Edinburgh Burgesses* 1929.
151. An example of this can be seen in L Inglebee Wood's book, *Scottish Pewter and Pewterwares*. Wood listed all of the known Edinburgh pewterers. According to his research, there were nineteen pewterers from 1550 to 1600, forty-two pewterers from 1600 to 1650 and sixty pewterers from 1650 to 1700. As we can see in table 1.4, the burgess rolls show fourteen pewterers from 1550 to 1600, thirty pewterers from 1600 to 1650 and fifty-four pewterers from 1650 to 1700. Wood 1905?, 175. Although this illustrates that the burgess rolls are not comprehensive, it also illustrates that they resemble the pattern of numerical growth and are therefore indicative of general trends.
152. *Edinburgh Burgesses* 1929.
153. ECA ED008/1/2, 274–5.
154. NMS Whitelaw EHMB.
155. Ibid.
156. ECA ED008/1/1–8.
157. Farr 2000, 24.

Chapter 2

The Crafts and Craftsmen

It has already been shown that the Incorporation of Hammermen as a single entity grew throughout the early modern period, but does this reflect accurately the demographic patterns for the individual crafts within the incorporation? Just as there was a burgh hierarchy and, inside that, a craft hierarchy to which the hammermen belonged, the Incorporation of Hammermen itself had an inner hierarchy. This hierarchy of crafts ranged from the numerous pewterers, down to the few swordslippers. There were also divisions of wealth ranging from the wealthy saddlers, down to the more humble spurriers. These divisions of wealth gave the Incorporation of Hammermen an aristocracy. Which crafts made up this aristocracy? Not all craftsmen in any craft were equal; there were wealthy locksmiths and poor locksmiths. These divisions ranged from servants up to guild brethren, with rich and poor divisions even in the masters of the crafts. What were the different levels to which a craftsman could aspire? How wealthy were the various branches of the hammermen? What does this tell us about Edinburgh's early modern metalwares market?

THE CRAFTS

The Incorporation of Hammermen as a whole was expanding between 1483 and 1750. But what was happening to the individual crafts that made up the incorporation? Were they all growing like the overall incorporation? Growth of single metalworking trades was not uncommon in early modern Europe. It has shown that in Reval, Estonia, the coppersmiths, clockmakers and locksmiths outgrew the Reval metalworking guild. They were able to break away from it and form into new specialized guilds,[1] just as the Edinburgh goldsmiths did.[2]

While the burgess rolls are not complete, they do give an interesting view of broad trends affecting the crafts. The goldsmiths are not included in the data, as the tables start with 1550 and they split off from the hammermen in 1525.[3] The hammermen minute books are complete and there are lists of freemen masters throughout, but there are only thirteen years for which the trade is listed with the name of the craftsman; the majority of the lists give only the master's name.[4] These thirteen years fall within a short time period between 1646 and 1717, providing a minute window which does not even cover one century out the whole 1483 to 1750 time frame. Albeit small, the data still gives a definite window into the demographic trends of the crafts that made up the Incorporation of Hammermen over two or three generations.

Table 1.4 was compiled from the burgess rolls.[5] The sixth column shows the total numbers of craftsmen to become burgesses, which was a necessary step to becoming a master, for each individual craft. 848 hammermen took burgess-ship between 1550 and 1750. The pewterers were the most numerous, with 143 burgess craftsmen. The pewterer craft was so small in 1483 that it was not even mentioned in the first seal of cause, though they were later mentioned in the 1496 seal.[6] Their omission in the former is in sharp contrast to their rise to the most populous single art in the 200 years covered by the burgess rolls.

The saddlers were the next biggest art shown by the burgess rolls, at 126. It would be interesting to see how numerous the saddlers were prior to 1550, but unfortunately the burgess rolls, which technically start at 1406, do not seem to be complete until the mid-sixteenth century.[7]

The saddlers were followed by the smiths at 120, the locksmiths at ninety-nine, the armourers at seventy-one and the cutlers at fifty-four. The other sixteen arts did not reach fifty burgess entries, though they might have had more burgess craftsmen who were not entered in the rolls. It appears that the pewterers, saddlers, blacksmiths and locksmiths, armourers and cutlers were the largest crafts in the hammermen numerically.

Looking at the second, third, fourth and fifth columns of table 1.4, there are some more subtle, specific trends. In the 1550–1600 period, the largest trades were the saddlers and cutlers. The lorimers and smiths were also quite numerous, followed by the pewterers and locksmiths. Neither of these crafts was even half the size of the saddlers. Many crafts, like the white-ironmen and the watch- and knockmakers, did not yet exist in Edinburgh. Many arts, like the damaskers, founders, sheathmakers and beltmakers only had one craftsman attaining burgess-ship in this period. Others had only slightly more.

The 1600–50 period saw the rise of the pewterers above the other arts, save the smiths. Closely behind them were the saddlers, armourers and locksmiths. The watch- and knockmaker trades started to provide burgesses and one smith took on the specialist description of 'farrier'. The sheathmakers made a slight comeback with four burgesses, while other arts, like the damaskers and swordslippers disappeared, never to be seen again in Edinburgh.

The 1650–1700 period was dominated by pewterers. They provided over fifty burgesses, while the next most numerous were the smiths and locksmiths, with thirty-four each. The saddlers, constant as always, made for thirty-one burgesses. The sheathmakers disappeared, while new trades like white-ironmen, or tinsmiths, pinmakers and stocking-frame makers were introduced to Edinburgh's list of occupations. Coppersmiths started to ascend to their 1700s place of importance, as did the watch- and knockmakers.

In the 1700–50 period the pewterers were still the largest single craft. The saddlers came in second, with the smiths and locksmiths right behind. While the lorimers and beltmakers dropped sharply, the coppersmiths and braziers nearly doubled. The founders, though still only nine in number, had tripled from the previous period and the farriers and white-ironmen quadrupled. The armourers had less than half of the burgess entrants that they amassed in the previous period.

The saddlers remained fairly constant in numbers of burgess entrants across the 200-year period. The smiths and gunsmiths also displayed continuity in numbers of craftsmen taking burgess-ship. Considering the size of Edinburgh, it is interesting that the gunsmiths' numbers were so low, though constant till the early 1700s. Other regions of Scotland specialized in the production of firearms.[8] It is possible that the numbers of Edinburgh's gunmakers show a reliance on other areas which specialized in this product; perhaps Edinburgh made only what was needed instead of competing.

Some crafts, such as the knockmakers, beltmakers, armourers, pewterers, coppersmiths, braziers and founders, showed growth. The locksmiths more than doubled the number of burgess entrants from the 1550–1600 period to the 1700–50 period. Growth of the crafts might indicate a growing consumer society.

While the cutlers were one of the biggest arts in the Incorporation of Hammermen in the 1550–1600 period, they soon declined rather severely. By 1715 the cutler craft was virtually gone; John Duncan was allowed to work in Edinburgh to pay his father's funeral expenses 'chiefly in respect there is no other freeman cutler residing in Edinburgh at present'.[9] They did have at least eleven new masters in the 1700–50 period. The lorimers, shearsmiths, swordslippers, sheathmakers and damaskers also declined.

Table 2.0 is a section of lists from the minute books of hammerman masters for various years between 1646 and 1749.[10] They are mostly complete, except for a handful of craftsmen whose trade was not listed and a group from 1693 onwards that is missing (see table 2.0 'missing' row). The numbers here do not reflect new men coming in, as in the burgess rolls; they are a tally mark of all the existing craftsmen alive and working that year. The last five lists – for the years 1693, 1705, 1717, 1741 and 1749 – show the crafts in groups.[11] Though only for a short time period, the data in this table does reinforce some of the general trends of the data from the burgess rolls.

Across table 2.0, the pewterers are always the most numerous single craft. When the crafts joined together into groups, the composite locksmiths took over as largest 'craft'. This might be because the craft included the knockmakers, who became more numerous in the early eighteenth century. The locksmiths themselves were growing[12] and were usually the second largest single craft in table 2.0.

Because these lists are more accurate, there are some subtler trends that appear. Notice that the smiths were very numerous in the burgess rolls, but in the minute books, the blacksmiths are usually not half the size of the locksmiths. 'Smith' is a general term and applies to both black- and locksmiths. Some of the smiths in the burgess rolls are actually locksmiths. The smiths are constant, though, just as the burgess rolls indicated.

Another interesting trend is the shortage of saddlers in the section of minute book lists. While the burgess rolls show them to be the second largest craft, they had only five or six practitioners in the late 1640s, possibly illustrating the disruption of trade brought by the Wars of the Covenant. By 1656 they started to pick up again and by 1674 they were up to twenty masters, though they fell away to eleven by 1717. The burgess rolls give an impression of stability, with a constant supply of between twenty to thirty-five new

THE LOCKSMITH CRAFT IN EARLY MODERN EDINBURGH

TABLE 2.0

Hammermen lists stating trade: numbers of masters (ECA ED008/1/1-8)

Trade	1646	1648	1654	1656	1660	1663	1668	1670	1671(?)	1674	1693	1705	1717	1741	1749
Blacksmith	4	5	6	8	7	9	6	6	5	7	7	7	5	7	7
Locksmith	10	14	14	13	15	14	14	17	12	16	48	49	38	37	45
Knockmaker	3	3	2	1	2	2	2	3	1	6					
Dagmaker	1	1	1	1	1	0	2	2	2	5					
Pewterer	7	15	20	21	21	20	20	19	17	28	40	NA	16	23	30
White–ironman						1	1	2		3					
Saddler	5	6	7	10	10	11	14	12	9	20	17	17	11	17	22
Armourer	5	7	7	7	10	9	8	12	8	9	10	NA	3	3	2
Lorimer	2	3	3	1	2	3	1	2	2	2	28	NA	16	18	23
Brazier	2	4	1	1	1	1	2	1		1					
Bell Founder/Founder		1													
Coppersmith			3	3	3	3	2	3	3	4					
Beltmaker	2	1	1	1	1	2	1	1	2	3					
Cutler		2	3	4	4	5	3	3	3	3	3	4		4	7
Shearsmith	3	3	4	4	3	5	4	4	3	4	4	NA	NA	NA	0
Sheathmaker	1	1	1												
Claspmaker	1	1	1	1	1	1	1	1	1	1					
Engraver									1	1					
Apothansherer pentr (painter?)		1	1							3					
No Trade Listed★	14	1		2	7	4	2	2	10	13					
Total Hammermen	60	69	75	79	88	90	83	90	79	129	157	77	89	109	136
Missing from list★★	1	0	0	0	0	0	0	0	0	0	3	78	4	NA	25

Lists of deacons and boxmasters not included in tallies, as they are already listed with trade
★ Unless craftsman was located in *Edinburgh Burgesses*, and assigned to their rightful trade
★★ Based on comparison with complete list of the same year – see table 1.10

saddlers per period. Perhaps Scotland's leather industry was a bit more volatile, but with enough reward to keep interest. With such a small window from 1646 to 1717, one can only speculate. The years with low figures might also represent old age or death pruning the saddlers' numbers.

The last sheathmaker seems to have passed away around 1654. The burgess rolls and the minute books' lists indicate that no more craftsmen took up this art. Other crafts such as the cutlers must have either made their own sheaths or bought imports.

CRAFT PRIVILEGE

Crafts guarded their privilege to work their section of a trade without others taking their business. In 1483 the seal of cause of the hammermen stated clearly that craftsmen were not allowed to 'exercise or use any more crafts but alanerly ane and to live thereupon, so that his other brother and craftsmen of the said crafts be not hurt through his large exertion and exceeding bounds'.[13] This was aimed at the freemen of the incorporation rather than unfreemen. It was a source of much argument in the meetings of the Incorporation of Hammermen at the Magdalen Chapel. The minute books are full of records of crafts trying to get craftsmen from different arts punished for working in their mediums.

The coppersmiths in 1734 were upset because a white-ironsmith had added a brass handle to a siphon he had made.[14] Brass is a copper alloy and therefore was the coppersmiths' and braziers' domain. There were of course other arts that used brass. The rules were constantly bent, but sometimes they were bent too far.

Sometimes it was not the material being used, but the method in which it was worked:

> Anent the complaint offered by the founders against the coppersmiths and locksmiths for encroaching upon their art and casting of founder work. The house upon searching into and hearing read the several acts of their incorporation, find that it is the uniform & useful practice of their incorporation that each art keep to and employ themselves in the exercise of their own proper art & branch of work they were admitted to ... and locksmiths, particularly William Richardson and William Auld, have all and each of them encroached upon and exercised the proper crafts of the founders. Therefore the house do discharge the said persons from exercising the casting of founder work in time coming, or any art exercising or working the proper art or work of ane other art in time coming whereupon this act is made ordered.[15]

With a forge, it would be easy to melt metal and cast various parts. By 1748 when this happened, brass lock cases for rim locks were in vogue and it might have been cheaper to make them than to buy them from the founders. Unfortunately, the clerk did not mention what the coppersmiths had done to encroach on the founders' work.

One of the bigger disputes was between the locksmiths and blacksmiths. The locksmith craft probably has its origins in the blacksmith craft and the one is just a mechanical version of the other. Their work often crossed over and their techniques and tools were very similar. In 1647, the locksmith and blacksmith arts had banded together in a dispute against a lorimer.[16] It was in both of their interests to stop the lorimers from doing work already covered by two crafts. The alliance did not last though.

In 1649 the blacksmiths started a dispute over the making of similar types of products with John Tweedie, Younger, who was a locksmith.[17] In 1654, some time after the troubles had calmed in Edinburgh, the blacksmiths made the dispute with all of the locksmiths. A supplication was handed in to the incorporation by the blacksmiths, complaining about the practice of the locksmiths of being 'hired daily to enter quays [and] sells all sort of chimneys only proper to the blacksmiths'.[18] The house ruled that no locksmiths were allowed to

> big any chimneys to the prejudice of the said blacksmiths to vent and sell again the same except so much as shall be for their ane proper use or what they shall work themselves of locksmith work ... and that under the pain of £10 totius quotus, or else they shall sell to the said blacksmith what chimneys they shall big that they work not themselves under the pain foresaid[19]

The locksmiths were noted in the minute books in 1612 as making chimney irons; it was not a new type of work that they suddenly decided to take over.[20] The judgement against the locksmiths did not go unopposed. The locksmith John Tweedie, Elder, protested against the act that they should have liberty to sell and 'big' chimneys, to which the blacksmiths also protested.[21]

The argument about chimneys did not rest there. It came up again in 1656.[22] Eventually the two arts came to an agreement. On 25 November 1682, there was an act appointing the agreement between the blacksmiths and locksmiths to be booked with the incorporation.[23] When the act was publicly read at a meeting of the Incorporation of Hammermen not one craftsman objected to it. The act had been written on 10 July 1682 and was to be contractual and final. Representatives from the blacksmiths on the one side and the locksmiths on the other, including in their number, his Majesty's Master Smith, John Callender, decided to finally conform to a previous 1622 decreet arbitral which had been given by the fourteen deacons of the Edinburgh incorporations. This decreet arbitral had also dealt with the conflict between the blacksmiths and locksmiths, but had gone beyond incorporation control to the other thirteen deacons.

The tone of the 1682 agreement was very formal and legal. This was to be a binding agreement to solve the dispute permanently. The agreement continued:

> viz, that the blacksmiths had good and undoubted right to the making of horse shoes, nails thereto and shoeing of horse, together with the making of chimneys and braces with racks thereto and [paterniks for the fire with couter sork and plough shoes] and that the locksmiths had good and undoubted right to the making and mending of locks and bands with all white work and filed work pertaining to the locksmith craft, with all sort of jointed bands and as for the door crooks and door bands then contraverted, they find the same to be ane indifferent and common piece of work to be wrought be both the said parties, as they should be employed therein and the mending of chimneys to be likewise common to both and the said fourteen deacons did discharge the said persons and parties and every one of them and their successors to intermell with or work ane other man's occupation, conform to the restrictions and limitation before set down and whatsoever is not expressly set down nor distinguished in name above written, the same to be wrought be them or any of them as they shall be employed as points of calling found to be indifferent and discerned the said persons and ilk ane of them and their successors to observe keep and fulfil to others the above written decreet arbitral in the whole ... and the party or person or their successors ... bound and obliged in payment of the sum of ten pounds Scots money ... as they should happen to transgress ... and now seeing the said blacksmiths ... and said locksmiths ... for themselves and their successors in their art, are all of them earnest willing and desirous to put away and remove all strife controversies and debates presently standing or which may hereafter arise betwixt the said two arts and to be united and incorporate in ane amicable and friendly society in all time coming, they all of them unanimously consent and agree to the following articles ... that all and whatsoever work which was distinguished and used formerly to be wrought be them separately conform to the said decreet arbitral, shall now and in all time coming be indifferent and common to both the said arts and every one of them and their successors have liberty to work the same as they shall be hereafter employed;

> Reserving to the said ... blacksmiths the horse shoes and nails to them allanerlie and to the locksmiths ... the locks and all other work whatsoever to be common to both said arts.[24]

The work they were arguing over, chimneys, door crooks and bands, were all parts of architectural hardware. It made sense for them to share domain over these work types and with the agreement sealed, the incorporation and the council did not need to worry about discord. By forming one 'amicable and friendly society', the governing was easier. It was a miniature incorporation in the incorporation. They still kept separate eldest and youngest masters for aiding the deacon and they kept several main items apart; horse shoes and shoe nails for the blacksmiths and locks to the locksmiths. All other smith-work from 1682 onwards was to be common.

This arrangement lasted about a year. On 23 August 1683, the incorporation's clerk recorded an act in favour of the locksmiths, watchmakers and gunsmiths against the blacksmiths, in the defence of their privileges. The petitioners went so far as to hire 'advocates, clerks and others for the managing of the said affair'.[25] Not even on paper were they an 'amicable and friendly society', but the types of work permitted kept the 1682 delineation and the two arts shared meetings at the Magdalen Chapel from then on.

One such shared meeting took place in 1745. On 30 May, before both the blacksmith and locksmith arts, the deacon informed the group of a letter he had received from a smith in Calton named Thomas Ainslie. The letter proposed that he should be honoured if they would receive him as a freeman of the incorporation and if found qualified, he would pay the house 25 guineas. The deacon asked the two arts for their resolution to the proposal.[26]

The two arts formed a craft committee to review the case. On 15 June they met again at the Magdalen Chapel. The committee reported that they had met with Ainslie and had talked him up to an offer of 500 merks Scots for upset money along with dues for the Trades Maiden Hospital. They decided that he had seemed a proper person to be admitted a freeman locksmith. The locksmith art then reported that they had agreed to admit Ainslie to an essay and to appoint him essay masters, with a landlord as was the usual manner required of ordinary entrants. However, a letter was produced stating that unless the blacksmith art would allow Ainslie to make his own essay and in his own shop he withdrew his proposal. This was argued upon amongst the locksmiths and they refused to alter either the type of essay or where it was normally made 'in the shop and under the eye and custody of some freeman'.[27] Therefore Ainslie's proposal was withdrawn. The two crafts worked together to decide on an issue which affected them both. In the end tradition and guarding of privilege won out over money.

A dispute between the locksmiths and one of the other crafts in 1733 illustrates how dramatic these inter-craft disputes could be. On 4 March

> George Aitken protested that the house should immediately proceed to consider the injury done to the locksmith art in their last proceeding. Thomas Richardson protested that since the house would not proceed to consider the said injury that the art could not be blamed if they should carry it before another Judicatory.[28]

What exactly happened with the threat of taking the dispute to another court is not apparent. There was more discussion a month later, though. The meeting included a reproach from the deacon for overstepping the house boundaries. Deacon Boswell protested 'that when once a member of the house has begun to speak, he shall not be interrupted till he be done and the deacon allowing the next man that rose to speak next'.[29]

When George Aitken spoke, he protested that the locksmith art should be able to retain the 'disposal of James Tweedy that was transferred to Deacon Dalgleish the sixth of March last', to which Thomas Richardson adhered and asked for a vote. Deacon Boswell then protested that there should not be a vote in regards that it had already been voted on, including Aitken and the locksmiths. Thomas Richardson then threatened that the locksmith art would not be liable any more for any of the burdens in the incorporation.[30] Sometimes the meetings could get heated.

Not all of the disputes were between crafts. Occasionally the argument was between incorporations. In 1665 the hammermen made a protest against the masons and wrights for 'building houses and furnishing the iron work thereto and saddlers' work by way of upholstery'.[31] Sometimes there were arguments between members of the same art. In 1740 Thomas Richard made a complaint for an unspecified master of the locksmiths against his own craft. This master alleged that some of his brethren were exposing faulty locks which did not include complete warding for sale in the market.[32] It was eventually decided that all ward-less locks were to be confiscated and every master was to put his initials or maker's mark 'in some convenient place' on the lock.[33] Thus the incorporation provided a practical vehicle for solving the inevitable disputes that arose in the day-to-day lives of craftsmen.

CRAFTSMEN

In the incorporations, below the deacons and office bearers, was the spectrum of ordinary craftsmen. This consisted of the masters, journeymen, apprentices and servants. The life of a craftsman was quite strictly regulated. They were forbidden from becoming merchants, or buying and selling goods, unless they renounced working their trades and obtained guild brethrenship. If caught breaking this law, all of the craftsman's merchandise was escheated, or confiscated. The council dictated prices and wages to them. If accused of charging exorbitant prices, punishments were handed out.[34] The craftsmen worked from five in the morning until eight o'clock at night.[35] They also worked 'on Saturdays and other vigils until 4 p.m.'.[36] The Sabbath, of course, remained work-free. To better understand the Incorporation of Hammermen, it makes sense to look at the smallest unit – the craftsman.

The career patterns of the trades were somewhat similar, so following the careers of two locksmiths in the early eighteenth century will give an indication of the experience of most Edinburgh hammermen. First, there are two fundamental steps in the career of an Edinburgh craftsman. Both were types of freedom, as a person living in a burgh was either a freeman or an unfreeman. The two types of freedom were freedom of the burgh and freedom of an incorporation. Both were necessary to practise a trade at the higher levels, but they were both separate institutions.

Freedom of the burgh was known as burgess-ship. This first type of freedom was not limited to craftsmen, but was open to all people in all occupations, provided they had the right connections and could afford to purchase it. Burgess-ship was part of early modern Scotland's middle class, or 'middling sort'.[37] At the bottom of the proverbial ladder were the poor and indigent. Above the poor were the labouring classes – the servants, apprentices, journeymen and day labourers. Above them came the burgesses. Being a burgess in Edinburgh meant that the person in question had paid a set sum of money to the dean of guild for his admission. The cost depended on whether or not the person was related to another person already admitted as a burgess. He could be a former apprentice of a burgess, the child of a burgess, or even married to a burgess's daughter. If he was not related to a burgess somehow, he was considered a stranger and the cost for burgess-ship was greater. By making burgess-ship selective, it protected the trade privileges of the few. This was the core level that all journeymen aspired to.[38] They wanted a shop, a house and the freedom to work their trade. In 1635, however, only 30 per cent of homeowners had managed to attain burgess-ship.[39]

The second type of freedom sought by a craftsman was the freedom of an incorporated trade. This was obtained by becoming a master in an incorporation. When a craftsman was skilled enough, he would petition the house for admission as a freeman. If the incorporation judged that he was ready and felt that the market could sustain one more master craftsman giving them a controlled amount of competition,[40] then an 'essay' would be set for him. Upon completion of a sufficient essay and payment of dues, the craftsman was then made a freeman and master of the incorporation.

Freedom of an incorporation protected business interests for the craftsmen. It kept strangers from producing goods or buying foreign goods and selling them cheaper in the burgh:

> The house desires the deacon to apply to the magistrates or council in order to get an effectual stop put to the hawkers and other persons going through the city and buying and selling old iron, brass and other things belonging to the hammermen and likewise to get a stop put to unfreemen exposing to sale hammermen's work of the market day.[41]

It also protected raw materials. If one was not allowed to work in iron then there was no point, other than personal profit, in buying up large quantities of it. This kept the available raw materials unofficially reserved for the craftsmen.

There was often some contention over the allowing of freedom to craftsmen. In 1736, Mr Andrew Dickie, a 'stranger' clockmaker, sent a letter to the incorporation craving both freedom of the incorporation and burgess-ship. The house nominated a committee consisting of several clockmakers and the former deacons and boxmasters. In this committee it was decided that five were to be a quorum. They met at two o'clock in the afternoon on 8 January to consider not only the answer to be given to Mr Dickie's letter, but also the possibility of admitting strangers to be freemen in general.[42] The committee recognised that it was 'a tender point to the generality of the arts to determine that point absolutely at present, but leaves it to the consideration of the particular arts when application is made to them upon that account'.[43] If there was another clockmaker in the Edinburgh market, it did not affect the business of the lorimers or coppersmiths, so why should the entire incorporation make decisions about the admission of strangers? Each art was to decide for itself on the distribution of freedom of its art. Dickie's burgess-ship was provided for him by the incorporation. This was unusual, but demonstrates how the incorporations could act as lobbyists to the council. Dickie must have had skills that Edinburgh needed, as he received both freedom of the burgh and freedom of the Incorporation of Hammermen.

Freedom was so jealously guarded that hammermen had to give an oath at their admission as masters. In 1685, James Gray was fined £20 'for packing and peeling[44] with an unfreemen contrary to his oath of admission'.[45] He was supposed to make 'ane iron sway for ane sign', for John Cope, periwigmaker. Instead, he bought one from James Horne in the Abbey, who was not a freeman of the Edinburgh Incorporation of Hammermen. He tried to make money by buying cheap goods from unfreemen and reselling them as his own work. If he had been a member of the guild and had gone through freemen craftsmen, this would have been fine. But he was only a burgess and a master and he paid unfreemen to do the work. He abused the freedom and it cost him a considerable sum.

UNFREEMEN

If only 30 per cent of homeowners were burgesses in 1635,[46] then there was a huge section of society that were lumped into the category of 'unfreemen'. Some of the unfreemen were 'foreign' unfreemen – merchants from unfree burghs, travelling craftsmen, apprentices come to Edinburgh from other areas and other such people from outside the burgh walls. Some of the unfreemen were locals. The children of unfreeman paid a higher rate than the children of freemen for an apprenticeship with a burgess. The small section of unfreemen that apply to this study are the apprentices, journeymen and servants of the Edinburgh Incorporation of Hammermen.

APPRENTICES

While there were incidences of an armourer's son and grandson also taking burgess-ship as armourers, it

THE CRAFTS AND CRAFTSMEN

TABLE 2.1
Number of apprenticeships booked (*Edinburgh Apprentices*)

Trade	1550–1600	1600–50	1650–1700	1700–50	Total
Locksmith	25	56	77	52	210
Gunsmith	7	8	6	4	25
Knockmaker	0	0	18	27	45

was not always the case that children followed in their fathers' footsteps and took the same trades. As can be seen in the 'Father's Trade' column of Tables 3.5, 3.6 and 3.7, many of the locksmiths, knockmakers and gunsmiths had fathers who were fermorers, merchants, tailors, wrights, writers, ministers, portioners and every other end of the occupational spectrum.[47]

Apprenticeship was a hands-on practical education, which served both parties involved. The master got help and the apprentice got skills, food, clothing and shelter. One of the rules for apprenticeship, laid out the 1483 seal of cause, was that 'it shall not be lawful to any master of the said crafts to reset or receive ane other man's apprentice as servant, nor give him any work, so long as he is bound to his master that he comes from and [is] paid of his duty and fee'.[48] Because of this clause, an apprentice who was bored or felt mistreated could not abandon his apprenticeship and simply go to work for another master. The apprentice had no choice but to stay the course and do his work. Apprenticeship was a contract.

The apprenticeship, or indenture, started when the child was about thirteen or fourteen.[49] It was supposed to last 'seven years and nay less'.[50] In 1739, a record in the hammermen minute books described how there was a period of two years after the indentures were over, in which the apprentice was to work as a journeyman for his master, to recoup lost money spent on his upkeep.[51] The length of apprenticeship was extremely variable. Tables 3.5, 3.6 and 3.7 show the lengths from the date of the apprenticeship booking to the date of freedom of the incorporation for several locksmiths, knockmakers and gunsmiths. The time elapsed ranges from three years, eight months and eleven days, to twenty-two years. The latter probably represents a normal apprenticeship and a long journeymanship, before finally attaining freedom of the incorporation. The three-year apprenticeship had probably already spent some time as a journeyman and was therefore skilled when he started. After three years he married a burgess's daughter and convinced the house to allow him freedom.

When an apprentice was ready for his essay, essay masters were assigned to him, as well as a booth to make the essay in. After 1653, it was decided 'that it should not be lawful in nae time coming for nae prentices to make their essay in their masters' booths and that because the locksmiths refused the above named William Jameson to make his essay in his said master's booth'.[52] The incorporation ensured that there was no possibility of cheating. This could have been somewhat unnerving, especially after the young apprentice had become used to the feel of the handles on the tools in his master's booth, or the way the vice at his master's bench worked. He would not have known how much pressure to put on the vice to keep the workpiece in without damaging it. Using someone else's tools at someone else's vice might have added a bit of pressure to the essay.

Table 2.1 was compiled by tallying the numbers of apprenticeships booked with locksmiths, gunsmiths and knockmakers, from 1550 to 1750.[53] Note that these three are broad categories, which include 'dagmakers', which were pistolmakers, watchmakers, 'hourmakers' and all other varieties under the general categories. Just like the burgess rolls, there is doubt as to how comprehensive they are, but the general trends should be fairly reliable. The locksmiths booked at least 210 apprentices from 1550 to 1750; the gunsmiths

TABLE 2.2
Apprentices' place of origin (*Edinburgh Apprentices*)

Trade	Edinburgh	Other	Unknown
Locksmith	39	158	13
Gunsmith	6	16	3
Knockmaker	15	26	4

TABLE 2.3
Comparison of incoming masters (shown by burgess-ship) and apprentices (*Edinburgh Apprentices, Edinburgh Burgesses*)

Trade	1550–1600	1600–50	1650–1700	1700–50	Total
Locksmith Masters	13	23	34	29	99
Locksmith Apprentices	25	56	77	52	210
Gunsmith Masters	6	6	7	3	22
Gunsmith Apprentices	7	8	6	4	25
Knockmaker Masters	0	3	7	26	36
Knockmaker Apprentices	0	0	18	27	45

had twenty-five and the knockmakers forty-five. In comparison with the numbers of locksmith, gunsmith and knockmaker apprentices to obtain burgess-ship in table 2.3, we see that there were more apprenticeships than incoming masters. The locksmiths produced only ninety-nine burgess entries and many of these had not been apprenticed. They produced more than twice that number of apprenticeships. While the gunsmiths and knockmakers are not as extreme in the difference, there were still more apprenticeship entries than burgess entries. If table 2.1 and table 3.5 are compared, the difference is even more apparent. Table 3.5 is a list of all master locksmiths listed in the Edinburgh Incorporation of Hammermen minute books.[54] There are only sixty-one masters listed that attained their freedom of the incorporation by right of apprenticeship. What happened to the other 144 apprentices? While there probably would have been some loss to death and some might have tried to attain a master position in another town somewhere, it is likely that most of them simply returned home, with skills that could be passed on to others.

Table 2.2 shows a tally of the place of origin for the apprentices. At least 75 per cent of locksmith apprentices were not from within the burgh walls, while 64 per cent of the gunsmiths and 58 per cent of knockmakers came from other areas. These included a few entries from foreign countries, like Ireland and England, but the mainstay of the entries were from Scotland, including Lewis, Turiff, Hillhead, Dundee, Dunbar, Culross, Stirling, Falkirk, Kelso, Peebles and so on. Many were from the suburbs of Edinburgh, like Leith, Bristo, Portsburgh and Canongate. Others were from nearby areas such as Gilmerton, Gorgie Mylne, and Dalkeith. It would seem that many of the boys from outside Edinburgh were booked into an apprenticeship in the capital, spent their six or seven years learning the trade until completion of indentures and then headed for home to set up as a master to train the local youths as apprentices. Some of their masters in Edinburgh had either come from or spent time in Europe gaining skill which they, in turn, brought back and passed on. In this way craft knowledge and skill from other areas and countries were disseminated throughout much of Scotland.

Drop-outs, whether part-way through an apprenticeship or at the end before taking freedom, were common in Edinburgh. One estimate for the surgeons states that only one fifth of surgical apprentices reached their final examinations[55] and, on average, only a quarter of apprentices in late seventeenth-century Edinburgh became burgesses.[56] Drop-outs were not only an Edinburgh phenomenon; a study of Bristol also found that a high number of apprentices did not become freemen. One sample of forty-seven smith apprentices yielded only one who took the freedom of Bristol. It is possible that the others decided to seek employment in the countryside at areas such as the Forest of Dean or the coalfields of South Wales.[57] In London, between 1540 and 1590, about 45 per cent of the apprentices in the carpenters' company did not finish their apprenticeships, let alone become freemen.[58] It was not guaranteed that an apprentice would carry on to become a burgess and freeman of a craft.

JOURNEYMEN

It seems that the term 'servant' referred to the journeymen. This is not as clear in the records as one would hope, but in a muster roll for the defence of Edinburgh in 1558,[59] there are 151 hammermen listed, of which sixty-six were masters. Eighty-five of the hammermen were listed as servants. If an apprentice started at fourteen and his indentures lasted seven years, then journeymen would have been in the twenty-one to thirty age group. They therefore would not have been missed out in town muster for defence. The word 'journeyman' does not appear in the 1558 muster roll, so servants and journeymen might have been the same thing.

Traditionally, Edinburgh journeymen were supposed to be preparing for the eventual outcome of attaining burgess-ship and then becoming a master in one of the incorporations. After apprenticeship, they worked for two to four years, earning money to set themselves up as masters.[60] In actuality, many never became masters, but instead worked all their lives as paid journeymen. This might have been due, in part, to the incorporations restricting the number of incoming freemen in order to protect craft privilege.

In Edinburgh, the traditional roles of journeymen were sometimes altered. Journeymen of the Incorporation of Mary's Chapel were at times allowed to take apprentices, so long as their booking fees were higher than that of booking with a master.[61] Due to the nature of building work, it made sense for a journeyman mason or wright to be training apprentices. There is also a mention of this practice from 1741 in relation to the locksmiths:

> Anent the complaint offered to the house by Thomas Richardson and Andrew Wilson masters of the locksmith art, complaining of the practice of some of the members of the house, their binding their journeymen as apprentices under indentures, entitling them to the freedom of the trade thereby and the taking of apprentices by some; while they work with others Masters under the pretence of transferring these apprentices themselves and craving the opinion of the house upon (thereupon). The house declared they find nothing inconsistent with the ancient practice in such usage nor that any thing derogatory or inconvenient can arise to the incorporation there anent and that every member may do therein as he pleases. Whereupon the said Thomas Richardson asked and took instruments.[62]

The 'ancient practice' was being redefined. Journeymen were being given privileges that originally they had been denied. They were skilled enough to train others, but usually they were not economically fortunate enough to be in the burgess level of society.

When a craftsman was booked as a journeyman, his name and his master's name were recorded in the minute books, such as the following 1704 entry: 'William Slowman is booked journeyman to John Lethem locksmith and present deacon of the incorporation, he paid the boxmaster 40s of booking money, 10s for the maiden hospital and the other dues.'[63] The sum of 50s was not too high, compared with the booking fee for Alexander Barclay in 1685. He paid £3, which was 10s more.[64]

It was a common practice in continental Europe for a journeyman to wander around from town to town, working in his trade and picking up experience. After his apprenticeship had finished, he would have been given papers certifying him as a journeyman. Various cities had different policies towards journeymen. Tallin, in Estonia, guaranteed every arriving journeyman at least two weeks work with a master.[65] In Nürnberg, incoming journeymen were forbidden from negotiating work with a master on their own. A deputized master received each journeyman and assigned him to a master. There would later be a banquet where the local journeymen would quiz the newcomer to investigate his background and qualifications. One of the rules for these banquets was that no journeyman was allowed to be armed at the table. Apparently, they could become heated events.[66]

How common travelling was for Scottish journeymen is unclear. There are at least two references to journeymen settling in towns other than those in which they did their apprenticeships. The Aberdeen Incorporation of Hammermen's minute books have a 1729 reference to journeymen joining the craft which states that 'no man shall be admitted as a freeman in this corporation until two years after expiring of his apprenticeship, and serving for that space as journeyman either in this burgh or somewhere else'.[67] In 1664, Thomas Montcuir was admitted to burgess-ship and in 1665 to the freedom of the Glasgow Incorporation of Hammermen. He had been trained in Aberdeen, and worked as a journeyman in Edinburgh.[68]

As Friedrichs points out, the blocked mobility of journeymen from protection of freemen's privileges and frustrated expectations would have undermined craft solidarity.[69] There was little incentive for the journeymen to be docile and keeping the journeymen in line proved to be a recurring problem for the Edinburgh council. One example of this can be found in the records for February 1686 and November 1688, when apprentices and journeymen were forced to sign a bond promising they would keep the peace.[70] In

December 1688, many journeymen participated in the anti-Catholic riots in Edinburgh and the sacking of Holyrood Abbey. The riots brought with them a loss of life, as well as a loss of property.[71] While there were burgesses and other unfreeman who also participated in the riots, the 1686 and 1688 bonds indicate that the journeymen alone were a large enough cause for concern. The bonds were another form of social control.

It might have been incorporation authority that kept hammermen journeymen in line during the 1745 uprising. There was only one journeyman from the Edinburgh hammermen, a watchmaker named John M'Naughton, who was out with Charles Edward. He boasted about having killed Colonel Gardner at Prestonpans and ended up a prisoner at Carlisle.[72] There were, however, at least eleven other Edinburgh journeymen and servants out. If they misbehaved, they could be fined or barred from work. The twelve that rebelled in 1745 did not prosper from their adventure.

Incorporation was also used as a means of control when journeymen simply refused to work. There was a complaint against the locksmith journeymen in 1750:

> The locksmith art represented that several of their journeymen had lately combined among themselves to give up working unless their masters would alter the hours of working from five to six in the morning and from eight to seven at night. The locksmith art met and engaged to one another not to fee any journeymen who should not work the ordinary hours and that under the penalty of five pounds sterling to be paid by the master.[73]

Even non-violent rebellion was crushed by withholding wages. Sometimes the council used oaths and bonds; sometimes it was through incorporation control of privilege and work. The journeymen were an underprivileged group who were often a thorn in the side of the council.

THE CAREER LADDER

The career ladder to the middle of Edinburgh society can be illustrated by reconstructing the lives of two Edinburgh locksmiths. While both ended up as Edinburgh burgesses and freemen locksmiths of the Edinburgh Incorporation of Hammermen, each took a slightly different path to get there.

Edward Bell was born in the first quarter of the eighteenth century. His father, James Bell, was a farmer in Craighall.[74] Unfortunately, his early years are mostly obscure. He did grow up on a farm, so Edward would have become accustomed to hard labour. Somewhere around the age of six, he might have attended the parish grammar school to learn basic reading, writing and arithmetic,[75] but being on a farm he might not have attended as regularly as he should have. After his education at the parish school was finished, if there was education given to him by other than his family, he went into Edinburgh to take up a trade.

The details of his trade experiences have several gaps in them, but can roughly be put together. On 10 January 1733, Edward Bell was put into the register of Edinburgh apprentices.[76] He was taken into the home and booth of George Aitkine, an Edinburgh locksmith. Aitkine had attained burgess-ship in 1720.[77] He therefore would have had another apprentice in his charge before young Edward came into his care, though the first apprentice was probably a journeyman by the time Bell arrived. Bell himself might have worked for him as a journeyman before his apprenticeship began in 1733.[78]

Bell's life as an apprentice would not have been easy; he would have been expected to earn his keep. All work was done for food, lodging and education; there was no payment for apprentices. Each day, work began at five in the morning.[79]

The master would give instruction at various phases of each new job set in front of Bell. At one moment, he would be swinging a sledgehammer while his master would move heated work – fresh from the forge box – around on the study, or anvil. In this way all the unskilled blows of the apprentice's hammer would fall in the right place, guided by the master's hand. At the next job Bell might have been stood next to the standing-vice at the workbench filing away at a crook band for some customer's door. As Aitkine walked by and noticed how short and futile his file strokes were, he would have given him a scolding and thus lessons were learned. By eight o'clock in the evening[80] – four on Saturdays[81] – the day was done and the booth was shut for the night. As the days went by, turning into years, Bell's hammer blows became more skilled and his filing technique more quick and efficient. His master found less and less to scold him for.

On 31 March 1739, six years after his indenture began, Edward Bell presented his bill to be admitted a freeman locksmith. The detailed account of this in the minute books of the hammermen gives some insight into the common practices followed in leaving apprenticeship and becoming a master. It is therefore expedient to reproduce the entirety of the account as follows:

> Edward Bell late prentice to George Aitken locksmith presented his bill for being admitted a freeman locksmith against admitting of Edward Bell, William Young protested that the same should not be received, because if this bill should pass every prentice should be entitled to the same advantage to George Begbie adhered. Simon Frazer counter protested that Edward Bell shall receive no damage from the above protest but admitted in the ordinary course and if stopped that he shall be liable for no damage that may follow their on to which George Aitken adhered. William Ormistoun protested that the bill may not be received in regard that the said Edward Bell has not served the two years prescribed by the acts of the house or immemorial custom after the expiration of his indentures and craves that a delay may be made until such time as the clerk be allowed to look into the corporation's records in order to satisfy the house anent the said acts ... Anent the bill presented by Edward Bell and the objections made thereupon in regard it's presumed that there are acts of the house against him and likewise the immemorial practice of the incorporation, the house puts it to the vote receive the bill or delay the consideration thereof; and it carried delay twenty six votes to twenty three ... The house delays the consideration of the bill presented by Edward Bell against which the said Edward Bell protested that he should receive no damage by the ... delay.[82]

The account starts off by stating that Bell was the 'late' apprentice of Aitkine; his formal period of apprenticeship was over at this date. The document then states that Bell was lacking the two years of service due at the end of an apprenticeship, which was often used to recoup money spent by the master on the apprentice during the indenture period. This amounts to an eight-year apprenticeship, which is odd, as a 1536 statute of Edinburgh apprenticeship states the norm as 'seven years and nay less'.[83]

After just over a month, on 5 May 1739, the bill was again discussed at the Magdalen Chapel:

> The house resuming the consideration of the bill presented by Edward Bell are of opinion that the same ought to be refused and that in consideration of the report made by the clerk that it was against the practice of the house in such cases and the house ordains the clerk betwixt and the next sederunt to draw an act in the strongest manner and terms declaring that for hereafter no prentice shall be admitted freeman of this house until eight years complete after the date of his indentures and that the said act shall ratify all former acts customs and ordinances of the incorporation relative thereto.[84]

The workings of the house were based on previous legislation, sometimes centuries old. There was a dilemma that the house could not immediately answer. The incorporation records were consulted and the house reached its decision based on acts from those records. When the decision was reached, forbidding Bell from taking freedom of the incorporation until the eight years were complete, the clerk was ordered to draw up another act before the next 'sederunt', or meeting, to have the decision on the books for future reference. Bell was going to have to keep working in Aitkine's booth for two more years before he could even consider setting up his own booth or taking on apprentices.

Bell still persisted. Two weeks later, on 19 May 1739, there was another meeting of the incorporation in the Cowgate. Bell tried to get an essay assigned early so he could start working on it:

> Upon the petition of Edward Bell, late prentice to George Aitkin locksmith craving that albeit the house would not admit him freeman immediately in respect of the usage of the incorporation in receiving none until two years expired after the date of the discharge of their indentures yet that they would please admit him in the mean time to the making his essay although the same should not be received until the house thought proper as the petition bears. The house taking the same to their consideration refused and hereby refuses the said bill and petition so presented by the said Edward Bell and delay judging thereof against which John Broun elder protested that whereas the said Edward Bell had served four years and six months a journeyman of this city, as would appear by the books of the house and six years ane apprentice, whereby the petitioner conceived himself entitled to be received a freeman of this incorporation and seeing the house has thought fit to delay granting the petition, therefore the said John Broun protested that notwithstanding the said delay it should no ways hinder the said Edward Bell from the exercise of his business within any part of the privileges and liberties of this city in regard he is willing to make his essay to testify his sufficiency to serve his majesties lieges and to pay the ordinary money due by prentices.[85]

While Bell might have seemed to be incessantly pestering, one can see why. He had done his six-year apprenticeship after four and a half years as a journeyman. If Bell applied for freedom in 1739, after his six-year apprenticeship, as proven by his entry in 1733 in the register of apprentices as stated above, then the four and a half years of journeymanship which John Broun, Elder, states is recorded somewhere in the various incorporation records, had to have started in about 1728.

After a childhood on the farm in Craighall, Bell moved into the capital and started working for a locksmith. By 1728 he was a journeyman. How much skill he had in his early journeyman years is not evident. It would have required money for the journeyman booking fee with the incorporation, which was £3 in 1685.[86] By 1733 he had become Aitkine's apprentice, eight years after Aitkine himself had attained burgess-ship. Six years later, Bell's apprenticeship was over, so he applied to become a freeman. 'Immemorial practice' dictated that he serve two more years as a journeyman, though Bell protested. The house was not swayed and Bell had to wait the two years, even though on 22 February 1740 he was allowed to attain burgess-ship and was listed as such in the burgess rolls.[87] It is not certain when his freeman's essay was assigned, but on 7 February 1741 he walked down into the Cowgate to the Magdalen Chapel and presented it:

> Compared Edward Bell, late prentice to George Aitkin, locksmith, present deacon and presented his essay viz a crook and crookband, a pass lock, with a round filled bridge not cut, nor broke on the backside and with brass knobs and jamband ... admitted freeman locksmith among them ...[88]

The essay was a very serious part of the initiation to the incorporation's freedom. In 1718 there had been a protest made to the incorporation that no one should 'be admitted freeman blacksmith or locksmith hereafter except the essay be narrowly looked to by the essay masters at the making and locked up at night and the essay masters strictly examined at the presenting of the essay'.[89] Freedom was a very serious honour and was not handed out lightly.

Bell then took the oath in front of the incorporation:

> By my part of paradise so help me God and by God himself, I, [Edward Bell], shall defend the true religion of Jesus Christ presently professed within this realm both with my body and goods and shall be well and true in my vocation and craft in serving of our [Sovereign Lord's] lieges without deceit and shall obey the deacon and masters whatsoever for the time and shall purchase no lordship nor other judges by them and shall skot, lot, watch and ward and bear all manner of portable charges with my brethren conform to my ability; and shall defend the liberty of the craft according to dignity at the uttermost of my power and shall keep all the general acts, ordinances and statutes made or to be made for utility and − of the said crafts without any reclaiming there from and shall forth from no unfreeman pack nor peel with them and shall take none of my brethrens houses, booths or works over their heads and shall not seduce nor tryst any of my brethren's prentices or servants from them nor reset nor free them without there license asked and given, lawful warning, compt and reckoning ab effect and I the said A. B. binds and obliges me faithfully to observe and fulfil the whole premises under the pane of perjury and defamation conform to this my oath of fidelity in all points as I shall answer in the presence of God.[90]

After the oath was sworn, according to the minute books, Bell would have taken 'the deacon by the hand'. The deacon that year, whose hand Bell happened to be shaking, was Bell's old master, George Aitkine. The essay to be inspected was a pass lock, or a door lock which was meant to be worked by a key for an already existing lock. In this way, one key – a 'pass key' - opened several different doors and a new lock could be added to an existing suite of locks. The warding in the essay, which was a series of obstacles inside the lock, could be varied so that another key, which was not a pass-key, would open only one of the doors and not both. The pass key would have been given to Bell to build the essay around. Aitkine would have taken this key and inserted it into the keyhole of Bell's pass lock essay. As he turned the key, it would have had to glide smoothly past the intricate warding inside. It then would have had to throw the bolt with minimal resistance, or else it would not have been accepted. The jamband, or keeper, brass knobs and bridge[91] would have all been checked. After the door crook and crook band had been deemed sufficient and the oath taken, Bell would have paid the dues, which were £10 Sterling and 20 merks Scots to the Trades Maiden Hospital and 'other dues' to the clerk and officer.[92] The last thing Bell had to do was produce his burgess ticket, which he had attained the year before. After at least twelve and a half years of apprenticeship and journeymanship Edward Bell was officially a freeman locksmith of the Edinburgh Incorporation of Hammermen. How long he lived and worked as a locksmith in Edinburgh is uncertain, but he was listed in 1752 as being a 'smith' at Mitchell's (land?) in Fishmarket Close.[93] This also illustrates the fact that 'smith' was often used as a generic term for various branches of the hammermen.

There were other routes to attaining freedom of the incorporation. Thomas Letham, like Bell, was born sometime in the early eighteenth century and, again, little is known about his early years. He might have been born outside the burgh, like Bell, but it is also possible that he was born inside the Edinburgh walls. If so, education would have been harder to get. T. C. Smout, citing Alexander Law's *Education in Edinburgh in the Eighteenth Century*, points out that municipal elementary schools in Edinburgh did not offer enough places to accommodate all the children who grew up there. There were only a few hundred seats between the High School, Heriot's, the Trade and Merchant's Maiden Hospitals and the Tolbooth Kirk Charity School, for the several thousand children in the area. He might have been lucky enough to attend one of the adventure schools, where education was paid for by the parents, but it is just as likely that he went without.[94] We do know that he learned to write his name. When he presented his essay on 3 May 1740, he signed his own name in the minute book.[95]

It would appear that Letham was never apprenticed to an Edinburgh locksmith, as his name does not appear in the *Register of Edinburgh Apprentices*.[96] There was no entry of Letham being booked an apprentice in the incorporation minute books either. He learned locksmithing somewhere, though, which might indicate that he started off as unskilled labour, working for a locksmith. This locksmith who employed and taught him might have been Alexander Fairbairn, as Letham took his daughter Jonet for a wife.[97]

It is also possible that he was born, raised and apprenticed in another burgh. He might have come to Edinburgh as a stallenger, or unfreeman allowed to sell wares in town, but not work.[98] Maybe he was an apprentice in Glasgow, or Dunfermline. He might have attained a stallenger licence for an Edinburgh fair. While at his stall, selling his locks, he might have met Jonet. Once married, he would have been allowed to join the incorporation as a locksmith, by right of her father, Alexander Fairbairn.

Whatever the case was, the first definite fact of Letham's career was recorded on 15 March 1740, when he presented his bill to become a freeman:

> Thomas Letham locksmith in Edinburgh presented his bill for being admitted ane freeman locksmith by right of marrying Jonet Fairbairn, daughter to Alexander Fairbairn, freeman locksmith, which was received accordingly. He paid the treasurer three pounds twelve shillings two pence and two thirds or a penny Stirling money as the half of his upset money and dues for the Maiden Hospital.[99]

The above entry in the minute books tells us that, even though he was not mentioned as being an apprentice in Edinburgh, he managed to become a freeman locksmith of the Edinburgh Incorporation of Hammermen by taking a different route; he married a freeman's daughter. Also by his marriage, he was entitled to buy burgess-ship seventeen days later, on 2 April 1740.[100] He was given a fancily scribed burgess ticket, as was the custom, and entered into the burgess rolls.

A month later, on 3 May 1740, Letham went down to the Magdalen Chapel and presented his essay:

> Compared Thomas Letham locksmith in Edinburgh and presented his essay viz a crook & crookband, a passlock with a round filled bridge, not cut nor broke on the backside and with brass knobs and a jamband which was found to be a well wrought essay able to serve his Majesties lieges and therefore they admitted him to be ane freeman locksmith among them. His essay masters were James Gardener John Wilson & Patrick Sibbald. His essay was made in Alexander Fairbairns shop and he landlord. He paid the treasurer the other half of his upset money making in whole seven pounds five shillings five pence one third of a penny Stirling money including the twenty merks Scots for the Trades Maiden Hospital and also paid the other dues to the clerk & officer and the said Thomas Letham in token of his consent to the acts of the incorporation conform to the oath taken by him there anent of the date hath subscribed these presents Thomas Letham.[101]

His essay, which was made in his father-in-law's booth, was the common essay. He too shook the deacon's hand and took the oath. Unlike Bell, he paid only £7 5s 5⅓d as upset, along with the 20 merks and other dues. Craftsmen who were apprenticed, such as Edward Bell, had to pay £10. For those that married a freeman's daughter, it was less. Could this have been to assure ease of 'disposal' for female children? Perhaps this practice of a 'tax-break' for craftsmen who married the daughter of a freeman was a burgh-controlled dowry of sorts, to ensure that female children in a patriarchal society were not left uncared for.

Thomas Letham was listed as living in Selkirk's (land?) in East Grassmarket in 1752.[102] When he took his first apprentice is not clear, but we do know that he took Robert Letham, son to one James Letham, tenant in Murehead, as apprentice on 7 February 1753.[103] It is not clear if James was kin, and how many apprentices Letham had throughout his career.

As the locksmith craft grew in importance, it would have become easier for a locksmith to climb the incorporation hierarchy to deacon or council member, unless he was content with plain freedom of the incorporation. There were also other directions to take, such as attaining guildry.

GUILDRY AND CRAFTSMEN

Once a locksmith had attained burgess-ship in Edinburgh, and subsequently become a freeman and master of the Incorporation of Hammermen, he was set up in a comfortable position in the burgh hierarchy. Freedom of an incorporation was a plateau in terms of a career in a craft. There were, however, higher rungs to climb on the proverbial ladder. The next step for a freeman was guildry. Guild brethren held a high position in burgh society. They had more privileges and power than common burgesses. Henceforth, guild brethrenship can be used to illustrate the position of the various hammermen crafts in Edinburgh society in terms of economic strength and status. This is particularly true of the locksmith craft. Records of guild brethrenship were included in the two volumes of *The Roll of Edinburgh Burgesses and Guild Brethren*.[104] Data was taken from these for the period of 1406 to 1750, which represents the earliest burgess/guildry entry, and marks the pre-Industrial cut-off point mentioned earlier. Were the hammermen wealthy? How did the various crafts rank in terms of wealth and status? What do these parameters tell us about the products and production of the hammermen? What does guild brethrenship suggest about the locksmith craft? The patterns of guild brethrenship in the Incorporation of Hammermen suggest answers to these questions and shed light on part of the hierarchy in the metalworking trades.

E. P. D. Torrie stated that the guild 'was a society for mutual self-help, conviviality and support of the church, retaining much in common with the early socio-religious guilds'.[105] The *Concise Scots Dictionary* defines the guild as 'an association formed within a burgh, enjoying exclusive rights of trading in it and taking a predominant part in its government'.[106] The principal concept behind the guild system is that of a fraternal group of individuals from a burgh, given a monopoly in their town for the buying of raw materials, the regulation of trade and the right to trade abroad.[107] It is important to note the difference between the guild and the craft guilds, or incorporated trades, which came about later in the fifteenth and sixteenth centuries. The guild to which burgesses became guild brethren was an older, larger economic organization, dealing mainly with the wealthier overseas merchants and the craft aristocracy. The Edinburgh guild was supposed to protect the Edinburgh guild brethren from receiving too little money for goods and services – perhaps due to foreign competition – while at the same time protecting the consumers against fraudulent dealers. Protection of trade went hand in hand with local political power. By influencing and participating in the burgh council, the guild obtained the power to further its own interests. Also, guilds took a fraternal role in burgh life, looking after guild brethren and their families when they were in need.[108]

Before the decreet arbitral in 1583, when craftsmen joined the guild they were supposed to renounce their trade. In an enactment of the Laws of the Four Burghs, before incorporations came about, there was a statement that dyers, fleshers, shoemakers and fishers should not be in the merchant guild unless they abstained from the practice of their trade with their own hands and conducted it exclusively by servants.[109] A craftsman that entered the guild was not to dirty his hands, but buy materials and employ servant craftsmen in his booth to make the wares for him; he was to be an employer. He effectively became a merchant of craftsman's goods. Since guildry brought with it foreign trade privileges, craftsman guild brethren might have hired journeymen to make the same products they once made, only for export instead of the domestic market. There are various lists of the customs rates for products leaving Scotland, including various metalwares.[110] Some craftsmen who joined the guild as employers may have become exporters.

After the decreet arbitral of 1583 the regulations were slightly more relaxed. In 1585 it was stated that there were different assessments of wealth for craftsmen entering the guild: 'the handy labourer using his craft in moveable goods to be esteemed worth five hundred merks of free gear by his craft and whatever he be that uses not the craft shall be worth one thousand merks free moveable gear'.[111] It would appear that after 1585 a craftsman could enter the guild and continue to work his trade.

Attaining the status of guild brethren in the early modern period indicated wealth, with the possible exception of receiving guildry 'gratis' from the council. The association between guildry and wealth is indicated by several details of brethrenship. Most significant was the cost of attaining guild brethrenship as opposed to the price of burgess-ship. Guildry was a higher social plane than burgess-ship; it was more prestigious, more politically powerful and therefore more expensive. By 1508 the price for the eldest son and heir of a burgess to attain burgess-ship was 6s 8d, while guildry cost 13s 4d, exactly twice as much.[112] By 1564 burgess-ship for an apprentice cost £5 and guildry cost £10. For a 'stranger', or unfreeman, the price was much higher: £20 for burgess-ship and £40 for guildry.[113] In 1647 burgess-ship for a stranger was £160 plus £10 for arms, while guildry for a stranger cost £240 plus £16 for arms.[114] If a burgess could afford guild brethrenship, then he was indeed wealthy.

Further proof of guildry equating to wealth is found in the act of council from 6 January 1585 which lists the levels of assessment for incoming brethren. It declares that no one is to be received guild brother from then on unless they meet certain criteria for their occupational category. For instance, a merchant had to have moveable goods worth 1,000 merks. At the very least, a craftsman had to be worth 500 merks even to be eligible for guildry. If he did not practise his craft but only employed other craftsmen to work in his booth then he had to be as wealthy as a merchant guild brother.[115]

One last indication of the connection between guildry and wealth is the arms that were required for burgess-ship and guildry in the sixteenth and seventeenth centuries. Every freeman in the early modern period was expected to 'bear the burden' with their neighbours as the town militia and watch. On 3 November 1591 a rule was set 'that anyone being made burgess must be sufficiently armed with ane furnished musket.'[116] From the late sixteenth century any burgess entered in the rolls has the word 'hagbut' or 'musket' listed after their name, until about 1644, when burgesses seem to have started giving money for the council to spend on arms instead of providing individual weapons and military service. While burgesses were expected to have only a musket, guild brethren were required to present an entire corslet, which was a suit of armour. The corslet is usually associated with pikemen in the military practices of the late 1500s and early 1600s. The pike was considered to be a more honourable weapon than the musket.[117] It is possible that the guild brethren were supposed to make up the pikemen of the Edinburgh defences, while the burgesses used the muskets. While a suit of armour was expensive and not everyone could afford it, muskets were considerably cheaper. Corslets were required for joining the guild for at least the first half of the seventeenth century, again indicating the level of wealth expected of guild brethren.

The guild was a highly selective group and it was considered both an honour and a privilege to join. The route to becoming a guild brother was easy, if one had the right connections and circumstances. The first step was to procure a burgess ticket. One could purchase burgess-ship and work for a while to save up money to purchase guildry at a later date. One could also purchase both burgess-ship and guildry at the same date. It appears that the costs remained the same, whether bought together or separately, but guildry was capital intensive and many could not afford both at the same time. Burgess-ship was a prerequisite to guildry, so when a person is listed as a guild brother, burgess-ship can safely be assumed.

As with burgess-ship, a candidate for guildry also needed connections. Marwick, in his indispensable book *Edinburgh Guilds and Crafts*, cites several examples of the various types of acceptable connections, which are similar to those linked with burgess-ship. Many acts of the Edinburgh council dealing with entry into the guildry mention candidates requiring 'right by their fathers, wives, or (as) apprentices'.[118]

The first way that one could obtain guild brethrenship was to inherit it 'in right of father'. In the medieval guild laws it stated that no one was to be admitted guild brother for less than 40s unless they were the son or daughter of a guild brother.[119] Price rates for guildry and burgess-ship written on 23 March 1508 start by listing that the eldest son of a burgess, entering as his heir, paid only 13s 4d for guildry. This was far cheaper than the £5 for an unfreeman to obtain the same.[120] If a person was seeking guildry and their father had been a burgess or guild brethren, they automatically had an advantage in price over someone who did not have a family relation with a burgess or guild brother. The 'right of father' entries into guildry indicate the selectiveness of the guild and their reluctance to admit large numbers of new brethren. Hereditary connections helped reserve the privileges for the select few in the burgh.

Another route to obtaining guildry was by 'right of wife'. This route was also semi-hereditary as it involved marrying a guild brother's daughter and therefore obtaining as a dowry of sorts the right to join the guild himself. Daughters in the early modern period were often seen as a cause for concern. Who would care for them in a patriarchal society when the father became old or passed away? By offering the passage of burgess and guild privileges through a daughter upon marriage, incentive was given to marry local daughters of burgesses and guild brethren. On 7 October 1462 John Chapellane received guildry by right of wife, after paying 20s.[121] On 29 January 1478 Thomas Haliburton was made burgess and guild brother by right of wife after giving spices and wine along with paying the 20s.[122] This was still a common practice in 1750. One example of this from 1751 is the deacon of the masons, Patrick Jameson, being received guild brother by right of his wife.[123]

Right of wife was sometimes obtained by marrying a burgess or guild brother's widow. A famous example of this is the infamous Major Thomas Weir. In 1642 he married Isobel Mein, the widow of a merchant named Bourdoun.[124] The marriage relieved the burgh of its duties in sustaining Bourdoun's widow and for Weir received burgess-ship and guild brethrenship gratis from an act of council.[125]

Another way that one could attain guildry was through apprenticeship. On 8 November 1564 an act was passed stating that former apprentices could purchase guildry for only £10,[126] while men who had not been apprenticed, or had not completed an apprenticeship, had to pay £40.[127] The reference to men who had not been an apprentice might refer to strangers only, not sons or sons in law of guild brethren, who attained guildry by the above-mentioned routes.

It would seem that prior to 1583, only those apprentices whose masters were guild brethren could join the guild. On 9 November 1583 the Edinburgh council passed an act which changed this.[128] Now, both guild brethren's apprentices and regular burgesses' apprentices had the option of purchasing guildry. Even if an apprentice's master was not in the guild himself, but was a burgess, that apprentice could climb to a higher societal rank.[129] Rather than making guildry even more selective, the 1583 act lifted a bar from guild membership.

Despite this, guildry retained a sense of hierarchy and privilege. Apprentices were subject to further legislation from the Edinburgh council in 1585 to ensure that the children of guild brethren enjoyed privilege over apprentices to guild brethren. On 28 April 1585 the council made the following act against apprentices seeking guildry:

> Item, anent the apprentices of guild brethren and burgesses, first, for their better trial and proof of their guild conditions; next, in respect they ought to be far inferior to their master's bairns twitching their right through their master ... therefore no apprentice be received burgess by right of his apprenticeship without he have served after the ische of his apprenticeship a freeman for the space of three year for meat and fie and than to be received burgess as an apprentice and also not to be received guild brother by that right without he have been a burgess for five year, so to abide thirteen year before he be guild brother by right of his apprenticeship.[130]

While the 1583 act was upheld allowing regular burgesses' apprentices to attain guildry, this act tempered the liberal entry regulations with a waiting period.

The 1585 act illustrates the position of apprentices in the guild entrance hierarchy: children of guild brethren, then sons in law of guild brethren and then apprentices. Thirteen years must have seemed like an eternity for apprentices when others gained entrance immediately due to family connections. Edinburgh's guild was a select group and they wanted to protect their privileges by keeping them in the family. Apprentices attaining guildry enlarged the group and diluted the privileges.

The apprentices were given an alternative route to the much sought-after guildry if they did not want to wait. Guild brethren wanted decent, respectable and trustworthy husbands to care for their daughters when they no longer could. Apprentices wanted a way around the long waiting period for guild entrance. The abovementioned act of council from 28 April 1585 set out to encourage apprentices 'to take in marriage their masters daughters before any others, which shall be a great comfort and support to freemen'. An apprentice could marry 'his master's daughter, or the daughter of any freeman burgess and guild and be found worthy and qualified, in that case to be received guild brother at any time by right of his wife'.[131] Quid pro quo. The master got a suitable son in law and the apprentice got guildry immediately by right of his wife.

Another route to guildry included brethrenship being given 'gratis', often for services rendered to the country, town, or guild. In 1562 Alexander Weyland, a lorimer from the Edinburgh Incorporation of Hammermen, was given guild brethrenship free due to his being injured in a French 'rage' in Edinburgh.[132] In 1459 Edward Boncle received guildry gratis for 'his aid and counsel'.[133] This continued throughout the early modern period, well beyond 1750. For example, in 1762 the five masters of the High School in Edinburgh were made burgesses and guild brethren 'dispensing with the dues, for good services done by them'.[134]

There are many examples of people being given guild brethrenship gratis at the request of various nobles. On 18 January 1555 Mr Robert Glen was given burgess-ship and guildry gratis at the request of Lord

Orkney.[135] On 1 February of the same year, Robert Lindesay was given guildry gratis at the request of the queen.[136] On 24 December 1563 a taverner named William Abercrummy was given burgess-ship and guildry gratis at the request of the abbot of St Colme's Inch.[137]

Because it spread the lucrative guild privileges quite thin, there were many attempts to curb the use of 'gratis' guild entrance. On the same day that the taverner William Abercrummy received burgess-ship and guildry free, the Edinburgh council decided that there was to be no more burgess-ship or guildry given gratis for one year under penalty of £10 'to be taken of the consenter and given without favour'.[138] On 26 September 1570 the council, bailies and provost considered all the gratis guild entries and declared that:

Understanding the great hurt that comes to the whole merchant estate of this realm by the solicitation of lords, great men and courtiers whose servants and kinsmen are made burgesses and freemen of burgh without paying of any duty therefore to the great hurt of the common well of all burghs and because such requests cannot commonly be refused for eschewing of the displeasure of the said great men and courtiers. Nonetheless the said provost, bailies and council statutes and ordains that in all times coming the heirs of such as are made burgesses or guild brother in manner above written shall not bruke the freedom and liberty of burgesses bairns nor be accepted nor admitted burgesses or guild [brother] without payment of the duty conform to the old acts notwithstanding their fathers freedom as said is and if the bailies, council or dean of guild consents or does in the contrary they to pay the said duty to the utmost but favour and that this act be observed for ever.[139]

TABLE 2.4
Method of attaining guildry (*Edinburgh Burgesses* 1929)

Trade	Right of father	Right of wife	Apprenticeship	Gratis	Unknown
Blacksmith	1			2	3
Pewterer	15	1	8	2	4
Saddler	10	3	4	4	4
Locksmith	4	1	1	3	2
Armourer	1	1			2
Lorimer				3	1
Spurrior					
Gunsmith	1		1		2
Watch/Knockmaker	3	2	1	2	3
Cutler	2	2	1	2	2
Coppersmith/Brazier	8	5		1	1
Beltmaker	1		3		2
Engraver		1		2	
Math. Instrmnt. Mkr.				1	
White-ironman		1			
Button-mould Mkr.					
Shearsmith					
Swordslipper					
Sheathmaker					
Farrier	1				
Bell Founder/Founder				1	2
Pinmaker					
Stocking Frame Mkr.					
Damasker					
Total	47	17	19	23	28

By declaring that the heirs of gratis guild brethren could not enter by right of father, the council ensured that the heirs would have to pay the full unfreeman price to join. As many could not afford this, the guild's numbers were controlled. The 'great men' still got what they wanted, but the guild had to tolerate only individuals.

Table 2.4 shows the numbers generated by the *Edinburgh Burgess Rolls* for the four main entry routes for guildry in the Incorporation of Hammermen: right of father, right of wife, apprenticeship and receiving it gratis from the council. The unknowns are those guild brethren where entry route was either not listed or unclear. These unknown entries are problematic in analysing the data. It is likely that they are a mixture of the first three types. Many entries for burgess-ship were via apprenticeship, with guildry coming at a later date with no entry route given. It would be easy to assume that these men attained guildry via apprenticeship, as they did their burgess-ship. The problem is that they might have attained a lower guildry price by marriage. If only the clerk had taken the time to mark down that it was in fact apprenticeship that entitled them to guildry, the task would be much simplified. It is unlikely that a gratis entry would not have been marked down, as the practice of giving guildry gratis was discouraged by the guild. They would have wanted records of those who gained entry without paying, so they would know not to allow the gratis guild brother's children in by right of father at the privileged price. Therefore, if all the unknowns were actually apprenticeship entries, right of father and apprenticeship would have been equally common as an entry route to guildry. It is unlikely that all the unknowns were of one type though, so it is a logical assumption that right of father was the most common entry route to guildry in the Edinburgh Incorporation of Hammermen. The gratis figure in table 2.4 is the only sure figure, as stated above. Twenty-three of the 134 hammermen, 17 per cent, received their guild brethrenship gratis from the council.

Just because someone had fulfilled the above requirements did not mean they could join the guildry at their leisure. As with burgesses, guild brethren were only admitted four times a year at the four head courts.[140] Other than at these four times, the 'locked book', where the names of burgesses and guild brethren were written, was 'put up in the charter house, not to be removed till two days before the said head courts, that the rights of fathers of applicants may be examined'.[141] This illustrates how keen the Edinburgh guild was to keep the numbers of guild brethren down to a controllable level.

On 22 March 1717 an act was passed by the council in hopes of limiting the number of people taking guildry by setting a time limit on entrance. Throughout the early modern period there were complaints about people carrying on trade without taking burgess-ship or guild brethrenship. The act seems to indicate that the people targeted were procrastinating, with the intention of becoming a burgess or guild brother at a later date. These people who were conducting private trade without entering, were reaping the benefits but were not contributing to the public taxes 'to the great prejudice of the neighbourhood and so several persons by their delaying to enter, [were] prevented by death, to the great prejudice of their widows and children'.[142] To prevent this, it was declared that from that point on each person having the right to enter as a burgess or burgess with guildry, either by their father, their wife, or as an apprentice, had to enter themselves in the guild books within the space of three years after either their majority, marriage, or the end of their indentures. If they did not enter in that time, then they lost the privilege. The act went on to declare that for each year that a person worked their trade without entering the guild, they would be fined 20s. By setting a three-year time limit, they were forcing conformity and control.

There are also several instances cited by Marwick that illustrate how selective the guild could be when considering candidates for brethrenship. On 23 April 1563 John Paterson, who was the deacon of the masons, asked the council to be made a guild brother. He stated that he had worked hard on the new Edinburgh tolbooth, and that other masons had received burgess-ship for their work. The council replied

> that they have not been in use to grant any such liberty or privilege to men unmarried; and therefore, when it should happen the said deacon to have ane lawful wife and married according to the order of the Kirk now present upon his good behaviour and service he should be considered in this his desire and satisfied to his pleasure.[143]

Marriage was also used against John Reid, servitor to James, Earl of Arran, when on 31 May 1581 he sought guildry. He was granted permission to

> exercise the trade of ane guild brother within the freedom of this burgh, not with standing that he be not admitted, but only free burgess and further promises so soon as he shall be married to admit him free guild brother for the request of the said earl.[144]

Early modern society hinged on institutions and all means were used to enforce societal norms.

On 6 March 1577, seven years before the decreet arbitral, Henry Blyth, a surgeon, and John Couper, a tailor, tried to join the guild. The council refused them unless they 'refused their crafts and boar boarding with the merchants'.[145] The decreet arbitral eventually brought equality in the guild for craftsmen and merchants, but this still illustrates how selective the guild could be.

There was also the ever-rising cost of purchasing guildry. Unfortunately, the recording of guild entry prices is random at best. In the 'Statutes of the Guild' of the late thirteenth century, the first mention of guild entry fees can be found.[146] It reads 'no one to be admitted into the guild of less than forty shillings, unless they be sons or daughters of guild brethren'. This might mean that the person had to have at least 40s of wealth in order to be eligible to join, or it might mean that they had to pay the 40s as an entry fee. Either scenario indicates the wealth that guildry represented.

In 1407 a duty of 10s was required for one to be made a guild brother.[147] By 1507 the price had been raised by 3s 4d for an eldest son and heir of a burgess to join the guild.[148] Other prices were also laid out for other entrance categories such as 20s for a second son of a burgess and 20s for a burgess's daughter. For an unfreeman's daughter it was £5 to join the guild. Unfortunately, it does not state how much it cost for an unfreeman's son to join the guild.

The entries on the price of guildry for 1564 and 1574 in the council records state that the duty payable for guildry was £40. It then states that for an apprentice it was only £10.[149] After the decreet arbitral the price for guildry through apprenticeship remained the same.[150] This decreet opened up the privileges of the guild to a greater pool of Edinburgh burgesses, but it seems that the guild did not respond by increasing the entry fees.

In the next century, there are several council entries from 1647 to 1654 that deal with guild entrance fees. The 1647 act begins by referring to the 'great damage and prejudice' the town was suffering by admitting burgesses and guild brethren 'at such low prices for the said freedoms'. The burgh was under much stress. The Bishops' Wars of 1639 and 1640 and the Scots armies sent to England, Ireland and the Highlands had severe monetary repercussions. One way that the burgh dealt with this was to increase the price for burgess and guild privileges. On 27 August 1647 the council stated that the price of becoming a guild brother would from then on be £240 and £16 for arms. The 1647 entry fees for guildry increased to a phenomenal amount and arms money replaced the physical provision of arms and armour for the town militia.[151]

On 8 October 1652 the council passed another act. In it several people who had been booked burgesses and apprentices 'in the time of trouble' were listed as desiring the council to ratify their burgess standing. It mentions that they were allowed to purchase burgess-ship and guild brethrenship 'as if they had been booked after the form and manner used of before'.[152] This was carried further in 1654:

> Forsameikle as the price and rate of the burgess-ship and guild-ship has been altered from the less to more and more to less, according to the exigency of the time…and seeing their times has their own pressing reasons for diminution of these prices therein contained, as the long continued troubles of a calamitous time, the great indigence and poverty of the people, who are not able to pay for their freedom at the late prices…therefore, to the effect the people may have ease for the time and these indirect ways and means may be prevented and removed and the guild box somewhat better supplied with money, the council has thought fit to reduce the price of the burgess-ship and guildship to the old rate during the councils pleasure; that is to say, the price of burgess-ship to be one hundred merks money and ten pounds for arms and the price of the guildship to be one hundred pounds money and sixteen pounds for arms, they paying the small dues over and above.[153]

These measures seem to represent necessity in hard times rather than guarded trade privileges.

Prices were set as a barrier to guild entry to keep the privileges reserved for a select group. They fluctuated as the council deemed necessary, in order to retain and maximise the effectiveness of those privileges. As shown in table 2.5, the cost for guildry varied widely with each category of applicant. Male children of those already in the select group had a definite advantage over apprentices and children of unfreemen. The cost also followed a general trend of increase over the early modern period, with a few decreases due to pressures of contemporary events. Guildry cost money and therefore represented wealth.

BENEFITS OF GUILDRY

There were various benefits that came with guild brethrenship. The most apparent of these guarded the trade privileges of the guild brethren. One such

TABLE 2.5
Cost of guildry (Marwick 1909, 9 & 135, *Edinburgh Burgesses* 1929, 1–3, 11)

Year	Entry route	Cost for burgess-ship	Cost for guildry
1200s	Unless guild son or daughter		40s
1407			10s
1507–8	Eldest son, heir	6s 8d	13s 4d
	2nd son	13s 4d	20s
	Burgess's daughter	13s 4d	20s
	Unfreeman's daughter	£3	£5
1564		£20	£40
	Apprenticeship	£5	£10
1574		£20	£40
1583	Apprenticeship		£10
1647		£160 + £10 arms	£240 + 20s + £16 arms
1654		100 merks + £10 arms	£100 + £16 arms
1694			£33 16s

privilege was that only guild brethren were allowed to have 'lot or cavil' with other guild brethren. This meant that a stranger, or unfreeman, could not come to an Edinburgh fair and set up a booth to sell wares in the best spots in the market place. The guild brethren were allowed to cast lots for the best positions first. Any remaining areas could then be divided up amongst unfreemen by lot and cavil amongst themselves.[154]

Only Guild brethren were allowed to trade abroad and they were also exempt from paying tolls in the king's burghs.[155] Certain goods were reserved for guild brethren to deal in. In the guild laws of Berwick, the buying of hides or skins for resale and the cutting of cloth were reserved.[156] In 1568, the doors of three booths were 'closed up' until their occupants purchased guild brethrenship, as they were selling spices that only guild brethren were allowed to sell.[157] Those who sold wine, wax, velvet, silks, or other fine wares, were threatened with the same in 1560.[158] While not all of these goods applied to the Incorporation of Hammermen, they do illustrate the privileges accorded to the guild.

Political power and prestige were other benefits of guildry. In 1681 the merchants of Edinburgh formed the 'Merchant Company' in an attempt to get a monopoly on retail for its members. This would have been an oligarchic super-guild in the guild. The crafts made the point that 'persons who wish may form voluntary societies, but a society on the lines proposed, destructive to other people's liberties, is against all reason and without parallel. The governors of such a company would be masters of the town'.[159] As it was, the guilds had economic power in the towns and after the Bishops' Wars, the power of burghs was great enough that the covenanters reduced their proportionate voting strength in parliament.[160]

Aside from guarding trade privileges and increasing political power, there were other benefits to becoming a guild brother. The guild was a fraternal organization, an extended family of sorts giving credence to the term 'brethren'. It was therefore expected that guild brethren were to act in a brotherly manner. Abusive language from one guild brother to another was fined 40d for the first three offences. After that the matter went before the aldermen, dean of guild and the remaining brethren of the guild. More serious assault cases were also handled by the guild itself.[161]

If a guild brother was in trouble with the law somewhere outside the burgh and his life was in jeopardy, three other guild brethren would go and stay with him, offering their services and support. He would have to pay for any extra errands he would have them go on, but it seems that the guild would pay the costs of the three brethren travelling to his aid. If it was decided that the guild brother was guilty, then the aldermen would decide whether or not the accused and condemned was liable for the expenses taken by his three guild brethren.[162]

Another aspect of the fraternal side of guildry was a form of insurance for guild brethren. If a guild brother fell 'sick or decayed', he was cared for by the other brethren. While sick, a person was incapable of earning a living for his family. The guild made sure they did not starve to death.[163] This is not to say that they alleviated all hardship for the family – going from a working state of wealth capable of affording guildry to a charity state of subsistence could not have been easy for the sick guild brother or his family.

When a guild brother died, all other guild brethren who were not out of the burgh on business were bound to attend his funeral. Failure to attend would have cost the absentee guild brother a boll of barley malt in earlier times.[164] If the guild brother died without leaving enough property or money to pay for his burial and the hiring of people to 'sing for his soul', he was buried at the expense of the guild.[165]

Apart from physical presence at funerals, the guild also provided part of the safety net set up for orphans in Edinburgh. Any burgess's child was eligible to gain entrance to Heriot's Hospital, which covered education. The guild then took up the cause of daughters of guild brethren who were sick, decayed, or had died in poverty. They were set up with a dowry for when they either got married or entered a convent.[166] The guild, though limited to the higher strata of urban society, was still integral to the social fabric of the early modern burgh.

GUILDRY AND THE INCORPORATED TRADES

In the earlier history of the incorporated trades, it was not common for craftsmen to join the guild. This changed after the 1583 decreet arbitral. This is illustrated by the number of hammermen who attained guildry prior to 1583. As can be seen in

TABLE 2.6
Hammermen attaining guildry (*Edinburgh Burgesses* 1929)

Trade	1450–1500	1500–50	1550–1600	1600–50	1650–1700	1700–50	Total
Blacksmith		1	2	1	2		6
Pewterer			3	7	9	11	30
Saddler	1	1	7	3	6	7	25
Locksmith				2	5	4	11
Armourer			1	1	2		4
Lorimer			1	1	2		4
Spurrier							0
Gunsmith				2	2		4
Watch/Knockmaker					3	8	11
Cutler			5	3	1		9
Coppersmith/Brazier					4	11	15
Beltmaker					5	1	6
Engraver						3	3
Math. Instrmnt. Mkr.						1	1
Whitesmith					1		1
Button-mould Mkr.							0
Shearsmith							0
Swordslipper							0
Sheathmaker							0
Farrier						1	1
Bell Founder/Founder					2	1	3
Pinmaker							0
Stocking Frame Mkr.							0
Damasker							0
Total Hammermen	1	2	19	20	44	48	134

TABLE 2.7
Percentage of freeman hammermen attaining guildry (*Edinburgh Burgesses* 1929)

	1450–1500	1500–50	1550–1600	1600–50	1650–1700	1700–50	Total
Ham. Guildbrethren★	1	2	19	20	44	48	134
Number of Freemen★			158	190	248	252	848
% Attaining Guildry			12%	11%	18%	19%	16%

★ Data from Tables 1.10 and 2.6

table 2.6, only three hammermen had become guild brethren from 1450 to 1550. From 1550 to 1600 nineteen hammermen took guildry. Therefore, until the 1550 to 1600 period, guildry has little meaning as an indicator of wealth for the Incorporation of Hammermen. From the decreet arbitral on, it will give a reasonable indication.

So were the Edinburgh hammermen wealthy? One way to answer this would be to compare the number of hammermen guild brethren to the number of entries for other occupational groups represented in the Edinburgh guild. This would involve taking a count from *The Roll of Edinburgh Burgesses and Guild Brethren* of every merchant, brewer, minister, glazier, farmer, shipmaster, bookbinder, gardener, cooper, baxter, naval officer, tailor, surgeon, wright, bonnetmaker and every other occupation to attain guildry from 1406 to 1750. This is beyond the scope of this book, so the guild membership numbers were taken for the hammermen only, from 1450 to 1750.[167] While this will not allow a comparison to other occupations it will still give a limited indication of wealth, first, for the hammermen as a whole, and second, for individual trades in the incorporation.

As can be seen in table 2.6, a total of 134 hammermen were listed in the burgess and guildry rolls as having attained guildry between 1450 and 1750. The same two volumes list 848 hammermen as attaining burgess-ship, which was equivalent to middle class and therefore not as wealthy as the 134 of them who attained guildry.[168] This would indicate that 16 per cent of the Incorporation of Hammermen was wealthy enough to afford guildry from 1483 to 1750.

Before 1550, only two saddlers and a blacksmith managed to become guild brethren. From 1550 to 1600 the number of hammermen guild brethren rose to nineteen. As can be seen in table 2.6, the number of hammermen guild brethren was fairly constant from 1550 to 1650. In the 1650–1700 period, the number more than doubled and then remained fairly constant until 1750. Table 1.4 shows that the population of hammermen masters, as shown by burgess-ship, increased in a similar fashion. From 1550 to 1750 the Incorporation of Hammermen was getting bigger and wealthier. More craftsmen could afford guildry.

Table 2.7 shows how the percentage of hammermen to attain guildry changed by half-century periods from 1550 to 1750. Using table 1.4, the numbers of incoming hammermen burgesses were taken for the fifty year segments to give the data in the 'Number of Freemen' row of table 2.7. Based on this, the percentage of hammermen to attain guildry climbed from 12 per cent in the half-century of the decreet arbitral, to 19 per cent in the 1700–50 period. The largest jump seems to have been in the 1650–1700 period, where the former 11 per cent rose to 18 per cent – a marked increase in wealth for the hammermen.

From 1550 to 1650, 90 per cent of the incoming freemen did not purchase guildry. While some of them might have had the capital to do so and did not, it would appear that only about 10 per cent of the hammermen held the amount of wealth required for joining. At this time they had to have at least 500 merks.[169] From 1650 to 1750, only 80 per cent of incoming freeman hammermen did not purchase guildry.

The data indicates that overall the Edinburgh hammermen were not wealthy, though their wealth did increase from the sixteenth to eighteenth century. The wealth rested with 10 to 20 per cent of the craftsmen at any fifty-year period. The 1700–50 period had the highest percentage of hammermen guild brethren, indicating that more hammermen had wealth in the latter days of the early modern period. Fourteen hammermen became guild brethren before 1583,[170] meaning that 89 per cent of them did so after the decreet arbitral.

Looking at hammermen guild brethrenship trade by trade will tell us much about the wealth and status of individual crafts in the Edinburgh Incorporation of Hammermen. Table 2.8 shows the hammermen crafts in descending order of number of guild brethren. This is for the whole 1450 to 1750 period and is based on data from table 2.6. The pewterers had the most guild brethren. This would indicate that they were the most lucrative craft in the Incorporation of Hammermen. When compared to table 2.6, though, it can be seen that this was a later development, as pewterers did not start taking guildry until the 1550 to 1600 period.

The second wealthiest hammermen craft, according to guild brethrenship, was the saddlers. This craft was stable in terms of numbers of guild brethren compared to the others. While most crafts started taking guildry after the 1583 decreet arbitral, the saddlers had a guild brother in 1463, twenty years before the incorporation of the metalworkers into the hammermen. While in the 1700–50 period the pewterers had almost twice as many guild brethren as the saddlers, over the whole early modern period the saddlers were a constant source of brethren and therefore a relatively wealthy craft in a hammerman context.

The third wealthiest hammermen craft was the coppersmith/brazier craft. In the 1450–1750 time frame, they were the third wealthiest craft in the hammermen. Like the pewterers, they developed their wealth later, from 1650 onwards.

Tied for fourth wealthiest craft were the locksmiths and knockmakers, though the knockmakers were technically part of the composite locksmith craft. The locksmiths started attaining guildry in the first decade of the seventeenth century; the knockmakers after 1650.

The fifth wealthiest craft would appear to be the cutlers. This is curious though, as the art was dying out in Edinburgh. In 1697[171] and 1715[172] measures were taken to bring this skill back into the burgh. The cutlers' guild brethrenship might reflect the council's attempt to make Edinburgh an appealing place for cutlers to settle.

These are the main crafts where guild brethrenship was attained. The saddlers were the main craft that show signs of wealth both before the decreet arbitral and after, but mainly after. The others seem to have attained wealth after 1600. While the saddlers had some wealth before 1583, it was the pewterers who ended up being the wealthiest by 1750.[173]

For the sake of tempering the idea that the pewterers were wealthy, which in a hammermen context they were, it will be interesting to look briefly at guildry for the Incorporation of Goldsmiths. According to the *Edinburgh Burgess Rolls*, from 1500 to 1750 there were 143 goldsmiths that attained guild brethrenship.[174] This one craft, which dealt with luxury items, left the hammermen to form their own incorporation within the first century of corporatism and went on to have nine more craftsmen, worth at least 500 merks, than all twenty-four hammerman crafts combined. As an incorporation, the hammermen were still not as wealthy as the goldsmith craft. Of course goldsmiths were always wealthy, throughout Europe.[175]

TABLE 2.8
Rank of hammermen crafts attaining guildry
(*Edinburgh Burgesses* 1929)

Trade	Total guildry
Pewterer	30
Saddler	25
Coppersmith/Brazier	15
Locksmith	11
Watch/Knockmaker	11
Cutler	9
Beltmaker	6
Blacksmith	6
Armourer	4
Gunsmith	4
Lorimer	4
Bell Founder/Founder	3
Engraver	3
Farrier	1
Math. Instrument Maker	1
Whitesmith	1
Button-mould Maker	0
Damasker	0
Pinmaker	0
Sheathmaker	0
Shearsmith	0
Spurrier	0
Stocking Frame Maker	0
Swordslipper	0

PRODUCTS AND PRODUCTION

What do the rank and status of the individual hammermen crafts reveal about Edinburgh metalware products and production? What metalwares appear to have been lucrative? What metalwares were in demand in Edinburgh? Using guildry as an indicator of wealth, table 2.8 would indicate that pewterware was a lucrative product. The pewterers had the wealth to supply thirty guild brothers from 1583 to 1750. The products that they were producing were not necessities. Wooden and horn table and flatware were easily available. The durability and aesthetically pleasing look of pewter made it a very nice medium for table and flatware. As pewterware often followed the styles of silver, it could provide the middling sort with some of the style that would otherwise be limited to those who could afford silver. An American study of Maryland from 1650 to 1720 showed that over 90 per cent of the top two-thirds of society in terms of wealth owned pewter. Over 88 per cent of the households in the study owned at least one item of pewter.[176] If the colonies were using that much pewter, it is likely that there was a strong demand for pewterwares in Edinburgh, a European capital. The trend of the numbers of pewterer guild brethren indicates a rise in demand for pewterwares in the seventeenth century, peaking at our cut-off date of 1750.

The saddlers' wealth illustrates the necessity of horse tack throughout the early modern period. Horses were used for transportation as well as war, which necessitated horse tack in the form of saddles, reins, stirrups and other hardware associated with the animals. Saddlers in Edinburgh were making money, which must reflect product demand.

The third wealthiest trade, the coppersmith/braziers, is interesting as the fifteen guild brethren they provided are limited to the 1667–1750 period, a late rise in wealth. Around the year 1700, there was a rise in the use of brass for lock cases and door knobs. The increase in importance of cheap durable tablewares such as pewter and white iron, or tin, provided equal demand for copper, a medium just as malleable, durable and attractive. Again, rise in wealth illuminates demand.

The two trades tied for fourth wealthiest are the locksmiths and knockmakers. The knockmakers were making a luxury item, yet the amount of money the knockmakers were bringing in by 1750 illustrates that the trade was thriving. This matches general patterns, such as Lorna Weatherhill's study of British material culture, which indicates that by 1715 clocks were mentioned three times more frequently in inventories than they had been in 1685.[177]

The demand for locksmith work is obvious. Everyone needed locks for doors. In 1747 William Hogarth made an engraving entitled 'The Idle 'Prentice return'd from Sea, & in a Garret with a common Prostitute.'[178] The dilapidated single-room house of the prostitute is the extreme of poverty, yet the door is clearly fitted with a lock. The fact that the locksmiths were tied for the fourth wealthiest trade illustrates that though the locksmith trade was labour intensive, it could also be lucrative. The demand was there.

So what do the burgess rolls and minute books show in terms of products and production? Table 1.4 shows burgess entries and therefore indicates craftsmen becoming masters and setting up their own booths for producing metalwares. In the first of the four periods shown, the two most numerous crafts were the saddlers and cutlers, indicating the importance of horse tack and domestic utensils in mid-to-late 1500s Edinburgh. There were fifty-four hammermen who worked on horse equipment (saddlers and lorimers), out of the 158 hammermen listed in the burgess rolls from 1550 to 1600. The blacksmiths also would have produced shoes and nails. On a rough estimate, using half of the 'smiths' as blacksmiths[179] and combining them with the saddlers and lorimers for an estimated total of sixty-five hammermen, this would indicate that a possible 41 per cent of the incoming masters in the Incorporation of Hammermen from 1550 to 1600 produced horse tack. This figure is based on the burgess rolls though, and is not completely accurate.

The cutlers accounted for 16 per cent of the hammermen. Knives were a common necessity. Most paintings of individuals in the early modern period show knives hanging from the waists of men and women.

In the 1600–50 period the pewterers became the largest craft, alone accounting for 16 per cent of the hammermen. Pewterware was on the rise. Horse tack in this period accounted for 24 per cent, using the same method as above.

In the 1650–1700 period the pewterers crafts boasted fifty-three burgess entrants; 21 per cent of the hammermen attaining burgesses. If the number of craftsmen working in the medium kept rising, there must have been a market for the product to feed the growth. Horse tack remained at a possible 24 per cent. It is still clear that the pewterers were growing, while the horse tack production was in a state of continuity, not growth.

The 1700–50 period shows the pewterers, still the largest single craft, falling slightly to 18 per cent of the hammermen burgess entrants. Horse tack was down to 22 per cent. The locksmiths account for at least 12 per cent, though some of the smiths might actually be locksmiths.

The last column in table 1.4 shows the complete totals for 1550–1750. The pewterers are the most numerous, followed by the saddlers, smiths and locksmiths. Cheap table wares, horse tack and architectural hardware, were the metalwares with the most producers as indicated by early modern Scotland's burgess entrants.

Both table 1.4 and table 2.8 illustrate that early modern Edinburgh had a large demand for pewterware and horse tack. These trades were lucrative. Guildry shows that there was also demand for locks, clocks and cutlery. Most of the items produced by the hammermen trades that had the most guild brethren were either domestic-related products, such as items for food consumption, architectural hardware and luxury timepieces, or horse tack.

GUILD BRETHREN AND THE LOCKSMITH CRAFT

So what does guild brethrenship tell us about the Edinburgh locksmith craft? Eleven locksmiths, eleven knockmakers and four gunsmiths attained guild brethrenship between 1406 and 1750. As individual trades, these are fourth and seventh wealthiest in terms of number of craftsmen who could afford guildry (see table 2.8). They were not as wealthy as the pewterers, saddlers, or coppersmith/braziers. By 1693, the Incorporation of Hammermen minute books started to group related trades together.[180] When this is taken into consideration and the locksmiths, knockmakers and gunsmiths, though separate trades, are viewed as one composite 'craft', the data is different. When the three trades are grouped together (see table 2.9) and compared to the other trades in their 1693 groupings, the locksmith craft (locksmiths, kockmakers and gunsmiths) is third wealthiest, just overshadowing the saddlers. Clockmakers in many European towns were part of the craft aristocracy. At Blois in 1666, the clockmakers were one of the first three crafts by prestige ranking in a general procession. The other two were the goldsmiths and drapers.[181] Locksmiths, however, were not as prestigious, especially in the late medieval period. In 1422, a ranking of London crafts in the Brewer's records lists the 'lockyers' in ninety-fourth place out of 111 crafts. The goldsmiths were number five, the saddlers number nine and the soapmakers were last.[182] The Edinburgh Incorporation of Hammermen's 1483 seal of cause did

TABLE 2.9
Hammermen groupings and guildry (ECA ED008/1/4)

Trade groupings 1693	Guild brethren★
Pewterer	31
White-ironman	
Lorimer	29
Brazier	
Bell Founder/Founder	
Coppersmith	
Beltmaker	
Locksmith	26
Knockmaker	
Dagmaker	
Saddler	25
Cutler	9
Blacksmith	7
Armourer	4
Shearsmith	0

★ 1450–1750 (*Edinburgh Burgesses* 1929)

not even mention the locksmiths.[183] They did grow in importance and wealth though.

On their own, the locksmiths appear to be tied for the fourth wealthiest trade in the Edinburgh Incorporation of Hammermen. They accounted for 8 per cent of the hammermen who attained guildry. The Incorporation of Hammermen was not exceed-ingly wealthy, though certain trades, according to the number of guild brethren, were lucrative. Locksmithing was labour intensive, but the demand for security provided eleven of the locksmiths with the means to attain the privileges of guild brethrenship.

CRAFTSMEN AND POWER

It has been argued that in the early sixteenth century the body that controlled burgh politics was a small, select oligarchy controlled by merchants.[184] While it is true that the merchant/craftsman friction can be

TABLE 2.10
Deacons of the Edinburgh Incorporation of Hammermen (ECA ED008/1)

Year	Name of Deacon	Trade	Boxmaster/Treasurer	Trade
1483				
1484				
1485				
1486				
1487				
1488				
1489				
1490				
1491				
1492				
1493				
1494	Robert Sheirsmyth	Shearsmith		
1495	Thomas Sparty			
1496	John Malesoun, younger			
1497	Andrew Muncur			
1498	Thomas Ra			
1499	John Letham			
1500	Andrew Muncur			
1501	Robert Selkirk			
1502	Thomas Sparty			
1503	Thomas Smyt	?		
1504	Robert Selkirk			
1505	William Auldjoy			
1506	John Locksmyth	Locksmith		
1507	Allan Cochran			
1508	Allan Cochran(?)			
1509	William Meil			
1510	William Meil			
1511	William Smyt			
1512	William Ra	Cutler		
1513	William Ra	Cutler		
1514	Henry Lorimer	Lorimer(?)		
1515	William Meil			
1516	Patrick Scot	Saddler		
1517	William Ra	Cutler		
1518	Thomas Smyt	Saddler		
1519	Christopher Wyntoin			
1520	Henry Lorimer	Lorimer(?)		
1521	William Smeberd			
1522	Andrew Hume			
1523	William Ra	Cutler		
1524	Patrick Scot	Saddler		
1525	Andrew Cochran			
1526	William Smeberd			
1527	William Ra	Cutler		
1528	Thomas Craufurd			
1529	Thomas Hunter(?)			

TABLE 2.10 (*cont*)
Deacons of the Edinburgh Incorporation of Hammermen (ECA ED008/1)

Year	Name of Deacon	Trade	Boxmaster/Treasurer	Trade
1530	John Smyt			
1531	William Smeberd			
1532	William Smeberd			
1533	James Frog			
1534	William Ra	Cutler		
1535	James Jonstone			
1536	James Jonstone			
1537	James Jonstone			
1538	William Smeberd			
1539	William Scot			
1540	William Ray	Cutler		
1541	W. Smeberd & J. Jonstone★			
1542	W. Smeberd & J. Jonstone★			
1543	James Jonstone★			
1544	William Scot			
1545	Mungo Hunter	Locksmith		
1546	George Peirsoun	Saddler		
1547	James Johnsoun			
1548	William Scot			
1549	George Peirsoun	Saddler		
1550	James Zoung	Cutler		
1551	Mungo Hunter	Locksmith		
1552	James Zoung	Cutler		
1553	James Zoung	Cutler		
1554	James Zoung	Cutler		
1555	Andrew Hamyltoun			
1556	James Zoung	Cutler		
1557	John Rynd	Pewtermaker		
1558	James Mure			
1559	James Cranstoun★			
1560	William Harlaw	Saddler		
1561	John Robesoun			
1562	James Zoung	Cutler		
1563	James Zoung★	Cutler		
1564	Nicholl Purves★			
1565	Nicholl Purves			
1566	John Weir	Pewterer		
1567	James Zoung★	Cutler		
1568	James Zoung★	Cutler		
1569	John Wilson	Pewterer		
1570	John Wilson	Pewterer		
1571	John Wilson	Pewterer		
1572	William Raa	Cutler		
1573	John Anan	Cutler		
1574	James Zoung	Cutler		
1575	James Zoung	Cutler		
1576	Robert Abircrumby	Saddler		

TABLE 2.10 (*cont*)
Deacons of the Edinburgh Incorporation of Hammermen (ECA ED008/1)

Year	Name of Deacon	Trade	Boxmaster/Treasurer	Trade
1577	Robert Abircrumby	Saddler		
1578	Robert Abircrumby	Saddler		
1579	John Richertsone★	Saddler		
1580	John Richertsone	Saddler		
1581	John Watt	Locksmith		
1582	John Watt	Locksmith		
1583	John Watt	Locksmith		
1584	?			
1585	Thomas Millar	Cutler		
1586	William Symonton	Saddler		
1587	Thomas Millar	Cutler		
1588	John Watt	Locksmith		
1589	John Watt	Locksmith		
1590	David Dyning	Saddler		
1591	David Dyning	Saddler		
1592	James Robeson	Cutler		
1593	James Robeson	Cutler		
1594	John Harlaw	Saddler		
1595	John Watt	Locksmith		
1596	John Watt	Lock. & Dagmkr.		
1597	William Symonton	Saddler		
1598	William Symonton	Saddler		
1599	Alexander Bruce	Cutler		
1600	John Harlaw	Saddler	Hew Meiklejohn	Locksmith
1601	William Weyllands	Lorimer	Thomas Weir	Pewterer
1602	William Weyllands	Lorimer	Thomas Weir	Pewterer
1603	Alexander Bruce	Cutler	James Sibbet (Sibbald)	Pewterer
1604	Alexander Bruce	Cutler	James Sibbet (Sibbald)	Pewterer
1605	William Symonton	Saddler	James Sibbet (Sibbald)	Pewterer
1606	William Symonton	Saddler	James Sibbet (Sibbald)	Pewterer
1607	Thomas Weir	Pewterer	Samuel Thomson	Cutler
1608	Thomas Weir	Pewterer	Samuel Thomson	Cutler
1609	James Sibbet (Sibbald)	Pewterer	Thomas Duncan	Locksmith
1610	James Sibbet (Sibbald)	Pewterer	Thomas Duncan	Locksmith
1611	William Weyllands	Lorimer	John Henderson	Lorimer
1612	William Weyllands	Lorimer	John Henderson	Lorimer
1613	Thomas Weir	Pewterer	Thomas Brown, Elder	Locksmith
1614	Thomas Weir	Pewterer	Thomas Brown, Elder	Locksmith
1615	James Sibbet (Sibbald)	Pewterer	David Brown	Saddler
1616	James Sibbet (Sibbald)	Pewterer	David Brown	Saddler
1617	Thomas Weir	Pewterer	Thomas Quhyt (White)	Armourer
1618	Thomas Weir	Pewterer	Thomas Quhyt (White)	Armourer
1619	Samuel Thomson	Cutler	Alexander Burrel	Lorimer
1620	Samuel Thomson	Cutler	Alexander Burrel	Lorimer
1621	Thomas Duncane	Locksmith	William Clarksone	Blacksmith
1622	Thomas Duncane	Locksmith	Robert Bruce	Saddler
1623	Thomas Weir	Pewterer	Robert Bruce	Saddler

TABLE 2.10 (cont)
Deacons of the Edinburgh Incorporation of Hammermen (ECA ED008/1)

Year	Name of Deacon	Trade	Boxmaster/Treasurer	Trade
1625	Thomas Quhyt (White)	Armourer	Thomas Brown, Younger	Locksmith
1626	Thomas Quhyt (White)	Armourer	Thomas Brown, Younger	Locksmith
1627	Thomas Brown, younger	Locksmith	Thomas Wilsone	Saddler
1628	Thomas Brown, younger	Locksmith	Thomas Wilsone	Saddler
1629	William Clarksone	Blacksmith	Richard Maxwell	Saddler
1630	William Clarksone	Blacksmith	Richard Maxwell	Saddler
1631	Thomas Quhyt (White)	Armourer	Alexander Thomsone	Cutler
1632	Thomas Quhyt (White)	Armourer	Alexander Thomsone	Cutler
1633	Richard Maxwell	Saddler	Andrew Halyburton	Blacksmith
1634	Richard Maxwell	Saddler	Andrew Halyburton	Blacksmith
1635	Thomas Weir	Pewterer	John Wast	Cutler
1636	Thomas Weir	Pewterer	John Wast	Cutler
1637	Thomas Whyt	Armourer	Thomas Inglis	Pewterer
1638	Richard Maxwell	Saddler	Thomas Inglis	Pewterer
1639	Richard Maxwell	Saddler	James Monteith	Pewterer
1640	John Ormistoune	Shearsmith	James Monteith	Pewterer
1641	John Ormistoune	Shearsmith	Samuel Burrell	Lorimer
1642	Andrew Halliburton	Blacksmith	Samuel Burrell	Lorimer
1643	Andrew Halliburton	Blacksmith	Andrew Borthwick	Pewterer
1644	Thomas Inglis	Pewterer	David Clark	Lorimer
1645	Thomas Inglis	Pewterer	James Monteith	Pewterer
1646	James Monteith	Pewterer	Adam Thomsone	Saddler
1647	James Monteith	Pewterer	Adam Thomsone	Saddler
1648	Alexander Lindsay	Armourer	Thomas Haliday	Brazier
1649	Alexander Lindsay	Armourer	John Tweedie, Elder	Locksmith
1650	No election?		John Tweedie, Elder★	Locksmith
1651	Adam Thomsone	Saddler	John Gaudie★	Locksmith
1652	Adam Thomsone	Saddler	John Gaudie	Locksmith
1653	James Monteith	Pewterer	John Gaudie	Locksmith
1654	No election?★			
1655	Andrew Halliburton	Blacksmith	John Harvie	Pewterer
1656	Andrew Halliburton	Blacksmith	Jonn Harvie	Pewterer
1657	No election?★			
1658	No election?★			
1659	John Gaudie★	Locksmith	Alexander Anderson	Coppersmith
1660	William Sibbald	Pewterer	Alexander Anderson	Coppersmith
1661	George Childers	Saddler	Thomas Waddel	Lorimer
1662	George Childers	Saddler	Thomas Waddel	Lorimer
1663	Robert Weir	Pewterer	James Thomsone	Armourer
1664	Robert Weir	Pewterer	James Thomsone	Armourer
1665	David Muir	Armourer	John Tod	Locksmith
1666	David Muir	Armourer	John Tod	Locksmith
1667	Robert Weir	Pewterer	Andrew Halyburton	Blacksmith
1668	Robert Weir	Pewterer	Andrew Halyburton	Blacksmith
1669	Alexander Anderson	Coppersmith	Alexander Cowstane	Pewterer
1670	Alexander Anderson	Coppersmith	Alexander Cowstane	Pewterer
1671	David Muir	Armourer	John Foreman	Blacksmith

TABLE 2.10 (*cont*)
Deacons of the Edinburgh Incorporation of Hammermen (ECA ED008/1)

Year	Name of Deacon	Trade	Boxmaster/Treasurer	Trade
1672	David Muir	Armourer	John Foreman	Blacksmith
1673	Alexander Cowstane	Pewterer	John Wilson	Armourer
1674	Alexander Cowstane	Pewterer	John Wilson	Armourer
1675	Andrew Halliburton	Blacksmith	Samuel Walker	Pewterer
1676	John Callendar	Locksmith	Samuel Walker	Pewterer
1677	John Callendar	Locksmith	John Ramsay	Pewterer
1678	Andrew Halliburton	Blacksmith	John Ramsay	Pewterer
1679	Alexander Anderson	Coppersmith	John Abernethie	Pewterer
1680	Alexander Anderson	Coppersmith	John Abernethie	Pewterer
1681	John Meikle	Coppersmith	Alexander Thomsone	Saddler
1682	James Prett	Locksmith	Alexander Thomsone	Saddler
1683	George Mitchell	Locksmith	William Andersone	Coppersmith
1684	George Mitchell	Locksmith	William Andersone	Coppersmith
1685	James Midletown	Armourer	Patrick Drysdale	Locksmith
1686	James Midletown	Armourer	Patrick Drysdale	Locksmith
1687	Alexander Thomsone	Saddler	William Brown	Locksmith
1688	Alexander Thomsone	Saddler	William Brown	Locksmith
1689	John Callendar of Craigforth★	Master Smith	Andrew Brown	Clockmaker
1690	John Callendar of Craigforth★	Master Smith	Andrew Brown	Clockmaker
1691	George Dalgleish	Lorimer	John Sympson	Gunsmith
1692	George Dalgleish	Lorimer	John Sympson	Gunsmith
1693	Alexander Thomsone	Saddler	Thomas Inglis	Pewterer
1694	Alexander Thomsone	Saddler	Thomas Inglis	Pewterer
1695	George Dalgleish	Lorimer	John Anderson	Coppersmith
1696	George Dalgleish	Lorimer	John Anderson	Coppersmith
1697	Alexander Thomson	Lorimer	John Letham	Locksmith
1698	Alexander Thomson	Lorimer	John Letham	Locksmith
1699	John Letham	Locksmith	James Herrin	Pewterer
1700	John Letham	Locksmith	James Herrin	Pewterer
1701	Samuel Walker	Pewterer	William Herrin	Pewterer
1702	Samuel Walker	Pewterer	William Herrin	Pewterer
1703	John Letham	Locksmith	Robert Tait★	Armourer
1704	John Letham	Locksmith	Robert Tait	Armourer
1705	Thomas Inglis	Pewterer	Thomas Brown	Locksmith
1706	Thomas Inglis	Pewterer	Thomas Brown	Locksmith
1707	James Lein	Saddler	David Symmers	Pewterer
1708	James Lein	Saddler	David Symmers	Pewterer
1709	David Symmers	Pewterer	Edward Bunkle	Beltmaker
1710	David Symmers	Pewterer	Edward Bunkle	Beltmaker
1711	John Anderson	Coppersmith	George Mitchel	Locksmith ?
1712	John Anderson	Coppersmith	George Mitchel	Locksmith ?
1713	William Herring	Pewterer	Murdoch Grant	Gunsmith
1714	William Herring	Pewterer	Murdoch Grant	Gunsmith
1715	George Dalgleish	Lorimer	David Hodge	Coppersmith
1716	George Dalgleish	Lorimer	Walter Davidson★	Saddler
1717	William Herring	Pewterer	Alexander Brown	Pewterer
1718	William Herring	Pewterer	Alexander Brown	Pewterer

THE CRAFTS AND CRAFTSMEN

TABLE 2.10 (cont)
Deacons of the Edinburgh Incorporation of Hammermen (ECA ED008/1)

Year	Name of Deacon	Trade	Boxmaster/Treasurer	Trade
1719	Walter Boswell	Saddler	John Dalgleish	Locksmith
1720	Walter Boswell	Saddler	John Dalgleish	Locksmith
1721	John Dalgleish	Locksmith	John Cunningham	Coppersmith
1722	John Dalgleish	Locksmith	John Cunningham	Coppersmith
1723	Alexander Brown	Pewterer	Alexander Brownlie	Watchmaker
1724	Alexander Brown	Pewterer	Alexander Brownlie	Watchmaker
1725	Thomas Gifford	Blacksmith	James Willson	Locksmith
1726	Thomas Gifford	Blacksmith	James Willson	Locksmith
1727	John Dalgleish	Locksmith	James Edgar	Pewterer
1728	John Dalgleish	Locksmith	James Edgar	Pewterer
1729	Edward Bunkell	Beltmaker ?	James Affleck	White-iron Smith
1730	Edward Bunkell	Beltmaker ?	James Auchinleck★	White-iron Smith
1731	John Dalgleish	Locksmith	John Lauder	Coppersmith
1732	John Dalgleish	Locksmith	John Lauder	Coppersmith
1733	James Wilson	Locksmith	George Aitken	Locksmith
1734	James Wilson	Locksmith	George Aitken	Locksmith
1735	David Hodge	Coppersmith	Simon Frazer	White-iron Smith
1736	David Hodge	Coppersmith	Simon Frazer	White-iron Smith
1737	Thomas Simpson	Pewterer	William Ormistoun	Coppersmith
1738	Thomas Simpson	Pewterer	William Ormistoun	Coppersmith
1739	George Aitken	Locksmith	James Gardner	Blacksmith
1740	George Aitken	Locksmith	James Gardner	Blacksmith
1741	Walter Boswell	Saddler	Wm. Armstrong	Coppersmith
1742	Walter Boswell★	Saddler	Wm. Armstrong	Coppersmith
1743	John Douglas	Armourer	Thomas Cleland	Saddler
1744	John Douglas	Armourer	Thomas Cleland	Saddler
1745	Thomas Gifford	Blacksmith	John Brown	Watchmaker
1746	Thomas Gifford	Blacksmith	John Brown	Watchmaker
1747	James Gardner	Blacksmith	Andrew Ranken	Coppersmith
1748	James Gardner	Blacksmith	Andrew Ranken	Coppersmith
1749	John Dalgleish	Watchmaker	James Yorkstoun	Cutler
1750	John Dalgleish	Watchmaker	James Yorkstoun	Cutler

★ see below:

1541–2 'in default of ane deacon'
1543 Johnstone replaced in May by Thomas Schort, who was 'cruelly slain with our old enemies of England at the invasion and burning of this burgh ... with ane young frenchman at the Netherbow Port. Ora pro animae sue', the Hertford Raid.
1559 No mention of election – just a deacon imposed by Reformation? (Smith 1906, 170)
1563 John Weir, pewterer, replaced by Zoung temporarily (Lynch 1981, 238)
1564 Purves replaced or replaced by Mungo Hunter (Lynch 1981, 239)
1568 James Zoung replaced (?) by Alexander Thomson
1579 John Richertsone replaced by Robert Abercrombie, Saddler, who supported the King in the 1570 – 73 civil war in Edinburgh (see Lynch 1981, 294)
1650 2 May to 5 December 1651 – John Tweedie, elder, remained boxmaster. No elections in 1650?
1651 October – William Sibbald, pewterer, unlawed for refusing to be boxmaster
1654 No election? September records of apprenticeships and freeman entries only.
1657 No election? Blank pages from 29 August to 15 October.

1658   No election? No September records.
1659   John Coll as deacon from 15 April 1660 to Michaelmas due to death of John Gauddie.
1689, 1690   John Callendar of Craigforth apparently is the same Locksmith deacon as in 1676. Perhaps Callendar bought land?
1703   Richard Miller, Clockmaker, was elected on the 11th, but by the 20th Robert Tait replaced him due to Tait's old age
1717   Walter Davidson recorded as 'continued' (?)
1730   James Affleck listed as continued boxmaster, only renamed as 'Auchinleck'
1742   Walter Bowell died in 1743 and George Aitken took his place till the next Michaelmas election.

overplayed, the 1483 seal of cause which started the Incorporation of Hammermen listed that their first complaint specified that the craftsmen were 'havely hurt by the daily market made through the high street in crames'.[185] While a great deal of progress was made with the 1583 decreet arbitral, the council and guild were still ruled by merchants. When in 1681 the merchants of Edinburgh formed the 'Merchant Company' in an attempt to gain a monopoly on retail for its members, the crafts spoke out, saying that such a society would be 'destructive to other people's liberties,' and 'against all reason and without parallel. The governors of such a company would be masters of the town'.[186] And so the merchants were. But the craftsmen did have a share in that power. So how powerful were the craftsmen? How powerful was the Incorporation of Hammermen? Which crafts in the incorporation wielded that power?

Power is a broad term and there were various types of power. In the Incorporation of Hammermen itself, there was an aristocracy. Table 2.11 shows the number of years a particular trade had one of its masters elected deacon. The highest rates of leadership go to the pewterers, saddlers, locksmiths and cutlers. Table 2.12 shows the office of boxmaster, which was also dominated by pewterers and locksmiths. Table 2.8 shows the highest frequency of guild brethrenship. Again, the pewterers were the most, with thirty guild brethren, followed by the saddlers, coppersmith/braziers, locksmiths and knockmakers. Table 2.0 shows that the largest crafts in terms of population of freeman masters were the pewterers, locksmiths and saddlers. There was a craft aristocracy.

Compared to the merchants, incorporations were not very powerful. The decreet arbitral in 1583 was supposed to make the craftsmen equal to the merchants. This meant equal representation in government, but this did not happen. On 9 May 1741 the Incorporation of Hammermen's clerk noted in the minute books a complaint that, although the merchants and craftsmen

TABLE 2.11
Number of times elected deacon 1494–1750
(ECA ED008/1)

Trade	Elected deacon
Pewterers	45
Saddlers	38
Locksmiths	36
Cutlers	29
Armourers	15
Lorimers	14
Blacksmiths	14
Coppersmiths	9
Shearsmiths	3
Beltmakers	2
Watchmakers	2
Unknown	45
No Election	5

TABLE 2.12
Number of times elected boxmaster 1600–1750
(ECA ED008/1)

Trade	Elected boxmaster
Pewterers	34
Locksmiths	31
Coppersmiths	17
Saddlers	15
Lorimers	9
Blacksmiths	9
Cutlerers	8
Armourers	8
White-ironmen	4
Gunsmiths	4
Watchmakers	4
Clockmakers	2
Beltmakers	2
Braziers	1
No Election	3

were each supposed to have their own representative in parliament, since 1707 the two groups had been restricted to one representative who had been a merchant ever since.[187] The Union had limited the number of representatives in parliament and instead of sharing, it was dominated by merchants.

Even though the burghs were ruled by merchants, the crafts had a voice, whether the council wanted to hear it or not. In 1737 the fourteen incorporated trades sent a petition to the house of peers in London to support a bill for barring Alexander Wilson, the provost of Edinburgh, from enjoying any office of magistracy in Britain, abolishing the town guard, taking away the gates of the Netherbow port and 'that they might be allowed to be heard by their Council'.[188] The deacon of the Hammermen asked the opinion of the house as to whether or not they wanted to subscribe to the bill along with the rest of the incorporated trades of Edinburgh, which they did. When the council would not listen, there were other channels to go through.

There were other ways in which the crafts were represented and even had a degree of influence. One example was the position of deacon convener of trades, who chaired the meetings of the fourteen deacons and represented their views to the council. From 1578 to 1730, thirty-eight surgeons acted as deacon convener, twenty-seven tailors, twenty-five skinners, twenty-two goldsmiths, nineteen hammermen, ten wrights and masons, three cordiners, three baxters and two bonnetmakers.[189] Crafts like the baxters and bonnetmakers did not have much political clout. Goldsmiths, hammermen, tailors, and others formed a craft aristocracy which could have influence. Many were in the guild. It is also significant that the convenery met at the Magdalene Chapel, which was the hammermen's meeting hall.[190]

In 1508 the crafts were given two seats on the town council.[191] Not all incorporations had representatives of their crafts as one of the two craft councillors. From 1551 to 1570 there were eleven hammermen councillors, seven goldsmiths, six skinners, five tailors, four barbers and furriers and one wright.[192] The poorest trades, the weavers, waulkers and bonnetmakers, never had their craftsmen as councillors,[193] though there were bonnetmaker deacon conveners of trades.

Some craftsmen even had royal positions, like the Mylnes acting as his Majesty's Master Masons, or John Callendar being his Majesty's Master Smith in 1682.[194] There were also Master Goldsmiths to kings, like George Heriot.

Overall, the craftsmen were not very powerful though they did have a political voice. The Incorporation of Hammermen seems to have fared better than many incorporations in terms of getting their masters onto the town council. In the incorporation itself, there was a small craft aristocracy, of which the locksmiths were a part. They were wealthy enough to enjoy guild privileges, numerous enough to supply a capital and astute enough to be in the top three in craft elections for deacon.

Incorporation was a social control, but considering the dramatic population increase across Europe in the sixteenth century, mirrored by the Incorporation of Hammermen's rise in master craftsmen, it is intriguing that the governmental structure of incorporation remained as unchanged as it did. While the system was tweaked from time to time, with craft councillors added, deacons removed and replaced and the decreet arbitral bringing nominal equality between craftsmen and merchants, the system did represent continuity. It guarded trade privilege and kept peace in Edinburgh throughout the early modern period, with fairly equal parts of 'social' and 'control'.

NOTES

1. Soom, A. 1971 *Zunfthandwerker in Reval*, as quoted in Friedrichs 2003, 155–6.
2. It was common in larger European towns that the goldsmiths were separate from the other metalworkers. Frankfurt am Main had a smiths' guild and a goldsmiths' guild in 1614. From 1617 to 1631, when corporatism spread through the town, separate corporations for the saddlers, goldsmiths and smiths were formed. Soliday 1974, 142–3. London was large enough that few of its crafts were incorporated together; single craft companies such as the armourers company or the pewterers company were more common. An account of London in 1598 describes a feast held at the Guildhall in which fourteen different metalworking companies attended. Stow 1994, 442–3.
3. Colston 1891, 27.
4. ECA ED008/1/–8.
5. *Edinburgh Burgesses* 1929.
6. Smith 1906, 181 and 184.
7. Many hammermen listed as masters in the earliest volume of the minute books are not listed in the burgess rolls. ECA ED008/1/1.
8. Doune is one example. Kelvin 1996, 91.
9. Whitelaw 1977, 107.
10. ECA ED008/1/1–8.
11. Certain crafts had work types in common and were therefore joined together under a broad heading. The gunsmiths, knockmakers and locksmiths were all part of the locksmith craft. See chapter 3 for more discussion.

12 Edinburgh was not the only European town in which the number of locksmiths grew significantly. In Dijon, between 1643 and 1750, the number of locksmiths almost doubled from 13 to 24. Farr 2000, 65.
13 Smith 1906, 182.
14 The essay was a 'siphon with a brass bow or curve'. ECA ED008/1/6, January 1734.
15 Ibid., ED008/1/8, 20 February 1748.
16 Ibid., ED008/1/3, 8 February 1647.
17 Ibid., ED008/1/3, 6 June 1649.
18 Ibid., ED008/1/3, 29 July 1654.
19 Ibid., ED008/1/3, 29 July 1654.
20 NMS Whitelaw EHMB, 76.
21 ECA ED008/1/3, 29 July 1654.
22 Ibid., ED008/1/3, 206.
23 Ibid., ED008/1/4, 340–3.
24 Ibid., ED008/1/4, 1682, 340–3.
25 Ibid., ED008/1/4, 351–2.
26 Ibid., ED008/1/7, 30 May 1745.
27 Ibid., ED008/1/7, 15 June 1745.
28 Ibid., ED008/1/6, 4 March 1733.
29 Ibid., ED008/1/6, 12 May 1733.
30 Ibid., ED008/1/6, 12 May 1733.
31 Carr 1954, 84.
32 ECA ED008/1/7, 3 May 1740.
33 Ibid., ED008/1/7, 37–8.
34 *APS* 1875, 382.
35 It is not clear if this was also true in winter. ECA ED008/1/8, 1 August 1750.
36 *APS* 1875, 382.
37 Dingwall 1994, 2.
38 Friedrichs 2003, 143.
39 Lynch 1981, 10.
40 Friedrichs 2003, 144: 'Membership in the guild was to be restricted, so that not too many people would compete in the same market. Complete equality was never envisioned, but each guild master was entitled to a fair opportunity to earn a living as the head of an autonomous unit of production.'
41 ECA ED008/1/6, 22 April 1738.
42 Ibid., ED008/1/6, 8 January 1736.
43 Ibid., ED008/1/6, 9 January 1736.
44 This means to 'have dealings with (unfreemen)' Robinson 1992, 467.
45 ECA ED008/1/4, 408–9.
46 Lynch 1981, 10.
47 In York from 1397 to 1534, 83 per cent of locksmiths' sons also became locksmiths. About a third, or 34 per cent of Parisian locksmiths' sons, became locksmiths between 1742 and 1776. Farr 2000, 248, 250. Unfortunately, the data in table 3.5 are not complete enough to attain similar statistics for Edinburgh.
48 Smith 1906, 183.
49 Carr 1954, 18.
50 Marwick 1909, 73.
51 ECA ED008/1/6.
52 Ibid., ED008/1/3, 191.
53 *Edinburgh Apprentices*, 1906 & 1929.
54 ECA ED008/1/1–8.
55 Dingwall 1994, 191.
56 Ibid., 193.
57 Ben-Amos 1991, 163.
58 Ibid., 155.
59 ECA 1558 Muster Roll, Burgh Records, Council Minutes, Vol. III, Folios 126v–137r.
60 Carr 1954, 18.
61 Ibid., 34.
62 ECA ED008/1/7, 72.
63 Ibid., ED008/1/5, 21.
64 Ibid., ED008/1/4, 380.
65 Friedrichs 2003, 98.
66 Strauss 1966, 100.
67 Bain 1887, 207.
68 Lumsden & Aitken 1912, 137.
69 Friedrichs 2003, 98.
70 ECA ED008/2/26. This bears the signatures and marks of over 170 journeymen and apprentices.
71 Houston 1994, 306–10.
72 Commissioners of Excise 1890, 252–3.
73 ECA ED008/1/8, 1 August 1750.
74 *Edinburgh Apprentices* 1929, 7.
75 Smout 1985, 438.
76 *Edinburgh Apprentices* 1929, 7.
77 *Edinburgh Burgesses* 1929, 3.
78 On 19 May 1739 John Brown, elder, stated that he had been a journeyman for four and a half years. See below. ECA ED008/1/6.
79 This was in summer, but it is not clear if it was true for winter also. Ibid., ED008/1/8, 1 August 1750.
80 In summer, but in winter? Ibid., ED008/1/8, 1 August 1750.
81 *APS* 1875, 382.
82 ECA ED008/1/6.
83 Marwick 1909, 73.
84 ECA ED008/1/6.
85 Ibid., ED008/1/6.
86 Ibid., ED008/1/4, 380.
87 *Edinburgh Burgesses* 1929, 14.
88 ECA ED008/1/7, 66.
89 Ibid., ED008/1/5, 190.
90 Ibid., ED008/1/4, 1662–1701. The oath is in the 1674–82 freeman lists.
91 The bridge probably refers to the warding, but is possibly a reference to the spindle, which connected the knobs through the lock and door. In the *Accounts of the Masters of Works*, there are several references to locks receiving new bridges, sometimes with a new key's bit. *MWA* 1982, 98, 187 and 327. On 29 June 1728, for 'the more security of the lieges', the essay of the locksmith art was changed to include the round filled bridge. ECA ED008/1/5, 29. Not being cut or broke might mean not leaving out the warding on the back of the lock, which was a problem addressed again on 3 May 1740. Ibid., ED008/1/7.
92 The payment was partly in Scots merks and partly in English pounds. Ibid., ED008/1/7, 66.

THE CRAFTS AND CRAFTSMEN

93 Gilhooley 1988, 6.
94 Smout 1985, 439.
95 ECA ED008/1/7, 29 and 30.
96 *Edinburgh Burgesses* 1929, 51.
97 ECA ED008/1/7, 26 and *Edinburgh Marriage Reg* 1906, 317.
98 Robinson 1992, 661.
99 ECA ED008/1/7, 26.
100 *Edinburgh Burgesses* 1929, 120.
101 His signature is in his own hand, not the clerk's. ECA ED008/1/7, 29–30.
102 Gilhooley 1988, 30.
103 *Edinburgh Apprentices* 1929, 51.
104 *Edinburgh Burgesses* 1929.
105 Torrie 1988, 258.
106 Robinson 1992, 252.
107 Lynch 1998 (unpublished Utrecht paper), 2.
108 This was also true of the craft guilds, which are referred to as incorporations throughout.
109 Marwick 1909, 25–6.
110 'Rates of Customs' 1867, 277.
111 Marwick 1909, 143.
112 The prices for burgess-ship and guildry are separate from upset costs for incorporation freedom. *Edinburgh Burgesses* 1929, 2
113 Ibid., 3.
114 Marwick 1909, 170.
115 Ibid., 143. This was the new situation after the decreet arbitral. After this, craftsmen were individually assessed for taxation, instead of paying a group rate through the incorporations.
116 *Edinburgh Burgesses* 1929, 15.
117 Reid 1998, 8.
118 Marwick 1909, 145–6.
119 Edinburgh's guild was based on Berwick's guild laws. *APS* 1875, 612.
120 *Edinburgh Burgesses* 1929, 2.
121 Marwick 1909, 44.
122 Ibid., 49.
123 *Edinburgh Burgesses* 1929, 106.
124 See Stevenson 1996, 64–77 for the details of his trial and execution for allegedly confessing to incest and bestiality. The case gained recognition from Walter Scott and R. L. Stevenson.
125 *Edinburgh Burgesses* 1929, 519.
126 Ibid., 3.
127 *APS* 18.75, 611.
128 Marwick 1909, 135.
129 This was seen as socially questionable though and in 1585 the council decided that for anyone to reach a higher station, such as guildry, while father, father-in-law, or master was only a burgess, they had to pay the highest entry price: 'Item, because the son, daughter, or apprentice can be in no better estate nor their father or master was by their right, therefore, where the master or father was no burgess or guild brother, the said apprentice, the son, or yet the husband of the daughter, not to be received burgess or guild brother but for the uttermost duty before mentioned'. Marwick 1909, 145–6.
130 Ibid., 145–6.
131 Ibid., 145–6.
132 Ibid., 96–7. This refers to the Siege of Leith in the spring of 1560.
133 Ibid., 44.
134 Ibid., 211.
135 The Lord of Orkney was the Bishop of Orkney.
136 Marwick 1909, 81.
137 Ibid., 98.
138 Ibid., 98–9.
139 *Edinburgh Burgesses* 1929, 4–5.
140 Prior to 1469, the head courts had been used by the burgesses to elect the common council. Lynch 1998 (unpublished Utrecht paper), 2.
141 *Edinburgh Burgesses* 1929, 6.
142 Marwick 1909, 198.
143 Ibid., 98.
144 Ibid., 123.
145 Ibid., 114.
146 *APS* 1875, 612.
147 *Edinburgh Burgesses* 1929, 1.
148 Ibid., 2.
149 *Edinburgh Burgesses* 1929, 3 and Marwick 1909, 110.
150 Marwick 1909, 135.
151 Ibid., 170–3.
152 Ibid., 172.
153 Ibid., 173.
154 Ibid., 8.
155 Lynch 1998 (unpublished Utrecht paper), 2.
156 *APS* 1875, 612.
157 *Edinburgh Burgesses* 1929, 4.
158 Marwick 1909, 95.
159 Houston 1994, 358.
160 Stevenson 1987, 169
161 Marwick 1909, 31.
162 Ibid., 31.
163 Ibid., 31.
164 Ibid., 31.
165 *APS* 1875, 612.
166 Marwick 1909, 31.
167 This data is presented in table 2.6. *Edinburgh Burgesses* 1929.
168 See table 1.4. The 134 were also included in the 848 as you had to first have burgess-ship to attain guildry. The goldsmiths are not included.
169 Marwick 1909, 143.
170 This does not include the goldsmiths. There were one blacksmith, six saddlers, one lorimer and five cutlers who became guild brethren before the decreet arbitral. *Edinburgh Burgesses* 1929.
171 Ibid., 458.
172 Whitelaw 1977, 107.
173 *Edinburgh Burgesses* 1929.
174 Ibid.
175 Stow's 1598 account of a feast from the time of Henry VIII at the London Guildhall lists sixty companies. The goldsmiths were listed in fifth place, illustrating their importance. Blacksmiths were number fifty-four. Stow 1994, 442–3.

[176] Smart Martin 1991, 167.
[177] Weatherill 1996, 25.
[178] Hallett 2000, 206.
[179] Some of the 'smiths' were actually locksmiths.
[180] ECA ED008/1/4, 1693.
[181] Farr 2000, 259.
[182] Unwin 1938, 370–1.
[183] Smith 1906, 181.
[184] Lynch 1981, 15.
[185] Smith 1906, 181.
[186] Houston 1994, 358.
[187] ECA ED008/1/7, 76.
[188] Ibid., ED008/1/6, 21 April 1737.
[189] ECA *An Historical Sketch of the Municipal Constitution of the City of Edinburgh* 1826, 75.
[190] Dingwall 1995, 36.
[191] Marwick 1909, 61.
[192] Lynch 1981, 24.
[193] Lynch 1998 (unpublished Utrecht paper), 4 & 5.
[194] ECA ED008/1/4, 340–3.

Chapter 3

The Locksmith Craft

> Historians, ancient and modern, not only record the martial achievements, but the singular sanctity of mechanics.[1]

There was a complex and dynamic relationship among the metalworking trades, not only in the Edinburgh Incorporation of Hammermen, but across Europe. In some cities, various trades or small groups of trades grew large enough to break away from the overall metalworkers' craft guild and formed their own corporations. This was the case with the corporation formed by the coppersmiths, clockmakers and locksmiths in Reval.[2] In London, many of the metalworking trades formed individual units of crafts. The blacksmiths and spurriers were separate from the armourers and braziers. The farriers had their own charter, separate from the blacksmiths, by 1674.[3] The clockmakers were also originally part of the Blacksmith's Guild, until they formed the London Clockmakers' Company in 1631.[4] By 1601, the Geneva watchmakers had formed themselves into a corporation, answering only to the town council.[5] Examples of this can be found in most early modern towns.

In Edinburgh, only the goldsmiths became rich and powerful enough to split away from the Incorporation of Hammermen;[6] other trades did not reach the level of strength required for independence. The locksmiths grew in importance, but never to the point at which they could have splintered off to form their own incorporation. Quite the contrary, their large numbers in the first half of the eighteenth century were due in part to their association with the gunsmiths, watchmakers and clockmakers.

As the incorporation expanded, new technologies were introduced to Edinburgh. This led to consolidation of trades and partitioning into groups which were, in effect, miniature incorporations inside the Incorporation of Hammermen. In the 1693 list of hammermen masters, a previously unseen type of categorization was used for grouping the craftsmen in the lists. Previously, the lists gave only of names of the masters, though after 1646, their trade was occasionally listed as well. The data from the lists with trades is in table 2.0. For the years 1693, 1705, 1717, 1741 and 1749, the data is given in terms of association with like crafts.[7] In the 1693 list, there were eight smaller lists with the titles 'Blacksmiths', 'Cutlers', 'Saddlers', 'Locksmiths and these joined with them', 'Lorimers and these joined with them', 'Armourers', 'Pewterers and these joined with them', and 'Deacons & Boxmasters'. There was also a complete list of all the hammermen's names, without mention of individual trade.[8] With new trades such as white-ironmen, watchmakers, knockmakers, dag-makers and coppersmiths, the incorporation needed to find places for them in the existing structure. They became 'allied' to established trades of similar work types. The coppersmiths, founders and beltmakers were joined with the lorimers. White-ironmen, or tinsmiths, were joined with the pewterers. Gunsmiths, framesmiths, knockmakers, watchmakers and an 'hourmaker' were all joined with the locksmiths. After 1750, there were also pinmakers and hookmakers joined with the locksmiths.[9]

This was not unique to Edinburgh; in Augsburg, clockmaking was associated with locksmithing.[10] The locksmiths, spurriers, gunsmiths, clockmakers and jackmakers of Ulm united themselves into a separate group within the overall Guild of Smiths (see figure 3.1).[11] Edinburgh termed this type of relationship as being 'joined' to a larger trade. These associations were an interesting phenomenon; a sub-culture of the overall incorporation experience, which was itself a sub-culture of the early modern craft guilds. Every city had a slightly different approach to craft structure and Edinburgh followed a system of association. The various trades joined with the locksmiths were not randomly selected, but were joined for very sensible reasons. What was the nature of the locksmiths' relationship with the 'joined trades'? To what extent were they combined and why were these trades associated with the locksmiths?

LOCKSMITHS

In the 1728 edition of Ephraim Chambers' *Cyclopaedia*, the entry for 'Lock' stated that

> The *lock* is reckoned the master-piece in smithery; a great deal of art and delicacy being required in contriving and varying the wards, springs, bolts, etc. and adjusting them to the places where they are to be used and to the various occasions of using them.[12]

One of the key factors that made it necessary for smiths to specialise in the production of locks is the fact that they had moving parts of a complicated, mechanical nature. While any smith could have made a pair of jointed tongs, a lock was considerably more complex. Temper of springs, precise travel of parts and proper contours of metal all had to be in complete harmony for a lock mechanism to work. On top of this was added the security measures taken in the form of 'warding' in the lock, which was a series of obstacles that only the true key could pass. A locksmith was in essence a mechanical engineer. This, however, took time to come about in Scotland.

Locks had been in use in Scotland many centuries before the Incorporation of Hammermen received its seal of cause. It is impossible to say when the first lock and key were used in Scotland. It is known that the Romans, who had taken Greek and Egyptian lock technology and improved on it, were quite adept at making them. They had settlements in various parts of Scotland, including Cramond and Mayfield, which are to the west and south-east of Edinburgh, respectively. Roman material has been found by archaeologists at Castle Hill, in Edinburgh, which at that time was occupied by the Votadini tribe.[13] It is fair to assume that Roman locks and keys could have been known to the residents of the area we now know as Edinburgh.

It is known that the Normans made use of locks and keys throughout England. When marrying into Scottish families and building keeps, they would have brought their lock technology with them. Locks and

FIGURE 3.1
Guild board from 1595 showing the relationship in Ulm, Germany, of the locksmiths, gunsmiths and clockmakers. (Ulmer Museum, Inv.Nr.A.B.344 as illustrated in Ribbert 1991, 55)

keys were probably known in Scotland by the early twelfth century, if not earlier.

It is harder yet to ascertain when locks and keys were first produced in Scotland. As stated earlier, the actual concept of a 'locksmith' denotes a unique specialisation of skill. Early locks might have been produced by a clever blacksmith. By the mid-eighteenth century, the locksmiths and blacksmiths were still closely related. In Aberdeen blacksmiths produced locks as essays for becoming masters.[14] The Edinburgh hammermen minute books give many examples of meetings of 'the black & locksmith arts', indicating that there was business transacted that did not concern the other crafts, such as pewterers, armourers and saddlers.[15] It is probable that the locksmith craft came from the blacksmith craft. The advent of a smith specialising in locks and keys was in itself a phenomenon, as a locksmith required

THE LOCKSMITH CRAFT

a steady market for locks and keys. Early blacksmiths must have encountered such a market, as some did eventually specialise. There is a reference from 1264 to 1266 in the *Exchequer Rolls of Scotland* to locks being used for the tower of Invernairn.[16] Another reference, from 1326, mentions a locksmith in Tarbert.[17] It can therefore be assumed that locks were definitely in use by 1266. By 1326, if not earlier, there was a smith specialising in lock and key production in Scotland.

There is an undated reference, somewhere between 1124 and 1423, in *The Acts of the Parliament of Scotland*, to a half-penny custom being paid for a dozen locks 'at the forth passing'.[18] This is a very important reference, as it tells us that locks were being exported from Scotland by 1423, sixty years before the Incorporation of Hammermen received its seal of cause. Not only was there a domestic demand for security devices, but also a surplus that could be traded abroad.

Even with a market for locks and a surplus of production to the point of exportation, the locksmith craft was still one of the lesser metalworking crafts of Edinburgh when the Incorporation of Hammermen first received its seal of cause in 1483. While no direct mention was made of the locksmiths in the founding document,[19] the very first page of the hammermen minute books, which started in 1494, mentions a hammermen called 'William Loksmyt'.[20] The locksmiths were there, incorporated with the other metalworking crafts, yet they were not important enough to mention by name in the seal of cause. The 1496 re-affirmation seal of cause did not mention them either.[21] They were still one of the 'others'. As time progressed, however, the locksmith craft grew in importance and size.

SIZE AND GROWTH OF THE EDINBURGH LOCKSMITH CRAFT

The growth of the locksmith art in the Edinburgh Incorporation of Hammermen is illustrated in particular by two sources. The charts and tables for the data from these sources are presented in chapter 1. The first source is the *Roll of Edinburgh Burgesses and Guild Brethren*. As has been shown in table 1.4, there was a considerable growth in the number of locksmiths from 1550 to 1750. From 1550 to 1600 only thirteen men attained burgess-ship as locksmiths. In 1600–50 there were twenty-three. From 1650 to 1700 the number was at thirty-four and in 1700–50 it dropped only slightly to twenty-nine. In the two centuries leading up to 1750, the number of locksmiths attaining burgess-ship more than doubled.

When put against the background of the overall growth of the total Incorporation of Hammermen as seen by the burgess rolls, we see that the locksmiths were growing at an even pace with the incorporation itself. Table 1.5 and chart 3.0 show the relationship of locksmiths attaining burgess-ship and hammermen in general attaining burgess-ship. Table 1.6 shows these figures converted over to percentages. In the 1550

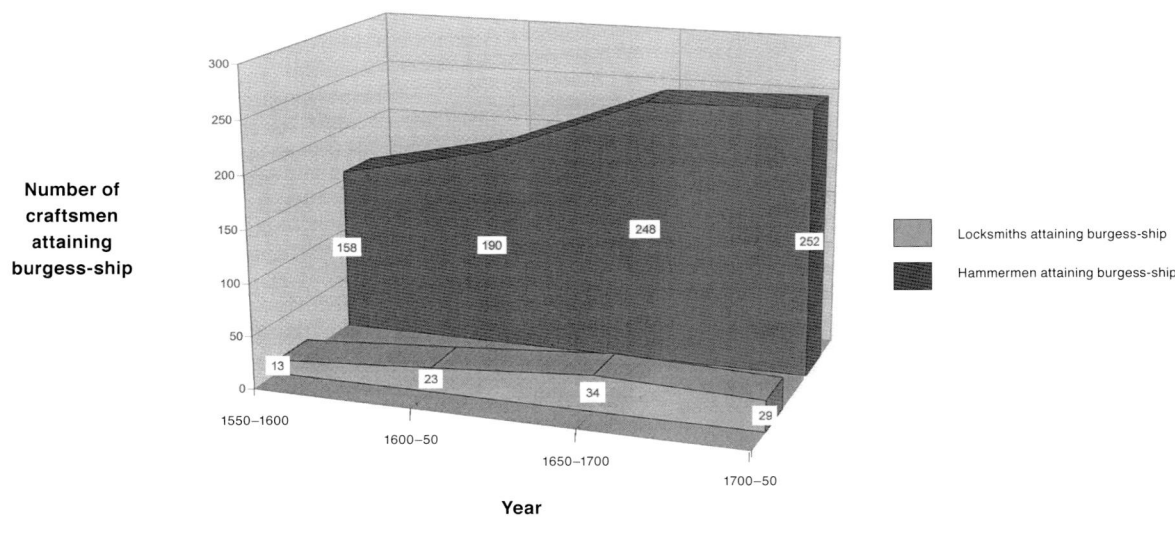

CHART 3.0
Growth rates – burgess rolls

TABLE 3.0
Edinburgh locksmiths

Year	Number of locksmiths	% of hammermen	Source
1646	10	17	ECA ED008/1/3
1648	14	20	ECA ED008/1/3
1654	14	19	ECA ED008/1/3
1656	13	16	ECA ED008/1/3
1660	15	17	ECA ED008/1/3
1663	14	16	ECA ED008/1/4
1668	14	17	ECA ED008/1/4
1670	17	19	ECA ED008/1/4
1671(?)	12	15	ECA ED008/1/4
1674	16	12	ECA ED008/1/4

ECA ED008/1/3–4

to 1600 period, the locksmiths accounted for about 8 per cent of the hammermen. From 1600 to 1650 they were around 12 per cent. In the 1650 to 1700 period they were about 14 per cent and in 1700–50 they were approximately 11 per cent. The percentages for all four periods were relatively close. From 8 per cent to 14 per cent is not a large jump, so it would appear that the locksmith craft from 1550 to 1750 was fairly constant in terms of percentage of the overall incorporation. Throughout, the average proportion of hammermen made up by locksmiths was 11 per cent. If the incorporation was growing and the locksmiths were constantly about 11 per cent of the incorporation, then the number of locksmiths had to be growing also.[22]

The second source that illustrates the locksmith craft's growth can be found in the incorporation minute books.[23] In table 2.0 we see the data from the fifteen freemen lists with denoted trade, as mentioned in chapter 2. Tables 3.0 and 3.1 isolate the data from table 2.0 for the locksmiths and several other related trades. From 1646 to 1674 both Tables 3.0 and 3.1 give ten counts of individual hammermen trades for ten of the years given in table 2.0. As seen by the data in table 3.0, the average number of freemen locksmiths, between 1646 and 1674, was fourteen. In 1648, they accounted for 20 per cent of the hammermen. In 1674, although their number had grown by two, they accounted for only 12 per cent of the hammermen. From 1693 onward, in terms of listed names of craftsmen, the locksmiths are listed as joined with several other crafts; namely, knockmakers, gunsmiths and framesmiths.

The freeman lists only give exact numbers of locksmiths for ten years in the period of 1646–74. Quantitatively, this is relatively weak evidence for growth of the locksmith craft from 1483 to 1750. Qualitatively, however, the freeman lists do show a growth of the locksmiths. In the 1483 and 1496 re-affirmation seals of cause, the locksmiths did not even warrant mention due to the small size of their craft. By 1693 (see table 2.0) they had other trades included with them. As technology advanced in clocks and firearms, the locksmith craft was the trade that these arts fell under. The reason for their inclusion with the locksmiths was the technical and mechanical nature of their work. In 1693 the locksmiths and the trades joined with them were the biggest craft grouping in the hammermen. This trend, as we can see in table 2.0, continued until 1749, if not later. While the numerical superiority is probably due to the watch and knockmakers (see table 1.4), the locksmiths were still seen as being important enough to have the many watch and knockmakers listed under their name. When taken with the burgess roll data from above, it is clear that the locksmith craft grew both in terms of raw numbers and in terms of importance between 1483 and 1750.

TABLE 3.1
Edinburgh locksmiths and trades joined with them
(Knockmakers, Gunsmiths and Framemakers)

Year	Locksmiths with joined trades	Source
1646	14	ECA ED008/1/3
1648	18	ECA ED008/1/3
1654	17	ECA ED008/1/3
1656	15	ECA ED008/1/3
1660	18	ECA ED008/1/3
1663	16	ECA ED008/1/4
1668	18	ECA ED008/1/4
1670	22	ECA ED008/1/4
1671(?)	15	ECA ED008/1/4
1674	27	ECA ED008/1/4
1693	46	ECA ED008/1/4
1705	49	ECA ED008/1/5
1717	38	ECA ED008/1/5
1741	37	ECA ED008/1/7
1749	45	ECA ED008/1/8

ECA ED008/1/3–8

THE LOCKSMITH CRAFT

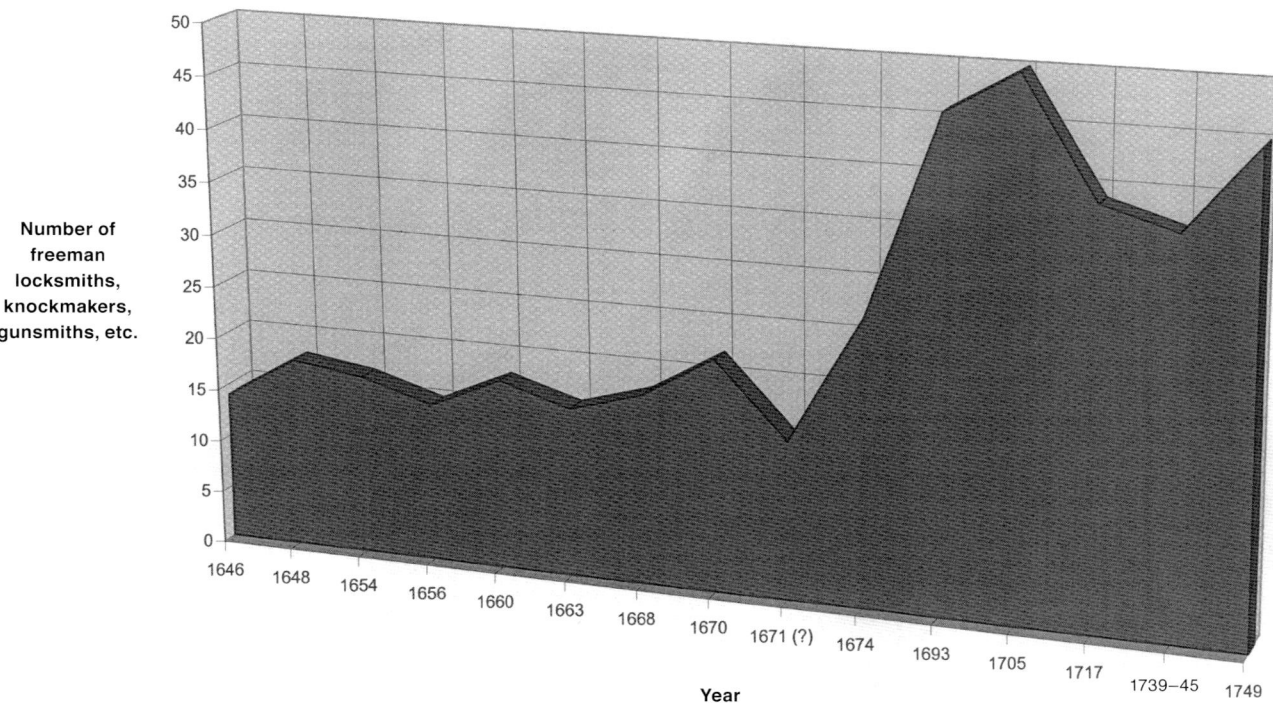

CHART 3.1
Edinburgh locksmiths and trades joined with them

DAGMAKERS AND GUNSMITHS

The first trade to be joined with the locksmiths seems to have been the dagmakers. 'Dag' is the Scots word for pistol, though dagmakers made other types of firearms as well and eventually became known as 'gunsmiths'. Their origin does not trace directly to the locksmiths though. They had roots in the melters, founders, potters, lorimers and locksmiths.

In the late medieval period, hand-held guns, or firearms, were rare. The first guns were more akin to cannon. The production of cannon in Edinburgh started in the fifteenth century. In the 1470s there was a royal foundry near Blackfriars,[24] which was on the south side of the Cowgate, near the town's High School Yard.[25] By 1511 a foundry was set up in Edinburgh Castle to make guns.[26] Melters, or founders as they were later known, were metalworkers who specialised in the casting of various metal objects, both domestic and martial.

The mediums used by melters and founders were bronze and iron. The bronze used for cannon is known as 'gun metal'. Sometimes misnamed 'brass', gun metal was made up of nine parts copper, one part tin and occasionally a part of zinc.[27] It was a strong alloy that could withstand the massive pressure of exploding gunpowder.

In 1505 a Frenchman named John Veilnaif was allowed to work in Edinburgh, because he 'said he could make guns'.[28] James IV (1488–1513) went to great lengths to bring in skilled craftsmen to bolster Edinburgh's trades. As artillery was the latest technology, he brought in craftsmen who had knowledge of making it.

In 1513 the term melter was applied to a craftsman who was casting guns. For example, Robert Borthwick was the 'gunner master melter of the king's guns'. He had six servants working under him, including a Frenchman named Peris Rowane who would, in 1532, take over as master melter.[29] In 1515 mention is made of a 'gunhouse', which was probably the Edinburgh Castle gunworks, formed in 1511.[30] A list of materials delivered to the gunhouse in 1515 includes: 'furnace stokkis, iron, charcoal and other necessaries for founding of certain guns in the castle'.[31]

In 1542 the gunhouse worked on a double culverin. This was made by the master John de Lyon and four servants. They were paid £16 10s and it took them about three months for 'casting thereof … boring and

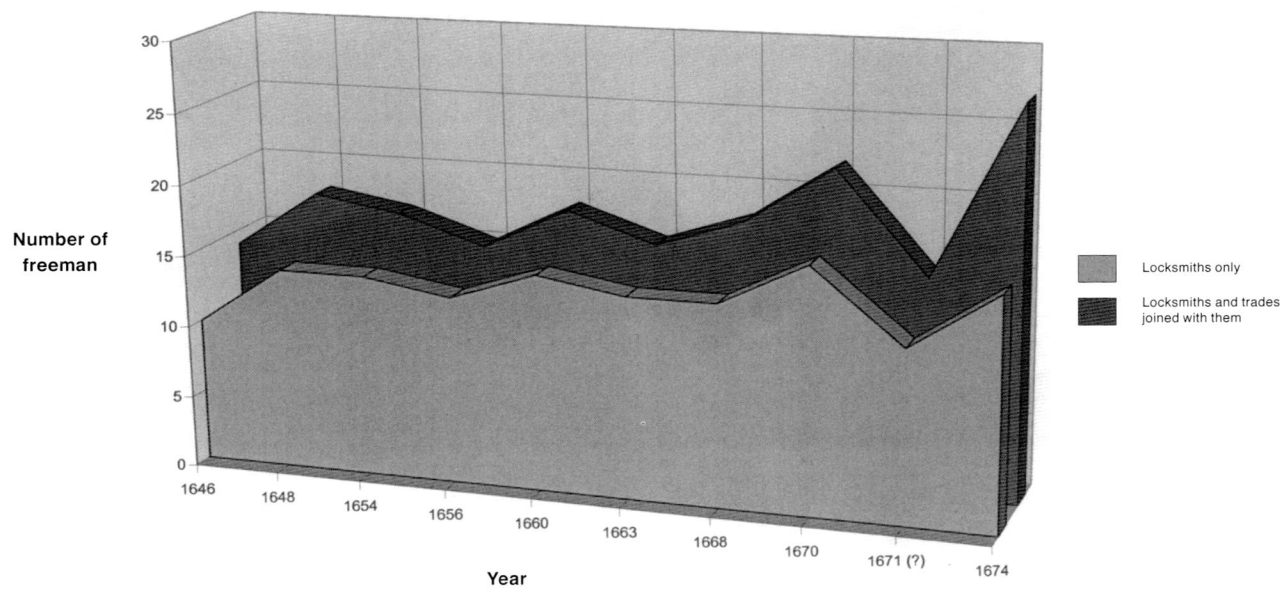

CHART 3.2
Populations of the locksmiths and those trades joined with them

cleaning'.[32] Boring and cleaning refer to the finishing processes involved in casting cannon. When the molten metal for a cannon was poured into a mould, the outside cooled faster than the inside, forcing the impurities towards the still molten core. After it was completely solid, the centre was bored out, leaving the hole where the charge and ball were put for firing. In this manner, the impurities were removed from the metal, leaving a strong cannon which could endure the massive forces of being discharged. This was the same method used for casting brass pistol barrels, like the ones made by some dagmakers. Cleaning, or 'clenging' refers to the outside being polished and made presentable. Polished surfaces on iron resisted rust.

In 1541 there was a Dutchman who worked in the castle making iron guns.[33] This is another example of the diversity of craftsmanship brought into Edinburgh by James IV and his son James V (1513–42). Within the next century French, Dutch and English melters and founders were allowed to work in Edinburgh. They also would have been exposed to the latest technology in ignition mechanisms on the continent and might have brought new ideas to Edinburgh.

DAGMAKERS

While mainly known for their pistols, dagmakers also produced other firearms such as hagbuts. A hagbut is simply an early type of hand firearm, the predecessor to the larger matchlock musket. In France they were called *arquebuse*, in Germany *Hackenbüchse* and in England either *hackbut* or *harquebus*. Scotland, being linguistically and geographically closest to England, used a word similar to theirs, 'hagbuit'.

Illustrated in *Scottish Firearms* are two pairs of dags of supposed Canongate craftsmanship, which date from 1589 and 1615. Both bear maker's marks on barrel and lock, which might indicate that the same person who cast the barrel also made the lock.[34] Considering that the various trades in the Incorporation of Hammermen were forbidden from using another craft's medium, this might indicate a link between the founders and the dagmakers. It is also possible that the dagmakers bought the cast gun-metal barrels and stamped their own maker's mark as a sign of quality.[35]

The locks which the dagmakers built had to have moving, mechanical parts. Henceforth they needed steel for springs and 'steels'. The springs provided the tension and potential energy to create sparks off of the steels for ignition of the powder. If the springs were not of correctly tempered steel, they would wear out and not function properly. If the steel was not correctly tempered, the flint would not make sparks, as the metal would not be brittle enough to chip away in small, heated shavings. It is doubtful that every

THE LOCKSMITH CRAFT

blacksmith could correctly temper springs, as this was a fine art. Locksmiths, however, considered this a daily part of their job. Dagmakers' and gunsmiths' work was therefore closely related to that of locksmiths.

At least six dagmakers became burgesses between 1550 and 1600. In 1570 David Cass became a burgess as a locksmith. In 1579 Gilbert Cass, who was listed as apprentice to 'David Cass, dagmaker', took burgess-ship.[36] In 1594 Gawine Furde, another of David Cass's apprentices, gave an essay which consisted of 'ane hagbut, ane dag and ane snap to be all perfectly outred'.[37] A 'snap' is a snaphaunce lock for ignition of the powder in a firearm. It had moving parts of a mechanical nature, very similar to a locksmith's type of lock. From early on, there was some correlation between dagmakers and locksmiths.

There were many dagmakers who did their apprenticeship with a locksmith, or started out as a locksmith themselves. William Nasmyth worked under Patrick Kennedy, a locksmith.[38] John Watt was admitted burgess as a 'smith' in 1575, a freeman of the Incorporation of Hammermen as a 'locksmith' in 1575 and a guild brother as a 'smith' in 1590. Five years later, he was described as a 'dagmaker'.[39] This could represent either changes in trade or generalisations from the clerk.

Mathew Watsone was booked apprentice to Peter Spens, a lorimer, in 1584. In 1594 Watsone gave his essay of 'ane hagbut, ane dag and ane snap' and was admitted freeman of the hammermen.[40] Lorimers also would have had the skills to make locks, as their trade involved hand filing and polishing, two of the necessary skills of dagmakers, locksmiths and any metalworking craft which involved fine work or moving parts.

It seems that the dagmakers came about by the combining of new technologies with the skills and knowledge from the melter and founder craft, the locksmith craft and the lorimer craft. The snaphaunce lock, or 'snap', was recorded in Edinburgh by 1575 and in Glasgow as early as 1578.[41] Whether or not it was produced earlier in Scotland is unknown. What is known is that by the 1590s dagmakers were making the snaphaunce locks, dags and hagbuts after being trained by locksmiths and lorimers who turned into dagmakers themselves, later in their careers. This might have represented the teacher learning as they taught, as it is possible that they passed on skills and new technologies that they were just learning themselves. However this is based on the assumption that 'locksmith' in this case meant a person who produced mechanical devices for preventing burglary and not a craftsman who made gunlocks.

There is one entry in the records of the Edinburgh hammermen which gives an insight into the nature of a 'locksmith'. In 1586 Patrick Kennedy, apprentice to Hew Brown, locksmith, was admitted freeman to the Incorporation of Hammermen with his essay of 'ane kist lock', or a chest lock. By 1587 he had burgess-ship as a locksmith. In 1592 he was described as a dagmaker. In 1593 two of Kennedy's colleagues, Alexander Adamson and David Edgar, who were both conventional locksmiths, were fined for buying unfreeman's hagbuts and finishing them.[42] In 1596 John Kennedy, Patrick's son, gave his essay of 'ane kist lock' and was admitted freeman dagmaker.[43] The locksmiths had the skills required for making gun locks. The question is, did the dagmakers come out of the locksmiths, or did they simply join with the locksmiths? Perhaps it was both.

At least one pair of John Kennedy's dags have survived.[44] The barrels, locks and belt clips have intricate engraving on them. It is possible that engraving could have been done through subcontracting with another craftsman who specialised in it. If Kennedy did it himself, it is a tribute to the many skills possessed by a dagmaker. Seeing as how Scottish pistols would become known for their metal construction and intricate floral engraving in the next few centuries, it is tempting to say that it was the dagmakers themselves who decorated their work. Much of the locksmith work from that time period is richly decorated, so it is possible.

The term 'dagmaker' survived into the late seventeenth century when it was replaced by the term 'gunsmith'. The latter had been in use before the mid-seventeenth century, but rarely. John Miller, senior, was admitted as a burgess dagmaker in 1646; that same year he was listed as a freeman gunsmith in the Incorporation of Hammermen. In 1693 he was again referred to as a dagmaker in a reference to his son, Archibald. His other son, James Miller, became a freeman in 1668 with an essay of 'ane brazine buckle with ane arrow head', showing possible links to the lorimer craft.[45] In 1674 James Miller was again listed as a dagmaker in the records of the Incorporation of Hammermen.[46] The gunsmiths were simply a continuation of the dagmakers.

After 1662 the term gunsmith came into normal usage. In 1662 Joshua Shushan received burgess-ship as a gunsmith. In 1668 he gave an essay of 'ane pair of sufficient pistols' and became a freeman in the

Incorporation of Hammermen.⁴⁷ The appearance of the gunsmiths represented a change in terminology for firearms, not a new and separate craft.

In 1675 John Simpson was admitted freeman to the Incorporation of Hammermen with his essay of 'ane mounted pistol with ane carbine buckle and ane arrow head'.⁴⁸ In 1668 the dagmakers' essay had been a buckle and an arrowhead. A carbine buckle was part of the arrangement for hanging a carbine at a mounted trooper's side while riding. In 1689 Simpson supplied samples of arms – thirteen firelocks and two matchlocks.⁴⁹ Matchlocks survived late in Britain. The mechanisms were basically the same as they were at the beginning of the century, though the shape of the lockplates followed the latest styles and the stocks resembled those of the more modern firelocks.

In 1677 Francis Henderson of the Canongate gave his essay of 'ane mounted pistol of the Scots fashion, ane carbine buckle and ane arrowhead' and was entered into the Edinburgh hammermen. The 'Scots fashion' refers to a pistol of all-metal construction. Unfortunately, the clerk did not go into detail about the pistol. It would be very interesting to know what kind of lock they were using at that time and what style of butt was used on the handle.

Many of the gunsmiths were involved in the re-mounting of old barrels into new guns. Military firearms are constantly exposed to the elements and therefore always in need of repair. In 1690 John McLurg was issued twenty-eight barrels to make into muskets,⁵⁰ while in 1691, James Gibson made up 206 firelocks from old musket barrels.⁵¹ This was a common practice.

The gunsmiths employed by the Edinburgh magazine also cared for the arms that did not need remounting. In 1688 John Simpson was employed at Stirling Castle for dressing arms that were 'spoiled with rain and salt water'.⁵² There were many instances of gunmakers being employed to care for functioning arms, both for the military, as well as for the civilian markets, which were only lately beginning to diverge.

In 1696 Robert Henderson produced an essay of a mounted pistol with a 'brigged' lock, a carbine hanger and an arrow head.⁵³ There were several craftsmen who gave the same essay. The bridged lock is particularly intriguing, as its meaning is elusive. It obviously had something to do with a flintlock mechanism. Bridged might have referred to the fact that the pan cover and steel, or striking surface for the flint, were one connected piece; in the earlier snaphaunces, they were two separate pieces.

The gunsmiths also made use of imported skill. In 1669 James Gullan was given £10 sterling 'in consideration of his coming from Holland and towards his maintenance until such time as he was settled in keeping of his Majesties magazine in Edinburgh Castle'.⁵⁴ Not only does this show an interest in continental gun technology, as the flintlock was about to make its appearance in the next few years, but also it shows early links with England's currency.

Sterling seems to have been the normal currency paid out to the magazine in Edinburgh Castle. From 1681 to 1682 Peter Sochon, or Shusan, was paid in sterling for his work there. In 1670 his father, Joshua Shushan, had been paid in Scots.⁵⁵ Throughout the last quarter of the seventeenth century the money used for the gunmaking in Edinburgh Castle was in pounds sterling, well before the 1707 Union.

Not all gunsmiths worked for the magazine, but this was one of the biggest markets for guns. Civilian guns were more decorative, so it would have taken more time to produce them. The military guns would have been easier to produce than those for civilians and therefore easier to make money from. There were craftsmen, known as 'gunstockers' who specialised in assembling the metal parts onto wooden stocks. They were more akin to the wright trade, not the hammermen. In 1692, Francis Henderson was paid 'for mounting up of fifty-five musket barrels with new firelocks and stocks'. This might indicate that the gunsmiths made not only the metal parts, but also the wooden stocks.

The dagmakers, or gunsmiths, were included in the craftsmen under the section of the 1693 list entitled 'Locksmiths and these joined with them'. Though unofficial, this association seems to have outweighed any previous associations with the founders or lorimers. Even before 1693, the gunsmiths had been in this association. On 15 September 1677, in a list of the two masters for each craft that worked with the deacon for that year, one of the two locksmiths was Francis Henderson, a gunsmith.⁵⁶ On 23 August 1683, there was an act in favour of the 'locksmiths and watchmakers and gunsmiths', in an argument between them and the blacksmiths.⁵⁷ Though not labelled until 1693, the association, which would last well beyond 1750, had started by the mid-seventeenth century.

None of the crafts seems to have been subordinate to the locksmiths, though. The house did on occasion deal directly with the gunsmiths, instead of the locksmith craft. On 17 May 1682, there was an act in favour of the gunsmiths recorded in the minute books:

'The house taking into their consideration a petition presented into them, by the gunsmiths of Edinburgh freemen amongst themselves'.[58] There were occasions when the gunsmiths were seen as an independent group and not as part of the overall locksmith craft.

PROGRESSION OF SCOTTISH GUNLOCKS

From the introduction of mechanical ignition on European firearms to the present day, there have been many innovations on the mechanisms. Scotland demonstrated the sophistication of her local craftsmen by the contribution of the 'highland lock' with its laterally-moving sear.[59] The production of several types of gunlocks throughout the early modern period also shows that Scottish craftsmen were not dependent on continental craftsmen for production; most types were made in Scotland's burghs. So far, the best study of lock mechanisms used on Scottish guns was done by Charles E. Whitelaw. His work was first published as a supplement in 1923 to Herbert J. Jackson's *European Hand Firearms of the Sixteenth, Seventeenth and Eighteenth Centuries*.[60] There was a later supplement published posthumously in 1977.[61] Whitelaw's original classification for pistols had two classes of pistols – snaphaunce and flintlock – with several types in each class. The later work published in 1977, elaborated on the second class and generalized Scottish gunlocks into the four categories shown in table 3.2.[62]

For the sake of clarity, the two systems can be combined and added to several other types of gunlocks on both pistols and long-guns to give a clearer picture of gunlock technology in early modern Edinburgh. It should be noted that not all of these types have been proven to have been produced in Scotland, but for the sake of forming a picture of the material culture of the trade, they merit mention. The various types often overlap in time of production.

TABLE 3.2
Whitelaw's four types of gunlocks (Whitelaw 1977)

Type	Description	Date
I	Early snaphaunce	early sixteenth to *c.*1686
II	Late snaphaunce	*c.*1647–*c.*1702
III	Doglock	*c.*1665–1700
IV	Flintlock	*c.*1700–*c.*1820

TABLE 3.3
General typology of gunlocks used in Edinburgh

Type	Description
I	Sear matchlock
II	Trigger matchlock
III	Wheellock
IV	Early snaphaunce
V	Late snaphaunce
VI	Doglock I
VII	Doglock II
VIII	Doglock III
IX	Highland lock
X	Conventional British lock

The first lock in table 3.3 is the sear matchlock. Mechanically, this is the simplest of the ten locks. A matchlock is a gunlock which held a burning cord, or match, in an arm mounted on the lockplate. Extending from the bottom of the hagbut was a lever. Upon the lifting of the lever, the arm would be thrust forward, putting the lit match into a small pan of gunpowder. The match would in this manner ignite the powder, which was connected via a touchhole to the powder in the barrel and therefore fire the gun.

The trigger matchlock retained most of the previous mechanism, but with the addition of a trigger and trigger guard. The long lever of the sear type could easily have snagged on something and caused an accidental fire. By reducing the size down to a simple trigger, a trigger guard could be added underneath the gun stock for safety. There was also another part added to the lock mechanism, showing early stages of the increasing complexity of gun locks. Matchlocks were not used on pistols, only long-arms such as hagbuts, calivers and muskets.

Another type of gunlock that might have been encountered by Edinburgh gunsmiths, at least for repairs, was the wheellock. There is not a single reference known to a Scot making a wheellock, but there are references to them being used here. They were possibly the most complex gunlocks of the early modern period and therefore likely to need repair. While it is possible that they were shipped off to a continental gunsmith, it is far more likely that a local dagmaker repaired them. A clergyman named Father Blackhill, writing in 1643, said 'I had behind my saddle a great cloach bag in which were my new clothes – and at the bow of my saddle two

Dutch pistolettes with wheele-workes and at my side two Scots pistolettes with snap works'.[63] It is interesting that the Father kept the Scottish snaphaunces by his side instead of the wheellocks.

The earliest known Scottish references to 'snapwork' being produced were in Edinburgh and Glasgow. In 1575 in an English intelligence report, Edinburgh was said to have supplied the most part of the gentlemen and horsemen of the realm with dags, otherwise called snaphaunces.[64] On 3 July 1578 in Glasgow, John Hannay, snapmaker, was ordered to serve John Barry, lorimer, in the making of snaps. There were earlier references to it being known in Scotland, as in the following modernized translation of a 1568 satirical poem:

> 'Now you are lamed from labour, I lament it,/Your pistols emptied and sprung back like a wand:/Snapwork, adieu, for dagmen do not stand,/And worse than that, you lack your priming-powder.'[65]

The mechanisms of snaphaunce locks were set upon thick plates of steel or brass. On this plate were mounted two arm-like pieces, various springs and a pan for powder; they were very complex mechanisms. The early snaphaunce lock had a characteristic sear which protruded through the lock plate to arrest the cock in the 'cocked' position. The cock, which was a spring-driven arm, held a piece of flint in a pair of jaws on one end.

When the trigger was pulled, the sear was pushed backwards, which caused it to withdraw into the lock plate. This released the cock, which swung forward, scraping the flint against the hardened steel. As the cock moved forward, an internal rod connected to the tumbler pushed open the pan cover, exposing the gunpowder to the sparks generated by the flint and steel. As the powder ignited in the pan, it spread through a small hole into the barrel and ignited the main charge behind the ball.

Compared to a match lock, the snaphaunce was far superior. Matchlocks had a constant open flame, whereas snapworks only ignited when triggered. For this reason, snaphaunces were issued to detachments guarding gunpowder in the Civil War.[66] Matchlocks also had to be kept lit, which was tricky in inclement weather and expensive for consuming match or 'lunt'.

Early snaphaunces did have two setbacks. First, there was no bridle to strengthen and brace the inner workings of the lock. Second, there was no half-cock position. When uncocked, the pan cover was automatically open and therefore it could not be carried primed. The gun was either uncocked and unusable, or cocked and ready to fire. If something accidentally tripped the trigger, then the piece would indiscriminately discharge.[67]

The late snaphaunce was used from c.1647 to c.1702. The predominant difference between late and early snaphaunces was the disappearance of the protruding sear. While this type of laterally-moving sear would be used late on the 'highland lock', in late snaphaunces, the sear interacted only with the tumbler on the back of the lock. The cock toe was removed, as the sear no longer came through the lock plate to engage it. The late snaphaunce had the same problems as the early snaphaunce, though.[68]

By 1612, in France, the snaphaunce had been evolved into the flintlock.[69] While the principle remained the same, the mechanism became much less complicated. In Scotland, the earliest flintlocks were of a type known as doglocks, due to a 'dog' catch which held the cock at the half-cocked position, which was a form of safety. The doglock was in use in Scotland from c. 1665 to c. 1700.[70] The first doglocks had the pan cover and steel combined into one piece – the distinguishing characteristic of the flintlock mechanism. Not only did this keep the powder in better, but it also greatly simplified the mechanism by removing the parts that connected the pan cover to the lock plate and the cock to the pan cover lever. When the cock fell on a flintlock, it pushed the pan open as it ran the flint against the steel. Gravity and inertia replaced a series of complicated parts, to make for a mechanism that was much easier to produce and maintain. Types I and III of the doglocks had sear and tumbler setups similar to the late snaphaunce lock. These show signs of the future conventional flintlock. Type II retained the laterally-moving sear from the early snaphaunce, though it was now catching on the breast, or front, of the cock as opposed to the toe which was behind it. By shifting the contact point to the front, a half-cocked position was achieved. This would later be an integral part of the highland lock. The doglock demonstrates that there was not one line of development in Scottish locks, but two simultaneous lines of development; one based on a sear and tumbler setup and one based on a laterally-moving sear. The earliest known example of a highland lock is dated 1678,[71] though by Whitelaw's estimation, this would be a Type II doglock. This represents the link between the doglock and the fully developed highland lock.

The final two stages of development were also flintlock mechanisms and were used from c.1700 to

TABLE 3.4
Approximate number of parts of gunlocks

Gunlock	Number of parts
Sear Matchlock	11
Trigger Matchlock	12
Wheellock	18
Early Snaphaunce	23
Late Snaphaunce	19
Doglock I	18
Doglock II	17
Doglock III	17
Highland Lock	17
Conventional British Flintlock	17

$c.$ 1820.[72] The first of these stages was the so called highland lock. With the laterally-moving sear catching the cock in the half-cocked position, there was a safety for the pistol. When the pistol was fully-cocked, or 'bended' in Scots,[73] the sear and tumbler acted very similar to a conventional flintlock. When the trigger was pulled, the sear was moved inside the lock plate and the cock was free to fall forward once the sear had disengaged the tumbler.

The term 'highland' should not be taken to mean that it was produced by highlanders as opposed to lowlanders. The very term has become something of a myth, with much of Scottish arms and armour currently being labelled as 'highland' or 'lowland'.[74] The term 'highland' was used in conjunction with Scottish weapons by their makers in the early modern period, but only to denote the clientele base. Edinburgh armourers produced 'highland hilt',[75] or basket hilt swords for sale to a market based on Highland cattle drovers. They were meant to be sold to them; they were not made by them. Almost all of the production of weapons happened in the burghs, not the Highlands, and therefore nearly all Scottish weapons are lowland. Who it was that coined the name 'highland lock' is uncertain, but it was a lowland-produced item, just as highland hilt swords were.

The conventional flintlock would eventually become the standard lock on all British military firearms. The most common example of this is the famous Brown Bess. It was much simpler than previous locks and was easily mass produced.

Initially, there was an increase in the complexity of gunlock mechanisms. As can be seen in table 3.4 and chart 3.3, the number of parts increased dramatically from the matchlock to the snaphaunce lock. While wheellocks were never produced in Scotland, they were used and their complexity, along with that of the snaphaunce, made for delicate firearms that needed much looking after. Throughout the early modern

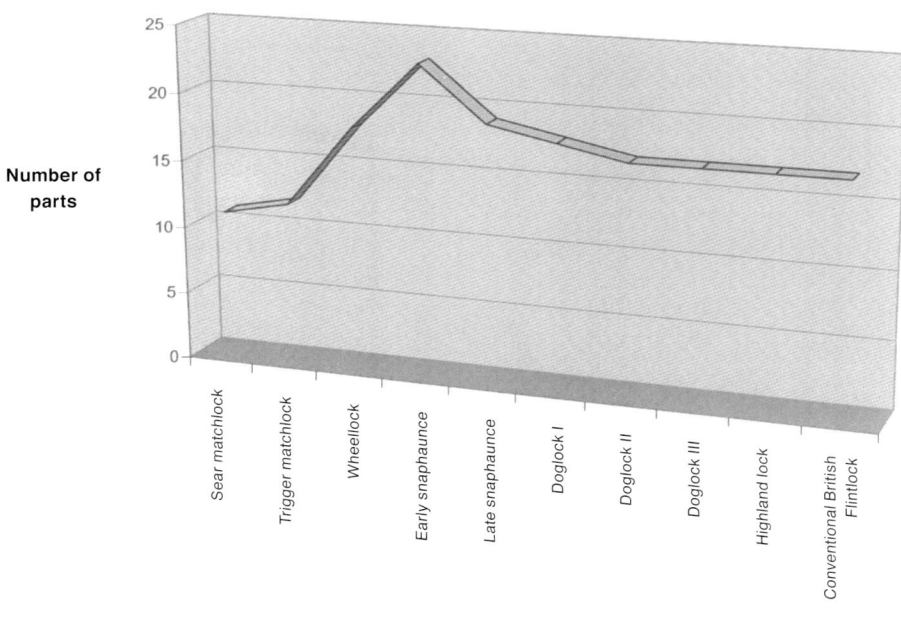

CHART 3.3
Number of gunlock parts

period, the approximate number of parts in a Scottish gunlock decreased slightly and levelled off. While still more complex than a matchlock, the later flintlocks were not as complex as the snap and wheellocks. They were, however, more sophisticated and easier to produce.

From the adoption of the snaphaunce in the sixteenth century, there was a line of Scottish gunlocks unique to Scotland. The snaphaunce was used across Europe though, and it is probable that there were connections between Scottish snaphaunces and those of other countries, representing borrowed technology. Still, there are many surviving examples which stand as a testament to Scottish craftsmanship and in some cases, Scottish ingenuity.

TOOLS AND TECHNIQUES

Dagmakers would have needed a smithy for heating metal, a study or anvil, several sizes of hammers, tongs, clamps for setting springs in locks and many files. They also would have needed long steel rods for welding the steel barrels together. A bar was wrapped around the rod like an overlapping coil, all the time impact welding the seam. It became a barrel formed like a paper-towel tube. Some type of device would have been needed for polishing the inside of the barrel. The mainstay of a dagmakers' work was probably done around a post-vice, which was a large vice mounted to a post in the ground. All parts for a lock would have been hand-filed and hand-fit to each other, as interchangeable parts were not common until the Industrial Revolution.

As with a locksmith, brazing was a necessary skill for a dagmaker. Brazing is a form of welding used for brass or steel. It was an extremely strong version of soldering and would have been used to join the various plates that made up the all-metal, hollow body of a pistol in much the same way that locksmiths would have used it for the hollow bodies of padlocks. Brazing would have been done in the smithy, by encasing the parts in clay with flux and bits of brass by the desired joints. When the lump was then heated to the proper temperature, the flux cleaned the seams while the braze material ran into the joint. As it cooled it formed a strong bond. In this manner, the body plates were joined together.[76]

Hardening and tempering of springs and frizzens would have been done in the smithy. Once the parts reached the proper temperature, which was gauged by the colour of the metal, they were quickly quenched in oil or water. This made them extremely hard and brittle. They were then tempered back to the proper level, much like an edged blade. Springs required a fair amount of skill to make properly.

Gun-barrels were case-hardened.[77] This was a hardening process which left the outside of the workpiece extremely hard, while the inside of the metal was still soft. This made for a better polish, which lasted longer and therefore was more resistant to rust. Case-hardening was described by Joseph Moxon in 1678 in the following manner:

> Take cow horn or hoof, dry it thoroughly in an oven and then beat it to powder. Put about the same quantity of bay-salt to it and mingle them together with stale chamberly, or else white-wine vinegar. Lay some of this mixture upon the loam ... and cover your iron all over with it; then wrap the loam about all and lay it upon the hearth of the forge to dry and harden. When it is dry and hard, put it into the fire and blow up the coals to it, till the whole lump have just a blood-red heat, but no higher, lest the quality of your mixture burn away and leave the iron as soft as at first. Then take it out and quench it. Or, instead of loam, you may wrap it up in plate iron, so as the mixture may touch every part of your work and blow the coals to it, as foresaid.[78]

Tempering and case-hardening were skills needed by gunsmiths, which required specialized knowledge not needed by pewterers or coppersmiths.

Their booths would have been small, as was the custom of all craftsmen's workshops in early modern Europe. Unfortunately, no contemporary

FIGURE 3.2
A Parisian gunsmith's shop, *c.* 1660 (Ricketts 1965, 42)

illustrations of a Scottish gunsmith's booth survive. Luckily, there are four engravings of the European counterparts. These images of gunsmith shops are from 1568 in Nürnberg, 1613 in Nürnberg, c.1660 in Paris and c.1694 in Amsterdam.[79] There are many similar elements. All of these shops have one or two workbenches, usually with at least one standing vice. All have finished products hanging in the shop, waiting to be sold. Production and sales would have had a direct correlation; if items were moving slowly, there would probably have been little rush in finishing work. All are well lit and open, with windows by the workbench, providing light for the workers. The forge would not have needed as much light, so it is farther away from the windows. The shops are small, because vast amounts of space were not needed. When work was taken out of the forge, it had to be put on the anvil immediately. If the anvil was on the other side of the shop, the work-piece would be cool by the time it got there.

The 1613 Nürnberg shop has only one worker, while the others have either two or three. The Parisian shop is interesting for the amount of detail it shows (see figure 3.2). Each of the three workers, a master, a journeyman and perhaps an apprentice, has his own standing vice. The apprentice is helping the master set up a small, bow-driven lathe in the standing vice, while the other worker uses a double-handled wrench to screw a breech plug onto a barrel. Like the locksmith trade, there was a lot of bench work involved in the gunsmith trade and a lot of the tools were common to both arts; the standing vices, the hand vice, the hammer, the files and the callipers could all be found in an Edinburgh locksmith's booth.

Like the locksmiths, the Edinburgh gunsmiths seem to have had little desire to stamp their mark on their work. Out of all the pistols that survive from 1550 to 1650, only five[80] can be ascribed to Edinburgh craftsmen.[81] Perhaps the craftsmen did not think it important to sign their work, until 1740, when the locksmiths were told to do so by the house.[82]

The dagmakers and gunsmiths had links to locksmiths, lorimers and possibly melters. New technologies entered Scotland and were incorporated into the Edinburgh hammermen by joining them with the trade that had the most in common with them. Taking knowledge of moving parts from the locksmiths' art, they produced mechanical devices that gave ignition to their firearms. Terminology was taken as well; 'lock', 'tumbler' and 'lock plate' were common to both arts. They also had skill in brazing and filing. The connection to the melters lies with the use of gun-metal barrels. It is uncertain as to whether the dagmakers cast the gun metal barrels themselves, or bought them from the melters. By 1693, they were firmly joined with the locksmiths only.

CLOCKMAKERS AND WATCHMAKERS

Clockmakers and watchmakers were also joined with the locksmiths. As with locks and gun locks, clocks and watches had mechanical, movable parts and often incorporated brass, iron and steel. Mechanical clocks had existed in Europe since medieval times. There are two types of clocks that apply to this study; weight-driven and spring-driven. The oldest known surviving weight-driven clock is in Salisbury Cathedral, in England. It dates to at least 1386 and is still functioning today.[83] In the early stages of clockmaking, these simpler weight-driven mechanisms were often made by blacksmiths. In London, the early clockmakers were in the blacksmiths' guild.[84] The problem with weight-driven mechanisms is that they depended on gravity and were not easily transported. If the mechanism could be turned upside down, the force driving the clock was interrupted and the mechanism slowed down. This type of clock had to remain still to work.

Spring-driven mechanisms had the advantage of a self-contained, easily moved power source. While gravity still affected the accuracy slightly, it was not as extreme. The earliest known spring-driven clock was made by Jacob Zech, or Jacob the Czech, in 1525,[85] though there are descriptions and illustrations of spring-driven clocks from the late fifteenth century.[86] The introduction of the spring might have been the link from locksmithing to clockmaking, as one of the locksmiths' necessary skills was the proper tempering of springs.

Spring-driven mechanisms opened up the possibility for smaller clocks, as the power supply took up less space. Smaller mechanisms were more easily transported, so the spring brought about the watch. The earliest known watch still in existence dates to 1548 and is probably German.[87]

EDINBURGH KNOCKMAKERS

Clockwork was an imported skill which was probably brought into Edinburgh after 1483. Many of Edinburgh's more famous horologists were of French and English origins (see table 3.6). Yet this is not to say that Edinburgh was void of clock- and watchmaking skill. Once it was established in Edinburgh, a thriving market for horologists grew and a sophisticated base of skill existed until the practice of importing and assembling bought parts prevailed. Several specimens of Edinburgh craftsmanship are still functioning today, in the National Museum of Scotland. It is also worth noting that Scotland had its own jargon for the parts of a clock, or 'knock'[88] as they were called up till the 1670s. 'Horologe brod' was Scots for the dial, or face of the knock; 'tows' were the knock ropes attached to the driving weights, which were known as 'pases'; and 'sails' was the Scots word for the quatre-foil fly, which looked like a pair of paddles and were used to cause wind-friction to slow the wheels.[89]

Prior to 1600, there is little evidence of clockmaking in the Edinburgh hammermen. One craftsman named William Purves was known to have worked in Edinburgh, Aberdeen, Stirling and Dundee. In his Dundee contract, it is stated that he was a burgess of Edinburgh.[90] There was a William Purves listed as having one of the three keys for the incorporation's box in 1542, and in 1546 he was given as William 'Purwes' in a list of masters paying 4s to the hammermen.[91] No mention is given that this Purves made clocks, but it has been pointed out that the minute book records accord with William Purves's movements as found in the Aberdeen notes.[92] Seeing as Scotland did not have the horological resources of the larger countries like France, or the Holy Roman Empire, it would make sense for a Scottish clockmaker to have the freedom of its largest metalworking guild in the capital city.

After Purves, there were no clockmakers listed in the hammermen minute books until the early 1600s. On 23 April 1585, a smith from Blantyre, with the surname of Smith, was brought to Edinburgh 'for repairing the knock of Lindores bought by the town, setting up thereof and dressing the same'.[93] Edinburgh had to bring in specialized craftsmen, because they did not have anyone in their local incorporation to do the job. There was a dearth of horological skill in Edinburgh.

On 4 January 1594, commission was given to the dean of guild and 'his council' to make an agreement with a craftsman named Fleming, 'for guiding and temperating of the town's knock in the steeple'. They granted him liberty to work his trade of 'monteris making' and to hold an open booth 'notwithstanding that his is no burgess nor free with any craft'.[94] It was recognised that the town needed clockwork skill and the rules protecting the privileges of the crafts were set aside to attain it. Not only would Fleming look after the common knock, but also he would be producing individual knocks, or 'munters', for sale in the burgh. As clock technology was moving out of the medieval period, blacksmith-made clocks were becoming a thing of the past. New specialists in spring-driven, personal clocks were coming in. They could work in steel for the springs of personal clocks as well as the iron for the larger tower clocks.

KNOCKMAKERS AND THE INCORPORATION OF HAMMERMEN

On 19 December 1604, a Canongate knockmaker named William Smith 'obliged himself [to] repair and uphold the town's knock in the steeple in all necessaries thereto'.[95] The fact that the Edinburgh council was using a Canongate craftsman, a stranger, could not have sat well with the Edinburgh incorporated trades. On 11 December 1607, another clockmaker named James Smith was given a salary of £10 a year to inspect the town's great clock twice a week and keep it in repair.[96] The council using an Edinburgh unfreeman was seen as equally bad. However, at some point around this time, Smith joined the Incorporation of Hammermen. His name was mentioned in a list of masters in 1606, but this is confusing, as he was still an unfreeman at that point. On 8 August 1610, by an act of Council, James Smith was given burgess-ship.[97] It just would not have done to see the rules broken, even if his skill was necessary to the burgh. But what about the Incorporation of Hammermen? Even with freedom of the burgh, he was still an unfreeman of the craft with servants working for him.[98] For the sake of keeping everything neat and tidy, Smith was made a master in the incorporation. The problem was that there was no knockmaker craft to put him in. Aside from Purves, seventy years earlier, this was new territory for the incorporation. He could have been put in with the blacksmiths, because the mainstay of his known work was the older type of weight-driven mechanism. The incorporation must have considered even these simple mechanisms too complex for the blacksmith art, so he was attached to the locksmiths. On 7 September 1613 'the deacon and masters with consent of the art of locksmith craft, admitted James Smith to his essay, to wit kist lock to be made in Abraham Hamiliton, his booth'.[99] His essay masters were Thomas Duncan and Thomas Brown, who were both locksmiths. They knew he could make clocks, but he had to prove himself on kist locks. He passed his essay, paid his upset of £40 and was the first knockmaker in the locksmith craft of the Edinburgh Incorporation of Hammermen.[100] The council continued to give him work on the town knocks. In 1614 he built a new knock for the town weigh-house.[101] In 1619 he was given by the council a new salary of £100 a year, for tending the town clocks, the great clock, the Netherbow clock and the weigh-house clock 'providing always [he] attend the tempering of the same by day and night and keep the same in good order so that they answer one to another in striking of the hour and keeping the just hour and measure winter and summer'.[102] He certainly had his work cut out for him. Until 1641 he was never referred to as a knockmaker in the incorporation minute books; he was referred to only as a locksmith.[103] An unofficial association had begun that would last well past 1750.

The practice was not immediately taken on as protocol in Edinburgh. There were still other knockmakers around the area. In the Canongate, William Smith became a Canongate Hammerman on 17 June 1615.[104] By 1627 he was joined by an English watchmaker named Cornelius Zet.[105] The Canongate records for 20 March 1627 state that before he was a freeman of their hammermen, he already had his own booth in which to make his essay.[106] In Edinburgh, a French knockmaker named Nicolas Funtanet attained burgess-ship in 1611, by marrying the daughter of a burgess.[107] He does not seem to have joined the Incorporation of Hammermen, though. The new technology brought with it a period of transition, where the incorporation had to adjust in order to incorporate it.

It was not until 1647 that knockmakers other than James Smith were recorded in the minute books of the Incorporation of Hammermen. On 11 August 1647 George and Robert Smith, who were both sons of James, attained burgess-ship of Edinburgh as knockmakers.[108] On 6 September 1647 they both became freeman locksmiths and knockmakers in the Incorporation of Hammermen.[109] George Smith is often given the honour of being the first hammerman admitted as a 'knockmaker',[110] but this is quibbling over terminology. George was not the first knockmaker in the incorporation and Robert was made a freeman 'knockmaker' on the same day as George. The same day they became freemen of the incorporation, the brazier art asked that the two brothers should not work in brass or copper 'but that allenerlie appertain to their essay'.[111] The incorporation was trying to make this new technology fit its established structure.

The first watchmaker in Edinburgh might have been the previously mentioned Fleming in 1594. It was stated that he had a booth for making 'monteris', which was another variation of the Scots word for watches and he was given permission by the council not to join the Incorporation of Hammermen.[112] He was a legal unfreeman, the perfect position to have been in. The first watchmaker listed in the minute books of the incorporation was the Frenchman, Paul Romieu, Senior.[113] Romieu is believed to have come from Rouen[114] to Edinburgh in the 1670s. He became a freeman clock and watchmaker of the incorporation on 2 June 1677, with his essay having been the movements of a watch. His essay masters were George Neill, a locksmith and Andrew Brown, a clockmaker.[115] It is doubtful that Neill had any technical expertise in regards to Romieu's essay; he probably was just a representative of the locksmith craft to ensure that Romieu made the essay himself.

Watchmakers continued in Edinburgh throughout the early modern period, though not in large numbers. In 1711, a clockmaker was given time off of his indentures due to his master's death and 'especially considering there are few watchmakers in this city at present'.[116] When a skill was needed, both the council and the incorporation were willing to bend the rules.

From 1613 on, all knockmakers, clockmakers, hourmakers and watchmakers were part of the locksmith craft, though the association usually went unspoken. In 1667 there is evidence that the practice continued, when Humphrey Milne, an English knockmaker in the incorporation, was listed as being one of the two masters for the locksmiths for that year.[117] In 1693, the practice became definite and recorded in the list of masters.

The section of the 1693 list entitled 'Locksmiths and these joined with them' listed several clockmakers and one 'hourmaker'. Several of the craftsmen had 'dead' after their name, but this is most likely a later addition to the 1693 list for finding the 1695[118] tally of living masters. It is also interesting that no craftsmen were listed as watchmakers in 1693, although Paul Romieu, Senior, was in fact a watchmaker. Perhaps the clerk was not bothered about the technical details.

The association between the watchmakers, clockmakers and locksmiths was never officially set down in the minute books. The most recognition it got was the 1693 entry of 'Locksmiths and these joined with them'. The association did not equate to the clockmakers being ruled by the locksmiths; they were not subordinate to them. In 1736, when Mr Andrew

Dickie craved admittance as a freeman clockmaker, it was the 'clockmaker art', along with the old deacons and boxmasters, who formed the committee to decide; the locksmiths were not involved.[119] The clockmakers asked the incorporation, not the locksmith craft, for protection of their privileges from strangers coming in. The house then provided Dickie with a free burgess ticket and, with the consent of the clockmaker's art, admitted him as a freeman.[120]

PROGRESSION OF SCOTTISH CLOCKS AND WATCHES

Early modern horology is not a field in which Scotland made any groundbreaking technological innovations, though one of Britain's finest clockmakers, David Ramsay, was from Dundee. He was given in 1618 the office of Chief Clockmaker to the King and was in 1631 one of the first masters to hold office in London's Clockmakers' Company.[121] But while Scots were far from unskilled in horology, the technology was imported. This can be said for most countries in the world, though and it is rather fortunate for Scotland that clockmakers from England and France settled in Edinburgh. In 1660 Humphrey Milne came from England to Edinburgh, where he produced many brass lantern clocks with balance wheel and verge escapements. It has been pointed out that Milne was rather conservative, as he tended to carry on producing the lantern clocks he knew instead of incorporating the latest technology from London. It was pointed out at the same time that Milne's real contribution to Scottish horology was taking a large number of local apprentices. He may not have used cutting-edge innovations, but he did help establish a base of skilled clockmakers.[122]

One of his apprentices, Andrew Brown, went to great lengths to incorporate the latest clock technology. The lantern clock in Scotland died with Milne. Brown kept up with London trends, making dependable mechanisms with the latest escapements. One of his clocks from c.1690 is capable of keeping time to within one or two minutes a month.[123]

While the new innovations from England, France, Germany, Holland and other European countries did help improve Scottish clockmaking, it is beyond the scope of this chapter to describe the entire technological history of Scottish horology, though it should be pointed out that this is a research project that needs to be done. Some of the more obvious technological details merit mention, however.

The most important component of horology was wheel cutting. If the 'wheels', or gears, were off by a fraction, the clock would not work properly. Precision was of the utmost importance.[124] The series of wheels in a clock was known as the 'train'. To achieve precision-cut wheels by hand-filing, the clockmakers had to have incredible skill. This was achieved by first marking out a wheel-blank on a 'division plate', which was a gauge for marking out where the teeth were to be cut. The problem of dividing up a circle into even parts for the cutting of the teeth was originally dealt with by geometry. By the 1500s Europeans had devised a mechanism for dividing a circle of metal with a known circumference. A division plate had various concentric circles with known numbers of teeth to be cut for each particular size. Once the metal disk had been attached and marked, it was then taken to a vice for cutting and filing.[125]

In 1609 there was a reference to an 'instrument to cut wheels' and by the 1670s there were references to engines that could cut them.[126] The division plate was incorporated into a hand-cranked milling machine. The oldest surviving illustration of a wheel-cutting engine is from France, in 1709.[127] When wheel-cutting engines first came to Edinburgh is impossible to say. They might have come with a Frenchman, like Paul Romieu, or with an Englishman, like Milne. If Andrew Brown cut his wheels by hand, then he was amazingly skilled.

Escapement was another area in which innovation was quite prolific. The earliest escapement was the 'foliot'. With a foliot escapement, there was a vertical crown wheel with teeth projecting forward. Resting right next to the wheel, was a rod with two flaps, or 'pallets', mounted at about a ninety degree angle to each other. The top of the rod had a 'T'-shaped section with weights on either end, which moved like a helicopter. As the clock moved, either due to weights or springs, the crown wheel would move, which would make the foliot oscillate from left to right. The pallets of the foliot would be caught one at a time by the teeth of the crown wheel and momentarily stop its turning. As this happened, the bar rotated and the other pallet would be pushed into the path of another tooth on the bottom of the crown wheel. As that pallet was stopped and pushed back, the process started again with the top pallet again arresting the vertical wheel as the foliot spun around and back repetitively. The escapement meant that the train could only move one tooth-space at time, slowing the mechanism down. The 'tick, tock' sound of a clock is actually the escapement putting the train in check.

The invention of the pendulum brought about a new type of escapement. It is debatable who invented the pendulum. Some say it was the famous astronomer Galileo,[128] while others believe it was a Dutch mathematician named Christian Huygens (1629–95). Others yet say it was Ahasuerus Fromanteel in 1658, who was born in Norfolk, of Dutch descent.[129] Whoever it was, the pendulum greatly increased the reliability of timekeeping.

The 'verge escapement' was invented around 1660.[130] The crown wheel was no longer vertical and that the rod with the pallets was placed across the top of the clock and attached to a pendulum. Instead of the foliot oscillating, the pendulum would swing. With each swing, a tooth of the crown wheel would be allowed to pass, slowly releasing the wound tension of the clock.

Eventually the system was simplified into a flat wheel with sharp teeth and an 'anchor' shaped escapement instead of the pallets. The anchor escapement, combined with a pendulum, is still in use today.

After 1750, clock- and watchmaking continued to advance. Mechanization took the art to new levels of ability. Machines were made for 'uprighting' the barrel, fusee and train wheels of a watch. To upright was to cut a work piece in such a way as to ensure the squareness of the parts to the movement plates in order to minimize friction and wear.[131] Uprighting gave perfect ninety degree angles at the edges of the parts. Without such a machine, it is hard to see how early watchmakers achieved this. The earliest known illustration of a tool for uprighting parts is in Diderot's *Encyclopedia* from 1765.[132] The earliest English mandrel is also from 1765.[133] The mandrel represents society moving over from cottage industry to the Industrial Revolution's mechanization and standardization of parts, which also affected the gunsmiths and locksmiths.

Clockmakers' shops on the continent were very similar to gunsmiths' shops. There are four surviving engravings of clockmakers' shops from Germany, Holland and France, from 1586, c.1600, c.1694 and 1748.[134] One of the most striking impressions given by the four engravings is how refined the 1748 shop is compared to the c.1600 shop. Clockmaking was becoming part of a European craft aristocracy. The 1748 shop illustrates the need for mathematical skills and the clean, elegant shop environment. The 1568 shop (see figure 3.3) shows hard, physical labour at the anvil, with the forge blazing away behind. The images of clockmaking betray hints of blacksmith roots, whereas the images which contain watchmakers show signs of goldsmith roots.

The multitude of parts from the various periods of horology was extremely technical. It only made sense that clockmakers in Edinburgh were joined with the locksmiths, as they were the only trade whose work was anything near as complicated. In the Canongate Incorporation of Hammermen, in 1619, there was a ten-year apprenticeship for a knockmaker, compared to the six years for a blacksmith.[135] The craft rules in Nürnberg also illustrate the complexity of clock and watchmaking. In 1629, a locksmith or a gunsmith was allowed to work as a clockmaker, but a clockmaker was forbidden from working on locks or guns.[136] If the smith was skilled enough, the town had another horologist at its disposal, but in practice, the skill level required would have limited the number of craftsmen doing this. The easier trades of locks and guns were forbidden to the clockmakers, because they could have

FIGURE 3.3
Der Uhrmacher, 1568 (Amman & Sachs 1973, 75)

done these jobs. Most smiths could not make a clock, so it did not matter if they were all allowed to. Skill kept the craftsmen in their respective places.

FRAMESMITH

The third art joined with the locksmiths in the 1693 list is that of the framesmith, or stocking frame maker, of which only one craftsman is mentioned in the Incorporation of Hammermen minute books, Mathew Downing. Though he was mentioned as a freeman in an earlier 1682 list and then again in the 1693 one under the locksmiths,[137] Downing did not officially receive burgess-ship until 1698. He is listed in the burgess rolls as a stocking frame maker, gratis, by act of Council on 4 September 1698: 'in respect there is none of his art can make these frames'. The entry in the rolls states that 'the Incorporation of the Hammermen … condescended to admit him freeman, gratis, he paying the clerk and servants dues and the poor box money'.[138] The condescension was due to the nature of the stocking frame, which was a wooden loom for mechanically making silk or woollen stockings. The frame was a wooden mechanism, with the only iron parts being the back and front joints and their arms and standards.[139] Wood was a medium for wrights, not commonly used by hammermen, but it was again the very nature of the stocking frame which allied it to the locksmiths. The trade was accepted into the incorporation because it was mechanical. It had moving parts like locks, clocks and guns. Framework knitting was of great importance in Scotland in the late seventeenth and early eighteenth centuries and Edinburgh needed the skills to maintain the frames.

To better understand the one framesmith's relationship with the locksmith craft, it is sensible to take a look at the origins of the stocking frame, which foreshadowed the Industrial Revolution of the eighteenth century. There are two versions of the story of the invention of the frame. One printed in 1831, by Gravenor Henson, is a written version of an oral history recorded from two stocking makers who served their apprenticeships in the early eighteenth century.[140] Henson's version of the events has the inventor of the frame as a minister and curate of Calverton, Nottinghamshire, in the late sixteenth century. Apparently the Reverend Lee was wooing a lady who dodged his advances by claiming to be too busy knitting stockings. Henson states that Reverend Lee

> became disgusted and he vowed to devote his future leisure, instead of dancing attendance on a capricious woman, who treated his attention with cold neglect, in devising an invention that should effectually supersede her favourite employment of knitting.[141]

The lady eventually realized her folly, as Lee then spent all of his time in the pursuit of an engine to remove the labour from the stocking maker trade, apparently even the time that should have been spent on his ministerial duties.

The technical side of his idea gave him some problems. He learned the basic principles of knitting from spending so much time with the lady as she knitted the series of loops into a web. Henson states that it was the round shape of the stocking that confounded him:

> making a whole series or course at once, having as many needles as loops; it seemed impossible to construct a machine to make a round web. Pondering in his mind the difficulties of his task, on one of his visits he found her knitting the heel of a stocking and using only two needles; one was employed in holding the loops whilst the other was engaged in forming a new series; the thought struck him instantly that he could make a flat web and then, by joining the selvages with the needle, make it round.[142]

As Henson's account, dramatic as it may be, shows, the frame was a highly complex mechanical device, as were locks, clocks and guns.

There is another account of the invention of the stocking frame from 1747, contemporary to the old stocking makers interviewed by Henson, though printed eighty-four years earlier. R. Campbell, a Scot, published his account in a book on the various occupations in London in the mid-eighteenth century. Chapter XL 'Of the Stocking Weaver' starts out by stating that the stocking weaver:

> is but of late invention; found out, as the story goes, by a young gentleman of Oxford. This gentleman happened to fall in love with a young woman, of fortune and family inferior to himself and married her without the consent of his relations, who abandoned him upon this undutiful step. The young couple were soon reduced to difficulties and in a little time had nothing to subsist on but a mere trifle the young woman earned by knitting of stockings. As this was their main support and that one hand could get very little by it, necessity set the young gentleman upon finding out a method more expeditious. He proved so happy in his enquiry as to fall upon the invention of the stocking loom, which he brought to great perfection and by it in a short time put himself in circumstances independent of his … inexorable parents.[143]

Much of the two accounts are similar, though the 1747 version is not as colourful. Some credence is given to the minister aspect of the 1831 version, by the arms of the London based Worshipful Company of Framework Knitters. In the centre of the arms is a frame, with a minister on the left and a woman on the right. Sheila Mason, in her book on the company, shows an illustration of these arms from the seventeenth century.[144]

Whether or not Lee was a minister, it would appear that he did invent the stocking frame by the year 1589.[145] He then took his idea to London, seeking patronage from Queen Elizabeth. She was excited at the prospect of such a machine, but disappointed when she found out that it only worked in wool and not silk,[146] as it was not until the seventeenth century that modified frames were used to make silk goods.[147] Though royal patronage did not come as easily as expected and Lee died in 1610,[148] framework knitting did eventually become a common enough trade for its London practitioners to incorporate. In 1655 the framework knitters in England petitioned Oliver Cromwell for official recognition. The necessity of incorporation was so that the 'just right to the invention may be preserved from Foreigners'.[149] While they did in 1657 attain recognition and form themselves into the Worshipful Company of Framework Knitters, they did not manage to preserve the stocking frame from foreigners. As early as 1608, Lee had shipped frames and workmen to France.[150]

In 1681, the Scottish parliament made the 'Act for Encouraging Trade and Manufactories', to provide protection for local wares by prohibiting the importation of various items, such as silk and woollen stockings. A company was formed under the protection of this act at New Mills in East Lothian, for the production of fine woollen cloth. By 1683 they had four silk-stocking frames, which had been purchased from Sir James Stanfield. They later bought more frames from England. Unfortunately, there were not enough orders for the company to thrive. In 1686 the company auctioned their frames. These frames and the frame-work knitters that ran them went to Edinburgh.[151]

By 1682 Mathew Downing, the stocking-frame maker, was listed in the Edinburgh hammermen's minute books.[152] He did not receive burgess-ship until 1698, when an act of Council recognized the need for his skills in the town. The entry in the burgess rolls states that 'the Incorporation of the Hammermen ... condescended to admit him freeman, gratis, he

FIGURE 3.4
Stocking knitters, 1698 (Weigel 1963)

paying the clerk and servants dues and the poor box money'.[153] Downing had been in the incorporation for sixteen years. The burgh establishment had been willing to turn a blind eye because they needed his expertise. He was not the only unfreeman in the burgh associated with frames; in 1690, John Burton, one of the New Mills framework knitters, was listed in the Register of Deeds as an 'indweller in Edinburgh'.[154]

While there was only one framesmith identified in the minute books prior to 1750, the use of knitting frames in Scotland became established enough to contribute to the decline of the Aberdeen hand-knitting trade after 1793.[155] In 1775, David Loch, who was concerned with promoting the native woollen industry, made a tour around Scotland in order to provide a report for the Board of Trustees on manufactures of textiles.[156] He reported that there were frames throughout Scotland. Stirling and Dumfries had thirty, Linlithgow had nine, and Ayr and Irvine twenty-five. Edinburgh and Leith had stocking frames which were 'increasing daily'. There were more than 119 stocking frames in Scotland in 1775.[157]

FRAME TECHNOLOGY

Due to the mechanical nature of the frames, Downing's art was listed as 'joined' with the locksmith craft in 1693.[158] The complexity of the framework knitting can be appreciated by studying figure 3.4, which shows hand-knitters at work on the various laborious phases of their operations. This was much simplified by the mechanization of one of the stages of the process. The frame was a labour saving device, but it was also far more technical. The frame of the stocking frame was made out of wood. Iron parts were added to this in a very complicated fashion. The following account of Lee's first machine gives the best possible description of the technical side of stocking frames and therefore merits inclusion in its entirety:

> His first operation was to drive his needles, eight to an inch, into a firm piece of wood, fixed upon a wooden frame (from which the machine has since taken its name): his next attempt was to form a wooden bar to press the end of the hooks into the groove at one motion; this he effected with facility and had the patience to make several inches by the hand with his new machine. However ludicrous such an apparatus may now appear, Mr. Lee thought he had effected wonders. Having thus become enabled to loop a series at once, lie next attempted to gain the thread to form the loop this presented still further obstacles, all attempts to gain the length of thread at the head of the needle, which he tried to effect by pins fixed upon levers, proved abortive; at length lie determined to gain the thread for the loop at the stem of the needle. Having constructed a lever made of wood for each needle, he found little difficulty in making an indented spring, from his needle wire, to balance the lighter end against the heavier and to prevent their falling. But to make an instrument to catch the thread, by passing between the needles and then, after carrying the thread to the head, to quit the work, presented no slight obstacle. Several ludicrous circumstances are related respecting his unsuccessful essays to frame the arch as well as the neb of the sinker; at length lie succeeded in framing from pieces of tin the present jack sinker. The only parts of the carcase of his frame made of iron, were the back and front joints and their arms and standards. The first frame ran only upon two trucks, whilst the half jack, which connected the movements of the jacks, combs and springs, was fastened to the verge bar, which stopped the heads of the jacks when the locker bar pressed them up after they had fallen. Mr. Lee's frames had no lead sinkers. The locker bar, to force up the jacks, was worked by the foot, as was also the frame, when sinking, to bring the thread to the head of the needle. The slur cock★ to force down the jacks, was worked by a lever, first by the hand, afterwards with the foot. The slur wheel is a later improvement.
>
> ★*The slur cock is an apparatus made to ride upon a long bar, called the slur bar, which is flat and the slur, having two sides like flaps and two wheels in the top to ease the motion, rides on the upper edge of the bar. In the middle of the cock, which is about six inches long, is a piece of iron, having two sides, cut a proper slant, which being forced against the jacks, from side to side, pushes them down in rotation and causes the hissing noise which frames make in that process.*[159]

Downing's occupation was every bit as technical and mechanical as that of a locksmith, gunsmith, or clockmaker. He would have had skills very similar to any of these trades.

In January 1693, the term 'locksmith craft' took on a new, broader definition. It became an incorporation inside the Incorporation of Hammermen, made up of mechanical trades. While this practice had been happening for some time, the first written proof of it being labelled as such is from 1693. The locksmiths, gunsmiths, clockmakers and the one framesmith all had specialist know-how in mechanical areas. Their products were absorbing new technology and becoming more complex and sophisticated. Incorporation control was already complicated. To avoid spreading out the power and control, new sub-incorporations were unofficially formed. New trades were joined into older, more established trades along work types. New associations, based on identity as a particular type of craftsman or similar materials and techniques, were formed and lasted well beyond 1750.

THE LOCKSMITH CRAFT

TABLE 3.5
Edinburgh freeman locksmiths list – servants and apprentices not included

Name	Place of origin**	Father**	Father's trade**	Apprentice date	Apprenticed to	Burgess date	Trade at burgess-ship	Burgess route	Date of freedom of incorporation	Length from apprenticeship	Trade at freedom	Date of death	Date of interment†	Place of interment†
Aikman, James	the Dean	Richard	Weaver	18 Mar. 1657	John Tod	31 Oct. 1666	Locksmith	Apprenticeship	23 Feb. 1720		Locksmith			
Aiken, George	Southsyde	William		8 Mar. 1710	George Auld	13 Jan. 1720	Smith	Apprenticeship	6 Feb. 1710		Locksmith			
Anderson, James	Lochhill	Robert	Fermorer	26 June 1700	John Letham	21 Dec. 1709	Hammerman	Apprenticeship						
Anderson, John	Yairdhead	David	Smith	29 Jan. 1679	Patrick Drysdale	11 May 1687	Locksmith	Apprenticeship						
Anderson, Patrick						31 May 1587	Locksmith	Good Service						
Armour, James						6 Sept. 1671	Locksmith	Right of Wife				9 Dec. 1675	Greyfriars
Auld, George	Wintoun	John	Smith			5 May 1708	Smith	Apprenticeship	8 May 1708		Locksmith			
Auld, William*	Edinburgh	George	Locksmith	29 Dec. 1697	Thomas Brown				1 March 1744		Locksmith			
Balfour, Alexander						30 Sept. 1696	Smith	Right of Wife						
Balfour, John						15 Feb. 1682	Smith	Right of Wife						
Balfour, William						30 July 1735	Smith	Right of Father	2 Aug. 1735		Locksmith			
Beghie, George						19 April 1738	Locksmith	Right of Wife	29 April 1738		Locksmith			
Bell, Edward	Craighall	James	Farmer	10 Jan. 1733	George Aitken	22 Feb. 1740	Smith	Apprenticeship	7 Feb. 1741	8 yr. 1 m.	Locksmith			
Booth, James		James	Merchant			3 Feb. 1619	Locksmith	Right of Father						
Booth, James		George	Merchant			6 Jan. 1636	Locksmith	Apprenticeship	20 Feb. 1636		Locksmith			
Braidwood, Alexander	Robertoun	Alexander	Fermerer	27 Dec. 1654	Robert Braidwood	19 Nov. 1662	Locksmith	Apprenticeship						
Braidwood, Robert	Robertoun	Alexander	Indweller	20 Dec. 1643	Andrew Brown	2 Feb. 1653	Locksmith	Apprenticeship						
Brown, Alexander		George	Smith	19 Aug. 1741	George Aitken	6 May 1747	Locksmith	Apprenticeship						
Brown, Andrew	Leith	Andrew	Smith	27 Feb. 1628	Thomas Brown, Eld.	16 June 1641	Locksmith	Right of Father	16 July 1641	13 yr. 4 m. 19 d.	Locksmith		23 Sept. 1687	Greyfriars, Heriot Gate
Brown, Daniel	Edinburgh	Thomas	Locksmith			26 Nov.1594	Locksmith	Right of Father	?		Locksmith* (see P. Kennedy)	1584*		
Brown, Hew*												1575	26 Jan. 1694	Greyfriars, West Side Causeway
Brown, John	Dunbar	William	Smith	11 Jan. 1665	Andrew Brown	23 Nov. 1670	Smith	Apprenticeship						
Brown, John		John	Smith			13 July 1723	Smith	Right of Father						
Brown, Robert	Kirknewton	Andrew	Fermorer	9 Jan. 1695	William Waugh	16 Dec. 1702	Locksmith	Apprenticeship	25 March 1703	8 yr. 2 m. 16 d.	Locksmith Locksmith Craft Master 1573			
Brown, Thomas	Leith, the Law, Abercorn	William	Halbertmaker	30 Oct. 1593	Adam Hamilton	16 Nov. 1602	Locksmith	Apprenticeship						
Brown, Thomas		Thomas	Baxter	4 Mar. 1600	John Thomson	24 May 1609	Smith	Apprenticeship						
Brown, Thomas		George		1 Feb. 1682	Patrick Drysdale	26 Mar. 1690	Smith	Apprenticeship						
Brown, William	Thornburne	William	Indweller	18 Jan. 1688	Patrick Drysdale	11 June 1679	Smith	Right of Wife						
Callender, John						4 Sept. 1695	Locksmith	Apprenticeship						
Callender, John (Craigforth)	Newmilnes	Alexander	Smith	8 Oct. 1662	John Tweedie	2 Sept. 1674	Locksmith	Apprenticeship	10 Sept. 1674	11 yr. 11 m. 2 d.	Locksmith		15 June 1695	Greyfriars, Brae Foot
Callender, John	Canongate(?)	John(?)	Locksmith(?)		John Callender, Eld.	10 Sept. 1690	Hammerman	Apprenticeship	28 May 1683					
Camochie, William*													11 Aug. 1673	Greyfriars
Carmichael, William	Robertoun	Roger	Indweller	30 Dec. 1657	Robert Braidwood	14 July 1669	Locksmith	Apprenticeship						
Cass, David						25 Jan. 1569-70	Locksmith	Apprenticeship						
Chalmers, James	Rochrig	Thomas		12 Nov. 1679	Alexander Braidwood	5 Sept. 1722	Locksmith	Apprenticeship						
Cherrie, Robert	Merchinstoun	John		19 April 1587	Mungo Dickson	19 Dec. 1598	Smith	Apprenticeship						
Cockburn, David	Dundee	David	Slater	10 Jan. 1655	John Tweedie	31 July 1667	Smith	Right of Wife						
Craw, James						22 June 1664	Merchant	Gratis						
Cuthbertoun, James*							(sic(?)				Locksmith	1575		
Dalgleish, John	Edinburgh	James	Locksmith	21 July 1697	William Brown	27 Feb. 1706	Smith	Apprenticeship	2 March 1706		Locksmith			
Dalgleish, Robert						3 Aug. 1737	Smith	Right of Father	15 Sept. 1737		Locksmith			
Davidson, John	West Port	William	Mealmaker	26 Nov. 1651	Andrew Brown	19 Nov. 1662	Locksmith	Apprenticeship						
Dickson, Mungo						15 Sept. 1574	Smith	Gratis						
Donald, Thomas				11 Aug. 1727	John Dalgleish	16 Nov. 1748	Merchant		5 Aug. 1749	22 yr.	Locksmith			
Drysdale, Patrick	New Battle	David	Farmer	14 Mar. 1666	Robert Braidwood	21 Jan. 1674	Locksmith	Apprenticeship				1715?		
Drysdale, Thomas	Johnsclewch	Robert	Indweller	1 Feb. 1693	Patrick Drysdale	29 Jan. 1707	Locksmith	Apprenticeship						

81

TABLE 3.5 (cont)
Edinburgh freeman locksmiths list – servants and apprentices not included

Name	Place of origin**	Father**	Father's trade**	Apprentice date	Apprenticed to	Burgess date	Trade at burgess-ship	Burgess route	Date of freedom of incorporation	Length from apprenticeship	Trade at freedom	Date of death	Date of interment†	Place of interment†
Duncan, David	Edinburgh	William	Locksmith			12 May 1559	Blacksmith	Right of Wife			Locksmith (*** p. 325)		23 Oct. 1596	
Duncan, Hew	Edinburgh	David	Locksmith			17 Oct. 1632	Locksmith	Right of Father	2 March 1633		Locksmith			
Duncan, John	Edinburgh	David	Locksmith			22 Feb. 1603	Locksmith	Right of Father						
Duncan, Peter	Edinburgh	David	Locksmith			8 May 1588	Smith	Right of Father						
Duncan, Thomas	Edinburgh	David	Locksmith			1 May 1599	Locksmith	Right of Father						
Duncan, William	Edinburgh	David	Locksmith			22 Feb. 1603	Locksmith	Right of Father						
Duncan, William	Edinburgh	William	Locksmith			27 Nov. 1639	Locksmith	Right of Father	30 Nov. 1639		Locksmith			
Edgar, David									25 Aug. 1586		Locksmith			
Fairbairn, Alexander						14 Oct. 1720	Locksmith	Right of Wife	15 Sept. 1721		Locksmith			
Fiddes, William						19 Nov. 1712	Smith	Right of Wife	13 Dec. 1712		Locksmith			
France, James	Edelwood Chaple (Hamilton)	Thomas		23 June 1587	Patrick Kennedy	3 Aug. 1602	Locksmith	Apprenticeship						
Gardner, William	Kinross	William	Baillie	17 July 1700	Patrick Drysdale	29 Dec. 1714	Locksmith	Apprenticeship	11 Jan. 1715		Locksmith			
Gilchrist, John	Dalkeith	Gavin	Smith	28 July 1587	John Thomson	4 Nov. 1595	Locksmith	Apprenticeship						
Goddie, John		George		7 May 1623	Thomas Porteus	25 Sept. 1639	Locksmith	Apprenticeship	18 Oct. 1639	16 yr. 5 m. 11 d.	Locksmith	1660		
Gottsoun, Andrew*									c1560		Locksmith			
Gray, Andrew	Parish of Robertoun	John	Indweller	11 Dec. 1661	Andrew Brown	9 July 1673	Locksmith	Apprenticeship						
Gray, James	Easter Dudingston	James	Blacksmith	27 Dec. 1671	David Cockburne	9 April 1684	Locksmith	Apprenticeship					2 Nov. 1674	Greyfriars
Gray, John	Libberton	Thomas	Smith			17 Jan. 1649	Smith	Right of Wife						
Greenlaw, Adam				21 Oct. 1668	David Cockburne	12 July 1682	Locksmith	Apprenticeship						
Haden, George						20 Jan. 1562-3	Locksmith							
Halyburton, Andrew	Edinburgh	Andrew	Blacksmith*			1 Feb. 1693	Locksmith	Right of Father						
Hamilton, Abraham						20 Oct. 1560	Blacksmith	Right of Wife	25 Aug. 1586					
Hamilton, Adam						29 April 1579	Locksmith	Right of Wife	3 May 1547 (sic)			1599–1600		
Hamilton, Archibald	Edinburgh	Archibald	Locksmith			30 Aug. 1609	Locksmith	Right of Father	27 May 1578		Locksmith			
Hamilton, Patrick						11 Aug. 1647	Locksmith	Right of Wife	6 Sept. 1647		Locksmith			
Harvie, Robert		Samuel	Wright			29 Aug. 1701	Hammerman	Right of Father				1748		
Hay, Alexander									1541–2		Locksmith			
Hopp, John*														
Hunter, John		James		4 Mar. 1612	Robert Cherrie	10 April 1622	Locksmith	Apprenticeship						
Hunter (Hunt), Mungo*									c1541		Locksmith	1577		
Jameson, William		John	Merchant			10 Aug. 1653	Locksmith	Right of Father	19 Aug. 1653		Locksmith		19 Nov. 1668	Greyfriars
Kello, John		Alexander	Merchant			4 Aug. 1665	Locksmith	Right of Father			Locksmith		8 May 1668	Greyfriars
Kennedy, Patrik					Hew Brown*	26 May 1587	Locksmith	Council, Act of	30 Dec. 1586		Locksmith			
Lauder, Robert					James Wilson	6 May 1747	Locksmith	Right of Wife	5 May 1747 1675		Locksmith	1749		
Lauder, Walter*											Locksmith			
Letham, John						4 July 1683	Smith	Right of Wife	29 Oct. 1717		Locksmith			
Letham, Thomas	Edinburgh	John	Smith			16 Oct. 1717	Smith	Right of Father	3 May 1740		Locksmith			
Letham, Thomas						2 April 1740	Locksmith	Right of Father	12 July(?) 1639		Locksmith			
Lithgow, John						2 Jan. 1639	Locksmith	Right of Wife	7 Nov. 1713		Locksmith			
Livingston, George						4 Nov. 1713	Locksmith	Right of Wife	10 May 1500		Locksmith	1739?		
Locksmyth, John						2 Mar. 1498–9	Locksmith		7 May 1496		Locksmith			
Locksmyth, Steven*									1 May 1494		Locksmith			
Locksmyth, William*											Locksmith			
Muir, Roger					Patrick Anderson(?)	13 April 1580	Locksmith	Servant(?)						
Marshall, Thomas	Edinburgh	Thomas	Mealmaker	13 Aug. 1628	Thomas Brown	10 July 1644	Locksmith	Apprenticeship	23 Aug. 1644	16 yr. 0 m. 10 d.	Locksmith			
Meggit, John		Archibald		2 April 1606	William Duncan	29 Nov. 1615	Locksmith	Apprenticeship						
Meggit, William	Edinburgh	John	Smith			10 Dec. 1628	Smith	Right of Father	4 July 1629		Locksmith			
Meiklejohn, Hew					Mungo Dickson	10 Jan. 1581–2	Locksmith	Apprenticeship						

THE LOCKSMITH CRAFT

TABLE 3.5 (cont)
Edinburgh freeman locksmiths list – servants and apprentices not included

Name	Place of origin**	Father**	Father's trade**	Apprentice date	Apprenticed to	Burgess date	Trade at burgess-ship	Burgess route	Date of freedom of incorporation	Length from apprenticeship	Trade at freedom	Date of death	Date of interment†	Place of interment†
Mertene, Adam*											Locksmith	1574		
Mitchel, George I	Edinburgh	George				30 June 1675	Locksmith	Right of Wife						
Mitchel, George II	Gilnerton	James	Fermorer			14 May 1701	Hammerman	Right of Father						
Mitchel, James				23 Mar. 1653	John Candie	8 May 1661	Locksmith	Apprenticeship						
Mitchel, Robert I	Edinburgh	Robert	Locksmith			28 May 1684	Smith	Right of Father	14 June 1684		Locksmith			
Mitchel, Robert II	Gilnerton	James	Portioner	9 July 1662	James Mitchel	30 Nov. 1670	Locksmith	Apprenticeship	13 June 1587		Locksmith			
Mitchel, Walter					Adam Hamilton	7 June 1587	Smith	Right of Wife						
Mossman, Alexander						31 Jan. 1672	Smith	Right of Father						
Neill, George	Edinburgh	Robert	Smith	19 Aug. 1674	George Neill	11 Nov. 1719	Smith	Apprenticeship						
Neil, John ?						5 April 1682	Smith	Right of Wife	26 Dec. 1646		Locksmith			
Neil, Robert						2 Dec. 1646	Locksmith	Right of Wife	12 Nov. 1640		Locksmith		15 Mar. 1661	Greyfriars
Nicolson, Patrick						28 Oct. 1640	Smith	Right of Wife						
Patoun, James	Uddingston	Andrew	Smith	7 Dec. 1608	Thomas Duncan	26 Jan. 1620	Smith	Apprenticeship						
Porteous, Thomas	Leithshield	William		18 Mar. 1663	John Davidson	26 April 1671	Locksmith	Apprenticeship						
Pratt, James	Litlegale	Alexander	Fermorer	13 Sept. 1682	James Pratt	23 June 1703	Blacksmith	Apprenticeship	24 June 1703	20 yr. 9 m. 11 d.	Locksmith	1703?		
Pratt, John				15 Dec. 1703	Alexander Hay	14 April 1714	Locksmith	Apprenticeship	17 April 1714		Locksmith			
Purdie, George	Edinburgh	Alexander	Locksmith*			30 July 1690	Smith	Right of Wife						
Ramsay, Alexander	Dumfries	William	Merchant	26 Sept. 1716	William Richardson	11 Sept. 1724	Smith	Right of Father	3 Oct. 1724		Locksmith			
Ramsay, Edward	Borrowstouness	Thomas	Indweller	18 Feb. 1708	William Brown	24 July 1728	Smith	Apprenticeship	25 Feb. 1716	8 yr. 0 m. 7 d.	Locksmith			
Richardson, Thomas						22 Feb. 1716	Smith	Apprenticeship						
Richardson, William	Edinburgh	William	Smith			5 June 1745	Smith	Right of Father	4 May 1745		Locksmith			
Richardson, William Jun.	Brunton	John	Calsaymaker	14 Aug. 1633	John Meggat	26 May 1647	Locksmith	Apprenticeship	1 June 1647	13 yr. 9 m. 18 d.	Locksmith		11 Feb. 1673	Greyfriars
Rob, John	Kirk of Menyie	David		12 June 1734	George Auld	9 Sept. 1747	Locksmith	Apprenticeship	11 June 1747		Locksmith			
Robertson, David		John	Blacksmith	15 Dec. 1675	Patrick Drysdale	16 June 1564	Blacksmith	Apprenticeship						
Robertson, James	Edinburgh	Patrick	Smith			9 Mar. 1687	Locksmith	Apprenticeship	1 March 1718		Locksmith			
Scott, John	Whyclaw	John	Tennant	6 Sept. 1732	William Richardson	22 Jan. 1718	Locksmith	Right of Wife	15 Sept. 1737		Locksmith			
Sheils, Robert						26 July 1693	Locksmith	Right of Wife	4 June 1743	10 yr. 9 m.	Locksmith			
Sibbald, Patrick						7 Sept. 1737	Smith	Right of Father						
Sibbald, Patrick						29 June 1743	Locksmith	Apprenticeship						
Sibbald, Thomas	Newmilnes	Thomas	Tailor			25 May 1715	Locksmith	Apprenticeship	25 July 1715		Locksmith (1606 Lst)			
Smith, James*	Turriff	Alexander	Mason		William Brown	2 June 1669	Locksmith	Apprenticeship			Locksmith			
Taylor, William	Edinburgh	Gilbert	Blacksmith		William Jameson	7 Sept. 1700	Blacksmith	Apprenticeship						
Thomson, Gilbert					Patrick Anderson	31 May 1587	Locksmith	Apprenticeship	9 June 1587		Locksmith			
Thomson, Gilbert	Stobo	James		30 June 1647	James Patton	25 July 1655	Smith	Apprenticeship	9 Aug. 1655	8 yr. 1 m. 10 d.	Locksmith		5 April 1674	Greyfriars
Thomson, John	Oliver	Thomas		29 Sept. 1613	John Thomson	8 Nov. 1620	Locksmith	Grats						
Tod, John	Edinburgh	John I	Locksmith		John Tweedie	1 April 1646	Locksmith	Right of Father	20(?) April 1646		Locksmith		?	
Tweedie, John I	Oliver	Patrick		29 Jan. 1645	John Tweedie	14 Sept. 1653	Locksmith	Right of Wife					?	
Tweedie, John II (James?)	Stobo	James	Mealmaker	10 June 1646	John Tweedie	10 Dec. 1656	Locksmith	Right of Wife	24 Dec. 1656	10 yr. 6 m. 14 d.	Locksmith		?	
Tweedie, John						17 May 1693	Locksmith	Right of Wife						
Ur, James	Not Edinburgh					18 July 1649	Locksmith	Grats	18 Aug. 1649		Locksmith			
Veatch, John						4 May 1670	Locksmith	Right of Father						
Walker, John	Edinburgh					11 May 1670	Locksmith	Right of Father						
Walker, Robert						26 July 1682	Locksmith	Right of Wife	7 April 1575		Locksmith (Dagmaker?)			
Watt, John*	Thunsland	Andrew	Farmer	16 Mar. 1726	James Wilson	26 June 1734	Smith	Apprenticeship	2 April 1734	8 yr. 0 m. 17 d.	Locksmith			
Wauch, William	West Port of Edr.(?)	James(?)	Fermorer(?)	30 Dec. 1646(?)	Andrew Brown(?)	28 Feb. 1705	Smith	Right of Wife	7 April 1705		Locksmith			
Wilson, Andrew						18 Aug. 1647	Locksmith	Right of Wife	25 Sept. 1647		Locksmith			
Wilson, James														
Wilson, James														
Wilson, John														

TABLE 3.5 (cont)
Edinburgh freeman locksmiths list – servants and apprentices not included

Name	Place of origin**	Father**	Father's trade***	Apprentice date	Apprenticed to	Burgess date	Trade at burgess-ship	Burgess route	Date of freedom of incorporation	Length from apprenticeship	Trade at freedom	Date of death	Date of interment†	Place of interment†
Winton, Adam*									c.1560		Locksmith	1577		
Young, David	Cowhallie	John		4 Feb. 1730	John Brown	30 April 1740	Smith	Apprenticeship	3 May 1740	10 yr. 3 m.	Locksmith			
Young, John		Alexander	Fermorer	26 April 1710	Alexander Hay	5 Sept. 1717	Locksmith	Apprenticeship	10 May 1718		Locksmith			
Young, William				15 Nov. 1727(?)	George Auld(?)	29 Mar. 1732	Smith	Right of Wife						

All smiths are referred to in various records as working on locks as opposed to blacksmith work
* indicates that craftsman was listed in ECA ED008/1, not *Edinburgh Burgesses* 1929
** other information found in *Edinburgh Apprentices* 1906
*** information found in Lynch 1981
† indicates that information was found in Paton 1902

TABLE 3.6

Edinburgh knockmakers/watchmakers list – servants and apprentices not included (from Smith 1903 & 1975, *Edinburgh Burgesses* 1929, ECA ED008/1, and Baillie 2002)

Name	Place of origin	Father	Father's trade	Apprentice date	Apprenticed to	Burgess date	Trade at burgess-ship	Burgess route	Guildry date	Inc. freedom date	Length from apprenticeship	Trade at freedom	Essay	Date
Alcorn, Richard	Edinburgh	Henry	Edr. Mint Essay Mr.	9 Feb. 1695	Andrew Brown	17 Sept. 1703	Watchmaker	Right of Father	17 Sept. 1703	25 Sept. 1703	8 yr. 7 m. 16 d.	Clockmaker	Pendulum clock with alarm and short swing, lock and key for the door	1739
Alexander, John						24 May 1671	Knockmaker	Right of Wife	24 May 1671	17 Aug. 1671			Knock, mounting, sun dial, kist lock and key	
Alexander, Robert	Edinburgh	John	Knockmaker	6 Dec. 1667	Robert Smith	8 Dec. 1708	Watchmaker	Right of Father	8 Dec. 1708	11 Dec. 1708	3 yr. 8 m. 11 d.	Clockmaker	Eight day pendulum clock, lock and key for the door	1707
Ancrum, Thomas		William	Writer	3 May/ 9 June 1703	Andrew Brown									
Arnot, Thomas	Balkelthy	George		23/29 March 1723	Thomas Gordon									
Barclay, Hugh	Sprouston	Mr. George	Minister	11 April 1717	Thomas Gordon	28 June 1727	Watchmaker	Right of Father		7 August 1727		Clockmaker		1749
Bell, Matthew		George	Merchant	8 Jan. 1690	Richard Mylne									
Binny, Daniel				11/24 June 1747	Andrew Dickie					1758?				
Brand, Alexander	Canongate?					4 Sept. 1743	Clock & Watchmaker		4 Sept. 1743	6 April 1727		Clockmaker	Pendulum clock, lock and key for the door	
Brand, James		Robert	Wright	19 July 1732	Alexander Brand									
Brown, Andrew	Langnewtoun	James		21 Dec. 1664/ 26 Feb. 1665	Humphrey Mylne	30 June 1675	Knockmaker	Apprenticeship		27 July 1675		Clockmaker	Knock with watch luminary	1712
Brown, John		Andrew	Tailor (?)	21 Oct. 1680	Andrew Brown (?)	14 Aug. 1689	Watchmaker	Right of Father		24 Aug. 1689		Clockmaker	House clock with watch alarm, lock and key for door	1719
Brown, John	Edinburgh	John	Watchmaker			20 May 1720	Watchmaker	Right of Father		21 May 1720		Clockmaker	Eight day pendulum clock, lock and key for the door	c 1762
Brownlie, Alexander	Edinburgh	Archibald	Indweller		Robert Alexander	28 Feb. 1718	Watch & Clockmaker	Right of Father	28 Feb. 1718	29 March 1718		Watchmaker	Movement of a watch	
Bruce, James	Edinburgh	Mr. Alexr.	Advocate	8 Nov. 1718 (?check)	Alexander Brownlie									
Coustelie, John					Paul Romieu					15 April 1715		Watchmaker	Movement of a watch	
Dalgleish, John	Edinburgh	John	Locksmith (Deacon)			11 Feb. 1747	Watchmaker	Right of Father		12 Nov. 1742		Watch and Clockmaker	White movement of a watch	
Dickie, Andrew					Richard Mylne	25 Aug. 1736	Watchmaker			28 Sept. 1736		Clock and Watchmaker	Eight day pendulum clock	
Drysdale, James	Edinburgh	Thomas	Locksmith			1 June 1743	Watchmaker	Right of Father		4 June 1743		Watch and Clockmaker	Eight day clock	
Duncan, Andrew														
Earns, James														
Fleming, *						No Burgess				No craft (* p. 107)			Monteris maker 1593–4	
Funtanet, Nicolas	France					1611		Right of Wife						
Geddes, James														
Goodoune, John														
Gordon, Patrick	Edinburgh									15 March 1715		Clockmaker	Eight day pendulum clock	1749
Gordon, Thomas														
Gordon, Thomas	Brigs?			28 Sept. 1688	Andrew Brown	8 Sept. 1703	Watchmaker	Apprenticeship	8 Sept. 1703	18 Sept. 1703	14 yr. 11 m. 21 d.	Clockmaker	Pendulum clock with a large and a short swing, lock and key for door	1743
Hogg, Thomas														
Hutton, James														
Irvine, Alexander														
Johnston, Alexander														
Johnston, David														
Johnston, John														
Kirk, Archibald														
Lawrie, Archibald														
Lawrie, Archibald yor.														
Mackerson, David					Paul Romieu	5 Dec. 1711	Watchmaker	Apprenticeship		9 Feb. 1712		Watchmaker		
Mathieson, Robert												Watchmaker	Movement of a watch	

TABLE 3.6 (cont)
Edinburgh knockmakers/watchmakers list – servants and apprentices not included (from Smith 1903 & 1975, Edinburgh Burgesses 1929, ECA ED008/1, and Baillie 2002)

Name	Place of origin	Father	Father's trade	Apprentice date	Apprenticed to	Burgess date	Trade at burgess-ship	Burgess route	Guildry date	Inc. freedom date	Length from apprenticeship	Trade at freedom	Essay	Date
Maxwell, William														
M'Kenzie, Kenneth														
Milne, George														
Milne, Humphry	Staffordshire ††													
Milne, Richard										5 Sept. 1678	1660 ?	Clockmaker	A clock, watch 2 lavum, with a lock	1695
Murray, William														1710
Myles, Gideon														
Neill, John														
Nicol, William					6 Dec. 1727	Patrick Gordon	2 Nov. 1748	Watchmaker	Apprenticeship		16 Sept. 1748	20 yr. 9 m.	Clock and Watchmaker	Plain eight day clock	
Paterson, Patrick														
Pearson, Emmanuel														
Penn, William														
Purves, William										c.1539				c.1560
Robertson, David														
Romieu, Paul Sen.	Rouen, France ††									2 June 1677		Clock and Watchmaker	Movements of a watch	1694
Romieu, Paul Jun.	France ?	Paul Sen.	Clock and Watchmaker							19 August 1692		Clock and Watchmaker	Movements of a watch	1710
Smith, George	Edinburgh	James	Knockmaker			11 Aug. 1647	Knockmaker	Right of Father		6 Sept. 1647		Locksmith / Knockmaker	Lock, key, sprent band, knock, mounts, dial	
Smith, James										7 Sept. 1613		Locksmith	Kist lock	1660
Smith, Robert	Edinburgh	James	Knockmaker			11 Aug. 1647	Knockmaker	Right of Father		6 Sept. 1647		Locksmith / Knockmaker	Chest lock, key, sprent band, knock, mounts, dial	
Steel, John					John Brown	13 Sept. 1749	Watchmaker	Apprenticeship		6 May 1749		Clock and Watchmaker	Plain eight day clock	
Stewart, Alexander														
Staton, Archibald				27 April 1726	Alexander Brownlie	12 Sept. 1739	Watchmaker	Apprenticeship		13 Sept. 1739		Watchmaker	Eight day clock	
Sutor, William				21 Nov. 1704	Richard Alcorn					14 Feb. 1713	8 yr. 2 m. 24 d.	Clockmaker	Eight day pendulum clock, lock and key for door	
Thibow, Jaques														
Thomson, Alexander														
Thomson, George														
Thomson, John														
Wilson, Thomas														
Wyllie, Alexander														

† indicates that information was found in Paton 1902
†† indicates that information was found in Loomes 1998
* indicates data found in Edin Recs 1869–1976

THE LOCKSMITH CRAFT

TABLE 3.7
Edinburgh freeman dagmakers/gunsmiths (partial list). All smiths are referred to in various records as working on dag or gun locks (from Whitelaw 1977)

Name	Place of origin	Father	Father's trade	Apprentice date	Apprenticed to	Burgess date	Trade at burgess-ship	Burgess route	Inc. freedom date	Length of apprenticeship	Trade at freedom	Essay	Date of
Adanson, Alexander				Jan. 1575	John Watt	19 Jan. 1581–2	Smith	Apprenticeship	27 Feb. 1581	7 yr.			1596
Archibald, Patrick											Dagmaker ?		Sept. 1579
Attinong, James	France					27 May 1674	Surgical/Mech. Inst.	Imported Skill?	19 Oct. 1676		Gunsmith	Mounted pistol, carbine, buckle, arrow head	1699
Bruce, Thomas						30 May 1632	Dagmaker	Right of Wife					
Carwood, John		John	Tailor			10 Aug. 1591	Dagmaker	Right of Father					
Cass, David				19 Feb. 1560	David Duncan	25 Jan. 1569–70	Locksmith	Apprenticeship	3 May 1569	9 yr. 2 m. 14 d.	Locksmith		18 March 1581
Cass, Gilbert					David Cass								
Clerk, David													
Clerk, David													
Clerk, James													
Edgar, David													
Fraser, John													
Furde, Gavin													
Gibson, James													
Grant, Murdoch													
Hadden, John	Edinburgh	John	Merchant			13 Nov. 1593	Dagmaker	Right of Father					
Henderson, Francis	Edinburgh	Francis	Gunsmith										
Henderson, Robert													1706
Herriot, William					John Wilson				6 April 1745		Gunsmith	Not listed	
Kennedy, John	Edinburgh	Patrick	Locks. / Dagmkr.		Hew Brown	22 Jan. 1601	Dagmaker	Right of Father	8 June 1596 (?)		Dagmaker	Kist lock	
Kennedy, Patrick				31 Oct. 1649	John Miller	26 May 1587	Locksmith	Act of Council	30 Dec. 1586			Kist lock	
Miller, James				7 May 1634	David Clerk	28 Jan. 1646	Dagmaker	Apprenticeshp	26 Sept. 1668		Gunsmith	Brazen buckle, arrow head	1668
Miller, John	Abberivan	John				26 Sept. 1598	Dagmaker	Right of Father	27 March 1646				
Muir, Alexander	Edinburgh(?)	John	Portioner										
Naysmith, John											Dagmaker in 1591		
Nicols, John						24 Sept. 1656	Gunsmith	Gratis					
Shousan, Joshua						3 Sept. 1662	Gunsmith	Act of Council	30 Sept. 1668		Gunsmith	Pair of sufficient pistols	
Simpson, John													
Spens, Peter													
Thomson, Alexander		George	Merchant		Murdoch Grant	1 Dec. 1708	Gunsmith	Right of Father	7 May 1709		Gunsmith	Mounted pistol with brigged lock and forged barrel, carbine hanger, arrow head	
Vaus, William													
Wallace, Nicoll													
Watsone, Mathew		John	Smith		Peter Spens	20 Jan. 1594–5	Dagmaker	Right of Father	28 Jan. 1595				
Watt, John													
Wisone, Charles													
Wison, John	Edinburgh	Charles	Gunsmith						14 June 1720		Gunsmith	Mounted pistol with brigged lock and forged barrel, carbine hanger, arrow head	

* indicates that information was found in ECA ED008/1, but not included in Whitelaw 1977
This may not include all freemen.

NOTES

1. Pennecuik 1722.
2. Soom, A. *Zunfthandwerker in Reval* 1971 as quoted in Friedrichs 2003, 155–6.
3. Melling 1988, 26, 28 and 40.
4. Clutton 1982, 70.
5. Christianson 2002, 68.
6. Colston 1891, 27. Colston states that the date is unknown, though their minute books, independent of the hammermen's minutes, start in 1525.
7. ECA ED008/1/1–8.
8. Ibid., ED008/1/4, 1693.
9. Colston 1891, 18–19.
10. Bruton 2000, 61.
11. Guild boards, Inv.Nr.A.B.344, Ulmer Museum, Ulm, Germany.
12. Chambers 1752, 'lock'.
13. Tabraham 1997, 20.
14. Bain 1887, 208.
15. One example of this is the meeting on 30 May 1745. ECA ED008/1/7.
16. *Exchequer Rolls* 1878, 29 'Rotuli Scaccarii'.
17. Ibid., 58.
18. *APS* 1814, 670 'Assisa De Tolloneis'.
19. Smith 1906, 181.
20. Ibid., 1.
21. Ibid., 184.
22. *Edinburgh Burgesses* 1929.
23. ECA ED008/1.
24. Caldwell 1981 (thesis), 303.
25. Harris 2002, 93.
26. Caldwell 1981 (thesis), 303.
27. Maryon 1971, 304.
28. Whitelaw 1977, 138.
29. Ibid., 138.
30. Ibid., 136.
31. Ibid., 138.
32. Ibid., 137.
33. Ibid., 136.
34. Blair 1995, 5 and 7.
35. Dr David Caldwell of the National Museum of Scotland is of the opinion that the brass barrels were being bought from Dundee and stamped later by the dagmakers who made the locks and stocks.
36. *Edinburgh Burgesses* 1929, 100.
37. Whitelaw 1977, 142.
38. *Edinburgh Burgesses* 1929, 285.
39. Whitelaw 1977, 161.
40. Ibid., 160.
41. Caldwell 1977, 321 and Blair 1995, 7.
42. Whitelaw 1977, 158.
43. Ibid., 150.
44. Kelvin 1996, 153.
45. Ibid., 152–3.
46. Ibid., 153.
47. Whitelaw 1977, 156.
48. Ibid., 157.
49. Ibid., 157.
50. Ibid., 152.
51. Ibid., 145.
52. Ibid., 157.
53. Ibid., 157.
54. Ibid., 146. In 1711 Edinburgh again took interest in continental gun technology, this time favouring imported firelocks to locally produced pieces. James Gibson imported firelocks from Holland instead of making them himself.
55. Ibid., 156–8.
56. ECA ED008/1/4, 248.
57. Ibid., ED008/1/4, 351–2.
58. Ibid., ED008/1/4, 321–2.
59. Blair 1995, 17.
60. Whitelaw 1923, 53–85.
61. Whitelaw 1977, 315–18.
62. Ibid., 315.
63. Kelvin 1996, 179.
64. Caldwell 1977, 321.
65. Blair 1995, 7 and 48–9, footnote 25, quoting a poem from George Bannatyne's manuscript collection of 1568 in the Library of the Faculty of Advocates, Edinburgh, published in Cranstoun 1891, 396.
66. Edwards 2000, 1.
67. Whitelaw 1923, 62–3.
68. Ibid., 64.
69. Ricketts 1965, 43.
70. Whitelaw 1977, 315.
71. Blair 1995, 17.
72. Whitelaw 1977, 315.
73. A 'half-bend' pistol is a pistol capable of the half-cock position, or safety. Kelvin 1996, 184.
74. Even Whitelaw makes this mistake: '… may, therefore, be looked upon as a Lowland type'. Whitelaw 1923, 63.
75. Whitelaw 1977, 86.
76. Moxon 1989, 12–13.
77. Ibid., 56.
78. Ibid., 56.
79. Amman & Sachs 1973, 74, Wagner 1980, 253, Ricketts 1965, 42 and Luiken 1704, 67 respectively.
80. The five are thought to be from Edinburgh. Caldwell 1977, 320.
81. There is also a lock plate with the initials 'GT' from the 1653 wreck of the *Swan*. It might have been made by George Thomson of Edinburgh. Martin 1998, 50.
82. ECA ED008/1/7, 37–8.
83. Duley 1997, 5–6.
84. Melling 1988, 33.
85. Clutton 1982, 20.
86. Ibid., 16.
87. Cutmore 1985, 9.
88. Knock and clock will be used interchangeably from here on.
89. Dareau 1997, 5.
90. Smith 1975, 304–5.
91. Smith 1906, 107, 130.

92. Smith 1975, 304.
93. *Edin Recs* 1892, 412.
94. Ibid., 107.
95. *Edin Recs* 1931, 8.
96. Ibid., 36.
97. *Edinburgh Burgesses* 1929.
98. *Edin Recs* 1931, 65.
99. ECA ED008/1/2, 7 September 1613.
100. NMS Whitelaw EHMB, 76.
101. *Edin Recs* 1931, 118.
102. Ibid., 196.
103. Smith 1975, 352.
104. ECA 69 SL.
105. Possibly Cornelius Yates of London? Baillie 2002, 351.
106. ECA 69 SL.
107. *Edinburgh Burgesses* 1929.
108. Ibid.
109. ECA ED008/1/3, 6 September 1647.
110. Smith 1975, 350, and Whyte 2001, 73.
111. Smith 1975, 366.
112. *Edin Recs* 1927, 107.
113. Smith 1975, 322.
114. Loomes 1998, 298.
115. Smith 1975, 322.
116. ECA ED008/1/5, 97.
117. Ibid., ED008/1/4, 101.
118. This is an arbitrarily picked, post-1693 date for example only.
119. ECA ED008/1/6, 8 January 1736.
120. Ibid., ED008/1/6, 9 January 1736.
121. Smith 1975, 307–8.
122. Dareau 1997, 6.
123. Ibid., 6.
124. It should be noted that early modern standards were not as precise as those of today, or even of the nineteenth century.
125. Wild 2001, 11.
126. Ibid., 9.
127. This refers to Nicholas Bion's *Traité de la Construction et des Principaux Usages des Instruments de Mathématique*, 1709, reproduced in ibid., 11.
128. Bray 2001, 35.
129. Greenlaw 1999, 9.
130. Dareau 1997, 6.
131. Baker 1999, 415–16.
132. Ibid., 415.
133. Ibid., 419.
134. See Amman & Sachs 1973, 75, Wild 2001, 20, Luiken 1704, 131 and Greenlaw 1999, 15 respectively.
135. ECA 69 SL, 1 January 1619.
136. Clutton 1982, 70.
137. ECA ED008/1/4.
138. *Edinburgh Burgesses* 1929, 159.
139. Henson 1970, 41.
140. Ibid., 39.
141. Ibid., 38.
142. Ibid., 40.
143. Campbell 1969, 214.
144. Mason 2000, 4.
145. Ibid., 15.
146. Henson 1970, 43.
147. Bennett 1981 (thesis), 47 and 174.
148. Henson 1970, 52.
149. Mason 2000, 25–6.
150. Ibid., 22.
151. Bennett 1981 (thesis), 173–5.
152. ECA ED008/1/4, 1682.
153. *Edinburgh Burgesses* 1929, 159.
154. Bennett 1981 (thesis), 175.
155. Ibid., 168.
156. Ibid., 178.
157. Ibid., 179.
158. ECA ED008/1/4, 17 January 1693.
159. Henson 1970, 40–2.

Chapter 4

The Locksmiths' Workplace

The activities of a locksmith, as with any occupation, had specific types of space in which they were enacted. In an urban environment, space was limited. On top of this, certain occupations were not welcome in certain areas of towns. Factors such as odour and levels of fire hazard were taken into consideration. Unfortunately, there are no directories showing the locations of occupations in early modern Edinburgh. It is a difficult and laborious task to isolate locations, involving blind searches through random sasines, minute books and burgess entries; a job far beyond the scope of this project. Could the locksmith art be practised anywhere in Edinburgh, or were there specific areas where their booths were clustered?

Not all activity of the locksmith craft involved production, though. There was also the retail side of the trade. This happened in either the booth or the weekly market. These two main areas of economic activity, markets and booths, were not well documented in terms of location. The various acts of the parliament, privy council or town council rarely go into such detail for any occupation. By looking at the practical requirements for the locksmith trade, it might be possible to make an educated guess at where the locksmiths could have been practised in the burgh. While this will be hypothetical until further research is done into the physical layout of Edinburgh's early modern occupational structure, it will at least give a more detailed view of a particular craft from pre-industrial Scotland.

MARKETS

Markets, or 'mercats', as they were called in Scots, were the main retail outlet for craftsmen. On 3 October 1477, King James III (1460–88) gave permission for Edinburgh to hold separate markets for animal feed, fish, salt, chapmen, along with hatmakers and skinners, wood and timber, shoes and leather, carcasses and mutton, fowls, livestock, meal, cloth, dairy products and used goods. Most pertinent to this study was the market for iron work 'belonging [to] cutlers, smiths, lorimers, lockmakers and all such workmen, to be used beneath the Netherbow, before and about Saint Mary Wynd'.[1] It is not known if it remained there through the early modern period.

By 1742, the Canongate's fleshmarket had moved from the head of the Canongate to an open square immediately to the north.[2] Edinburgh's markets were also moved occasionally. In 1477 the market for skins was on the south side of the High Street, from the Bellhouse down to the Tron.[3] On 11 February 1558 it was decided to shift the market to 'beneath the Salt Tron, betwixt Walter Scott's Close and Nidrie's Wynd on both sides'. In 1559 there was further legislation by the bailies and council 'for down taking of the skin market from the place where the same was used to be had to the Freir Wynd head and from their further to the Nether Bow'.[4] In 1477 the fish market was on the High Street, from Frere Wynd to the Netherbow,[5] but in Rothemay's 1647 map it was down Fish Market Wynd, between the High Street and the Cowgate.[6] In 1477, there were at least seven markets in the Edinburgh High Street.[7] In the 1647 and 1742 maps, it is evident that at least three of these markets had been cleared from the High Street: the poultry, fish and meal markets. Metalwares were not as messy, nor as odorous, as chicken and herring, so perhaps the market that the locksmiths attended was left where it had been in 1477.

Markets were highly regulated. In the Hammermen's 1483 seal of cause it was stated that

> there shall [be] no open market used of any of the said crafts, or work pertaining to them of their craft, upon the high street, nor in crames upon boards, nor bachlit[8] nor shown in hands, for to sell in no part fore nor backside within this burgh, but alanerly on the market day.[9]

In the 1496 reaffirmation, it was again stated:

> … no open market made nor used by whatsomever persons of any work pertaining to the said Hammermen of their craft in showing thereof in hands upon the High Street nor in crames nor on boards nor other ways within the said burgh nor in their booths except alanarly the market day.[10]

and reaches commonly through the wholes breadth of the forge and is broad and deep as you think good, as at 'D'.[42]

Forges could reach such a heat as to completely liquefy iron. In this heat, it was possible that even brick could burn; henceforth the tewel iron was set to cover the main area where the heat would be most intense on the brick wall behind the forge. The trough was for keeping water to control the heat of the fire, cooling workpieces or hot tools and tempering steel. Moxon continued with his description of the forge setup:

> The bellows is placed behind the back of the forge and hath as aforesaid, its pipe fitted into the pipe of the tewel and hath one of its boards fixed so that it move not upwards or downwards. At the ear of the upper bellows board is fastened a rope, or sometimes a thong of leather, or an iron chain or rod, as 'E'; which reaches up to the rocker and is fastened a cross a rock-staff, which moves between two cheeks upon the centre pins, in two sockets, as at 'G'. So that by drawing down this handle, the moving board of the bellows rises and by a considerable weight set on the top of its upper board sinks down again and by this agitation performs the office of a pair of bellows.[43]

The bellows were a device for directing a high-speed stream of air directly into the centre of the fire. This increased the amount of oxygen, creating even more heat as it was burned. The increased heat brought the workpiece up to any temperature the smith desired and if not careful, melted it. Apparently, all early modern forges were side-blown, as opposed to the more modern method of having the air blown up from below the fire.

One of the other main components of a smith's booth that Moxon illustrated was the anvil. The anvil's purpose was to offer a solid surface on which the metal could be pounded into shape. A soft surface would have given way, leaving the work only mildly marked. The anvil was hardened though and therefore did not move. The hot metal which was struck with the hammer was flattened between the two. With a bit of skill, the 'squishing' could be controlled. On the anvil Moxon commented:

> Its face must be very flat and smooth, without flaws and so hard that a file will not touch it (as smiths say, when a file will not cut, or race it.) The upper plain ... is called the face; it is commonly set upon a wooden block, that it may stand very steady and solid and about two foot high from the floor, or sometimes higher, according to the stature of the person that is to work at it.[44]

Moxon's diagram shows only one of the variety of anvils available in the early modern period (marked 'Fig. 2A' in figure 4.6). While there were other varieties, such as those shown in figures 3.1, 4.4 and 4.5, the basic setup shown in figure 4.6 seems to have been universal; the anvil was always mounted on a wooden stump, with its face at a height so that the smith could work comfortably while standing.

Moxon did not go into much detail about the bench itself; only the tools on it. The bench was a very important part of the locksmith's booth, though. It was a desk; a place where a great deal of the locksmith's work was done. It is significant that almost all early modern prints of trades show a bench in the workshop. For a locksmith, the bench had to be absolutely stable. If it was not, then the vice would rock back and forth as the craftsman attempted to saw, or file the workpiece, resulting in wasted energy and time. Often, benches were secured to a wall of a shop. It is interesting that figure 4.3, the 1528 locksmith's shop from Nürnberg, shows a freestanding bench. Perhaps it was secured into the floor; perhaps the picture is only representative.

TOOLS

The same sources which illuminate the physical space of a booth also give a clear picture of the tools and techniques employed by Edinburgh locksmiths. First, there are the tools associated with the forge. This group of tools were usually intended for working with hot metal. Locksmiths needed to be able to heat the iron parts they worked with in order to shape them. Tongs allowed the locksmith to reach into the fire to place the part in the section of the fire which would give him the specific heat desired. Tongs then enabled the smith to retrieve the glowing workpiece and keep a constant purchase while hitting it with a hammer at the anvil. Moxon stated that there were only two types of tongs:

> There are two sorts of tongs used by smith; the one the straight-nosed tongs, used when the work is short and somewhat flat and generally for all plate iron. The other crooked-nosed tongs, to be used for the forging small bars, or such thicker work, as will be held within the returns of their chaps.[45]

Since every part had a different shape, some parts were easier to hold than others. If a locksmith needed to hold an odd-shaped piece and did not have tongs that would grasp it correctly, then he would simply make tongs with specialist jaws.[46] Moxon probably did not

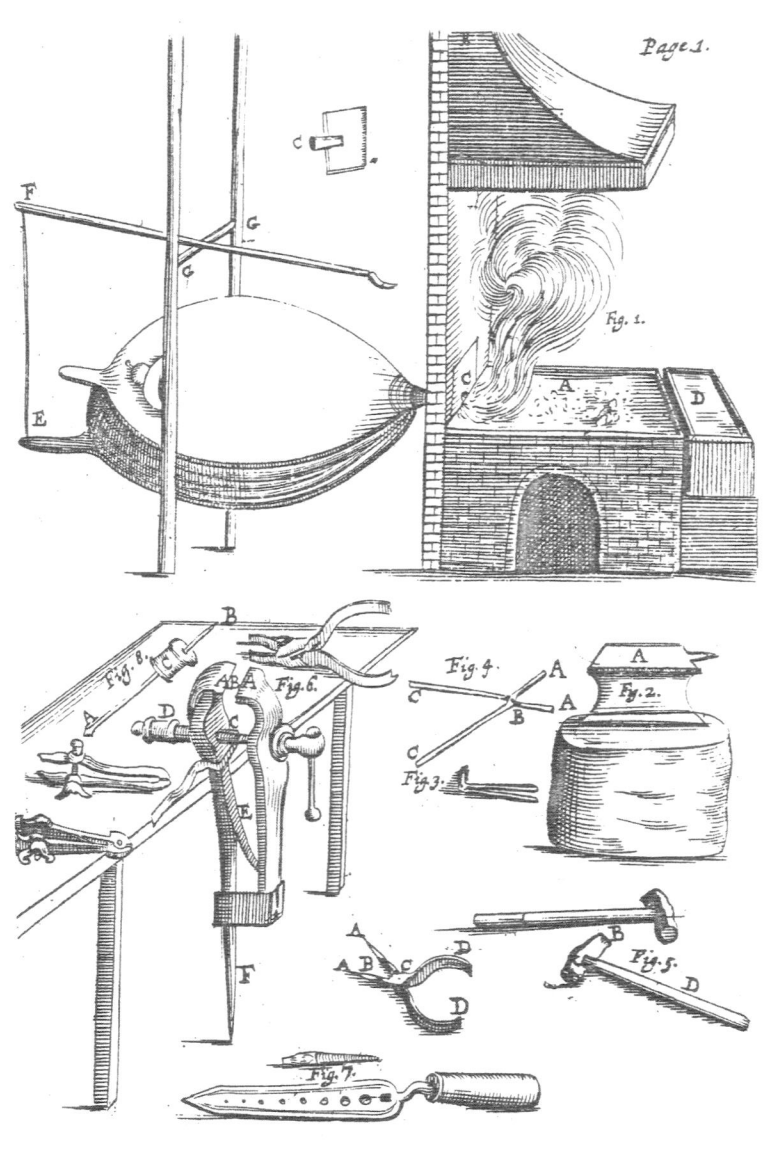

FIGURE 4.6
Moxon's illustration of a smith's forge from 1678 (Moxon 1989, 1)

as a whole. Much of early modern locksmiths' work is very similar across Europe though, and the engravings of other trades from various cities and towns are similar. It is unfortunate that the Edinburgh town council did not see it as a necessity to the town's honour to have a series of pictures done of Edinburgh crafts.

Although it is not specifically of a locksmith's shop, there is an English diagram of a 'smith's forge' which confirms the basic setup described in the aforementioned shops (see figure 4.6). Joseph Moxon's book, *Mechanic Exercises*, was first published in 1678. In it, Moxon set out to explain how several trades worked. He stated in the preface:

> I intend to begin with smithing, which comprehends not only the blacksmith's trade, but takes in all trades which use either forge or file, from the anchorsmith, to the watchmaker; they are all working by the same rules, tho' not with equal exactness and all using the same tools, tho' of several sizes from the common blacksmith uses.[39]

Though he often referred to areas used by 'blacksmiths', the mainstay of the work is described as being for 'smiths'. None of the work deals with horses, but nine of the thirty-eight pages and one of the two diagrams devoted to smithing (see figures 4.6 and 5.4) deal specifically with the production of locks and keys.[40] Moxon's diagram of a smith's forge should therefore be taken as representative of a typical locksmith's forge.

As can be seen in figure 4.6, Moxon's diagram of a smith's forge can be divided up into three main components: the forge, the anvil and the bench. The forge was 'to be built up from your floor with brick about two foot and an half, or sometimes two foot nine inches high, according to the purpose'.[41] If it was for making anchors, it would have been necessarily larger. Locksmith's work was rarely so large that it could not be carried in hand, so his forge's dimensions would have followed suit. Further describing his diagram, Moxon wrote:

> The back of the forge is built upright to the top of the ceiling and enclosed over the fireplace with a hovel, which ends in a chimney to carry away the smoke, as 'B'. In the back of the forge against the fireplace, is fixed a thick iron plate and a taper pipe in it about five inches long, called a tewel, or (as some call it) a tewel-iron, marked '★', which pipe comes through the back of the forge, as at 'C'. Into this taper pipe, or tewel, is placed the nose, or pipe of the bellows. The office of this tewel, is only to preserve the pipe of the bellows and the back of the forge about the fireplace from burning. Right against the back is placed at about twenty inches, or two foot distance, the trough

common activity in a locksmith's booth was filing at the vice. All three pictures show at least one locksmith at work at the bench, demonstrating the importance of bench-work to the trade. It is interesting that all show them as being seated while working at the vice; a practice which would be scorned by a modern-day Edinburgh locksmith. Did Edinburgh locksmiths in the early modern period sit while working at the vice? Considering the hours worked, maybe it should be expected that they sat when at the workbench. Of the seven locksmiths illustrated in the three pictures, five are shown filing at a vice.

All three of the pictures show similarities in the dress of the locksmiths. All seven of them are wearing aprons to protect their clothes. Clothing was expensive and it would be interesting to know whether a locksmith owned a set of clothing just for the workshop, or whether they had to wear the same outfit for work and for everyday life. Five of the seven wear hats while working. Their outfits seem to indicate that locksmiths wore normal clothes, as opposed to special work attire.

The seven locksmiths also highlight some variations in the three shops. The 1528 shop shows only one locksmith working, while the 1568 shop has four smiths. The 1698 shop shows only two. Only the 1568 shop shows all three of the main components: forge, anvil and bench. Perhaps the other pictures, which only illustrate certain aspects of the locksmith's shop, did not include all the workers in the shop. Perhaps they are mere generalizations of the locksmith's environment. If they are taken on face-value, then perhaps the difference in numbers indicates a variation in wealth of different locksmith's shops, with the 1528 shop showing a tradesman who did less business than the 1568 shop. Edinburgh locksmiths had a degree of variation, as only eleven of them purchased guildry in the early modern period, indicating an inequality in wealth (see table 2.6).[38] The booths of these eleven would have been more akin to the 1568 shop, while the booths whose master did not attain guild brethrenship might have looked more like the smaller-scale 1528 shop.

The discrepancy in numbers of locksmiths in the three images of shops could also illustrate a growth in the Nürnberg locksmiths in response to the greater demand for locks brought about by the population expansion of the 1500s in Europe. This type of growth was certainly the case in Edinburgh, where the numbers of locksmith-entrants to burgess-ship more than doubled from 1550 to 1750 (see table 1.4 and chart 3.0). Perhaps the 1528 shop evolved into the larger 1568 shop as a response to market pressures. But did Edinburgh locksmith's booths take on more craftsmen per booth?

All three pictures show tools, though they become better illustrated in the later shop. The 1528 picture shows only two files, a vice and what appears to be a square-drive wrench for tightening the vice. The 1568 shop has anvils, hammers and tongs, as well as the omni-present files. The 1698 shop shows a plethora of the tools used. There are two anvils, two vices, a hand drill, lock picks, a saw, callipers, files and engraving tools. There are files stored up above so as to not allow them to touch each other, which causes them to go dull much faster. What appears to be another wrench for tightening the vice, is sitting behind the nearest one.

The work being produced in the three shops is fairly standard. All are producing door locks, keys and hinges. The 1568 booth also has several padlocks on display. Locks, keys and architectural hardware seems to have been the normal work of locksmiths' booths, though the 1568 booth has surplus stock on display to the public, above the bench. More craftsmen meant more production.

The physical buildings occupied by the three shops all share one feature: they all have at least one window. On a practical level, windows allowed in light, which maximised vision while minimizing the costs of artificial lighting by candles, rush lights and the fuel-consuming forge. Windows also allowed air circulation, which would have been necessary when working with any type of chemical in the forge. In winter the craftsmen probably stayed as close to the forge as possible. Equally practical was the fact that a view to the outside helped the morale of the workers.

The 1528 shop shows a wooden floor, a stone wall with one window visible from the bench, a stone forge and a timber ceiling. The 1568 shop seems to have a dirt floor, a timber ceiling and one large window. The window sill doubles as the bench, while the window is used to display the shop's wares. The 1698 picture gives no indication about the building materials of the booth, though two large windows are clearly present. One has a screen, possibly to prevent people entering through the window and removing valuable tools, materials, or work.

It is a shame that there are not more engravings of locksmith's booths to compare. All three of the above mentioned, figures 4.3, 4.4 and 4.5, are from Nürnberg and therefore not necessarily representative of Europe

FIGURE 4.5
A locksmith's booth in 1698, Nürnberg, Germany (Weigel 1963)

components of a booth are not present in all three shops; all picture a bench with at least one vice and sundry tools. The 1698 shop does not show a forge, though with the anvil and hammers, it can be assumed to be elsewhere in the shop, out of view. The 1528 and 1568 shops both show the forge area behind the locksmiths. In the 1528 shop, there in no anvil pictured, though with the forge present, it can again be assumed to be there. Whether shown or not, the prints all show that the main components of a locksmith's booth were the forge, the anvil and the bench.

The seven locksmiths illustrated in the three shops also show several concurrences, as well as some differences. Judging from these images, the most modern Edinburgh, one needs only to enter one of the many shops on the High Street. They are often small; typically long and narrow, with a shop front consisting of one or two small windows and the door.

Examples of surviving booths can also be seen underneath Mylne's Court, in the Lawnmarket. When built in 1690, the ground floor section of the building was a line of shops.[34] One shop, a jewellery store today, was in 1883 a baker's shop.[35] The inner walls were not easily changed, as that would involve changing the entire building, so like water, businesses filled the existing container. Edinburgh's booths can still be examined today.

Archaeological excavations in Exeter have shown the size of a brass foundry. Thomas Pennington started the foundry in Paul Street *c*. 1625, with the production of domestic wares and bells happening until *c*. 1720. The space taken up by the foundry was about nine metres by twenty-three metres.[36] While this is not a small area, a foundry was a larger-scale occupation

FIGURE 4.4
A locksmith's booth in 1568, Nürnberg, Germany
(Amman & Sachs, 1973, 69)

than a locksmith's shop. Still, one would expect a vast complex for as technical a process as happened in that nine by twenty-three metre space. It would make an interesting study to look at floor plans of surviving buildings and compare them with tax rolls to figure out what space was used for what occupation. Perhaps there is a correlation between booth size and trade, or perhaps space was parcelled out randomly, depending on the space available in the property up for sale. Most likely, there was a degree of both involved in the upset of a booth.

While there are no surviving engravings or prints of an Edinburgh locksmith's booth and it is unknown which surviving shops were at one stage a locksmith's booth, it is possible to look at the general structure of a locksmith's booth by turning to Europe. As with Edinburgh, small booth size was not uncommon in Europe, though there was no standard space requirement for a shop in any early modern city. In Nürnberg, there are many shop frontages still visible with the single window and door façade which also survived in Edinburgh. It is thought that in Nürnberg, this was due to high ground taxes.[37] Luckily, there are three surviving images of Nürnberg locksmith's shops (see figure 4.3 from 1528, figure 4.4 from 1568 and figure 4.5 from 1698). There are certain key elements of a locksmith's booth which are either figured or can be deciphered from the three shops. The main

FIGURE 4.3
A locksmith's shop in 1528, Nürnberg, Germany (Wagner 1978, 117)

the most spacious booth in the building. It also tells something of the prestige of Edinburgh merchants that the best booth in the building was described as a 'merchant's booth', regardless of the occupant. It was taken for granted that merchants commanded more prestige than the humbler crafts, but in this case, a member of the craft aristocracy was usurping their standing.[29]

Judging by the small size of Maistertoun's booth, it is possible that he was a wholesaler, with his goods kept in a warehouse in Leith. Perhaps he was a more humble merchant, selling small wares. His stone shop was the only space in Mossman's Land that he owned, which probably indicates that he resided elsewhere; his dealings with the building were purely business. Smyth, the spurrier, might have been the opposite. He owned three 'laigh cellars'. His work space was underground, accessible from a stair leading into Murdoch Brown's house. There was a domestic hearth in the southern most cellar, indicating a possible residence of the Smyth family. It would seem that work and home were in the same three cellars.[30]

Murdoch Brown and John Baxter were different, in that they had their booths on the ground floor and lived on the ground and first floors, respectively.[31] It is interesting that a bonnetmaker would have owned such a house while a spurrier, which was one of the minor trades in the Incorporation of Hammermen, was living in the cellar. This might be because the spurrier needed the space for his trade, while the bonnetmaker needed only the two small booths on the southern face of Mossman's Land. On the other hand, Brown might have been wealthier than Smyth. Perhaps even a humble incorporation like the bonnetmakers[32] had its own aristocracy. The fact that the tailor, John Baxter, lived above the others, yet not on the top floor, fits the usual pattern of wealth being concentrated in the middle floors of Edinburgh tenements.[33] The general trends of booths and chambers fit into a wider pattern of wealth and standing in the urban environment. Where a locksmith's booth would have fitted into Mossman's Land, is more difficult to say.

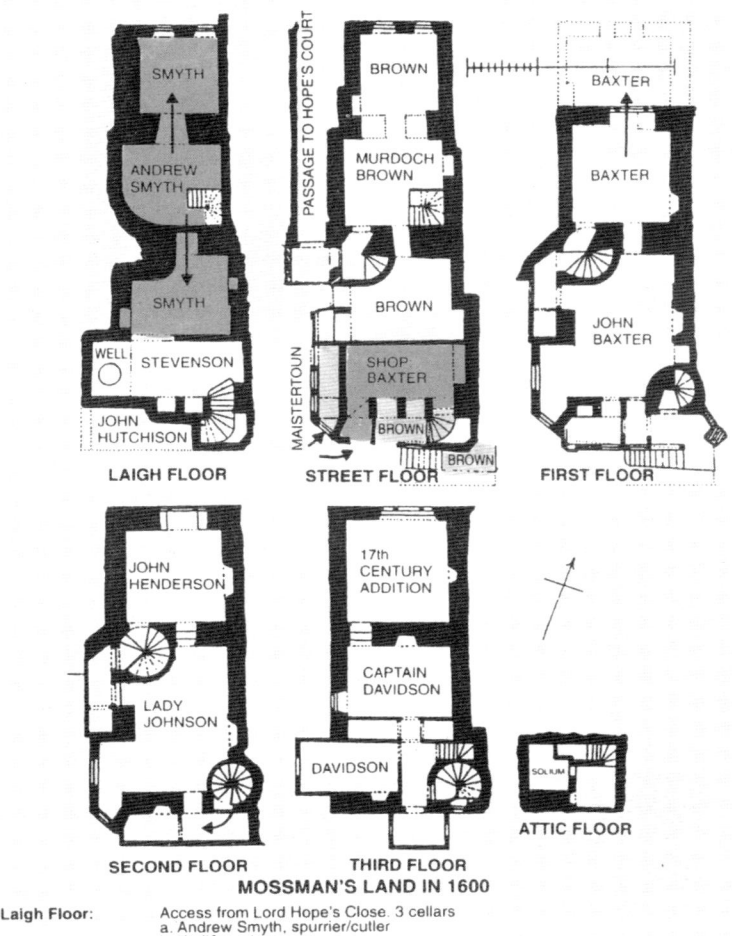

FIGURE 4.2
Floor plan of Mossman's Land (John Knox House) in 1600 showing four booths. (With kind permission of Dr Smith, from Smith 1996, 57)

It seems that booths in general were not large spaces. As it was, with the population increase of the sixteenth century, space within the city walls was precious. If the space was not needed, then it was not taken. To get a feel for the size of a booth from early

In Glasgow the hammermen could sell from either their booths or the market, and were even allowed to vend their work on the High Street.[25] Closer yet, in the Canongate in 1614, Walter Smyth, a servant to James Nasmyth, dagmaker, was charged with 'coming to Thomas Glen, dagmaker, his booth, with a pistolet in his lap and took ane gentleman away which was standing therein, which was proven by the brother of the said Walter'.[26] Not only could customers buy directly from booths, but their custom was protected from rivals enticing them away. Smyth was fined 20s. Customers were nearly sacrosanct.

In France, it was noted that merchants who worked from warehouses did not 'have open shops or any display counter and sign at their doors and houses'.[27] Warehouses could indicate an overseas trader, or a local 'merchant' who sold goods brought in from the surrounding countryside. Merchants with a shop would have relied on the counter and sign to advertise their wares, as would have craftsmen. The ultimate goal of producing wares was to sell them and the display aspect of booths, as opposed to the storage aspect of warehouses, was therefore very important. A craftsman who had his booth on the High Street had a distinct advantage to one who had his booth tucked away down a side close.

Unfortunately, there are no surviving prints, engravings, or representations of an Edinburgh locksmith's booth. There is one representation of an Edinburgh Goldsmith's booth engraved in the stone above the north entrance to George Heriot's School (see figure 4.1). The c.1630 representation shows the goldsmith blowing the fire with a pair of hand-held bellows. Behind him is his anvil and to the right of the hearth is his bench. The bench is typical of the goldsmith craft, with bags for catching the filings from the precious metals. Bench tools line the wall and cover the bench, while tools for working with heated metal lie beside the hearth. The anvil, hearth and bench are all in close proximity, to avoid losing heat while transporting work from one to the other. This was an aspect common to all crafts using heat.

A floor plan from Mossman's Land, which is today known as the John Knox House, shows the booths of a small, uneven sample of Edinburgh burgesses from around 1600 (see figure 4.2).[28] Mossman's land had workspaces for a merchant, a spurrier, a bonnetmaker and a tailor. Their shops make an interesting study of booths, as these four trades can be ranked according to theoretical wealth and standing. James Maistertoun, the merchant, should have been the most wealthy of the four; followed by John Baxter, the tailor, Andrew Smyth, the spurrier and then Murdoch Brown, the bonnetmaker. The merchants were a very diverse group though, and the merchant's 'stone shop' on the west side of Mossman's Land is only a third of the size of the tailor's shop. Baxter's booth was listed as the 'main shop or merchant's booth', yet it was occupied by a tailor. Tailors were usually part of the craft aristocracy and it is no fluke that a tailor would occupy

FIGURE 4.1
Detail of stonework above north doorway to Heriot's Hospital, showing a goldsmith's booth, c.1630. (Dalgleish & Maxwell 1987, 8)

It was a matter of privilege to be able to produce and sell a certain type of product and incorporation was meant to protect the Hammermen's right to certain wares. By limiting the selling of those wares to a specific market day, it was easier to ensure that unfreemen would pay stallenger's fees for the right to sell Hammermen's work, making it more difficult to usurp their privilege.

On the market day applicable to a specific craft, the craftsmen would bring their wares from their booths to the designated market place. Goods were allowed to be sold only from the individual's specific stand in the market, though it was a common complaint that hucksters walked up and down the town plying their wares. There were exceptions to this rule; stallengers who sold woven goods were allowed to sell from only their market stall, whereas the makers of the wool were allowed to walk up and down the market selling their goods.[11] Freemen burgesses were allowed to buy whole webs of cloth on any day of the week and unfreemen were allowed to sell whole webs to free burgesses. These inconsistencies in the burgh's market policies illustrate the importance of cloth to Edinburgh's economy.[12]

The market would open at nine in the morning and go until one in the afternoon.[13] In 1740, it appears that the market for metalwork lasted until two.[14] The market time was an important part of burgh privilege and measures were taken to ensure that the selling of goods happened only in the market place at the market time. There were fines for leaving goods on display past the close of the market. In 1740 work was seized from a stallenger named Chalmers in Potterrow 'for not razing his stall in the market when two of the clock in the afternoon struck.'[15] In order to prove that one was a freeman of the burgh, it was required in 1664 that burgesses brought along their burgess tickets to the market.[16]

Another place where craftsmen could sell their wares was at one of the two burgh fairs. Fairs were like markets, only far less frequent; the markets were weekly, but the fairs happened only once or twice a year. During fairs, freedom seems to have been open to all. Unless someone was an outlaw 'beyond sanctuary', the burgh's freedom was suspended and all had licence. These fairs would have been golden opportunities for unfreemen, as they would have been able to sell their wares in Edinburgh, though the freemen of the burgh had first pick of selling space.[17] While limited in time, fairs were still usurpations of much guarded burgh freedoms.

The market was a very important institution in early modern Edinburgh. Markets required open space, such as the High Street, or the Fishmarket Close. Some would have needed a ready source of water. In a wet climate, the Hammermen probably would have needed covered stalls. While the burgh did relocate the less desirable markets which involved strong odours or mess, away from the High Street, the unoffensive markets remained where they had been in 1477.[18] Perhaps the Hammermen's market for finished metalwares remained by St Mary's Wynd.

BOOTH

The markets and fairs, which were common areas, open to all freemen and those unfreemen who paid stallenger's fees, were purely for retail. Booths were the other main economic areas in the early modern burghs and were owned by both merchants and craftsmen. They had several functions, but the main activity in a craftsman's booth was production. Craftsmen worked from five in the morning until eight o'clock at night on weekdays[19] and till four o'clock on Saturdays.[20] All the raw materials and tools, or 'worklumes' as they were known,[21] would have been kept in the booth. When locksmiths did outside jobs, such as picking open a lock for someone who lost a key, the booth was a base of sorts from which the job could be solicited. At night, the booth could be locked up in an effort to prevent work or tools being stolen, though this undoubtedly did happen from time to time.

Another role of the craftsman's booth was the education of apprentices, which is hinted at by the anvil having been commonly called the 'study'.[22] The anvil and the bench in their master's booth were where apprentice locksmiths learned their trade. Booth space also might have doubled as sleeping space for apprentices, servants, or even the family members of masters, especially when the craftsman's booth was located next to his house. Beds and chambers were expensive.

Booths were also showrooms for the craftsman's wares. While there is no direct evidence from Edinburgh that hammermen could sell directly from their booths,[23] there is evidence from other towns in Europe. Nehemia Wallington, a London turner in the mid-seventeenth century, kept a journal in which he thanked God for customers coming to his shop and making 40s worth of purchases on a day when other shopkeepers had shut their doors and windows for fear of fighting in the streets.[24]

mean that there were only two types; he probably was making a reference to the two most common. Diderot, in his mid-eighteenth-century encyclopedia of trades, illustrated four different types.[47] All smiths had to be self-reliant and show ingenuity in the work place.

Locksmiths also needed hammers at the forge, for shaping metal on their anvil. There were many different shapes and sizes of hammers. Moxon described several different varieties:

> as first the hand-hammer, which is sometimes bigger, or less, according to the strength of the workman; but it is a hammer of such weight, that it may be wielded, or governed, with one hand at the anvil. Secondly, the up-hand sledge, used by under-workmen, when the work is not of the largest, yet requires help to batter or draw it out; they use it with both their hands before them and seldom lift their hammer higher than their head. Thirdly, the about sledge is the biggest hammer of all and is also used by under-workmen, for the battering, or drawing out of the largest work; and then they hold the farther end of the handle in both their hands and swinging the sledge above their heads, they at arms end let fall as heavy a blow as they can upon the work. There is also another hammer used by them, which they call a riveting-hammer. This is the smallest hammer of all and very rarely used at the forge, unless your work prove very small; but upon cold iron it is used for riveting, or setting straight or crooking small work.[48]

If a locksmith tried using a heavy sledge hammer to straiten the delicate pin of a key hole, he might have crushed it completely. If he tried using a light riveting hammer to shape steel, even when glowing red, just out of the forge, it would barely have dented the workpiece. Specific tools had specific jobs and therefore there were several hammers in a locksmith's booth.

Various types of chisels would have been used for cutting hot metal. One type is known as a hardy and was set into a hole on the anvil.[49] The heated workpiece was set on top of the wedge-shaped hardy and struck by the hammer. This caused the hardy to be driven into the workpiece like a knife, cutting it in two. There were also handled chisels for cutting the top of the heated iron.[50]

The second group of tools were usually meant to be used with cold metal at the bench. The main feature of a locksmith's bench was the vice (see figures 4.3, 4.4, 4.5 and 4.6). While work was held steady in the vice, the locksmith changed its form. Hammers were used for light hammering. If the iron was thin enough, heat was not needed to shape the piece and the hammering could take place at the bench.

Files were some of the main tools used by locksmiths. Files came in all shapes, sizes and cuts. Moxon explained them as follows:

> The several sorts of files that are in common use are the square, the flat, the three square, the half round, the round, the thin file, etc. All these shapes you must have of several sizes and of several cuts. You must have them of several sizes, as well because you may have several sizes of work, as for that it sometimes falls out that one piece of work may have many parts in it joined and fitted to one another, some of them great and others small; and you must have them of several cuts, because the rough-toothed file cuts faster than the bastard-toothed file, the fine-toothed file faster than the smooth-toothed file.[51]

Different shapes were required for different shaped jobs; a square file was not suited for making a rounded cut. Different sizes were needed for different sizes of work. A large file took off a lot more metal than a small file and would therefore have eaten small workpieces. With different cuts, the locksmith could gauge how much metal would be taken off the workpiece, as well as bring the surface to a good finish:

> The rough or course-toothed file (which if it be large, is called a rubber) is to take off the unevenness of your work which the hammer made in the forging; the bastard-toothed file is to take out of your work the deep cuts, or file-strokes, the rough-file made; the fine-toothed file is to take out the cuts, or file-strokes, the bastard-file made; and the smooth-file is to take out those cuts, or file-strokes, that the fine file made. Thus you see how the files of several cuts succeed one another, till your work is so smooth as it can be filed. You may make it yet smoother with emerick, Tripoli, etc.[52]

When used in succession from rough-cut down to fine-cut, the metal attained a polished finish which resisted rust better than a rough surface.

When a locksmith wanted to cut iron plates to shape, one method involved a large pair of shears, with one leg mounted in a large wooden block. Another method was to use cold chisels, which were wedges of steel that could be struck by a hammer to cut iron that had not been heated in the forge.[53] The workpiece was set on a soft iron plate, the chisel set in the position desired and a heavy blow was struck down on the top of the chisel. The ward clefts on key bits were often cut out by chisels:

> The ... wards [are] made, or at least entered at the forge, when the iron had a blood, or almost a flame heat, yet sometimes smiths do it on cold iron, with a thin chisel ... but you must take care that your chisel be neither too

thick, or too broad, for this punching of wards is only to give the thin files entrance to the work; which entrance you then have, you may easily file your … wards, wider or deeper, as your work may require.[54]

Saws were also used, as can be seen by the picture of the 1698 locksmith's shop from Nürnberg (see figure 4.5).

When a locksmith needed holes put in a workpiece, he had two main options. The first involved using a punch, which was a long, thin piece of hardened steel, the end of which was round in section, but flat on the tip. The punch was set over the workpiece, which was in turn set over the open jaws of the vice and struck with a hammer. In much the same way that a paper punch puts holes in paper, the steel punch was driven through the iron plate, leaving a clean, round hole. Other shapes could also be punched in iron, depending on the needs of the locksmith. Rectangular holes for mortice and tennon joints of lock-case walls required punching.[55]

Another option for making holes was the hand drill. This item was a simple device, akin to the method of starting a fire with sticks. By making a hardened steel bit spin on the softer iron workpiece, a hole was eventually bored through. There seem to have been several methods of powering the spinning motion. One involved a downward force on two handles, which caused the bit to unwind (see the triangular shaped drill hanging on the wall in figure 4.5). The bit was first wound up and then placed in the spot where the hole was desired. When downward pressure on the handles caused the two cords to unwind, the bit was forced to spin. Another type was the bow powered drill (see figure 4.6, 'Fig. 8'). As the bow which was looped around the bit was pushed forwards, the spool rotated, causing the bit to bore through the workpiece.

The bow powered mechanism was also used on small hand lathes, for accurately turning shapes in metal, or boring evenly spaced holes for pipe keys (see the vice mounted lathe in figure 4.7, 'Fig. 27').

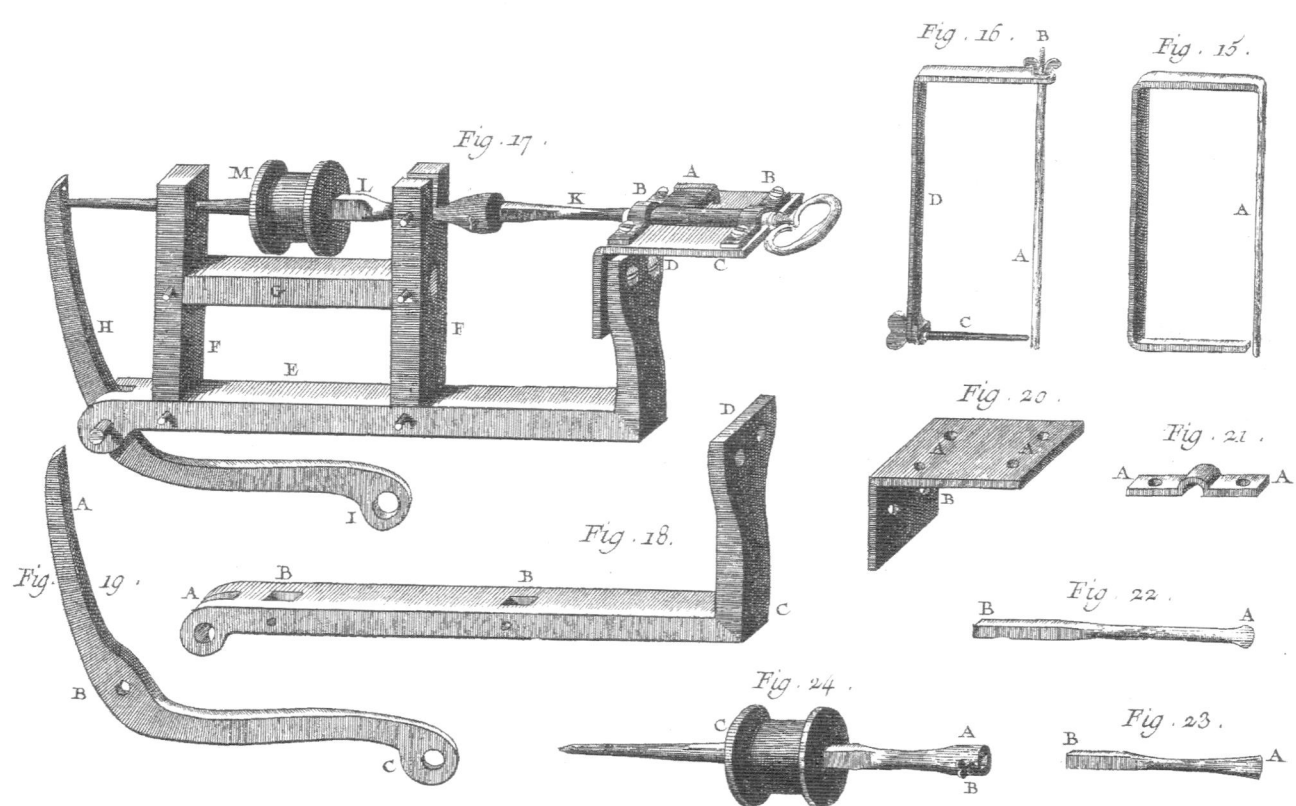

FIGURE 4.7
Diderot's picture of a hand lathe for boring pipe keys (Diderot 1966, plate XX)

THE LOCKSMITHS' WORKPLACE

These were common tools, used by many trades (see the gunsmith's booth in figure 3.2 – the apprentice is setting one up). As the part spun, metal was removed evenly, leaving a symmetric and smooth surface. This is how locksmiths made the turned decoration on key stems and pots.

There were various other tools for different purposes. There were hand-vices, of which Moxon commented:

> Hand-vices are of two sorts, one is called the broad-chapped hand-vice, the other the square-nosed hand-vice. The office of the hand-vice, is to hold small work in, that may require often turning about; it is held in the left hand and each part of your work turned upward successively, that you have occasion to file with your right. The square-nosed hand-vice is seldom used, but for filing small globulous work, as the heads of pins that round off towards the edges, etc. And that because the chaps do not stand shouldering in the way, but that the flat of the file may the better come at the edges. Their chaps must be cut as the vice aforesaid and well tempered.[56]

Hand-vices had a wing-nut, which held tension on the jaws so that they held a constant grip. If the locksmith wanted to be able to change the position of the workpiece without constantly opening and tightening the wing-nut of the hand-vice, he would use pliers:

> Pliers are of two sorts, flat nosed and round nosed. Their office is to hold and fasten upon all small work and to fit it in its placed. The round nosed pliers are used for turning, or bowing wire, or small plate, into a circular form. The chaps of the flat nosed pliers, must also be cut and tempered, as the chaps of the vice.[57]

Hand-vices and pliers were simply hand-held vices (see figure 4.6). They used leverage to provide a grip which the human hand was not strong enough to give.

Another necessary tool in the locksmith's booth was used for cutting threads for screws and bolts (see figure 4.6). Moxon wrote the following of screw plates and taps:

> The screw plate is as plate of steel well tempered, with several holes in it, each less than other and in those holes are threads grooved inwards; into which grooves, fit the respective taps that belong to them. The taps that belong to them, are commonly made tapering towards the point, as 'Fig. 7' shows.[58]

When a locksmith made a bolt for attaching a lock to a door, he would run the end of the bolt into the screw plate. As the soft iron bolt turned in the hardened steel plate, it was forced to form threads. The corresponding tap was then forced to turn inside the nut for the bolt, leaving it with the same thread pattern. The nut and bolt then fit together.

TECHNIQUES

Locksmiths employed several important techniques in their work. The first techniques dealt with cold work, such as hammering and filing. Other techniques dealt with joining metal parts. The rest of the major techniques dealt with the preparation of iron and steel for certain tasks.

Hammering was one of the most basic of skills for any locksmith. In fact, it was important for the entire Incorporation of Hammermen. If hammer blows did not land squarely, then half of the hammer's face would have been indented into the heated iron, while the other half of the hammer's face was suspended in air above the work. This would have resulted in deep, half-circular indentations and misshaped metal. If the hammer blow landed with the entire face equally touching the work, then the blow was evenly spread across the work and the surface was not left scarred with indentations. By learning to control the hammer blows, the smith saved much time and effort in filing the surface smooth later. All depended on the intended plane of the hammer's face when it contacted the workpiece. All this took time to learn.

The importance of filing to the locksmith craft is demonstrated by the amount of space – three pages – which Moxon spent discussing it. Apprentice locksmiths had to learn to take long, heavy, level strokes when filing. The importance of aesthetics in early modern metalwork demanded control in this element of the art.

One of the first lessons Moxon gave was control over how much metal was removed, by learning not to file too much:

> when you file upon the prominent, or rising parts of your work, with your course cut file, you must also take care that you file them not more away than you need, for you may easily be deceived; because your course file cuts deep and makes deep scratches in the work.[59]

Moxon stated that the deep scratches could be removed with finer files, though this would have taken a great deal of time. It was important that the locksmiths paid attention to which tools they were using; the larger, rough-cut files removed metal much faster than the medium and fine-cut files, but they could also damage the workpiece and create more work.

Another lesson in filing was keeping the file level, so as not to curve what should be a flat surface:

> If it be a square bar, (or such like) you are to file upon, all its angles, or edges, must be left very sharp and straight. Therefore ... you must, in your filing, athwart over the chaps of the vice, be sure to carry both your hands you hold the file in, truly horizontal, or flat over the work; for should you let either of your hands mount, the other would dip and the edge of that square it dips upon would be taken off; and should you let your hand move never so little circularly, both the edges you file upon would be taken off and the middle of your intended flat would be left with a rising on it. But this Hand-craft, you must attain by practice; for it is the great curiosity in filing.[60]

Moxon went on to explain how one should not keep their file level when making a round surface, as that would create flat spots on it. Instead, the file should have followed the contour. All surfaces are in certain planes and the file needed to stay in that plane in order to attain the correct surface and finish. A well-known maxim in metalwork states that one cannot put the metal back on once it is removed.

The locksmith apprentice was not to file gingerly, though:

> When you thrust your file forwards, lean heavily upon it, because the teeth of the file are made to cut forwards; but when you draw your file back, to recover another thrust, lift, or bear the file lightly just above the work; for it cuts not coming back.[61]

If one kept pressure on the file on the backstroke, the files went dull sooner, resulting in increased expense. Heavy, level strokes, using the entire length of the file on the push and an ease of pressure when drawing it back, resulted in quick, controlled and effective filing. Bad filing was un-economical in time expenditure, but also in the cost of buying a new set of sharp files to replace the ones that were dulled.

There were several options for joining metal parts; some were done cold, others involved heating the parts in the forge. Cold joining was a broad technique, that entailed forming a mortice tab of iron on one piece and putting it through a tennon, or slot, which had been punched into another piece. The protruding end was then smashed with a hammer, which riveted it into place. This was known as peening and was a very strong method of joining. Another variation involved making a rivet, which resembled a nail and putting it through the two work pieces. The protruding end was then peened over, making an 'H'-shaped fastener.

The most common hot joins were welding and brazing. Welding entailed first cleaning the surfaces which were to be welded, coating them in a chemical flux, such as borax and then heating them until they reached a welding-heat. This type of heat could be seen, as the metal was glowing white and sparking profusely. The parts were then removed to the anvil as quickly as possible and smacked firmly with a hammer. The metal would then fuse together. This is known as either impact welding or forge welding.

The other common hot joins was brazing and soldering. Moxon describes the way in which these processes took place:

> You may have occasion sometimes to braze or solder a piece of work; but it is used by smiths only, when their work is so thin, or small, that it will not endure welding. To do this, take small pieces of brass and lay them on the place that must be brazed, ans strew a little glass beaten to powder on it to make it run the sooner and give it a heat in the forge, till (by sometimes drawing it a little way out of the fire) you see the brass run. But if your work be so small, or thin, that you may frear the iron will run as soon as the brass and so you lose your work in the fire, then you must make a loam of three parts clay and one part horse-dung and after they are wrought and mingled very well together in your hands, warp your work with the brass and a little beaten glass upon the place to be brazed closed in the loam and laying it a while upon the hearth of the forge to dry, put the lump into the fire and blow the bellows to it, till you perceive it have a full heat, that is, till the lump look like a well burnt coal of fire; then take it out of the fire and let it cool: afterwards break it up and take out your work.[62]

The glass acted as a flux, cleaning the edges and making the brass flow into the seam. Padlocks, keys and some lock parts from the early modern era often show remnants of this process. It is interesting that glass and manure were both involved in this process, showing both a lack of waste through recycling and a reliance on animal products in the early modern urban environment.

There were other techniques that were equally important to hammering, filing and joining. Two of the most important were methods of iron preparation, known as hardening and tempering. The two usually happened in conjunction in the order mentioned. Iron is a soft metal in its purest form. Items like springs cannot be soft; they need to return to their original position when moved in order to be effective. The way to achieve this was to shape the spring from a suitable steel, rather than iron and heat it in the fire. The locksmith could tell how long to heat the part by the colour of the metal. Once it was heated, it was removed from the forge and quickly quenched in the water trough. This sudden cooling caused the steel to become extremely hard, to the point that a file would not cut it. At this point, however, the steel was too hard; it was brittle and would break under pressure. Tempering was the process of gently bringing the steel from too hard back to the point where it was springy. Moxon describes it thus:

> If your steel be too hard, that is too brittle ... [it] will be subject to break; or if it be a spring, it will not bow, but with the least bending it will snap asunder: Therefore you must let it down (as smiths say) that is, make it softer by tempering it. The manner is thus, take a piece of grinstone or wet-stone and rub hard upon your work to take the black scurf off it and brighten it; then let it heat in the fire and as it grows hotter you will see the colour change by degrees, coming to a light goldish colour, then to a dark goldish colour and at last to a blue colour; choose which of these colours your work requires and then quench it suddenly in water.[63]

The blue colour was the correct one for springs.

If tempered steel was at the middle of a spectrum, with 'brittle' at the hardest end and 'malleable' at the softest end, then the next technique was the farthest end possible on the softening side of the spectrum. When steel was properly tempered, it was near untouchable with a file. This also meant that it was virtually unworkable at the bench. If a locksmith needed to alter the shape of a piece of steel, he first needed to make it soft enough to work with. This was achieved by a process called 'annealing'. Moxon simplified the process in his book on smithing:

> Having chose your steel and forged it to your intended shape, if you are either to file, engrave, or to punch upon it, you ought to anneal it first, because it will make it softer and consequently, work easier. The common way it to give it a blood-red-heat in the fire, then take it out and let it cool of itself.[64]

With the metal in a softer state, the locksmith could shape the workpiece to the required dimensions. He would then harden and temper it to the point where it would serve its purpose.

The amount of skill required to master these techniques is illustrated by the length of apprenticeship, which was supposed to be at least seven years.[65] If the work week was more than eighty hours,[66] and it took seven years to be ready to train others and open one's own booth, then it is apparent that these skills were not to be taken for granted. They took time to develop. There were no charts, or gauges to explain when the metal was ready for a specific task; all was done by a careful combination of eye and experience.

MATERIALS

Locksmiths used a range of raw materials in their trade. They needed iron stock for lock and key production, as well as for making or repairing tools. By the late seventeenth century, lock cases, as well as door knobs and other bits of architectural hardware, were increasingly made of brass. While wrought iron was more rust resistant than some higher carbon metals, tin was often used for coating work as a rust preventative. Fuel options included coal and charcoal and there were many other chemicals and items that added to the overhead expenditures of a locksmith's booth. Some of these items were produced locally, but most had to be imported by merchants, illustrating both the dependency of the burgh on foreign trade and the dependency of craftsmen on merchants.[67]

The primary material needed in a locksmith's booth was iron. Iron was obtained in various forms, including plates and bars. While there was iron production in Scotland prior to the Industrial Revolution, it was on a small scale. In 1610, there was a colony of English workmen under Sir George Hay, which made iron and cast canon in the woods of Letterewe in Gairloch parish, Wester Ross.[68] There was also an iron mill set up in Dalkeith in 1648.[69] The mill was set up on the River North Esk, so that its trip hammers could be water-powered. The Statistical Account of 1845 states that the corn mill, which was previously the iron mill, was formerly used for manufacturing iron bars, sheet iron and all sorts of heavy smith work.[70] The heavy smith work that they produced included finished wares, such as cart and wheelbarrow wheels, ploughs, shovels, spades, picks, gates, railings, and other such items.[71]

While Scotland's main source of iron ore was the inferior bog ore, certain industrious Scots imported scrap iron and refined it using local fuel. In 1724, Alexander Graham of Duchray noted a new iron works in the parish of Callendar. He stated that the site 'made very good iron partly of tar got in the country and partly of iron scraps got from Holland by managers of the work'.[72] The fuel for the refining process was charcoal made of the birch timber cut down in the woods nearby. While there were other areas in Scotland producing iron prior to 1750, iron production, as opposed to usage in making finished goods, was very limited in Scotland prior to the Industrial Revolution.

The bulk of iron used by Scottish smiths came from abroad. Joseph Moxon, commenting on English sources of foreign iron, had the following to say about the vast network of European suppliers:

> English iron, is generally a course sort of iron, hard and brittle ... unless it be about the Forest of Dean and some few places more, where the iron proves very good. Swedish iron is of all sorts, the best we use in England. It is a fine tough sort of iron, will best endure the hammer and is softest to file; and therefore most coveted by workmen, to work upon. Spanish iron, would be as good as Swedish iron, were it not subject to red-sear, (as workmen phrase it) that is to crack betwixt hot and cold. Therefore when it falls under your hands, you must tend it more earnestly at the forge. But though it be good, tough, soft iron, yet for many uses, workmen will refuse it, because it is so ill and unevenly wrought in the bars, that it costs them a great deal of labour to smooth it; but it is good for all great works that require welding, as the bodies of anvils, sledges, large bell-clappers, large pestles for mortars, & all thick strong bars, etc'.[73]

While Scotland would have had different trade networks than England, the sources of the iron would have been the same for all countries across Europe. From 1740 to 1749, Sweden exported 42,700 tons of iron, with 53.5 per cent going to the British market, 10.5 per cent going to Holland, 24 per cent going to the Baltic area and 12 per cent going to the Latin market.[74] Sweden did not sell to England alone.

Moxon was also quite interesting about where the best sources for steel were to be found:

> The difficulty of getting good steel makes many workmen (when by good hap they light on it) commend that country-steel for best, from whence that steel came. Thus I have found some cry up Flemish-steel, others Swedish, English, Spanish, Venice, &c. But according to my observation and common consent of the most ingenious workmen, each country produces almost indifferently good and bad; yet each country doth not equally produce such steel, as is fit for every particular purpose ... The Flemish-steel is made in Germany, in the country of Stiermark and in the Land of Luyck: from thence brought down to Cologne and is brought down the river Rhine to Dort and other parts of Holland and Flanders, some in bars and some in gads and is therefore by us called Flemish-steel and sometimes gad-steel. It is a tough sort of steel and the only steel used for watch-springs ... I cannot learn that nay steel comes from Sweden, but from Danzig comes some which is called Swedish-steel: it is much the same quality and fineness with Flemish-steel. The Spanish-steel is made about Biscay. It is a fine sort of steel, but some of it is very difficult to work at the forge, because it will not take a good heat; and it sometimes proves very unsound, as not being well curried, that is well wrought. It is too quick (as workmen call it) that is brittle for springs or punches, but makes good fine edged tools. Venice-steel is much like Spanish-steel, but much finer and works somewhat better at the forge. It is used for razors, surgeon's instruments, gravers, etc.[75]

Steel was a different thing altogether from iron and also had to be imported.

There are a few known sources of iron which fed the Scottish burghs. Records from Edinburgh mention Swedish, Danish and Spanish iron. In Edinburgh, Swedish iron cost 24s a stone in 1600 and 30s a stone in 1607. Danish iron was also 30s a stone in 1607.[76] In the 1612 rates of valuation and customs for imported goods, 'Spanish spruce and Swedens iron' cost 13s 4d the stone weight.[77] Iron and steel were important commodities, both to locksmiths and all other metalworkers and illustrate the dependence of Scotland on foreign trade. The Baltic trade was especially important.

Other metals were also needed by Edinburgh locksmiths. Tin was a common coating for rust-proofing iron. The 1612 rates of valuation and customs state that unwrought tin by the hundred weight cost £30.[78] It would seem that only the more expensive locks and keys would have been coated in tin. Brass was also used by locksmiths, increasingly after the last quarter of the seventeenth century.[79] In 1612, the rate for imported brass, by the hundred weight, was £40.[80]

Metals were not the only raw materials needed by locksmiths. Fuel was another large overhead cost for a locksmith's booth, as in order to shape the metal into usable parts, heat had to be applied. Coal was a fuel which was found readily in Scotland. Production was increased ten fold from 40,000 tons during the 1551–60 period, to 475,000 tons in 1681–90.[81] In Bo'ness, in the late seventeenth century, coal mining employed 2.9 per cent of the male pollable population.[82] One of the more productive early coal mines was Sir George Bruce's mine at Culross, Fife. Bruce was granted the lease of Culross Abbey's mine in 1574. After gaining technical expertise in Europe, he introduced several innovations to the mine, including his 'Egyptian wheel' mechanism for draining the water out of the lower levels. The monks before him had managed to work the coal at thirty feet in depth. Bruce's miners got down to 240 feet, with drifts that reached a mile under the Firth of Forth.[83]

It is interesting that in the 1612 book of customs and valuations, the import list does not mention coal,[84] though the export list does. The rate for exported 'smiddy coals the chalder' was £4.[85] In the early eighteenth century, coal cost 6d for eighteen stones.[86] Charcoal, which was wood, burned to the point where all moisture was gone, was also a possible fuel for running a forge. It is doubtless that there were other raw materials needed by locksmiths, which the records do not directly name.

Many of the details found in an Edinburgh locksmith's booth would also have been found in the booths of other European cities. Often, the booths were similar to those of other trades. Several of the locksmith's tools and techniques were similar to those of closely related trades, such as blacksmiths. It is unfortunate that the early modern locksmith craft was not better recorded, but with the sources available, it is still possible to piece together the workplace of the Edinburgh locksmiths. Their tools and techniques can be studied in a roundabout way, all the time pointing to the required knowledge of basic metallurgy and the patiently learned skills that produced security for the early modern burgh.

NOTES

1. *Edin Recs* 1869, 34–5.
2. Edgar 1742.
3. *Edin Recs* 1869, 35.
4. Colston 1891, 89.
5. *Edin Recs* 1869, 34.
6. Today, this is called Fish Market Close. Gordon of Rothemay 1647.
7. There were fourteen markets in total in 1477; seven of them were located on the High Street. *Edin Recs* 1869, 34–5.
8. 'Resold'? Robinson 1992, 32.
9. Smith 1906, 182.
10. Ibid., 182.
11. Marwick 1909, 194.
12. Ibid., 190.
13. *Edin Recs* 1869, 35 and Marwick 1909, 189 and 193–4.
14. ECA ED008/1/7, 43.
15. Ibid., ED008/1/7, 43.
16. Marwick 1909, 182.
17. Ibid., 8.
18. Such was the case with the lawnmarket, or land-market; land referring to 'country'. *Edin Recs* 1869, 35 and Marwick 1909, 193. This particular continuity might also reflect the importance of cloth to Edinburgh's economy.
19. This was in summer; it is not mentioned if the hours were the same in winter. ECA ED008/1/8, 1 August 1750.
20. *APS* 1875, 382.
21. As in the 1645 testament of David Clark, dagmaker, reprinted in Whitelaw 1977, 300.
22. Whitelaw 1977, 300 and 'Rates of Customs', 1867, 329 and 359.
23. There is a reference in the Incorporation of Goldsmith's seal of cause stating that they could sell from either booth or market, and they were originally part of the hammermen. Colston 1891, 30.
24. Seaver 1985, 122.
25. Lumsden & Aitken 1912, 74.
26. From Canongate Hammermen Records, as transcribed in Whitelaw 1977, 207 and accidentally described as coming from the Incorporation of Hammermen of Edinburgh in Kelvin 1996, 177.
27. Friedrichs 2003, 145.
28. Dr Smith was kind enough to allow me to use research from his book: Smith 1996, 35 and 57.
29. Ibid., 35 and 57.
30. Ibid., 35–7, 57 and 60.
31. Ibid., 57.
32. Bennett 1981 (thesis).
33. Pinkerton & Windram 1983, 29.
34. Ibid., 26.
35. Ibid., 36, 'Fig. 3'.
36. Crossley 1990, 20.
37. Strauss 1966, 21.
38. There were 150 different locksmiths listed between 1494 and 1750 in the hammermen minute books. ECA ED008/1.
39. Moxon 1989, Preface.
40. Ibid., 1–38.
41. Ibid., 1.
42. Quotation marks around symbols referring to Moxon's diagrams were added by myself for the sake of clarity. Ibid., 2.
43. Ibid., 2.
44. Ibid., 3.
45. Ibid., 3.
46. Streeter 1980, 17.
47. Diderot 1966, plate LIII, figures 39–41.
48. Moxon 1989, 3–4.
49. Diderot 1966, plate LI, figure 4 and Streeter 1980, 12.
50. Ibid., plate LII, figure 14.
51. Moxon 1989, 15.
52. Ibid., 15.
53. Ibid., 22.
54. Ibid., 29.
55. Streeter 1980, 15.
56. Moxon 1989, 5.
57. Ibid., 5–6.
58. Quotation marks around 'Fig. 7' were added by me for the sake of clarity and refer to figure 4.6. Ibid., 7.
59. Ibid., 16.
60. Ibid., 16–17.
61. Ibid., 17.

62 Ibid., 12–13.
63 Ibid., 61.
64 Ibid., 60.
65 Marwick 1909, 73.
66 5 am to 8 pm on weekdays, ECA ED008/1/8, 1 August 1750, and till 4 pm on Saturdays. *APS* 1875, 382.
67 It would make an interesting study to compare craftsman/merchant relations in conjunction with import duties on raw goods. Perhaps there was some correlation between the growth of merchant power and dependence on them for raw materials.
68 Stell & Hay 1995, 9.
69 Dennison & Coleman 1998, 86.
70 *Statistical Account* 1845, 503.
71 Smith 1985, 7.
72 Joynson 1996, 98.
73 Moxon 1989, 13–14.
74 Hildebrand 1992, 26.
75 Moxon 1989, 57–8.
76 Coutts 1987, 152–3.
77 'Rates of Customs' 1867, 316.
78 Ibid., 331.
79 Hume 1969, 246.
80 'Rates of Customs' 1867, 292.
81 Kelvin 1996, 56.
82 Whyte 1987, 233.
83 Sked 1999, 3.
84 'Rates of Customs' 1867, 295.
85 Ibid., 336.
86 Kelvin 1996, 57.

Chapter 5

The Locksmiths' Work

What did the locksmiths do and what did they make? While the very term 'locksmith' would seem to be sufficient to answer this, with smith meaning worker and in this case a worker of locks, there is still no depth to this answer. Modern-day locksmiths retain the term, but do not build locks. In fact, they only repair locks and cut keys from blanks which were made in other countries, such as Italy. Unfortunately, the sources for the locksmiths in Edinburgh rarely went into any great detail as to what they were producing. When they did, the jargon used in the records is still rather opaque to twenty-first century minds. While some of the words can be found in Scots dictionaries, many are too technical; no doubt the average person on a seventeenth-century street would not have fully understood the technological labels of all the lock parts. With the records using forgotten terminology, when used at all, it is hard to get a precise understanding of what the locksmiths did. Luckily, there is another type of source available to historians – artefacts. By using the material culture which survives, in conjunction with contemporary paintings and the written documents, it is possible to piece together a picture of what products and services the locksmiths provided for early modern Edinburgh. Was the work of Scottish locksmiths the same as that of European locksmiths? This chapter will first look at the written records of locksmiths' work and then the material records, in order to get a better understanding of the work done by both Edinburgh locksmiths and European locksmiths in general.

There were two main categories of work done by locksmiths in the early modern period: production and services. Production activities in a locksmith's booth could cover a range of different items. It is known that in some European towns, there were craftsmen who specialized in a certain area of a particular trade. For example, in Nördlingen, in 1615, there were seven locksmiths and one padlocksmith.[1] The market for padlocks in that area of Germany was strong enough that the one smith could specialize in making only padlocks. By contrast there is nothing in Edinburgh's records to indicate that any locksmith ever specialized in the production of just one item. Production in Edinburgh encompassed all facets of locksmiths' work.

PRODUCTION

The main written source for locksmiths' work is the Incorporation of Hammermen's minutes. The fourteen incorporated trades all made use of the office of boxmaster, who kept the boxes in their care which held the important papers and money of the incorporations. The first volume of the Incorporation of Hammermen's minute books lists an entry in 1500 'for the lock making and the key of the little box to John Anderson, xvj d'.[2] If the boxes were to be secure, they needed to be locked. Usually, there were three different keys given out to different officials in the incorporation, so that the boxmaster alone did not have complete access to the money and deeds. The very institution of incorporation gave work to the locksmith craft.

The Incorporation of Hammermen also owned various tenements and properties. These often needed repairs for locks and architectural hardware. One of the earlier locksmiths, a man named John Loksmyt, was given 6d for two locks and bands by the incorporation.[3] Bands were large iron hinges that stretched across the door and rested on crooks, which were 'L'-shaped spikes of iron mounted in the wall. Throughout the early modern period, the Hammermen's minutes are peppered with listings of payments to locksmiths for architectural hardware,[4] along with wrights' and masons' bills for installation.

The minute books laid out the work for locksmiths after a dispute with the blacksmith craft over the rights of production.[5] When the issue was resolved, locksmiths' work was defined as 'the making and mending of locks and bands with all white work and filed work pertaining to the Locksmith craft, with all sort of jointed bands'. It then went on to state that the door crooks, door bands and mending chimneys were common work for both blacksmiths and locksmiths.[6] Locksmiths not only made lock and keys; they also made other types of architectural hardware.

TABLE 5.0
Locksmiths' essay (ECA ED008/1)

Date	Locksmiths' essay
1586	Kist lock
1587	Kist lock
1587	Kist lock
1609	Kist lock, a hinge, boss lock, and double plate lock
1629	Kist lock
1633	Kist lock
1636	Kist lock
1639	Kist lock
1639	Kist lock
1639	Kist lock
1640	Kist lock
1641	Kist lock
1644	Kist lock
1646	Lock, key, sprent band
1646	Chest lock, key
1647	Chest lock, sprent band, key
1647	Chest lock, key, sprent band
1647	Chest lock, sprent band, key
1649	Chest lock, key, sprent band
1653	Chest lock, key, sprent band
1655	Chest lock, key, sprent band
1656	Chest lock, key, sprent band
1674	A great chest lock with a sprent band and a key
1675	A great chest lock with a sprent band and a key
1683	A crook and crookband, a chest lock, and sprent band
1684	Double iron lock, crook, crook band
1684	A double iron lock with a crook and crook band
1684	A pass lock with two brass drawers, crook and crook band
1687	A pass lock with two brass drawers, the lock polished, crook and crookband
1690	A pass lock with two brass drawers, the lock polished, crook and crookband
1690	A pass lock with polished knobs and the lock polished, crook and crook band
1693	A pass lock with polished knobs and the lock polished, crook and crook band
1693	A pass lock with polished knobs and the lock polished, crook and crook band
1695	A pass lock and key, cruik and cruik band
1698	Double iron lock, crook, crook band
1700	Crook, crook band, pass lock, brass knobs, jamb band
1703	Crook, crook band, pass lock, brass knobs, jamb band
1703	Crook, crook band, pass lock, brass knobs, jamb band
1705	Crook, crook band, pass lock, brass knobs, jamb band
1706	Crook, crook band, pass lock, brass knobs, jamb band
1708	Crook, crook band, pass lock, brass knobs, jamb band
1710	Crook, crook band, pass lock, brass knobs, jamb band
1712	Crook, crook band, pass lock, brass knobs, jamb band
1713	Crook, crook band, pass lock, brass knobs, jamb band
1714	Crook, crook band, pass lock, brass knobs, jamb band
1715	Crook, crook band, pass lock, brass knobs, jamb band
1715	Crook, crook band, pass lock, brass knobs, jamb band

TABLE 5.0 (cont)
Locksmiths' essay (ECA ED008/1)

Date	Locksmiths' essay
1716	Crook, crook band, pass lock, brass knobs, jamb band
1717	Crook, crook band, pass lock, brass knobs, jamb band
1718	Crook, crook band, pass lock, brass knobs, jamb band
1718	Crook, crook band, pass lock, brass knobs, jamb band
1720	Crook, crook band, pass lock, brass knobs, jamb band
1721	Crook, crook band, pass lock, brass knobs, jamb band
1724	Crook, crook band, pass lock, brass knobs, jamb band
1734	Crook, crook band, pass lock, brass knobs, jamb band
1735	Crook, crook band, pass lock, brass knobs, jamb band
1737	Crook, crook band, pass lock, brass knobs, jamb band
1737	Crook, crook band, pass lock, brass knobs, jamb band
1738	Crook, crook band, pass lock, brass knobs, jamb band
1740	Crook, crook band, pass lock, brass knobs, jamb band

Some of the most detailed accounts of locks produced in early modern Edinburgh were the essays set for apprentice locksmiths to become masters and freemen of the Incorporation of Hammermen.[7] The minute books started listing essays in the late sixteenth century. A sample of essays for the locksmiths is shown in table 5.0. There were two main components of the essays: kist locks[8] and pass locks. There were occasionally different essays set. In 1609 one essay included a kist lock, a boss lock and a double plate lock and from 1684 to 1698 there were several double iron locks. Besides these few exceptions, the essays from 1586 to 1683 were variations of a kist lock and from 1684 to 1749 variations on a pass lock.

Moreover, for a century, the essay remained a lock for one of the various types of boxes. It is interesting that the term 'chest' replaced the Scots term 'kist' before the Cromwellian occupation. One of the components was a 'sprent band', which was a form of shackle mounted on a hinge (see figure 5.1). It is an integral part of most kist locks, so the 1646 essay of a 'lock' shown in table 5.0 probably referred to a kist or chest lock also. Why it was that kist locks were seen as being important enough to be the test for mastership is unknown. The 1612 list of rates and customs for imports and exports shows that imported kists ranged in price from 20s up to £30.[9] Kist locks were either seen as a luxury item, or a staple product; we do not know with certainty which of the two.

Door locks, of which pass locks are a complex variety, were not luxury items. There is a Hogarth engraving from 1747 entitled 'The Idle Prentice Returned from Sea, & In a Garrett with a Common Prostitute'. The door clearly shows a lock, though the rest of the interior shows extreme poverty.[10] Pass locks are locks that are made to pass, which means that one key will open all of the locks; it will pass them all. By keying alike three different locks, one key could open them all; a person needed only one key to have access to all the rooms. Alternatively, one of the locks might have been made on a master system. In a master system, a master key will open all of the locks, while other servant keys will open only a certain number of the locks. This was achieved by altering the warding inside the locks; the mastered lock had the most warding and the master key was the only one cut broad enough to pass all of them. The servant keys were cut to pass only some of the warding, giving restricted access.

The earlier essays of pass locks often stated that they were to have 'brass drawers' and be polished. Drawers probably refer to the knobs for drawing in the bolt and latch. Brass was becoming more common on Edinburgh locks. Around the late seventeenth century it became the fashion in England and America to make lock cases out of brass.[11] Brass knobs started to replace the loop handles. Brass was more resistant to the elements than iron. The polished cases and brass fittings on Edinburgh locks might indicate that fashion in Scotland paralleled that in England. The brief change from brass knobs to brass handles from 1743–5, as shown in table 5.0, might reflect trends in fashion.

FIGURE 5.1
Sprent band for a chest lock dated 1664, England.
(Courtesy of Holy Trinity Church, Stratford-upon-Avon)

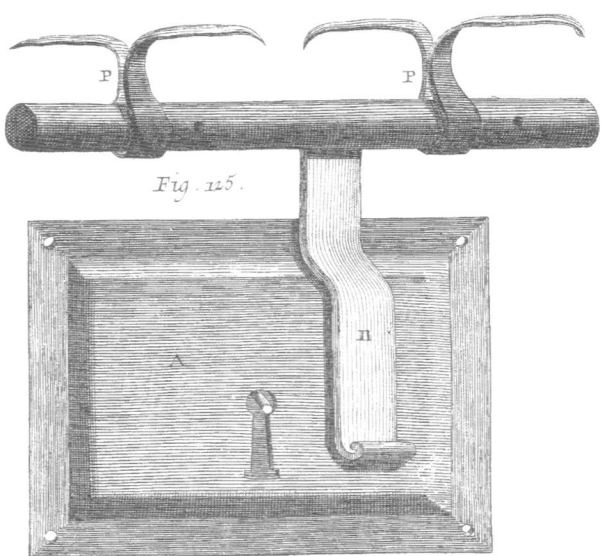

FIGURE 5.2
Boss lock – *serrure à bosse*. France, *c.* 1751 (Diderot 1966, plate XXIX)

It is interesting that the 1609 essay involved making three different locks. One wonders if the Incorporation was angry at the poor apprentice! The boss lock part of the essay was either for a door, a chest, or a padlock. An example of a boss lock for a door can be seen in figure 5.2. Boss padlocks can be seen in figure 5.59. This type of lock was also used on kists, chests and other such boxes. They were of simple construction, as the body is a single a piece of iron plate shaped into a concave dish, with the mechanism mounted inside. The main or draw bolt then had a sprent band attached that was captured by the internal bolt of the lock mechanism, keeping the main bolt and the door in the closed position.

The 1609 double plate lock is a bit more mysterious. A plate lock usually indicates a simple mechanism mounted on an iron plate for internal doors. The adjective 'double' might indicate that it was large, as in the contemporary term 'double musket'. It might also have been a technical term for a type of iron plate. In the 1612 list of rates and customs, doubles are stated as 'harness plates or iron doubles'.[12] Armour, or 'harness', was made of iron plates. Perhaps a double plate lock refers to a thick type of plate used for a specific type of lock? Whatever the term means, the setting of an essay consisting of a double plate or an iron lock seems to have occurred only in the seventeenth century and they often included door furniture.

The problem with essays is their lack of explanation. Were they setting essays of difficult items to make which would indicate the extent of their abilities, or were they setting items that were in high demand and would therefore show a basic level of proficiency? It is doubtful that essays were market driven, as door locks would have been in huge demand during the population boom of the 'long' sixteenth century. More houses meant more doors. Perhaps it also meant more chests for keeping the goods of all the people. A further study on chest and door lock ownership through the use of testaments would shed light on the relationship between essays and markets. What essays do indicate is that Edinburgh locksmiths had the skills for producing kist locks and door locks.

THE LOCKSMITHS' WORK

Another interesting source for what kinds of locks were being produced in Scotland comes from the *Accounts of the Lord High Treasurer of Scotland*. The majority of the accounts are a running list of expenses incurred for various building projects in Scotland and give a good amount of detail as to what was used in terms of architectural hardware. In 1491 a new 'inlock' was added to the castle door where charters were kept. It cost 3s.[13] In 1517 two small stock locks were purchased for use at Craigmillar. The pair cost 5s 2d.[14] A slightly more detailed entry for 1541 lists three stock locks for the dungeon of Blackness Castle.[15] A 1548 entry lists payments for 'three great through locks to the palace of Holyroodhouse, price of the piece xxij s., summa iij li. vj s.'[16] A 'great through lock' is most likely the sixteenth-century term for a large pass lock to be mounted on a door. It is unfortunately more common for locks to be given more ambiguous names in the records, such as the 1518 reference to 'great locks'.[17] The adjective refers to size.

There is evidence given in the accounts of a range in quality of door locks. In 1507, a lock was put on the 'turngree door' of an unspecified abbey, which cost 14d,[18] but a lock put on the queen's chamber door at Linlithgow in 1506 cost 14s.[19] There was a spectrum of cost for Scottish locks, ranging from simple stock locks up to more grandiose works of art.

Another job which one would think would be at the high-end of the cost spectrum was the production of yett locks. While the average burgess would have owned at least one door, not everyone would have owned a large iron 'yett', or gate. Governmental buildings and the houses of the nobility would have required yett locks. Yet surprisingly, a 1505 entry suggests that yett locks were not as expensive as one would think; 2s 6d was paid for 'the mending of the east and west park yetts and a lock to one of them'.[20] The 2½s not only bought a new yett lock, but got two yetts repaired as well.

The accounts make many references to padlocks, which came in multiple types and sizes. Again, the records do not give a great amount of detail. A 1497 entry lists a payment of 4s 2d for 'two hanging locks to the treasure kist'.[21] Larger hanging locks seem to have been considered higher security. In 1541 there was a payment 'for three great hanging locks to the prison house door in the castle and ane to the head of the tower upon the iron yett, price the piece xx s'.[22]

Size was not the only differential in padlocks. There were various forms of padlocks available at any given time. This might be represented by terminology. As shown above, some padlocks were called hanging locks. Others were known as paddock locks, as a 1568 payment for 'paddock locks to the castle of Dunbar' shows.[23] A paddock was a frog. This is probably where 'padlock' comes from. In Germany, the word for padlock is *Vorhängeschloß*. Whether or not hanging and paddock locks were different is not disclosed by the records.

The accounts also mention chest locks. In 1503, there was an entry for locks and keys to two pairs of coffers, which cost 10s.[24] In 1504, seven locks and seven keys for 'the kists in the wardrobe' cost 14s.[25] In 1503 a kist lock was about 2s.

Press locks, which were locks for cabinets, are also listed. In 1512 there was a payment of 28s for six bands and three locks for the queen's presses. Each cabinet door needed two bands, or hinges and one lock.[26] The furniture for a single cabinet door cost 9s 4d.

There were various entries for new keys being made. Keys were not mounted to buildings and therefore easily lost or damaged. One example of many is the 1491 payment of 12d for 'ane new key and the mending of ane other lock'.[27] It is unfortunate the clerk did not give separate prices for the entries of new keys. Perhaps new keys were only ordered when other work had to be done?

Aside from locks, the accounts make references to architectural hardware which might have been made by locksmiths. Locks needed fixtures in order to work. One 1495 entry illustrates this by mentioning a payment of 2s for a lock, staple and nails.[28] The nails were for fastening the lock to the door. Once through, the ends of the nails would have been peened over to prevent their removal. The staple was a 'U'-shaped iron bar with each end set into the door jamb to give the lock's bolt purchase on the jamb. A 1503 entry refers to Edinburgh locksmiths making locks and bands for 'the Friars of Stirling'.[29] In 1504, twelve bands and twelve crooks were purchased for Lochmaben, along with six locks. This would have kitted out six doors for the price of 8s.[30]

A later entry from 1513, gives some insight into how crooks and bands were mounted. A payment was made for 'lead to the crooks'.[31] After the hole was bored in the stone, lead would have been inserted. The spike of the 'L'-shaped crook would then have been driven in, forcing the lead into the crevices and creating a tension hold on the iron crook. The door, which would have had the bands attached by nails, would then have been set on the crooks.

TABLE 5.1
Sample of prices for locksmiths' products (MWA 1957)

Item	1532	1539–41	1558–94	1612	1616–19	1623
Great stock lock					54s 4d	3 li. 6s 8d
Stock lock		5s	8s	16s–20s	24s–40s	
Chamber door lock	1s–5s			20s	32s	
House door lock	4s–5s		4s			
Double plate lock						
Button lock						
Paddock lock	5s				6s 8 d.	
Key	16d–18d	12d	1s 4d	6s 8d–8s	12s	

Item	1624	1625–41	1627	1629	1633	1640
Great stock lock	3 li.		3 li. 6s 8d		20s	
Stock lock	27s 2d	32s	18s–26s	10s–30s	33s 4d	18s–30s
Chamber door lock				24s		
House door lock				18s	13 li. 6s 8d	
Double plate lock		4 li.			16s–4 li.	
Button lock			36s		2 li.	2 li.
Paddock lock						
Key					10s–30s	6s–12s

The *Accounts of the Masters of Works* is a similar source to the Lord High Treasurer's accounts, dealing only with the building and repairs done on royal palaces and castles. It lists many similar references to locksmiths' products, though often with more detail and better descriptions. The door locks included pass locks, through locks, great through locks, chamber door locks, privy locks, stable door locks, plate locks, double plate locks, boss plate locks, stock locks, pipe stock locks and great stock locks. Padlocks included hanging locks, hanging boss locks, great hanging boss locks, paddock locks, great padlocks, lesser padlocks, little padlocks and padlocks for yetts. Cabinet locks included press locks, button locks, single button locks, bordered button locks and almrie locks. There were kist and chest locks. There were pipe keys, great keys, stock-lock keys, triple, double and single keys. Shields were often included.[32] Crooks, bands, snecks, sneckheads, staples and jamb bands are all mentioned.[33]

Table 5.1 shows a partial sample of prices for a few varieties of locksmiths' products listed in the *Accounts of the Masters of Works*. The evidence is too sporadic and varied to be positive, but the data does seem to indicate a pronounced increase in the cost of locksmiths' work from the 1530s to the 1630s, which was, for the most part, significantly greater than the rise in price over the same period of basic foodstuffs. In 1540, a basic stock lock cost only 5s. By 1612, the price was 16 to 20s. In 1640, a stock lock cost 18s to 30s. Chamber

TABLE 5.2
Sample of prices for locksmiths' services (MWA 1957)

Item	1530	1536	1612	1623	1633	1640
Key and mending	1s 4d	1s 6d	10s–16s	12s–16s	4s–18s	8s

door locks also increased. In 1532, they were 1s to 5s a piece, but by 1629, they were 24s. Larger house door locks went from between 4s to 5s, up to £3 6s 8d. Keys are the most striking, as they went from 16d or 18d, all the way up to between 6s and 30s. Within any of these categories there would have been variation of quality. Locksmiths' products were becoming more expensive.

Table 5.3 is a sample of daily wages taken from Gibson and Smout's *Scottish Economic History Database, 1550–1780*.[34] The daily wages for all four categories – smiths, wrights, masons and workmen – significantly increased between 1559 and the early decades of the seventeenth century. The rise in wages for skilled craftsmen such as smiths, however, was significantly greater than that for ordinary labourers and the gap between these two groups in the workforce continued to widen in the 1620s and 1630s. As can be seen in table 5.4, the increase in the price of bread was broadly in line with the rise in wages of ordinary workmen over the same period, part of a deliberate policy on the part of the council to keep the price of wheat bread stable in real terms. If the prices of locks, as shown in table 5.1, were increasing while the income of smiths was also increasing, and the price of a staple such as bread was stable, then it would appear that locksmiths in the later early modern period would have had more disposable income than their sixteenth century counterparts. This is corroborated by the increase in locksmiths attaining guild brethrenship.[35]

EUROPEAN LOCKSMITHS' PRODUCTS

There are many foreign sources for looking at the metalwares produced by locksmiths. These are important, because a comparison of surviving locks and keys with foreign provenance shows that Scottish locks were not that dissimilar from other European types. An interesting English account, written by Richard Neve in 1726, lists the following types of locks:

Stock locks plain from 10d to 14d per piece or more
S-bitted stock locks with a long pipe, 1s 6d
S-bitted and warded stock locks very strong, 7s
Brass locks from 5s 6d to 9s
Brass-knobbed locks in iron cases, 3s
Double-springed locks, 1s
Closet-door locks, 1s 4d
Pad, (or secret) locks with slits instead of pipes, 1s
Plate stock locks 3s 8d some ditto for half that price
Plate stock locks in shute, 4s 6d
Brass-knobbed locks in shute, 6s 6d
Iron rimmed locks very large, 10s 6d
Some locks, made of iron and brass of 50, nay £100 per lock[36]

Neve states that it was 'endless to mention them all', so his list is not comprehensive. It does give an interesting sample of what was commonly available in eighteenth century England. Stock locks seem to have been the most common, as Neve listed six varieties of them. Rim locks, such as the brass and iron locks, accounted for four types. Smaller locks, such as spring locks and closet door locks only gave two entries and the padlock only one. Neve was writing a builder's dictionary, so the fact that ten of the thirteen locks discussed were substantial door locks might represent Neve's bias; the sample might not represent the English lock market, so much as the builders' section of that market. Chest

TABLE 5.3
Daily wages in shillings (Gibson & Smout 2005)

Year	Smith	Wright	Mason	Workman
1559	36	36	36	18
1616	107	144	144	80
1617	107	120	144	80
1618	107	107	144	80
1625	107	107	160	80
1626	107	107	144	80
1628	107	160	160	80
1629	120	120	160	80
1633	144	144	168	80
1639	160	160	160	80
1640	160	160	160	NA

TABLE 5.4
Price of wheatbread in pence per ounce
(Gibson & Smout 2005)

Year	d/oz
1559	0.18
1616	0.86
1617	0.86
1618	0.86
1629	0.86
1633	1
1639	0.86
1640	0.86

locks and the many varieties of padlocks are not represented.

The prices given by Neve show that plain stock locks were the most economical. Spring locks, which were usually for chamber doors,[37] and padlocks were the next cheapest at a shilling each. Above these came closet-door locks, s-bitted stock locks and brass-knobbed locks in iron cases. An 's-bitted stock lock' refers to the shape of the key hole. The profile of the key's bit was 'S'-shaped. The key hole was therefore an 'S' under a round hole. The long pipe refers to the length of the key. Brass-knobbed locks in iron cases were more expensive due to the amount of metal used, compared to a wooden stock lock.

Plate stock locks were basic plate locks which were set inside a wooden case, or 'shute'.[38] Like plain stock locks, they were not encased completely in metal; unlike stock locks, the metal parts were mounted on a single iron plate. Plate stock locks, such as 'MJ 234', in figures 5.40, 5.41 and 'MJ 292' in figure 5.42, clearly used more metal that plain stock locks, such as the one in figure 5.45. Reduction of iron lowered the cost, but even plate stock locks got slightly more expensive with the addition of the protective wooden shute.

The brass-knobbed locks in shute are more curious. This might indicate that they were a form of plate stock lock with brass knobs and a latch bolt. Perhaps the term shute had another meaning as well.

Brass-cased locks were in use from the late seventeenth century,[39] and were expensive due to their solid, cast brass case. Brass and wood were more resistant to the elements. Many of these locks survive today on Edinburgh doors.

While plain stock locks were the cheapest lock listed by Neve, their fancier s-bitted and warded counterparts were among the more expensive locks. Stock locks were also resistant to the elements, due to their wooden case. Particularly strong ones with good warding were ideal for municipal buildings.

The most expensive locks were the large, iron-rimmed locks and the £50 to £100 iron and brass locks. These had more metal and probably better construction. The latter group probably cost so much due to fancier workmanship.

The pattern of cost shown by Neve's account of English locks closely resembles some of the price

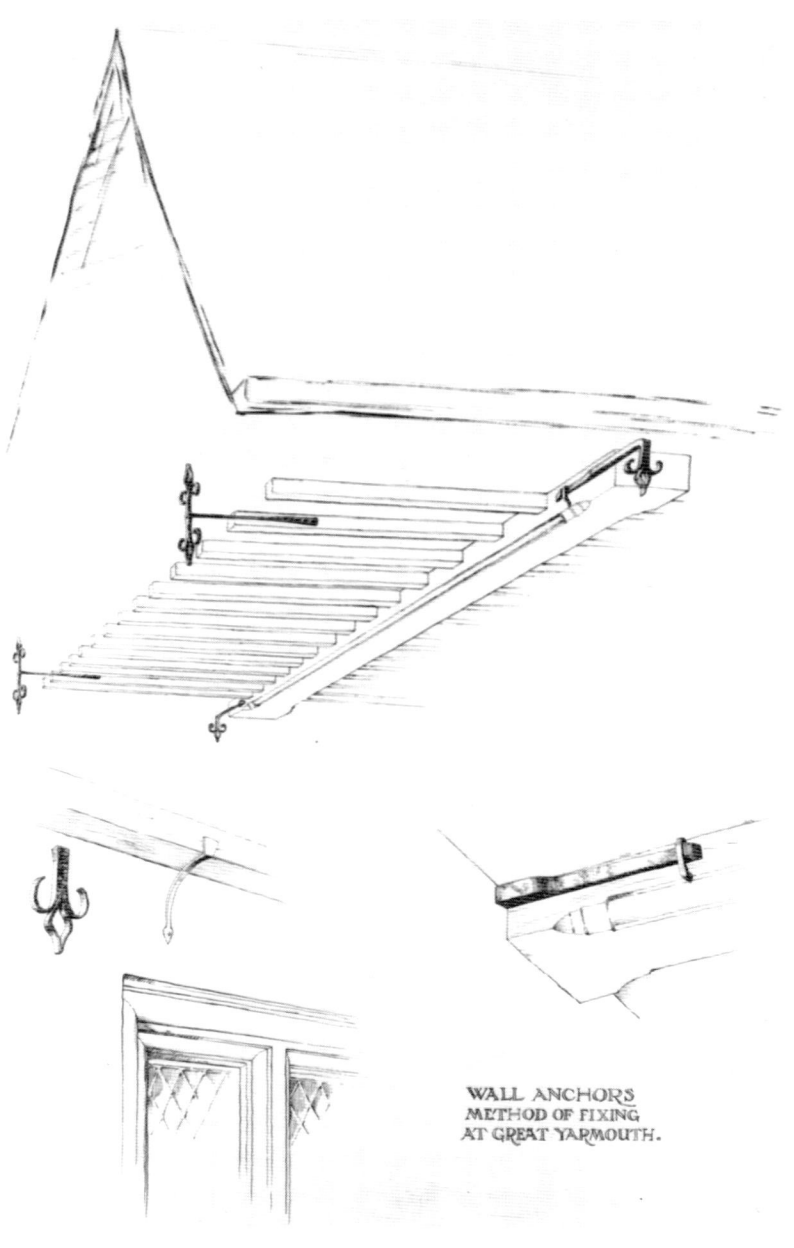

FIGURE 5.3
Wall anchors shown in cutaway illustration.
Drawing by J Seymour Lindsay (unpublished, author's collection)

differentials shown in Scotland's, *Accounts of the Masters of Works* (see table 5.1). English stock locks in 1726 varied from 10d to 7s.[40] Scottish stock locks in 1629 varied from 10s to 30s.[41] There was a spectrum of quality available.

Diderot's eighteenth-century encyclopaedia of trades is another source of locksmiths' work. The section entitled 'Serrurier' includes fifty-seven plates and twelve pages of notes on mid-eighteenth century locksmiths' work in France. The plates include pictures of locks, keys, architectural hardware and tools. One interesting item shown in three figures from plate IV, is the wall anchor.[42] Wall anchors were an architectural feature used for holding walls together. Due to the weight of roofs, walls often get pushed outward. Wall anchors were iron anchors attached to inner beams (see figure 5.3). They kept the walls from spreading. The fact that Diderot included wall anchors under 'Serrurier' is significant, as this might indicate that locksmiths in other countries also made wall anchors. In James Court, off of the Lawnmarket in Edinburgh, there are three wall anchors visible on the back-side of one of the High Street buildings.[43] If French locksmiths made wall anchors, it is possible that the ones in James Court were made by Edinburgh locksmiths.

SERVICES

The second category of locksmiths' work was services. The Incorporation of Hammermen's minute books not only talk of the products of the locksmiths, but also the services they provided. One early entry from the first volume talks of a payment for 'mending of the weekly box, the lock and the key…vij d.'[44] As it was only a repair, there was little overhead cost from iron expenses and the cost of the job was less than half the cost of a new lock and key. Iron was precious and needed to be recycled when possible.[45]

The *Accounts of the Lord High Treasurer of Scotland* also give details of the service side of locksmiths' work. In this source, many of the entries were for repairs of locks. In 1488 there was a payment for the mending of the locks and keys to the boxes 'that the Abbot of Arbroath had, iii s'.[46] In 1501 there was a payment 'to auld Alexander Tulloch for mending of two locks in the king's place in the abbey … ij s'.[47] The frequency of lock repairs in the Lord High Treasurer's accounts might be indicative of how valuable iron was at this time.

Another service shown in the Lord High Treasurer's accounts is lock picking. Keys were easily lost and locksmiths had the technical knowledge to open the locks. In 1488, there was a payment to a smith who opened several locks. The entry states that the smith was paid 'in gold forty demyis'.[48] One demy was equal to 9s,[49] so the smith received 360s for picking an unspecified number of locks. Just as is the case today, there was a high fee for a locksmith travelling to open locks. This is due to the time consumed by a smith leaving his work to go to the site where the locks to be opened are, and the overhead for obtaining or making the lock picks to open the mechanism.

Locksmiths also travelled to deliver work that was contracted from outside the burgh. In 1501 there was a payment 'to the locksmith of Edinburgh, for carrying of part of locks to Stirling to the Gray Friars, … viij d'.[50] Considering that the smith was paid only 8d, it is hopeful that he was going that way anyway.

One service that the locksmiths did not provide was installation of locks. In 1491, the *Accounts of the Lord High Treasurer of Scotland* list the following: 'Item, for a bolt of iron and lead and to a mason to make a hole and put the bolt in … viij d'.[51] The iron bolt would have been made by a smith, but the installation required a mason. Such a bolt hole can be seen in a door jamb at Mylne's Court, which was apparently built in 1690.[52] Bolt holes, slots and staples were used to hold the locked bolt when it extended from either the door's lock or its draw bolt. The nature of bolt holes required masonry skills and therefore the locks were probably installed by craftsmen in the building trades rather than locksmiths. In 1507, a wright was paid for a key, which he probably had paid a smith to make for him.[53] Other entries in the Lord High Treasurer's accounts show wrights being paid for locks. In much the same way that lorimers made parts for saddlers, locksmiths made parts for builders; they did not install the locks themselves.

The *Accounts of the Masters of Works* also gives references to locksmiths' services. The main service was repairs. Locks were mended and new keys made. Sometimes the warding was changed and the key redone to suit. Table 5.2 shows a partial sample of prices listed in the *Accounts* for having a locksmith repair a lock and make a new key. As with the prices of locksmiths' products shown in table 5.1, the data for table 5.2 also seems to indicate an increase in the cost of locksmiths' work from the 1530s to the 1630s. In 1540, the price for mending the lock and making a new key was only 1s 4d. By 1612, the price was 10s to 16s. In the 1630s, the service cost between 4s and 18s. The prices would have varied, depending on the extent of the lock's damage and the complexity and size of the key. Locksmiths' services were becoming more expensive in real terms.[54]

LOCKSMITHING: A LOOK AT THE PROCESSES

To be able to fully understand the work of a locksmith would require doing an apprenticeship and working in the trade day by day. While this study may never fully appreciate the experience of early modern locksmiths, it can attempt to look at some of the more intricate concepts involved in making locks and keys. Due to the nature of their work, these might never have been labelled or recorded; they may have taken these fundamental concepts for granted.

The first concept is security. When making the locks and keys, the smith was trying to outsmart criminals. A locksmith could have looked at a lock and known right away how high of security the mechanism was. Unfortunately, a thief who knew how to pick locks also understood this concept.[55] Much of early modern security was therefore based on deception. Hiding the key holes, or putting false key holes, were common examples.

Another important concept was that of 'mechanical motion', or 'travel'. Locks were complex mechanisms. If one part was slightly misplaced, then there would be friction on the parts and the mechanism would bind up, in either the locked or unlocked position; travel was impeded. Locksmiths therefore had to ensure that all parts moved exactly the way they were supposed to move, to exactly the correct distance. This concept could also work in favour of a locksmith. If a lock was not working, the smith could simply use reason to discover the problem. Due to the mechanical nature of the locks, it was guaranteed that there would be a logical explanation somewhere in the workings of the mechanism.

Sometimes, it was more economical to sell a new one. The old, malfunctioning lock could be recycled, as iron was valuable. If a locksmith spent all day fixing a lock which would bring him only 7d, when he could have been producing a new lock that would bring in 14d, then it is obvious which job should be given precedence. Locksmiths were businessmen and the shrewder the smith, the more wealthy and affluent he would have been. Along with the skills taught in the master's shop, the apprentice would have had to learn these concepts to make his trade viable, let alone profitable.

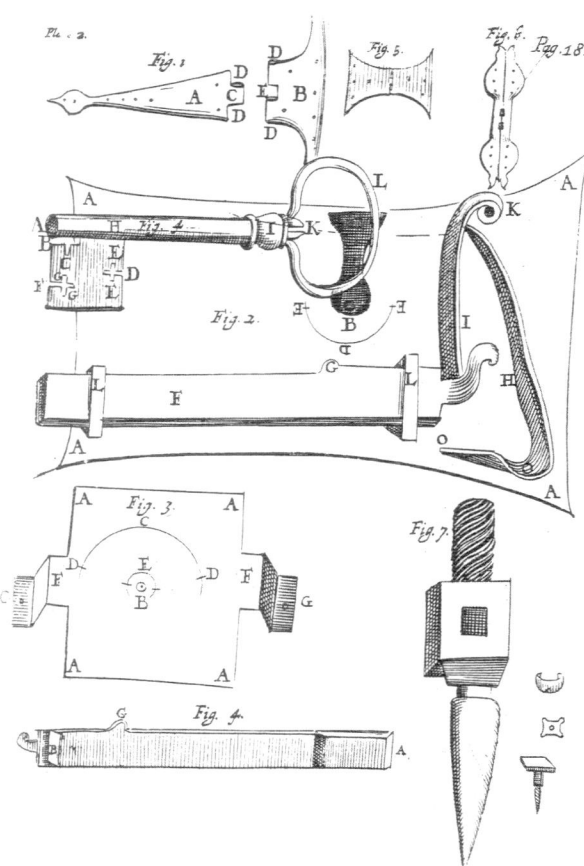

FIGURE 5.4
Moxon's illustration of a spring lock from 1678. Note the bolt, below, and key are both marked 'Fig. 4'

Joseph Moxon, in his 1678 book *Mechanic Exercises*, gave a detailed account of how a type of chamber-door lock, known as a 'spring lock', was made in England. Chamber-door locks were intended for use inside houses, on doors for chambers. They are often differentiated from house-door locks, which were used on the main door to the close, turnpike or street. Moxon's text was accompanied by a detailed picture, reproduced in figure 5.4. The explanation of Moxon's illustration is key to understanding the process and is therefore given in whole:

> In Fig. 2. 'AAAA' the main plate, 'BC' the key hole. 'EDE' the top hook, 'EE' cross wards, 'F' the bolt, 'G' the bolt toe, or bolt nab. 'H' the draw-back spring, 'I' the tumbler, 'K' the pin of the tumbler, 'LL' the staples.

> In Fig. 3. 'AAAA' the cover plate, 'B' the pin, 'BCD' the main ward, 'DD' cross wards, 'E' the step ward or dap ward.

In Fig 4. 'A' the pin hole, 'B' the step, or dap ward, 'C' the hook ward, 'D' the middle, or main cross ward, 'EE' the cross ward, 'F' the main ward, 'GG' cross ward, 'H' the shank, 'I' the pot, or bread, 'K' the bow ward, 'L' the bow, 'BCDEEFGG' the bit.[56]

The first step, according to Moxon, was to cut out a section of iron plate for the main plate (Fig. 2. 'AAAA'). This was done using either a large pair of shears or a cold chisel and cutting plate set on the anvil.

The locksmith then decided what 'depth', or length, he wanted the key's bit (Fig. 2. 'BCDEEFGG') to be. This refers to the distance from the centre of the key to the edge of the bit. This decided how big of a radius the key's orbit would have and therefore determined where the bolt would have to be put. It also decided the size of the key hole. The depth was marked out on the main plate with a compass. The centre was where the key would rest in the lock and the other arm was where the bit would travel around to engage the bolt. Moxon told his readers to leave 'about half an inch of plate between the bottom of the key hole and the lower edge of the main plate'.[57]

With the main plate set aside, the locksmith next cut out another section of iron plate for the cover plate (Fig. 3. 'AAAA'). The cover plate formed a backing for the lock. The pipe key would pass through the key hole in the main plate, make contact with the cover plate and stop in the correct position to turn around inside the lock. The cover plate was to be cut out with two wing-like pieces which were bent at right angles (Fig. 3. 'FF' and 'GG') in the vice. These formed legs so that the cover plate could stand off of the main plate. The distance between the two plates was to correspond with the size of the key's bit, which travelled around in between the two plates. On the foot of each leg of the cover plate (Fig. 3. 'GG') a hole was punched for later riveting to the main plate.

In the middle of the cover plate, the centre was found. A compass was used to find the positions of the warding. The first arc (Fig. 3. 'DCD' in figure 5.4) marked out the position of the main ward in the lock. The compass was then set to a little more than half the diameter of the key's shank and another arc was scribed onto the cover plate. This arc (Fig. 3. 'E') marked out the position of the step ward, or dap ward.

With the positions laid out on the cover plate, the smith next had to make the actual wards. Moxon described this section of the process as follows:

> you must take thin plate and with hammering and filing make them both ... hammer-hard and of equal thickness all the way. Then file one edge very straight, by laying a straight ruler just within the edge of it and drawing, or racing with a point of hardened steel, a bright line by the side of the ruler. File away the edge of the plate to that line, then draw ... another straight line parallel to the first straight line, or which is all one, parallel to the filed edge, just of the breadth you intend the wards shall be and file as before, only, you must leave two, or sometimes three studs upon this plate, one near each end and the other in the middle, to rivet into the main plate, to keep the ward fixed in its place.[58]

The wards started out as rectangular strips of thin iron plate, with two or three studs projecting uniformly from one side. Moxon stated that the wards were to go on the main plate, though he had originally started off talking about the cover plate. His illustration (figure 5.4) shows the warding on both plates.

The smith next had to shape the strips into a partial circle, or 'C' shape. This happened at a small type of anvil, known as a 'bickern'. Moxon carried on describing this process:

> Then laying the plate a-thwart the pike of the bickern, hold your hand even with the face of the bickern and hammer this plate down somewhat by the side of the pike and by degrees you may (with care taken) bring it unto a circular form, just the size of that circle you described on the main plate; which when done, you must apply this ward to the circle you described on the main plate; setting it in the position you intend it shall be fixed and marking with a steel point where the studs stand upon that circle, in those marks punch holes to rivet the studs to.[59]

This process was repeated as many times as there were wards in the lock. Once in place and the holes punched, the work would have been turned over, set on an anvil and tapped with a hammer until the studs collapsed around the outside of the hole; in this manner the wards were riveted onto the plate.

The next stage of the spring lock was the pin, or post, in the centre of the key hole (see the post in the centre of the key hole of the boss lock in figure 5.2). First a hole had to be punched through the centre of the cover plate,

> somewhat smaller than the wire you are to make your pin of, because you may then file one end of the pin away to a shank, which must fit the smaller hole on the plate and the whole thickness of the pin will be a shoulder, which will keep the pin steady in the centre hole of the plate, when the pin is riveted to the plate.[60]

With a small section of the end of the pin filed down to a smaller diameter, the end was then put through the hole until it could not go any further. The cover plate was then turned over and the pin set on the anvil or in the vice. A hammer was used to crush the protruding, filed-down end of the pin around the hole of the plate. This process was known as peening, or riveting. As the metal was hammered, it expanded, making it impossible to be withdrawn through the hole again. In this manner, the pin was fastened upright onto the cover plate.

The cover plate section was then set to the side, while the key hole was either punched or drilled. This depended on how delicate the warding around the key hole was. If drilled, then two small holes were drilled close to one another and a series of files used to expand the hole until it was the correct diameter for the key.

At this point, Moxon mentioned the making of the key, which he did not go into much detail on. Sometimes the key was already made before the lock; sometimes the key was made to an existing lock. Moxon describes the key-making process in several broad steps: forge the key, drill the end of the shank to form the pipe (see figure 5.4) and cut the wards, which were the clefts for passing over the warding. Moxon states that the wards were made by heating the key and punching out the clefts. Files were then used to bring them to the required width and depth. The key would then be cleaned and polished.[61]

The bolt (Fig 2. 'F') was the next step in making a spring lock. Moxon wrote 'you must forge the bolt of a considerable substance, thick and square at the end that shoots into the staple in the frame of the door, that it may be strong enough to guard the whole door ... '.[62] The rest of the bolt was a complex shape, which is not easily deciphered from Moxon's illustration (Figure 5.4). His description is slightly clearer:

> the rest of the bolt that lies between the two staples on the main plate, may be made very thin inwards, that is, the side that lies towards the main plate, which because it cannot be seen when the bolt is fixed upon the plate, I have made a figure of it and turned the inside to view, as in 'Fig. 4.' where you may see, that the end 'A', hath a considerable substance of iron to guard the whole door, as aforesaid and 'B' is a square stud, which doth as well keep the outside flat of the bolt on the range, as serve for a stud for the spring 'H' in 'Fig. 2.' To press hard against and shoot the bolt forwards: This bolt must be wrought straight on all its sides, except the topside, which must be wrought straight only as far as the shoulder 'G', called the toe, or nab of the bolt, which rises, as you see in the figure, considerably high, above the straight on the top of the bolt.[63]

The purpose of the toe, or nab, was to catch on the end of the key's bit when it was turned around in the lock. The key pushed on the toe, which made the bolt slide over to the open position.

Once the bolt was forged and cleaned with files, the hollow side was placed against the main plate for fitting. The placement of the bolt required precision 'that when the key is put into the key hole and turned towards the bolt, the bottom of the bit may fall almost to the bottom of the nab and shoot the bolt back so much, as it needs to enter the staple in the door frame'.[64] The bolt was attached by staples, or small 'U'-shaped brackets, which had to be perfectly placed so that the key met the bolt at the exact distance of the key's bit from the key's stem. When the key was vertical, it should have been about a half of a millimetre away from the bottom of the bolt. When the bolt's 'true place' was found, the holes for the staples which held the bolt were punched and the staples riveted over the bolt to the main plate. The bolt was then attached, but able to move back and forth easily; this was the concept of 'travel'.

Next, a hole was punched in the main plate for the tumbler pin (Fig. 2 'K'). This pin was to hold the tumbler (Fig. 2 'I') in place on the main plate. The tumbler was a long piece of iron which had a round hole at one end for pinning to the lock. The tumbler acted as a lever and transferred the energy from the spring (Fig. 2 'H') to the bolt; it kept the bolt in the closed position until moved by the key.

The spring was made of steel. It was held in place by two small tabs which fit into punched holes in the main plate. The tabs were riveted in place at 'O' and 'O' at Fig. 2 in figure 5.4. Four holes were then punched in the four corners of the main plate for screws or nails. Last of all, the cover plate was riveted in place over the key hole, and finishing work done for aesthetics.[65] Similar types of locks and keys are found in collections across Europe, indicating that the English methods were employed elsewhere.[66] Spring locks were basic mechanisms for internal doors which illustrate many of the methods used to produce all locks.

SURVIVING MATERIAL CULTURE

In 2002 I was given the opportunity to do some voluntary work for the National Museum of Scotland, cataloguing its collection of locks and keys. This task

TABLE 5.5
NMS locks and keys

Category	Scottish objects	Foreign objects
Keys	163	28
Door locks	17	0
Padlocks	54	3
Chest locks	7	0
Cabinet locks	1	0
Other	3	0
Total	245	31

TABLE 5.7
NMS keys percentages

Keys	% Scottish	% Foreign
Stock-lock keys	18	11
Pipe keys	51	54
Shank keys	23	32
Safe keys	0.006	0
Ceremonial	1	0
Groups of keys	4	4
Latch keys	1	0
Watch keys	0.006	0
Other keys	0.006	0

took about two and a half years and yielded 282 pages of data.[67] The majority of the NMS collection is used here as a rough sample of lock and key material culture. For the work of Edinburgh's locksmiths, it is not an entirely representative sample, but it is the best sample available. It does represent the material culture used in Scotland and in many cases Edinburgh. Material culture is an often neglected historical record. Alone, it can fall short of being an accurate historical picture, but used in conjunction with the previously discussed records, the NMS sample can give a new perspective to understanding what the locksmiths did in the early modern period. The sample can also give a clearer view as to how close Scottish lock and key material culture matches its European counterparts.

NMS SAMPLE

The NMS sample consists of 276 objects.[68] They are sometimes single pieces and sometimes groups of up to 25 connected pieces. An object might be a fragment of a lock, a lock with a key, or a key chain with eleven keys on it. The term 'object' is meant to represent an isolated unit. In actual numbers, there are more than 302 keys, 82 locks and 3 key-related items, but for statistical purposes the sample was grouped into 276 objects; 245 of these are thought to be Scottish in origin and 31 to be foreign. The 245 were used in Scotland, but with a thriving merchant community throughout the early modern period, it is difficult to be sure that they were in fact produced here. Several objects are very similar in style and form, possibly indicating that they were made in the same booth.

Table 5.5 and charts 5.0 and 5.1 show the breakdown of the NMS sample. It consists of 163 Scottish keys, 28 foreign keys, 17 Scottish door locks, no foreign door locks, 54 Scottish padlocks, 3 foreign padlocks, 7 Scottish chest locks, no foreign chest locks, 1 Scottish cabinet lock, no foreign cabinet locks and 3 'other' lock and key related items from Scotland.

TABLE 5.6
NMS locks and keys percentages

Category	% Scottish	% Foreign
Keys	67	90
Door locks	7	0
Padlocks	22	10
Chest locks	3	0
Cabinet locks	0.004	0
Other	1	0

TABLE 5.8
NMS padlock types percentages

Padlock type	% Scottish	% Foreign
Medieval (?)	7	0
Modern	2	0
Boss	4	33
Barrel	22	33
Ball	9	0
Bag	15	0
Triangular	4	0
Half-heart	11	0
Combination	4	0
Other Padlocks	22	33

One problem with using objects as historical documents is the question of survival and representation. Scotland's climate is not conducive to the survival of iron objects, especially ones mounted on external doors. Keyholes, windows, cracks in walls and anything that allowed a draught, brought moisture to un-tinned metal surfaces, encouraging corrosive rust. Another factor in survivability was the comparable poverty of Scotland. Metal was expensive and therefore recycled whenever possible. If locks were fancy, then they were saved and no doubt there are many beautiful locks held in private collections across Scotland; the NMS hold a fraction of the surviving material culture. Whether destroyed by the elements, recycled, or kept as heirlooms, the majority of Scotland's locks and keys did not make it into the NMS collection, which makes the sample even more unrepresentative. It has already been discussed that kist and chest locks were the primary essay for apprentice locksmiths seeking freedom of the Incorporation from at least 1586 to 1684, but only seven chest locks are included in the NMS sample.[69] Pass locks were the essay from the late seventeenth century to well beyond 1750, though only seventeen door locks are shown by the NMS sample.

Another factor in survival and representation is that people often save the aesthetically pleasing items and therefore collections are missing everyday, plain objects. While museums today are better at realizing that it is not always the 'pretty' objects that tell the best story, many of the articles probably belonged to the early collections of the Society of Antiquaries of Scotland, which was founded in 1780, and are therefore already biased.[70]

These problems do not make the NMS sample irrelevant though; written documents often do not survive either. There are no specifically urban records for Scotland predating 1398,[71] though burghs had been in Scotland since at least the time of David I (1124–53). Many burgh records do not predate the sixteenth century.[72] While the historical documents, both written and material, do not always give a complete picture, the patterns of survival in themselves can be interesting.

KEYS

As can be seen in table 5.6, keys make up 67 per cent of the NMS sample of Scottish objects, and are therefore by far the most numerous objects in the NMS sample. Their survivability is probably so high due to their size. They were easily lost and therefore highly replaceable, leading to more keys. They were also easily found with metal detectors and archaeology. Their size made for unobtrusive antiques. While a lock might have been recycled, keys were easier to keep, as they did not get in the way, were aesthetically pleasing and made 'pretty' collections. There are more keys than locks in the NMS sample, because more keys were made and more were kept.

Keys are a difficult object to classify, as there are dozens of variations. They could have been shank keys, pipe keys, or latch keys. Each of these types also could have been either a cabinet key, a rim key, a padlock key, or even a stock-lock key. The combinations of just these few examples are bewildering. For the purposes of this study, the keys will be divided into the following broad categories: shank keys, pipe keys, stock-lock keys, key groups, ceremonial keys, latch keys, watch keys, safe keys and 'other'.

SHANK KEYS

Shank keys is a broad reference to the basic type of pivot key used since Roman times. There are two particular types of shank keys relevant to this section: plain shank or rim-lock keys and stock-lock keys. figure 5.17 shows the first variety in 'MK 38'. figure 5.53 shows the stock-lock type in 'MJ 284'. Shank keys are usually noted by having a solid, cylindrical section which is thrust inside the lock. Extending from this section, known as the 'shank', is the flag-like 'bit'. Shank keys fall under the even broader category of pivot keys, as they are meant to be turned on a central axis to operate the lock. Shank keys are still used

TABLE 5.9
NMS keys

Keys	Scottish objects	Foreign objects
Stock-lock Keys	30	3
Pipe keys	83	15
Shank keys	37	9
Safe keys	1	0
Ceremonial	2	0
Groups of keys	6	1
Latch keys	2	0
Watch keys	1	0
Other keys	1	0
Total	163	28

today, though greatly modified. Of the 163 keys in the Scottish objects of the NMS sample, thirty-seven were grouped into shank keys, or 23 per cent.

PIPE KEYS

Pipe keys are keys with hollow stems. The locks they operated had pins or posts in the key holes (see figure 5.2). Pipe keys offered greater security due to the pins blocking the key hole. While a pipe key could enter the lock by sliding over the pin, lock picks had to find a way to circumvent it. The only other alternative was to make a key with the exact same outer and inner diameters as the true key; a task not easily done without arousing suspicion while going back and forth to check the progress of the pick. Pipe keys, which had a hollow, pipe-like stem, were also pivot keys. It is interesting how many pipe keys are in the NMS sample. They account for 51 per cent of the Scottish key-objects (see table 5.7). While more complicated to make than shank keys, their security was better.

STOCK-LOCK KEYS

Stock-lock keys are a specific type of shank key. It should be noted that not all stock locks used stock-lock keys; some used pipe keys, as in figure 5.45, while others used plain shank keys. The distinctive characteristic of a stock-lock key was the positioning of the shoulder.[73] Figure 5.53 shows a plain shank key, 'MJ 298', at the bottom and several stock-lock keys, with their distinctive mid-bit shoulders, above. The shoulders lined up the key to pivot around the warding towards the bolt. On rim-lock type shank keys, the shoulder was behind the bit. The shoulder stopped against the outer metal plate of the lock, with the bit completely inside. Stock-lock keys had the shoulder half or a quarter of the way across the bit. The entire shank, shoulder and part of the stem entered the lock and came to rest on the main ward. While a shank key needed at least three plates of iron, two outer plates to stop the shoulder from either side, and an inner main-ward plate to ward off false keys, stock-lock keys only needed one iron plate. The main ward stopped the key and warded off false keys at the same time.[74]

Stock-lock keys made up 18 per cent of the Scottish key-objects in the NMS sample. This is a remarkable survival rate considering the inexpensive nature of stock-locks. In 1640, a key for an iron lock was 12s, but a key for a stock lock was only 8s. A pipe key for a piped stock lock was 6s.[75] Stock lock keys are shown in figures 5.36 to 5.54.

KEY GROUPS

Groups of keys offer an interesting challenge to classification in material culture studies. One such group, 'K 2002.348', shown in figure 5.37, consists of four types of keys: shank (.2, .3), stock-lock (.1), pipe, (.4, .5, .6, .7, .8) and a possible safe key (.4). Two of the keys are for more modern lever locks (.2, .4), while the others are all of the warded type common in the early modern period. This group, however, probably dates to the nineteenth century. Should this group be broken up and added to the data of each individual item? No, this study will view the group as a whole; a single object of great importance. Not only does this group show us the physical signs of manufacturing processes, but they also show us what locks the consumer used. The owner probably did not know the difference between a stock-lock key and a pipe key, but they did know what kept their doors secure. The owner of this group, if in fact the group was not altered before entering the National Museum's care, might have had a safe, two modern lever locks and several large door locks. They had eight doors with large, modern locks. Apparently this group was found unregistered in the museum, illuminating one of the problems of using objects as documents. One of the keys was stamped by Bryden, though, so this tells us that they probably have an Edinburgh origin. Bryden was a bell hanger in Rose Street in the early 1800s.[76] The fact that a group of such expensive, large locks was used in Edinburgh in the nineteenth century offers a stark contrast to the large quantity of cheaper stock-lock related keys. Perhaps at this time, Edinburgh was more affluent. Edinburgh definitely was keeping up with the latest technology, as one of the lever locks came from a Rose Street shop in the New Town.[77]

Another, equally interesting group is 'L.1927.14'. This group of six keys belonged to the Edinburgh Incorporation of Candlemakers. It is dated 1812 and consists of one shank key for a door and five pipe keys for either doors, cabinets, trunks, or padlocks. The Candlemakers were one of the humblest incorporated trades, yet by 1812 they owned or rented at least one property. They also had possessions valuable enough to be locked up with a state-of-the-art lever lock. They were organized enough to have keys belonging to the whole incorporation, not individuals. Keys are often shown in paintings as status symbols. Town magistrates often posed for portraits holding them. The keys to Edinburgh were conventionally presented to the monarch at the Overbow or West Port at royal entries.

Pictures of towns surrendering after a siege often show the town's mayor or provost handing over the keys of the city. Incorporation officials received keys upon taking office.[78] This group of keys (see figure 5.34) had a great deal of significance to a group of craftsmen.

CEREMONIAL KEYS

Two of the Scottish key-objects are purely ceremonial. When town magistrates or conquering generals were given keys as a symbol of gratitude, these keys were often functional too. Ceremonial keys are different in that they are not intended to open any lock; they are simply for show. One of these, 'MJ 265', is shown in figure 5.36. Note the flat section of stem where a nameplate once was. These two keys make up about one per cent of the Scottish key-objects in the NMS sample.

LATCH KEYS

There are two Scottish keys which can be classified as latch keys, 'MJ 202' and 'MJ 297' in figure 5.36. The latter is for a type of lock commonly called either a 'French latch' or an 'Edinburgh latch'.[79] The Edinburgh name is due to the extensive use of this type of lock in Edinburgh's Georgian New Town. Many escutcheon plates of this type of lock are still visible on doors leading onto the streets there. 'MJ 297' was found in East Lothian.[80] The other latch key, 'MJ 202', is of another type. This one has an 'S'-shaped section which pivots to slightly beyond a right angle to the stem. Eric Monk, in his book, *Keys Their History and Collection*, states that

> The plain but strange key had a simple solid shank loosely pivoted at the last 20 mm and turning back at right angles to the main stem. The key entered a round hole of some 9 mm diameter, the end was pushed back by a spring and the key was turned to raise the latch.[81]

This latch key came from a house in Edinburgh.[82] Latch keys account for only one per cent of the Scottish key-objects in the NMS sample, despite their common use in Georgian times. There are, however, probably a great many in private collections.

WATCH KEYS

One of the Scottish key-objects is a key for a watch. 'MJ 182' can be seen in figure 5.32. It is only 0.006 per cent of the Scottish key-objects in the limited NMS sample.

SAFE KEYS

While there are several keys in the NMS sample which might have been for safe locks, many are either included with another object, such as a safe lock, or impossible to definitely call a safe key. Perhaps they only resemble safe keys. One Scottish key is known to have been a safe-lock key, but is unattached to one of the two safe locks in the NMS sample. It is 'T'-shaped, as if it were a removable turn-crank (see 'MJ 70' in figure 5.31). This means that the 0.006 per cent represented by the safe key is artificially low. There are three other safe keys, at least, included as part of the two safe lock objects.

SCOTTISH KEYS IN THE NMS SAMPLE

The key-objects in the NMS sample represent a long period of time. They include Roman keys and modern keys. There is a great variation in the quality represented; there are cheaper stock-lock keys, expensive watch keys and fancy shank-type keys with names of various members of the royal family engraved on them. The majority of them are of the higher security pipe form, demonstrating an attempt to maximise the rather weak security of early modern lock technology.

DOOR LOCKS

As can be seen in table 5.6, door locks make up 7 per cent of the NMS sample of Scottish objects. By the 1680s, pass locks were the main essay piece for Edinburgh locksmith apprentices who wished to become masters, so 7 per cent is lower than might be expected. As shown in table 5.10, the seventeen door locks in the NMS sample can be divided into four main categories: rim locks, stock locks, plate stock locks and safe locks.

TABLE 5.10
NMS door locks

Door locks	Scottish objects	Foreign objects
Stock locks	9	0
Plate stock locks	2	0
Rim locks	4	0
Safe locks	2	0
Total	17	0

THE LOCKSMITHS' WORK

RIM LOCKS

Rim lock is a term for any door lock which sits on the face of a door. They were usually placed on the inside of the door, with a hole bored through for the key to reach the lock. These four locks range in date from possibly the early sixteenth century ('MJ 6' in figure 5.40 and 5.41) to the early nineteenth century ('K 2002.333', which is not pictured). Three of the four appear to have been higher quality locks, while 'MJ 291', as seen in figure 5.39, was less substantial and possibly a cheaper lock. The sizes and weights of the other three rim locks, not to mention the decorative work, indicate that this section of the door-lock objects was dominated by the 'survival-of-the-prettiest' phenomenon.

'MJ 6' is of very heavy construction. It resembles a plate stock lock, but similar locks found at Lacock Abbey, in England, suggests that it was not used like a plate stock lock. Instead, it was probably installed directly to the door. Wood was first removed, creating a crater in which the mechanism sat. Plate stock locks often had a separate block of wood, resembling a plain stock lock, into which they were mounted. The entire unit was then fastened to the door, making a sandwich around the plate stock lock.[83] 'MJ 6' seems to have been mounted directly to the door, like the Lacock Abbey locks.

'MJ 8' is probably the finest lock in the NMS sample (see figures 5.5 and 5.6). With its all-metal construction and intricate decoration, this would have been a very expensive lock. The mechanism had a snib, which could be set to keep the spring bolts inside the lock so that the door could be opened with only

FIGURE 5.5
Large iron door lock.
(Courtesy of the National Museums of Scotland, MJ 8)

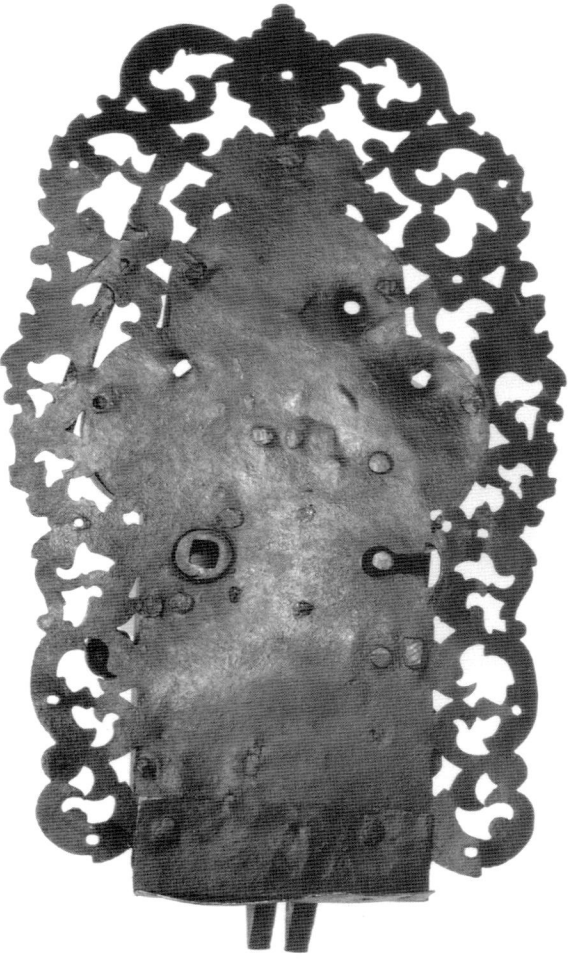

FIGURE 5.6
Back of large iron door lock.
(Courtesy of the National Museums of Scotland, MJ 8)

123

the lever handle (see the central, vertical bar with spherical finial protruding from the top of the lock in figure 5.5). It is interesting that there is only one set of warding, though there are two separate ward boxes. The key was a pipe key and could only operate the mechanism from one side. There was a ward box for each side of the door, though both were mounted next to each other. It was doubtful that anyone would ever think about picking the lock from inside the house, so warding was not included in that ward box. Metal was expensive, so even the finest of locks demonstrate economy in production.

Underneath the lever handle of 'MJ 8' is a circular stamp with the letters 'AM'. It is possible that this might stand for Alexander Mossman, an Edinburgh locksmith, but this is making a broad assumption. It is not known if this was, in fact, made in Edinburgh and whether it dates to the early seventeenth century, as Mossman did. There are somewhat similar locks in the Old Ashmolean building in Oxford, which probably date to 1683. It is possible that the decorative floral border on 'MJ 8' might pre-date the non-bordered Oxford locks, but it should be noted that border work was still being used in Ulm in 1732.[84] Unfortunately, the finest lock in the NMS sample has no provenance.

STOCK LOCKS

Of the seventeen door locks in the sample, stock locks are the most numerous, with nine objects. The inexpensive nature of stock locks and minimalist usage of iron parts in a wooden frame has already been discussed, so why do these cheap, wooden locks survive so well? It might be because the environment was kinder to the wooden case than the metal rim locks. Moxon stated in 1678 that stock locks were used on outer 'street doors'[85] but this might have been a generalization. In 1623, stock locks were listed in the *Accounts of the Masters of Works* as being put on inner chamber doors.[86] Stock locks were already less affected by the environment than iron cased locks, so indoor stock locks had a better chance of survival.

Stock locks were certainly recycled. In 1633 there were several references to mending stock locks in the *Accounts of the Masters of Works*. One lists a payment of 16s for 'ane key for ane stock lock and for translating of the lock', meaning that they changed keys and made the inside of the lock match the new key.[87] The same year, Robert Grenock was paid 24s 'for mending of five locks two of them new stocked and keys the rest mended in the work'.[88] If stock locks were so cheap,

why did they get mended? Even more interesting is the fact that a stock lock was put on the Prince's chamber door in 1633.[89] Would the king's son be given a cheap lock for his door? It seems more likely that there was a range of quality even for cheaper stock locks. Richard Neve, in 1726, did list a type of stock lock that cost 7s, compared to the plain variety at 10d.[90] The *Accounts of the Masters of Works* listed many as selling for over £3 Scots.[91] Ivor Noël Hume noted that most of the surviving stock locks he had encountered had a type of warding inside known as a collar ward. This added metal, which meant increased expense and time. Hume noted that few of the cheaper collarless main wards showed up in the surviving stock locks.[92] Perhaps so many stock locks survive, because these are not the cheaper variety. Maybe the nine stock locks, or at least part of them, represent the high end of the cost spectrum?

PLATE STOCK LOCKS

Plate stock locks do not survive as well as their fully wooden counterparts. There are two plate stock locks in the NMS sample. One, 'MJ 234', is a pipe-key lock, as seen in figures 5.40 and 5.41. It was only operated from one side of the door. The other, 'MJ 292', is a through lock, meaning that it can be opened with a key from either side, and is shown in figure 5.42. It has been noted by Donald Streeter that plate stock locks did not use the forward shoulder feature found on stock-lock keys.[93] With two plates already present in the lock, it was not necessary to save metal by making the key act off of one plate.

'MJ 234' indicates that plate stock locks were also recycled, as there is a solder visible on the back of the cover plate (see figure 5.41). It is doubtful that a locksmith would have tried to sell a lock with such a visible defect, so this would seem to be evidence of a repair and continued life.

SAFE LOCKS

This category is represented by two locks, which are both thought to date from the early nineteenth century, as they were made by Bryden in Rose Street, Edinburgh. 'K 2002.341' has a double bolt mechanism with a wheel which transfers the power of the first bolt to the second bolt. 'MJ 296' is an even more complex mechanism, combining levers and warding. These locks represent the transition of Edinburgh out of the warded age of lock technology.[94]

SCOTTISH DOOR LOCKS

It is interesting that of the seventeen door locks in the NMS sample, the majority of them are stock locks. While not as numerous as the cheaper stock locks, there are several medium to high quality locks in the NMS sample. It is possible that the stock locks are high-quality in their cost spectrum. The door-lock objects in the Scottish sample seem to represent a collection of the nicer artefacts, with only one or two lower quality locks. The periods covered by them are equally interesting, as they might span from the early sixteenth century to the nineteenth century.

PADLOCKS

As can be seen in table 5.6, padlocks make up 22 per cent of the NMS sample of Scottish objects. Padlocks survive very well, as they are small enough to store easily, but are more substantial than keys. The fifty-four padlock objects are the most diverse group of Scottish objects. Using a broad typology, there are ten categories of padlocks, as shown in table 5.11. Some of these types of padlocks were specific to certain time periods. Often, they overlapped and at least one type, the barrel padlock, was used across the world from the ninth century until the twentieth.[95]

BARREL PADLOCKS

As can be seen in table 5.8, barrel padlocks account for about 22 per cent of the Scottish padlocks in the NMS sample. Barrel padlocks were a very simple type of lock. The entire mechanism is encased in an iron tube, or pipe, with a shackle going from side to side (see figure 5.56). The actual mechanism was simple; a plate with two to three arms with springs mounted on them passed through corresponding holes in the shackle. Once through, the springs expanded, trapping the plate and arms inside the lock and barring the shackle from moving. A key had to be inserted into the opposite end to depress the springs so they could be withdrawn to release the shackle. This type of mechanism is illustrated in a 1767 plate from a French book on locksmithing (see the various components marked 'Fig. 6' at the top of figure 5.7). Bolt-type padlocks, similar in mechanism to door locks, are thought to have come into Europe in the fifteenth and sixteenth centuries, though spring-type padlocks such as the barrel and half-heart types remained common.[96]

There is a sixteenth-century engraving of torture implements from Nürnberg, Germany, amongst which is a picture of a barrel padlock which held stocks closed.[97] Another German example from *c.* 1511 is found in one of Albrecht Dürer's prints, *Der Engel mitt dem Schlüssel zum Abgrund*. Sweden also used barrel padlocks, such as the 1644 slide-key type example in the Victoria and Albert Museum's collection.[98]

Barrel padlocks are found with a variety of mechanisms, so it is expedient to make a new barrel padlock typology. The items in the NMS sample are of four main types, as can be seen in table 5.12. These types are slide-key, screw-key, 'T'-turn-key and side-entry. One of the twelve cannot be identified, as it is heavily corroded.

TABLE 5.11
NMS padlocks

Padlocks	Scottish objects	Foreign objects
Medieval(?)	4	0
Modern	1	0
Boss	2	1
Barrel	12	1
Ball	5	0
Bag	8	0
Triangular	2	0
Half-heart	6	0
Combination	2	0
Other padlocks	12	1
Total	54	3

TABLE 5.12
NMS barrel padlocks

Barrel padlocks	Scottish objects	Foreign objects
Slide-key type	5	1
Screw-key type	3	0
T-turn-key type	2	0
Side-entry type	1	0
Unknown	1	0
Total	12	1

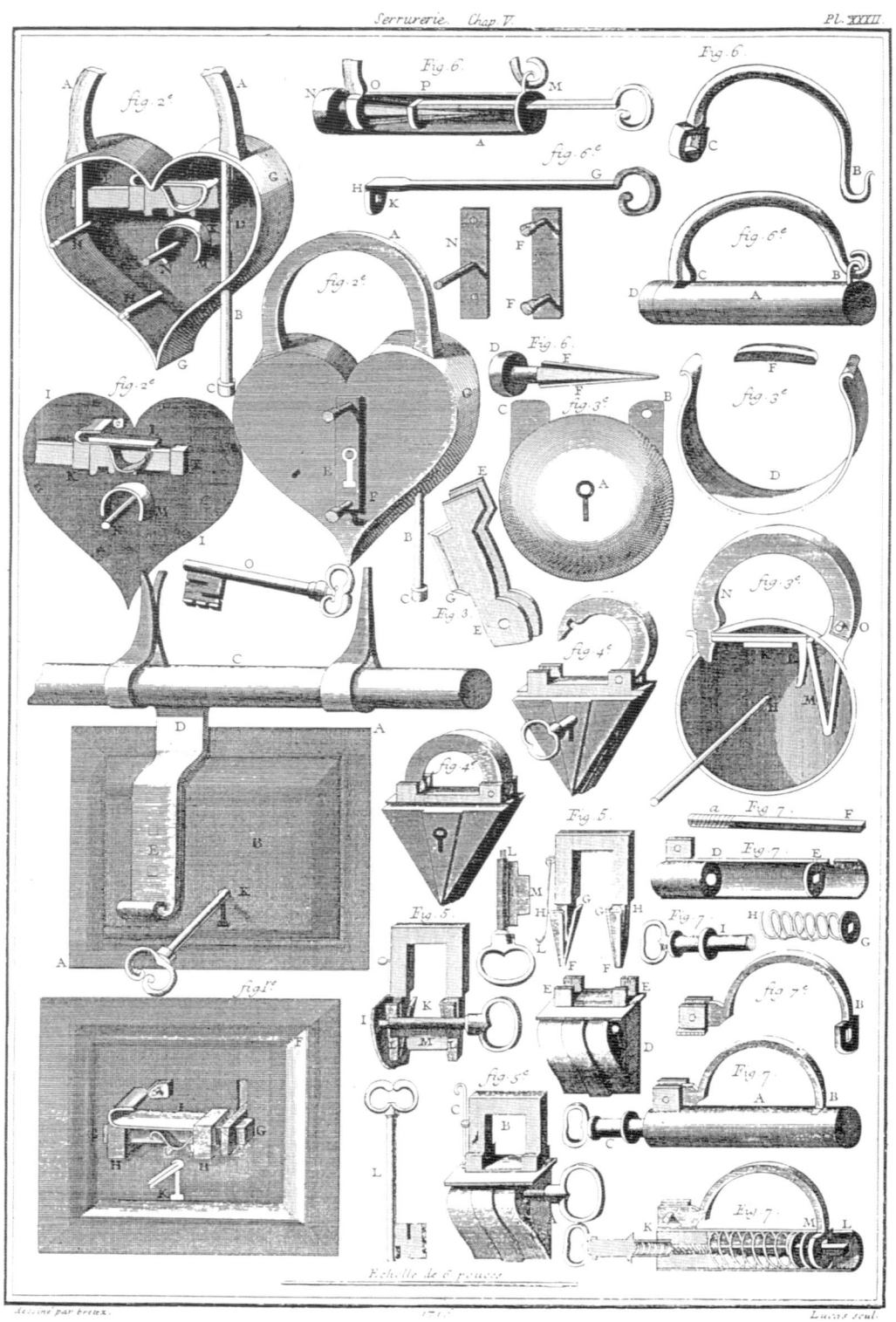

FIGURE 5.7
Plate from Monceau's *Art du Serrurier*, 1767 (Mandel 2001, 188)

Slide-key Type
Slide-key mechanisms account for five of the twelve barrel padlocks in the NMS sample. This is probably the oldest version of barrel padlock, as it was the type used by the Vikings.[99] As stated above, the mechanism's internal workings can be seen in 'Fig. 6' at the top of figure 5.7. Hume has shown that slide-key type mechanisms have been excavated in America from mid-eighteenth-century contexts.[100] This type of barrel padlock was long-lived. Figure 5.56 shows only one slide-key; the barrel padlock that went with it is now missing ('MJ 28'). The thin construction of the keys might account for their low survival rate.

Screw-key Type
Screw-key mechanisms make up three of the twelve barrel padlocks in the NMS sample. These padlocks had coil springs inside. When the key, which consisted of a pipe with an internal screw thread, was inserted into the padlock and repeatedly turned, the threaded internal pin was drawn up into the key like a corkscrew. This depressed the coil spring and eventually released the shackle.[101] A diagram of this mechanism from 1767 can be seen in 'Fig. 7', in the bottom right-hand corner of figure 5.7. See also, 'MJ 214' and 'K 2002.347' in figure 5.66, which are screw-key type barrel padlocks.

'T'-turn-key Type
There are two, 'T'-turn-key mechanisms in the twelve barrel padlocks in the NMS sample. This type of key combined the principle of the slide-key type, with a double-bitted pivot key (see 'MJ 26', in figure 5.56). The key was inserted to the back of the lock, in between two springs and then turned ninety degrees, forcing the springs above and below to compress. The arms could then be removed, freeing the shackle.

Side-entry Type
There is only one side-entry type barrel padlock in the NMS sample. This type is a combination of the screw-key type mechanism with a pivot key. 'MJ 209' can be seen in figure 5.56. Note the placement of the key hole. In 2004, the National Museum of Scotland were kind enough to have some x-rays done of several padlocks (see figures 5.8 and 5.9). 'MJ 209' has an internal coil spring, but instead of a threaded rod being turned, a hooked rod is 'caught' by the key and pulled out of the shackle. The end of the key was drilled, evidenced by how off-centre it is.

BAG-SHAPED PADLOCKS

After barrel padlocks, the second largest category of Scottish padlocks was bag-shaped padlocks, which accounted for 15 per cent of the padlock sample. The eight objects of this type in the NMS sample can be seen in figures 5.63 to 5.65. According to Hume, this type of padlock developed in the late seventeenth century and was characterized by escutcheons that swung forward and up, instead of swivelling to one side of the key hole.[102] One such early bag padlock can be seen in figure 5.63, 'MJ 22'. The NMS sample would indicate that these became the dominant padlock type in the later eighteenth and nineteenth centuries. They are of heavy construction, with finely-made keys. A Glasgow example, 'MJ 194', even has a counting mechanism to show the owner how many times the lock had been opened. Interestingly, the case has been pried open at some point. This might have been to reset the counter with the consent of the owner. 'MJ 171' and '183' also have complex mechanisms, with secret levers to expose the key holes (see figure 5.65). Hume reckons that brass escutcheons on iron padlocks were a nineteenth-century innovation, 'most of them dating no earlier than 1840.'[103] He does not state if this is based on excavations or surviving pieces.

HALF-HEART PADLOCKS

Half-heart padlocks had spring-type mechanisms, like slide-key barrel padlocks. Figure 5.7, 'Fig. 5', shows three views of how half-heart padlocks worked. On either side of the upside-down 'U'-shaped shackle were two to four arrowhead-like springs. When pushed through the top openings of the padlock body, they expanded, trapping the shackle. A key was then inserted from the side and turned ninety degrees towards the shackle, which depressed the springs so that the shackle could be removed.

There are six half-heart padlocks in the Scottish sample, accounting for 11 per cent of the padlocks. Figure 5.55 shows that these padlocks came in different sizes. Hume's study of early modern locks and keys showed a time frame of 1730–1820 for half-heart padlocks. There is a *c.* 1726 painting of two half-heart padlocks in the Magdalene Chapel in the Cowgate of Edinburgh.

BALL PADLOCKS

There are nine ball padlocks in the NMS sample, which are shown in figure 5.58. These account for 9

THE LOCKSMITH CRAFT IN EARLY MODERN EDINBURGH

FIGURE 5.8
X-rays of padlocks.
(Courtesy of the National Museums of Scotland)

128

per cent of the padlocks. Ball padlocks, or 'globular', as they are sometimes called, might have been in Europe as early as the late medieval period.[104] The Ashmolean Museum, in Oxford, states in a display of ball padlocks that they are thought to range from the 1400s to the 1600s.

There are several paintings and drawings that show ball padlocks. Lorrain's drawing, *The Liberation of St Peter*, which dates from 1640–1, is in the British Museum, London. In it, there is a ball padlock by St Peter's feet.[105] A 1658 painting, *The Siege of Spanish-occupied Dunkirk*, shows a ball padlock on a chest.[106]

Archaeology has shown ball padlocks excavated in various mid-seventeenth century contexts. They have even shown up as late as 1730.[107] Diderot decided to illustrate them in the mid-eighteenth century.[108] They were very common in Europe and America.

Another French source, Monceau's, *Art Du Serrurier*, from 1767, is shown in figure 5.7 and shows how ball padlocks were constructed.[109] The x-rays taken in the National Museum of Scotland also show construction details. The side view of the ball padlock in figure 5.8 shows that there are two parallel seams running longitudinally around the padlock in line with the shackle. The padlocks' bodies were made by forming two dish-shapes, or half-spheres, and brazing them onto a 'C'-shaped strip of metal (see figure 5.7, 'Fig. 3e'). These would have been simple to make and therefore possibly inexpensive. They would have been rust-proofed, by browning, as was done to the NMS examples, or tinning, as was done to a German example in the Germanischen Nationalmuseum, Nürnberg.[110]

'MEDIEVAL' FORMS

These four padlocks appear to have been spring mechanisms, similar to barrel padlocks in principal and half-heart padlocks in structure. 'MJ 25' is too badly corroded to get an impression of its inner workings, but 'MJ 20', '187' and '302' all seem to have been operated by slide-keys. As Hume pointed out, bolt-type padlocks in which a key turned to push a bolt out of a shackle did not enter Europe until the fifteenth century.[111] Until proof is found otherwise, it would appear that these four locks, shown in figure 5.55, were the height of padlock technology before the early modern period. It should be noted that turn-key, bolt-type locks were used on doors, so it would not have been a far jump to transfer that technology into a padlock.

Triangular Padlocks
The two triangular padlocks in the NMS sample, which are shown in figure 5.58, account for 4 per cent of the padlocks. Triangular padlocks were in use from at least the sixteenth to the eighteenth centuries, across Europe.[112] These padlocks were depicted in several mediums from c.1530 to 1629.[113] In America, they have been found by archaeologists in seventeenth-century contexts.[114] In France, they were depicted in eighteenth-century locksmithing books. Diderot decided to illustrate them in the mid-eighteenth century.[115] Another French book which shows them, was Monceau's, *Art Du Serrurier*, from 1767. It is reproduced in figure 5.7.[116]

The NMS x-rays show a few construction details for triangular padlocks. Figure 5.8 shows different angles of a series of padlocks. The straight-on view of the smallest triangular padlock in figure 5.8 shows the simple v-spring mechanism inside, confirming Diderot's eighteenth-century plate.[117] The padlocks' bodies were made by brazing together thin iron plates into the triangular form. It appears, from the largest triangular padlock in figure 5.8, that the upper section (which resembles 'Fig. 3 EGE' in the centre of figure 5.7) was recessed into the top plate of the triangular body. These would not have been difficult to make for a locksmith in the early modern period.

Boss Padlocks
In the early records, these were referred to as 'hanging boss locks', but for clarity's sake they shall be referred to as boss padlocks.[118] Boss padlocks are quite simply a boss lock with a plain square of iron riveted to the back to make an enclosed mechanism. Where the sprent band would have gone, a shackle was put instead, with the other end looping through the far side of the padlock body (see figure 5.59). There are only two boss padlocks in the NMS sample, but this should not reflect the importance of boss padlocks. One of these two padlocks, 'MJ 13', was used on the 'cage' of the Edinburgh Tolbooth.[119] This was the type of lock used in 1707 to secure the Scottish crown jewels. They were later cut off the chest by Sir Walter Scott.[120] The government certainly had some faith in the security of these locks.

Combination Padlocks
There are two brass combination padlocks in the NMS sample. Both have letter combinations, as opposed to the more modern numbered wheels. One opens to 'Farm' and the other to 'Lever'.[121] See figure 5.66.

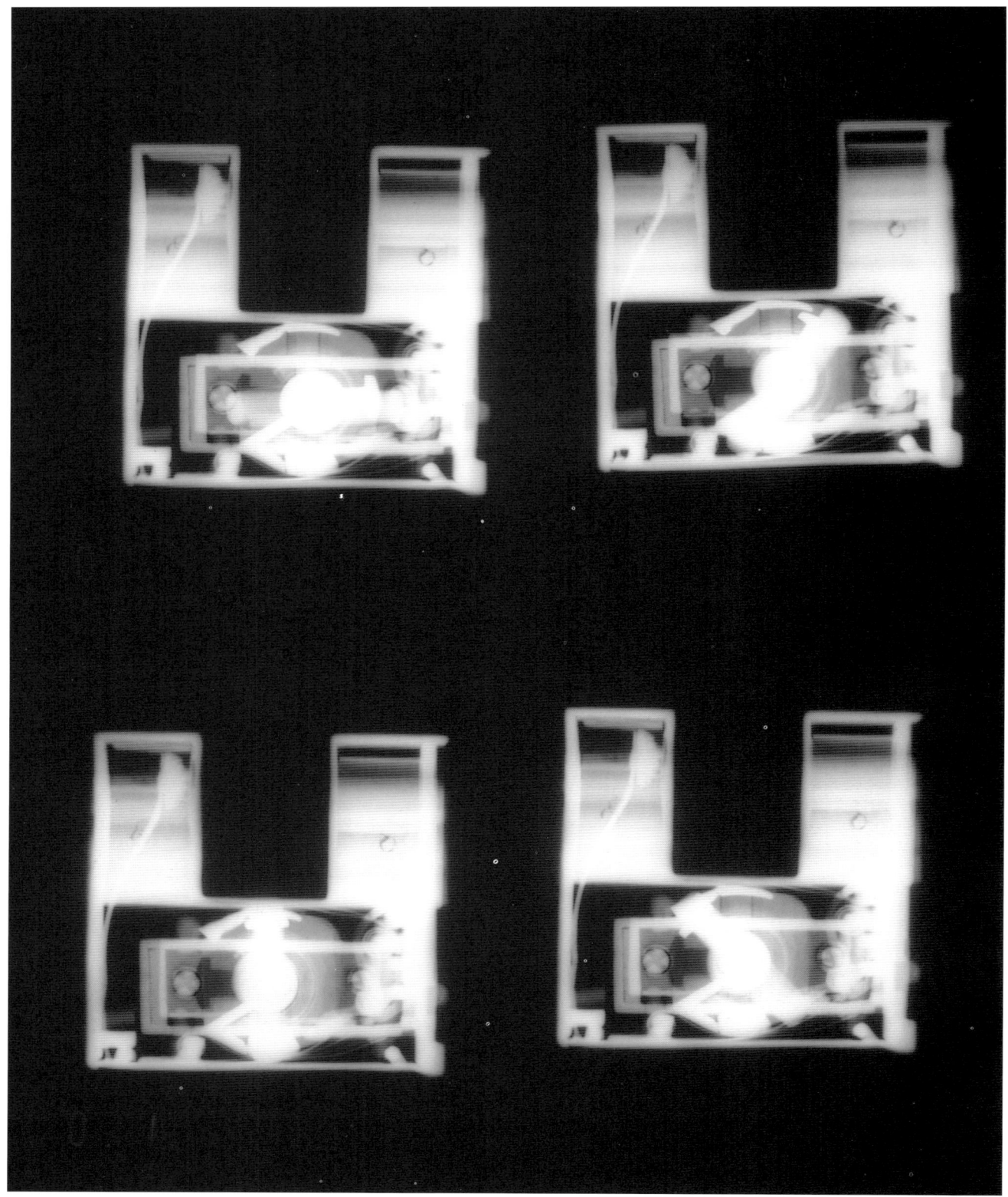

FIGURE 5.9
X-rays of padlock 'MJ 19', front view with key in four different positions. (Courtesy of the National Museums of Scotland)

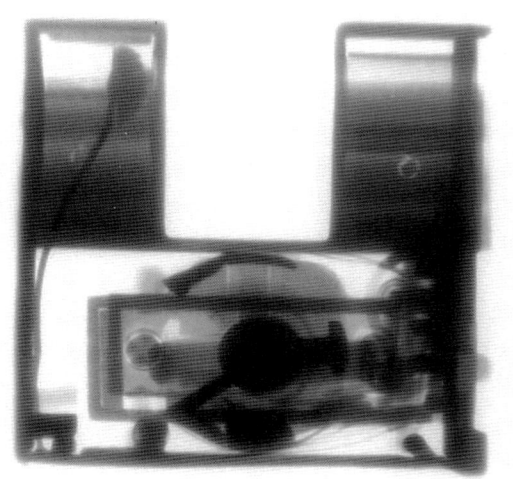

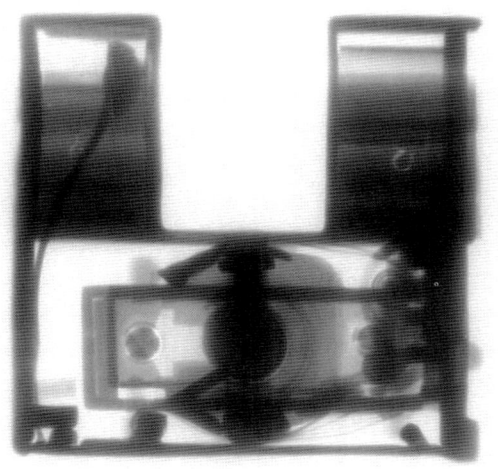
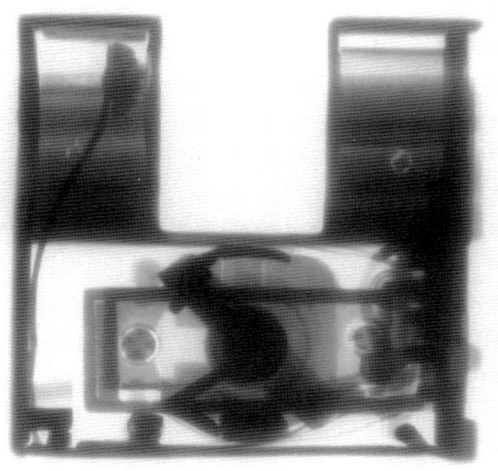

FIGURE 5.9
X-rays of padlock 'MJ 19', front view with key in four different positions. (Courtesy of the National Museums of Scotland)

Beaumont and Fletcher's play, *The Noble Gentleman*, from 1615, includes the line 'with a strange lock that opens on A.M.E.N'.[122] It is doubtful that the two combination padlocks in the NMS sample are as old as 1615, but they do represent a subsection of lock technology that came into Scotland.

'Modern' Padlocks
There is one padlock in the NMS sample which can be considered modern. It is flat and circular and made of cast iron. It probably dates to the nineteenth or twentieth century. Though beyond the time span of this study, it is still an interesting look at one of the directions locks took after the warded age. It is simpler and far less aesthetically pleasing than early modern locks. See figure 5.66.

OTHER PADLOCK OBJECTS

This category lumps together twelve padlocks that are harder to classify. Some are spring locks, like 'MJ 31' in figure 5.66, though this particular lock does not appear to be European in origin. Others, such as 'MJ 108' in figure 5.62, are of the sliding-bolt type. There is a late eighteenth century engraving of such a padlock in Diderot.[123] A few are of smaller size, while two in particular, 'MJ 18' and '19' in figure 5.57, are massive. These types of locks were found across Europe. 'MJ 19' in particular, is very similar to a Spanish example which was used to lock the town gates at night.[124] These were high security locks in their day.

The mechanism of 'MJ 19' is extremely complex. The NMS x-ray in figure 5.9 shows that there are at least two different coil springs, one main spring for pushing out the bolt when released, several bolts and various levers. An interesting item, pointed out by the Museum's clock expert, is that there is space for three rungs of warding and the key is cut with three ward clefts, but the x-rays show what might be a lack of the middle and back set of wards. The front cleft seems to be filled, but the middle and back clefts appears to be empty. Economy of metal and selling only partially filled locks were problematic in 1740s Edinburgh; apparently it was also a problem at the time and place where this padlock was made.

SCOTTISH PADLOCKS

Padlocks range from the medieval period up until modern times in the 54 Scottish objects in this category. Though there are diverse types, mechanically there are only two types: spring and bolt. The former was activated by a key which depressed a spring. There were many variations on this. The latter, which is thought to be a later development in Europe,[125] was operated by a turning key which pushed a bolt out of the shackle, so that it could be withdrawn. The NMS sample shows that both types carried on throughout the early modern period.

CHEST LOCKS

Table 5.6 shows that chest locks make up 3 per cent of the NMS sample of Scottish objects. This is intriguing, as this type of lock was one of the main essay pieces for becoming a master locksmith in Edinburgh. The records in Edinburgh often mention kist locks, chest locks and locks for coffers, but the means to tell these locks apart are apparently lost in history. The seven locks in this category (see figures 5.67 to 5.70) range in date from the medieval period ('MJ 132' in figures 5.69 and 5.70) to the seventeenth century ('MJ 9' in figure 5.68 and 'MJ 11' in figures 5.69 and 5.70). Several might be later ('MJ 149' and 'MJ 150' in figures 5.69 and 5.70). This early grouping is unusual in the NMS sample, which has a high concentration of eighteenth and nineteenth century objects.

The size and quality also varies. 'MJ 132' was intended for a small casket, whereas 'MJ 12' and 'MJ 138', in figure 5.67, were part of large trunks. 'MJ 9' is incredibly elaborate and ornate, whereas 'MJ 149' is quite plain. 'MJ 9', with its hidden lever-releases worked into the mechanism, might have been an essay, as much time and effort went into it. It is thought to date to *c.* 1627, based on a comparison with a similar dated key, 'MJ 66' (see figures 5.15 and 5.22).

Another possible essay is 'MJ 11', which is shown in greater detail in figures 5.10, 5.69 and 5.70. The construction is rather simple, but decoration was added to the cover plate on the front. The key is what makes this a possible essay. It is very ornate compared to other pipe keys in the sample. The bow is attached to the stem of the key by 'rabbit ear'-shaped bow supports, which seem to have been common in the seventeenth century. Whether or not 'MJ 11' is a seventeenth century locksmith's essay is now impossible to say with certainty, but it might have been.

CABINET LOCKS

As seen in table 5.5, there is only one cabinet lock in the NMS sample. Table 5.6 shows that this equals only 0.004 per cent of the Scottish objects. Cabinets

THE LOCKSMITHS' WORK

FIGURE 5.10
Front of chest lock. Seventeenth-century?
(Courtesy of the National Museums of Scotland, MJ 11)

were quite common in Edinburgh in Deacon Brodie's time and Brodie himself was a cabinetmaker. This type of lock was part of the essay for clockmakers in the Edinburgh Incorporation of Hammermen.[126] The one example of a cabinet lock, 'K 2002.432', might not even be Scottish. The key greatly resembles a type often referred to as English, which D'Allemagne described as 'English export keys'.[127] They are found in collections across Europe. This example might have come from a piece of furniture where the door folded down to become a writing surface. The back of the lock is extremely ornate, with floral engraving and a dragon head terminal (see figures 5.71 and 5.72). It is difficult to say why so few cabinet locks are present in the NMS sample. No doubt there are many of these locks *in situ* on furniture in the NMS collections, but only this one is in their collection of locks and keys.

OTHER LOCK AND KEY-RELATED ITEMS

As evident in table 5.6, the 'other' section makes up 1 per cent of the NMS sample of Scottish objects. The three objects included are a sliding bolt latch (not pictured), a belt hook with eleven keys and a solitary belt hook. The latter two objects are shown in figures 5.23 and 5.24. Suspension from belts was the common way to carry keys in the early modern period, as depicted in many contemporary paintings and engravings. It is surprising that more key-suspension devices are not present in the sample. The sliding bolt latch is somewhat more modern, but illustrates a common door fastening that is also underrepresented in the NMS sample.

FOREIGN OBJECTS

Were Edinburgh and European locksmiths doing the same work? The NMS sample also includes thirty-one objects given an accession number beginning with 'MK'. This designation denotes that the object is foreign. While many of the 'Scottish' objects appear to actually have come from other lands, the 'MK' group is known to have come from abroad. The foreign objects fall into only two categories: keys and padlocks.

Twenty-eight of the thirty-one foreign objects were keys. These were of similar varieties to the Scottish keys: shank, pipe, stock-lock, etc. Their places of origin range from England to Italy. Many of them are high-quality (see figure 5.13 for example). Sometimes, foreign keys were reworked in Scotland; the *Accounts of the Masters of Works* show a payment of 20s Scots for the dichting and tinning of seven English keys on 11 May 1629.[128]

Three of the foreign objects are padlocks. 'MK 7', a boss padlock is from Norway (see figure 5.59). 'MK 45' is a barrel padlock, also from Norway (see figure 5.56). 'MK 6', shown in figure 5.58, is from Sebastopol, Crimea. When they came to Scotland is hard to say, but the foreign objects do show that lock technology across Europe varied only slightly.

NMS SAMPLE: WHAT'S MISSING?

The NMS sample, while it does include a great deal, is not comprehensive. So what locksmiths' work did not survive, or is not in the sample? Keys, the most heavily represented of the artefacts, show a lack of certain types of specialist keys. There is only one watch key and two latch keys. These deficiencies can be seen by the number of watchmakers in early modern Edinburgh, or the number of 'Edinburgh latches' on New Town doors.

Door locks are one area in particular that is severely underrepresented. Only four rim locks are in the sample, though this was an essay piece. There are no brass-cased rim locks or mortice locks. A brass rim lock from *c.*1731 can be seen in a painting by Gawen Hamilton (*c.*1697–1737) entitled *Nicol Graham of Gartmore and Two Friends Seated in a Library*.[129] By this time, Britain favoured rectangular rim locks for doors. These would eventually be superseded by the mortice

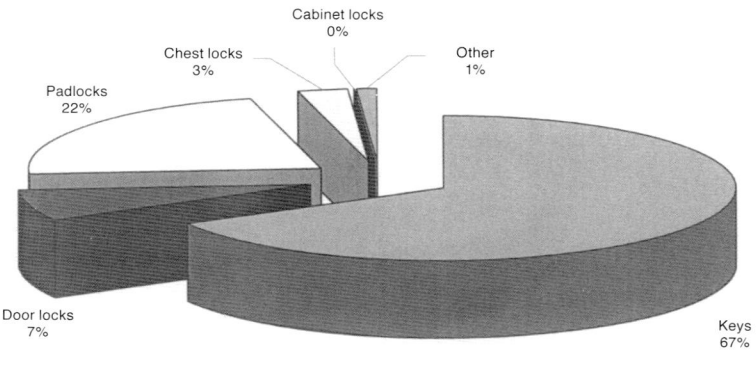

CHART 5.0
NMS Scottish sample

lock, which fit inside the door, instead of resting on it. Mortice locks were in use by the mid-eighteenth century. G. Bernard Hughes states that

> Thick, solid mahogany doors of the period prompted the introduction of the mortice lock, concealed from view by inserting it into the edge of the door. In most early mortice locks only the brass knob was visible against the polished mahogany and the keyhole masked by a swinging escutcheon.[130]

For some reason, both brass rim locks and mortice locks are not present in the National Museum's collection and therefore absent from the sample. No doubt many are still in use on doors in private houses.

Padlocks are heavily represented as a whole, but taken as individual types, there are deficiencies. It has been mentioned that there are only two Scottish boss padlocks. Padlocks were not always as well-constructed as other locks, and this lead to many being discarded and later found in excavations.

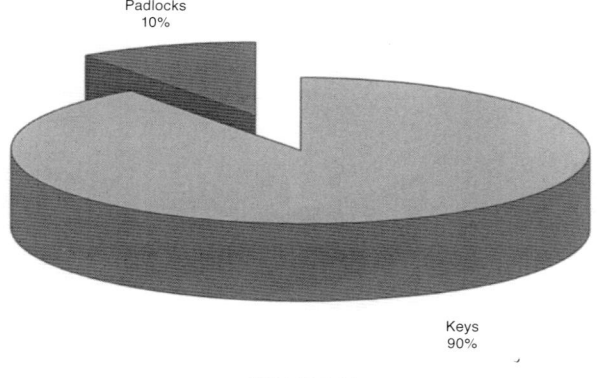

CHART 5.1
NMS foreign sample

Chest locks and cabinet locks are both underrepresented. They were both essay pieces and there are references in governmental records to new ones being purchased.[131] It is possible that the portable nature of furniture lead to them being taken away from Scotland, or kept *in situ* and away from the collection of locks and keys.

The NMS sample shows that several periods are underrepresented; the objects become more prolific towards the later Georgian era. The sample might reflect survivability increasing as the time approaches our day, or it might reflect changes in wealth as Scotland entered the 1707 Union of Parliaments and increased trade overseas.

Of all lock and key material culture, keys and padlocks survive the best because they were the most prolific and easiest to care for. This may represent a skewed sample, but it also reflects a consumer market with a high demand for replacement components of previously bought goods; a sharp contrast to the celebrated rise in demand for luxury goods.

OBJECTS *IN SITU*

There are only a few original locks left *in situ* in Edinburgh. One notable example is a chamber door lock in John Knox House. It is thought to be from the seventeenth century. Countless Georgian and later examples can be found in the Edinburgh tenements. There is a large rim lock from *c.*1810 at the Customs House in Leith. Many of these types of locks are brought in for repair at locksmith shops which specialize in making new keys for them, such as Edina Lock and Key in Canonmills. This illustrates that many warded-type locks are still in use. Outside Edinburgh, one of the finer examples is a brass rim lock thought to date from *c.*1740–50. It is *in situ* at the Old Rectory, Dunkeld. At Hopetoun House in West Lothian there are several locks, fire places and railings made by William Aitken in 1708.[132] Aitken was not a freeman of the Incorporation of Hammermen,[133] but he was a locksmith living in Edinburgh.[134]

Edinburgh also has *in situ* architectural hardware which might have been made by locksmiths. Wooden doors and their locks were often removed and replaced, but their keepers, staples, sneckheads and other fixtures sometimes remain in the stone door jambs. Sneckheads

THE LOCKSMITHS' WORK

were keepers for door latches. Door latches often involved simple handles with a sneck going through the door to lift a fall bar out of the sneckhead.[135] This system kept the door closed, but the locks were separate components on the door. A sneckhead which probably dates to 1690 can be seen in Mylne's Court in the Lawnmarket (see figure 5.11).[136] Mylne's Court also has several staples which survive in the door jambs. These would have kept the lock's bolt. Stirling Castle also has *in situ* architectural hardware from the early modern period.

LOCKSMITHS' WORK

Lorna Weatherill, in her book *Consumer Behaviour & Material Culture in Britain 1660–1760*, stated that 'Material goods such as furnishings made physical and visible statements about accepted values and expected behaviour. They were used to draw lines in social relationships, at the same time providing shelter and subsistence.'[137] This statement describes perfectly the work of the locksmith craft. Locks made a very visible statement, to the point that intricate decoration adorned much of their work and at least some simple file work graced the more humble pieces. Locks were a statement of security. They were meant to exclude the majority while giving access to a privileged few. They were a physical statement that unlawful entry was not socially acceptable. Keys were a symbol of trust and status. They were given to family members in homes and officials in organizations. Keys meant that a person had access. The problem with artefacts being used as documents is making the bridge from an abstract concept to a tangible view of people's lives, but when objects are used in conjunction with written documents, our picture becomes much more clear.

Most importantly, the sample can tell us a great deal about how the locksmiths made the items; braze seams and welding seams are visible. Evidence of wrought iron can be seen on certain keys. Spreading of metal can indicate when holes were punched instead of drilled. While not completely representative, the NMS sample can still give a large quantity of information about early modern locksmiths and their work.

THE END OF THE WARDED AGE

While there were isolated incidents of locks being made with slightly more security than others, they still all relied on warded type keys. The era of warded lock technology did not start to wane until 1778, when a locksmith named Robert Barron patented a new form of lock.[138] While the tumbler mechanism had been an integral part of the warded lock for centuries before Barron, he took the concept and modified it. By making the tumbler act inside the bolt, the tumbler had to be raised to a specific height; if pushed too high, it would bind inside the bolt. This added another critical dimension to the key and made the locks harder to pick.

Barron took this idea farther by adding two tumblers which had to be lifted to different levels before the bolt could be thrown.[139] This invention marked a revolution for lock technology. Barron's idea caused warding to fall into disuse, though this process took a long time. New technology is always expensive, so alongside a period of remarkable invention, older, cheaper warded technology held on.

Aside from Barron, there was a series of other great inventors who helped bring lock technology out of the warded age.[140] Joseph Bramah's famous 'Bramah

FIGURE 5.11
Door jamb with original sneckhead. From Mylne's Court, Lawnmarket, Edinburgh.

Lock' is still made today and still highly respected. His system was patented in 1784 and involved a pipe key with notches all around its mouth of varying depths. Each notch corresponded with a different sliding lever inside the lock. When the key was pressed down, the inner levers all fell to their required depth, which lined up a series of cuts. The bolt was then free to be moved by turning the key. Versions of this lock, known today as tubular locks, can be found on almost any payphone, vending or washing machine.

In 1790, a Mr. Rowtree took out a patent for a lever lock, which is the basic idea behind Barron's invention. Rowantree's tumbler lock used wheels inside the mechanism. A Mr. Bird, in the same year, introduced a four-lever lock, which was the predecessor of today's lever locks.[141] Cotterill's 1846 patent for the 'Patent Climax-Detector Lock' involved the principles of Bramah's lock, only with the inner sliders being positioned at right angles to the key.[142] The century between 1750 and 1850 saw some of the most ingenious lock modifications since medieval times, if not Roman. Many were chain reactions, based on variations of their competitors' products. Eventually, an American named Yale came up with a cylinder lock, based in part on Bramah's lock and in part on ancient Egyptian locks.[143] This lock is widely used around the world today. In Britain, these locks are usually used in conjunction with a modern form of the lever lock.

Edinburgh was not isolated from the renaissance of lock technology; innovation came from Scotland's capital as well. One particular example was the Bryden family, who were not locksmiths, but bell-hangers. With the Reform Bill of 1832, the road was paved for a later act on 14 May 1846, which abolished exclusive privilege of trading in Scottish Burghs.[144] The once powerful incorporations became friendly societies, concerned only with insurance for their elderly members, widows, and orphans.[145] No one could tell a bell hanger not to make locks; all occupations were open to anyone who could practise them.

The Bryden family business, in 1806, consisted of only John, who was a bell-hanger in Cowan's Close, Crosscauseway in Edinburgh.[146] In 1811, one of John's sons was working with him at their new shop at 53 Rose Street in the New Town.[147] The shop expanded with other sons, and moved to 82 Rose Street by 1827.[148] By 1832, the business not only specialized in bell-hanging, but also Venetian-blind manufacturing.[149] In 1834, they moved to 80 Rose Street, with one of the sons, William Bryden, continuing at the shop at number 82.[150] John Bryden and Sons opened a shop in Glasgow in 1852. Their trade there included bell-hanging as well as Venetian and spring-roller blind making. They kept the 80 Rose Street shop, in conjunction with their shop at 112 Buchanan Street in Glasgow,[151] a practice which would never have been allowed by incorporations.

There are several locks and keys in the NMS sample that came from Bryden and Sons, 80 Rose Street. The locks were predominantly safe locks, which combined warding and levers in complex mechanisms. The keys which Bryden and Sons produced had a particular type of bit, with an extending arm which would lift a series of levers as the key turned through the warding (see figure 5.36, 'MJ 213' and 'MJ 215'). These were made before warding had disappeared, but after new technologies were being introduced to locks. They were made not by locksmiths of the Incorporation of Hammermen, but by bell-hangers in the New Town. Edinburgh was exiting the warded age, and the incorporations were losing power.

THE LOCKSMITHS' WORK

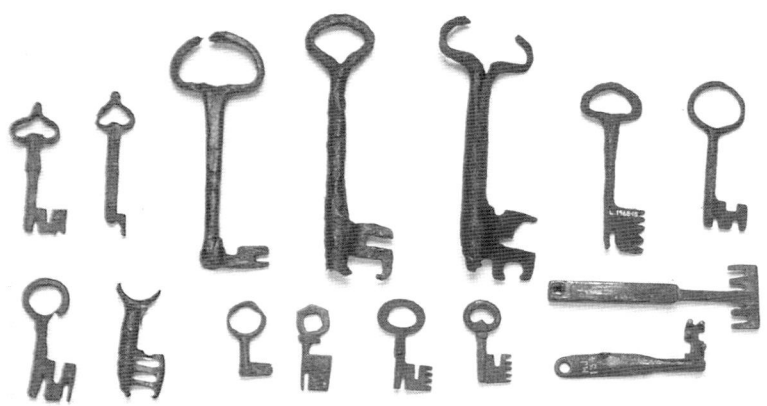

FIGURE 5.12
Keys. (Courtesy of the National Museums of Scotland)

FIGURE 5.13
Keys. (Courtesy of the National Museums of Scotland)

FIGURE 5.14
Keys. (Courtesy of the National Museums of Scotland)

FIGURE 5.15
Lock and keys. (Courtesy of the National Museums of Scotland)

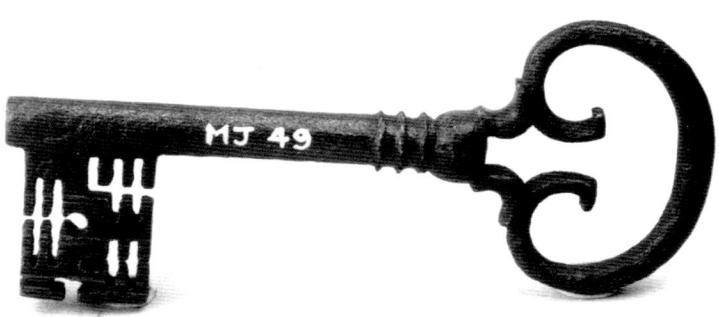

FIGURE 5.16
Key. (Courtesy of the National Museums of Scotland)

FIGURE 5.17
Keys. (Courtesy of the National Museums of Scotland)

THE LOCKSMITHS' WORK

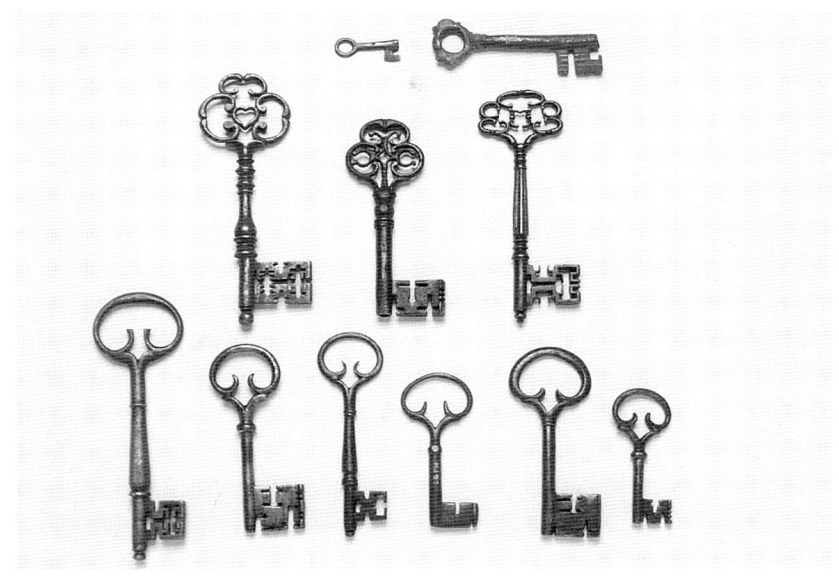

FIGURE 5.18
Keys. (Courtesy of the National Museums of Scotland)

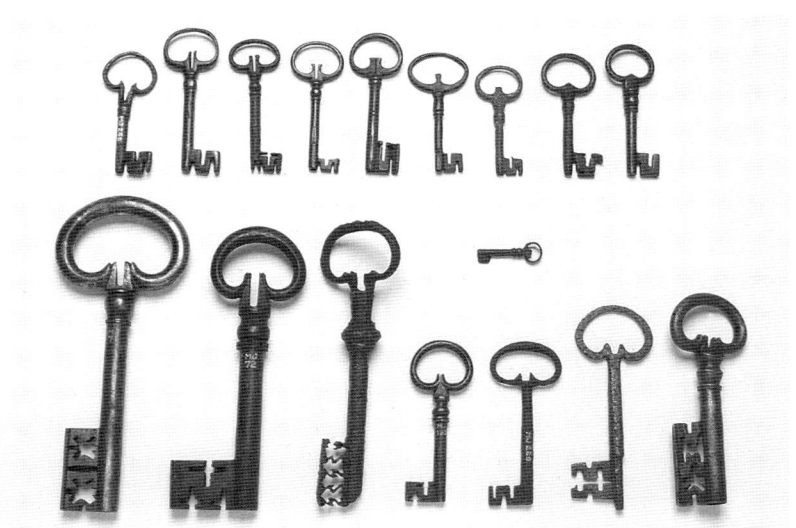

FIGURE 5.19
Keys. (Courtesy of the National Museums of Scotland)

FIGURE 5.20
Keys. (Courtesy of the National Museums of Scotland)

FIGURE 5.21
Keys. (Courtesy of the National Museums of Scotland)

FIGURE 5.22
Datable keys – 1627, *c.* 1660, *c.* 1810. (Courtesy of the National Museums of Scotland)

FIGURE 5.23
Belt loop and keys. (Courtesy of the National Museums of Scotland)

FIGURE 5.24
Belt loops. (Courtesy of the National Museums of Scotland)

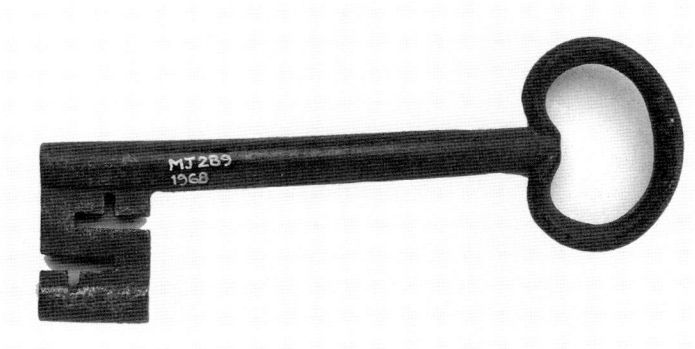

FIGURE 5.25
Key. (Courtesy of the National Museums of Scotland)

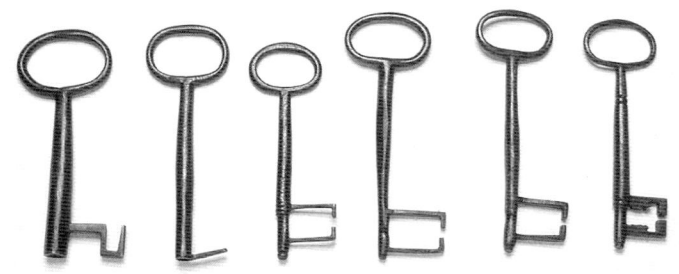

FIGURE 5.26
Deacon Brodie's picks. (Courtesy of the National Museums of Scotland)

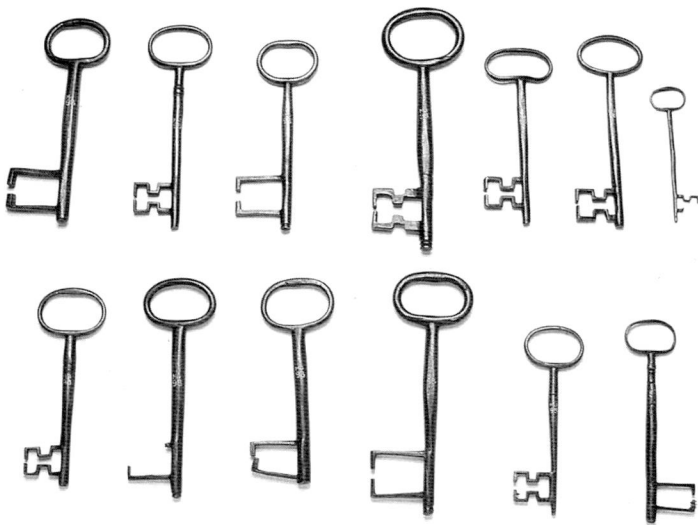

FIGURE 5.27
Deacon Brodie's picks. (Courtesy of the National Museums of Scotland)

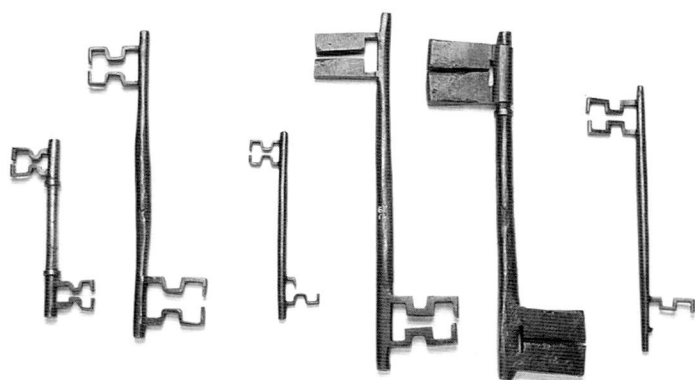

FIGURE 5.28
Deacon Brodie's picks. (Courtesy of the National Museums of Scotland)

THE LOCKSMITHS' WORK

FIGURE 5.29
Deacon Brodie's picks – detail showing thread wrapped around tops of bits. (Courtesy of the National Museums of Scotland)

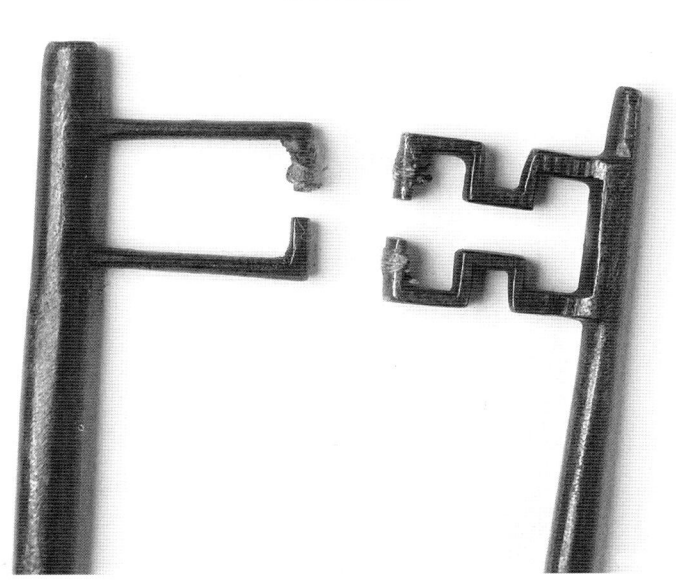

FIGURE 5.30
Key. (Courtesy of the National Museums of Scotland)

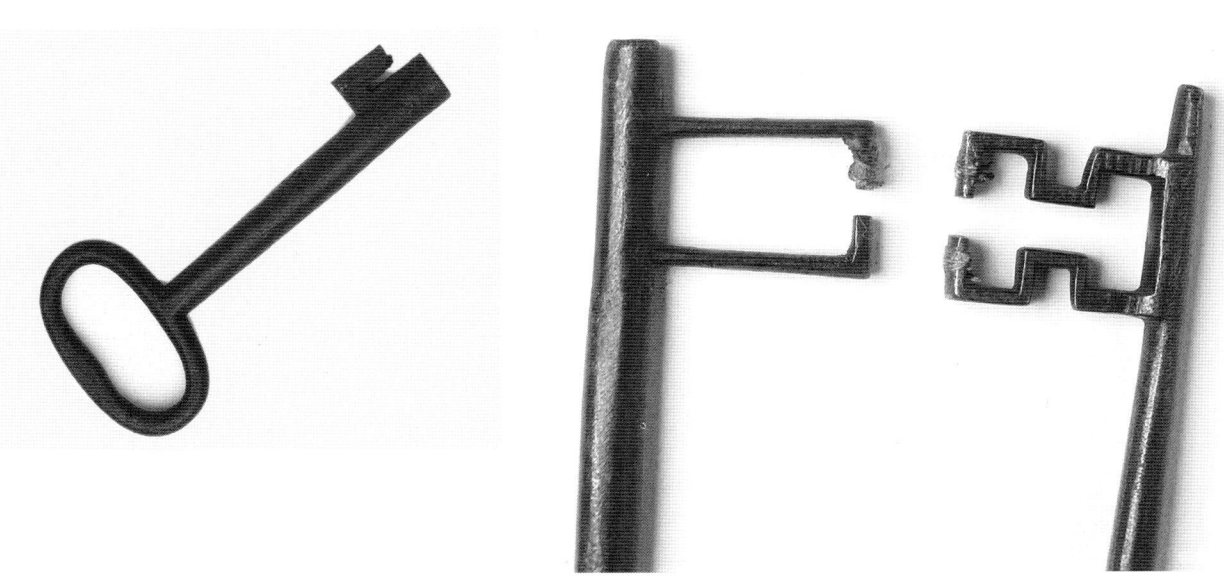

FIGURE 5.31
Keys. (Courtesy of the National Museums of Scotland)

FIGURE 5.34
Keys, 1812. (Courtesy of the National Museums of Scotland)

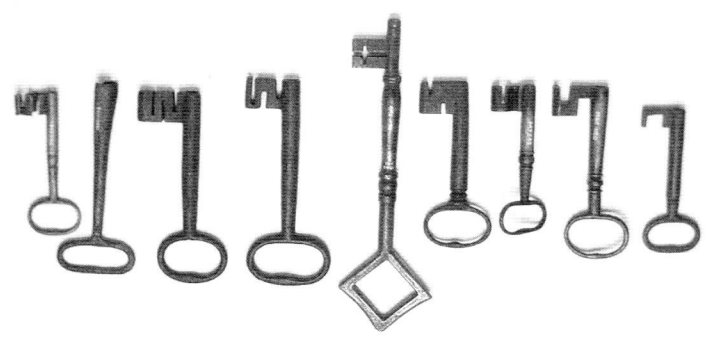

FIGURE 5.33
Keys. (Courtesy of the National Museums of Scotland)

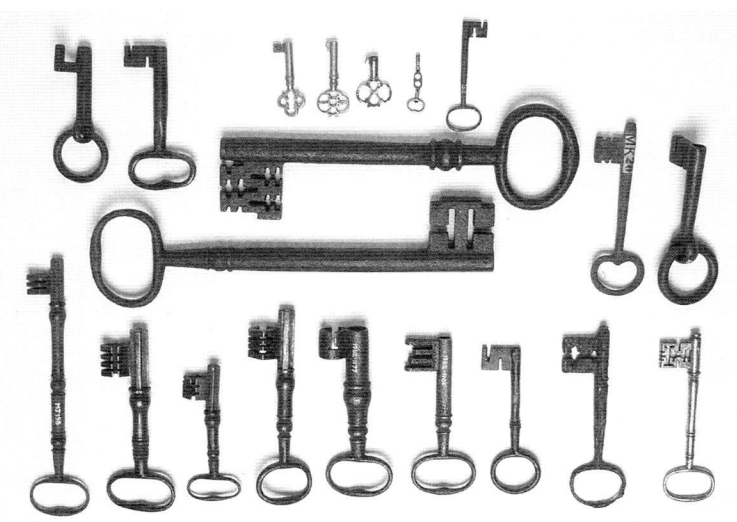

FIGURE 5.32
Keys. (Courtesy of the National Museums of Scotland)

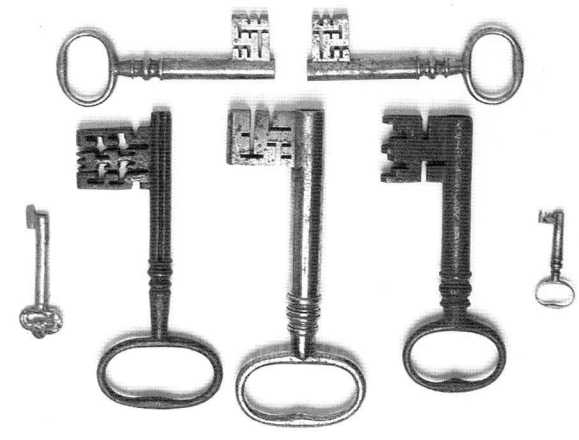

FIGURE 5.35
Keys. (Courtesy of the National Museums of Scotland)

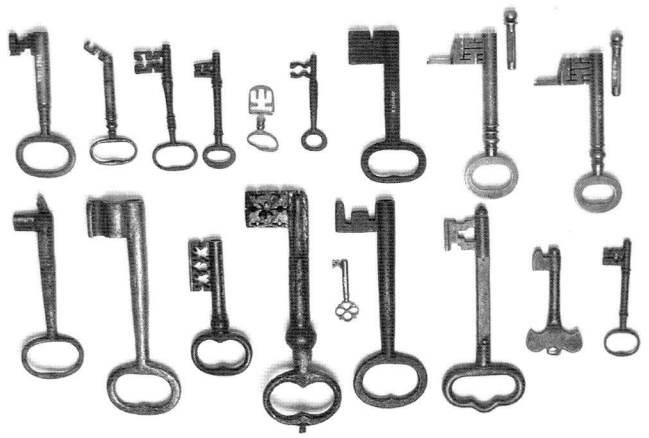

FIGURE 5.36
Keys. (Courtesy of the National Museums of Scotland)

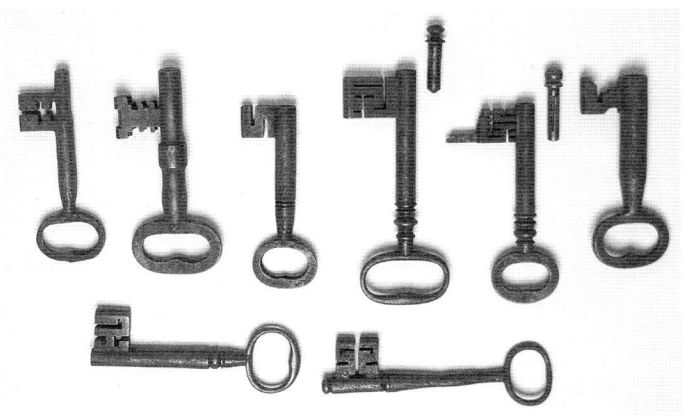

FIGURE 5.37
Keys. (Courtesy of the National Museums of Scotland)

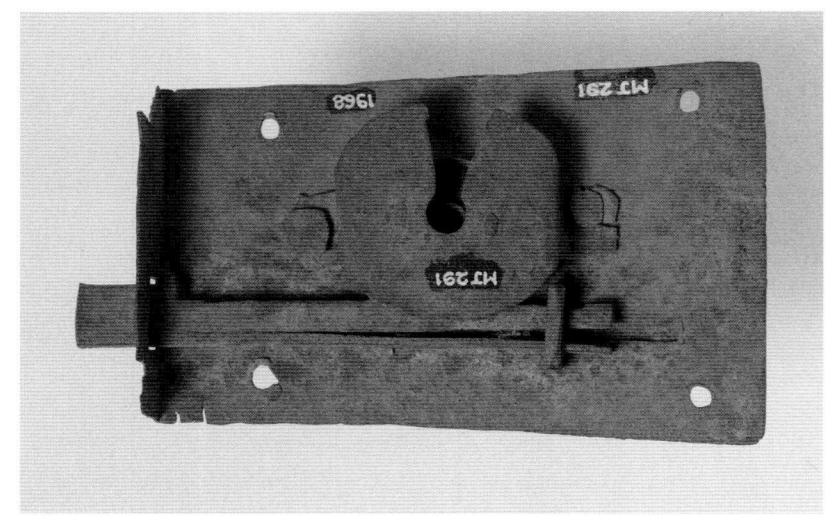

(Front)

FIGURE 5.39
Door lock. (Courtesy of the National Museums of Scotland)

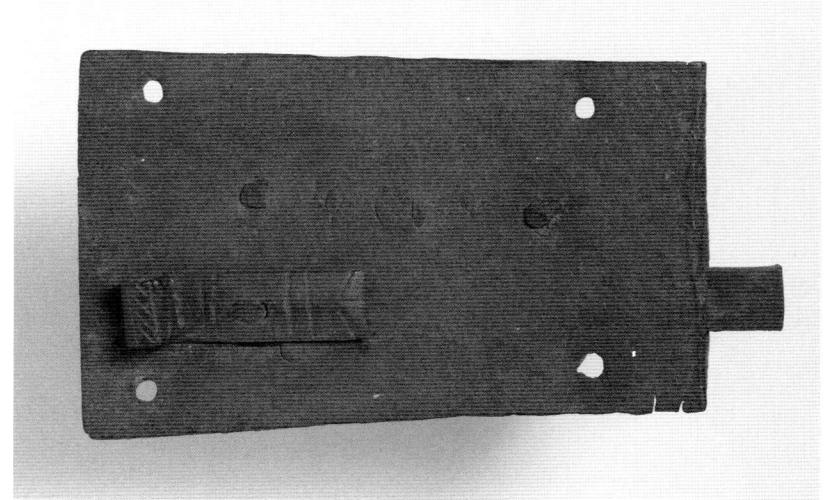

(Back)

FIGURE 5.38
Group of keys. (Courtesy of the National Museums of Scotland)

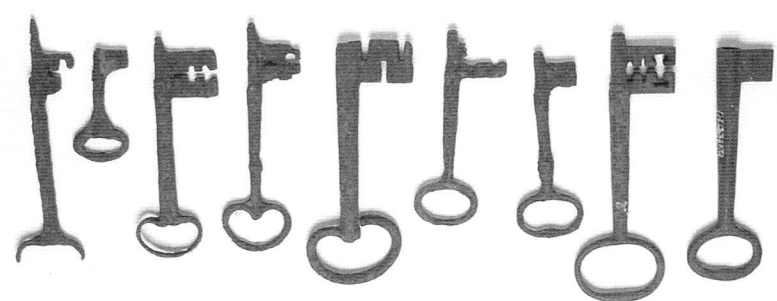

THE LOCKSMITHS' WORK

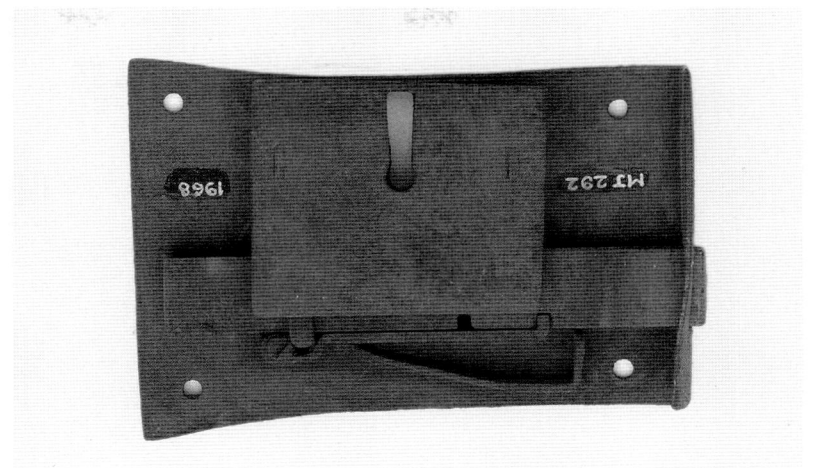

FIGURE 5.40
Door lock and plate stock lock. (Courtesy of the National Museums of Scotland)

FIGURE 5.41
Door lock and plate stock lock. (Courtesy of the National Museums of Scotland)

FIGURE 5.42
Plate stock lock. (Courtesy of the National Museums of Scotland)

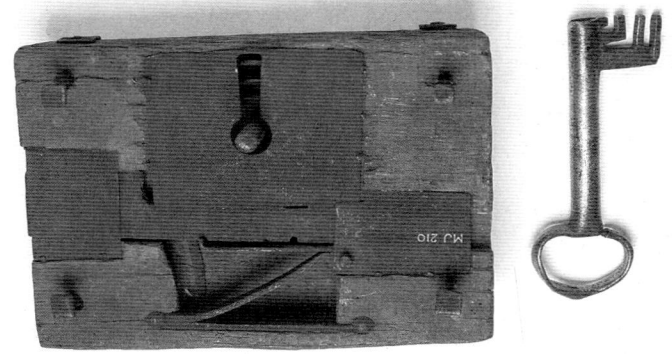

FIGURE 5.43
Stock lock. (Courtesy of the National Museums of Scotland)

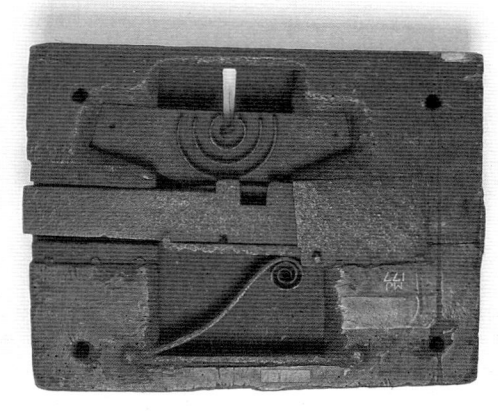

FIGURE 5.44
Stock lock. (Courtesy of the National Museums of Scotland)

FIGURE 5.45
Stock lock. (Courtesy of the National Museums of Scotland)

THE LOCKSMITHS' WORK

FIGURE 5.46
Stock lock. (Courtesy of the National Museums of Scotland)

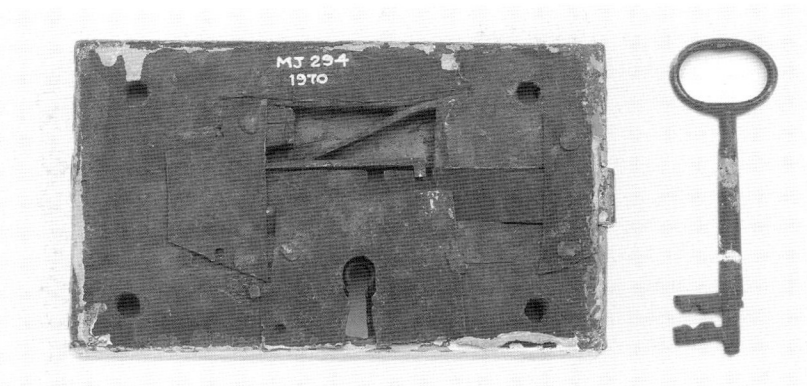

FIGURE 5.47
Stock lock. (Courtesy of the National Museums of Scotland)

FIGURE 5.48
Stock lock. (Courtesy of the National Museums of Scotland)

FIGURE 5.49
Stock lock. (Courtesy of the National Museums of Scotland)

FIGURE 5.50
Stock lock. (Courtesy of the National Museums of Scotland)

FIGURE 5.51
Stock-lock keys. (Courtesy of the National Museums of Scotland)

FIGURE 5.52
Stock-lock keys. (Courtesy of the National Museums of Scotland)

FIGURE 5.53
Stock lock and stock-lock keys. (Courtesy of the National Museums of Scotland)

FIGURE 5.54
One pipe and two stock-lock keys. (Courtesy of the National Museums of Scotland)

FIGURE 5.55
Padlocks. (Courtesy of the National Museums of Scotland)

THE LOCKSMITHS' WORK

FIGURE 5.56
Barrel padlocks. (Courtesy of the National Museums of Scotland)

FIGURE 5.57
Padlocks. (Courtesy of the National Museums of Scotland)

FIGURE 5.58
Padlocks. (Courtesy of the National Museums of Scotland)

FIGURE 5.59
Boss padlocks. (Courtesy of the National Museums of Scotland)

FIGURE 5.60
Padlocks. (Courtesy of the National Museums of Scotland)

THE LOCKSMITHS' WORK

FIGURE 5.61
Padlock. (Courtesy of the National Museums of Scotland)

FIGURE 5.62
Padlock. (Courtesy of the National Museums of Scotland)

FIGURE 5.63
Padlocks. (Courtesy of the National Museums of Scotland)

FIGURE 5.64
Padlock. (Courtesy of the National Museums of Scotland)

FIGURE 5.65
Padlocks. (Courtesy of the National Museums of Scotland)

THE LOCKSMITHS' WORK

FIGURE 5.66
Padlocks. (Courtesy of the National Museums of Scotland)

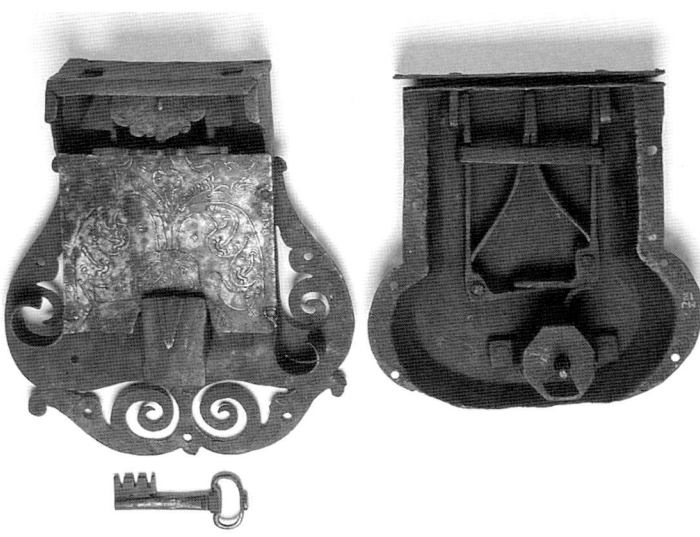

FIGURE 5.67
Chest or kist locks. (Courtesy of the National Museums of Scotland)

FIGURE 5.68
Chest or kist lock.
(Courtesy of the National Museums
of Scotland)

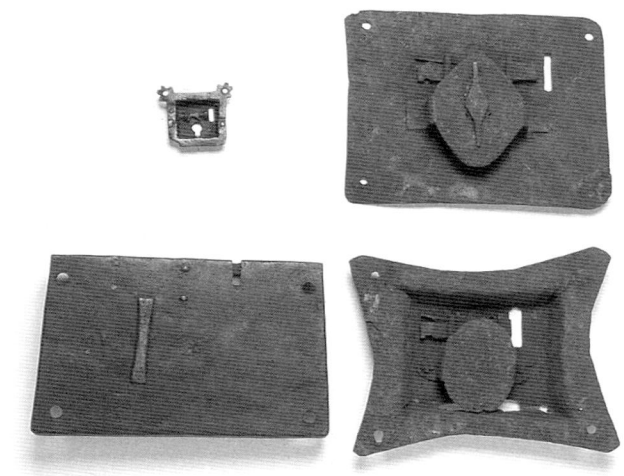

FIGURE 5.69
Chest or kist locks. (Courtesy of the National Museums of Scotland)

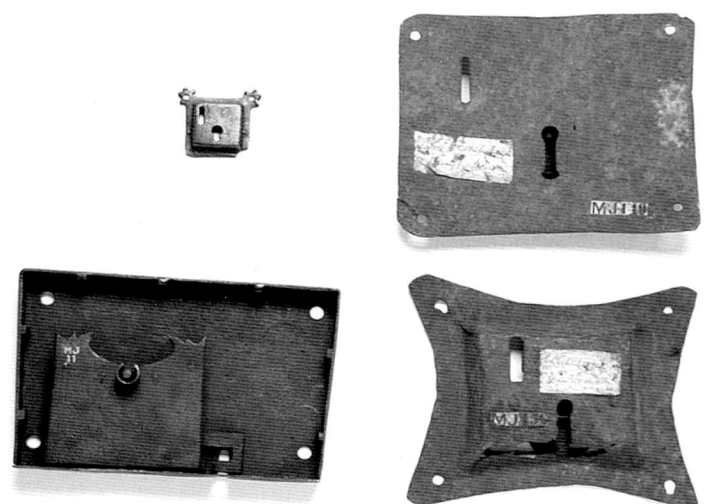

FIGURE 5.70
Chest or kist locks. (Courtesy of the National Museums of Scotland)

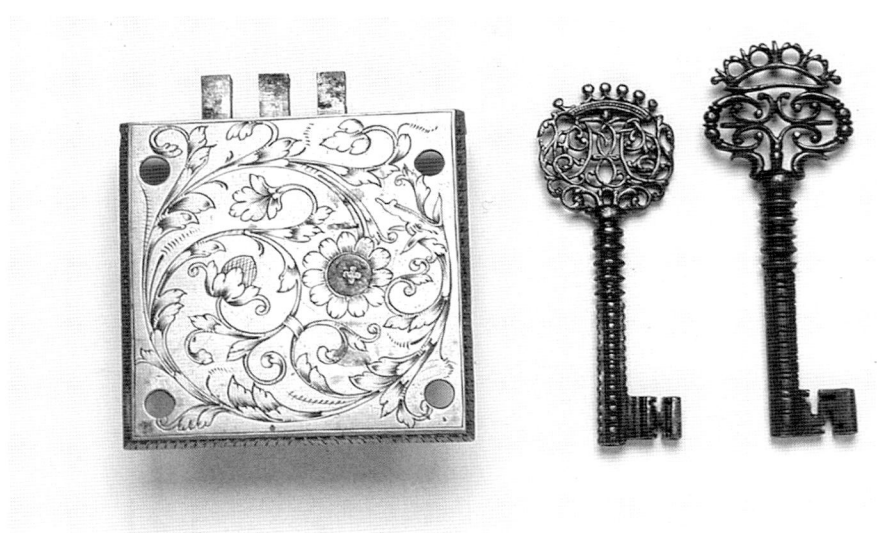

FIGURE 5.71
Cabinet lock. (Courtesy of the National Museums of Scotland)

FIGURE 5.72
Cabinet lock. (Courtesy of the National Museums of Scotland)

NOTES

1. Friedrichs 1979, 313.
2. Smith 1906, 19.
3. Smith 1906, 46.
4. ECA ED008/1.
5. Ibid., ED008/1/3, 6 June 1649 and 29 July 1654.
6. Ibid., ED008/1/4, 340–3.
7. The following discussion of essays comes from the minute books. Ibid., ED008/1/1–8.
8. 'Kist' is Scots for chest.
9. 'Rates of Customs' 1867, 297.
10. Hallett 2000, 206.
11. Hume 1969, 246.
12. 'Rates of Customs' 1867, 297.
13. *TA* 1877, 184.
14. Ibid., 1903, 130.
15. Ibid., 1907, 474.
16. 22s and £3 6s Ibid., 1911, 167.
17. Ibid., 1903, 148.
18. Ibid., 1901, 366.
19. Ibid., 1901, 348.
20. Ibid., 1901, 164.
21. Ibid., 1877, 365.
22. Ibid., 1907, 487.
23. Ibid., 1970, 120.
24. Ibid., 1900, 362.
25. Ibid., 1900, 423.
26. Ibid., 1900, 378.
27. Ibid., 1877, 184.
28. Ibid., 1877, 228.
29. Ibid., 1900, 250.
30. Ibid., 1900, 280.
31. Ibid., 1902, 523.
32. A shield was an escutcheon, or a small metal plate which reinforced the key hole. Pride 1996, 69.
33. *MWA* 1957 & 1982.
34. Gibson & Smout 2005.
35. See Chapter 2.
36. Neve 1969, 194.
37. Moxon 1989, 22.
38. The best discussion of stock locks, both plain and plate, can be found in Hume 1969, 245.
39. Ibid., 246.
40. Neve 1969, 194.
41. *MWA* 1957 & 1982.
42. Diderot 1966, plate IV.
43. Similar wall anchors can be seen in Molander 1985, 36.
44. Smith 1906, 5.
45. A 1709 English locksmith's bill with entries for repairs is reproduced in Eras 1974, 60.
46. *TA* 1877, 88.
47. Ibid., 1900, 112.
48. Ibid., 1877, 83.
49. Bateson 1987, 8.
50. *TA* 1900, 112.
51. Ibid., 1877, 184.
52. This is from the third floor, north side, west flat off the common stair. The north side of the Mylne's building might be earlier than 1690. Pinkerton & Windram 1983, 22.
53. *TA* 1901, 382.
54. *MWA* 1957 & 1982. This is again shown by Gibson and Smout's database as presented in table 5.3. Gibson & Smout 2005.
55. Remarkable examples of lockpicks survive in the NMS collection – see figures 5.26 to 5.29.
56. Inverted commas added, punctuation and spelling modified for the sake of clarity. Moxon 1989, 23.
57. Ibid., 23.
58. Ibid., 24–5.
59. Ibid., 25.
60. Ibid., 25.
61. Ibid., 28–9.
62. Ibid., 29.
63. Ibid., 29.
64. Ibid., 30.
65. Ibid., 31.
66. There is a double-bolted version of a spring lock *in situ* in Johannes Keppler House in Regensburg, Germany.
67. This data can be found in the appendices of my PhD thesis. Allen 2005 (Thesis).
68. This is only a sample of the locks and keys in the NMS; objects which were either on display or grossly outside the time period of this study were avoided.
69. Note that the NMS holds several boxes and chests with locks which were not included in this study, most notably the celebrated Darien chest.
70. McKean 2000, 6.
71. Lynch 1988a, 173.
72. Flett & Cripps 1988, 18.
73. Hume 1969, 245, 248.
74. The best study of stock locks was done by Ivor Noël Hume, in his book *A Guide to Artifacts Of Colonial America*. Ibid., 243–52.
75. *MWA* 1982, 396.
76. See below for more information on the Brydens. NMS.
77. NMS K 2002.348.4.
78. ECA ED008/1/1–8.
79. Monk 1994, 41–3. There is a superb specimen of an Edinburgh latch mechanism on display at the Writers' Museum, Lady Stair's Close, Lawnmarket, Edinburgh.
80. NMS.
81. Monk 1994, 42.
82. NMS.
83. Hume 1969, 245.
84. See object INV.Nr.A.B. in the Ulmer Museum, Ulm, Germany.
85. Moxon 1989, 22.
86. *MWA* 1982, 144.
87. Ibid., 333.
88. Ibid., 366.
89. Ibid., 357.
90. Neve 1969, 194.
91. *MWA* 1957 & 1982.

92. Hume 1969, 245.
93. Hume 1969, 245.
94. Neither are pictured.
95. Hume 1969, 250.
96. Ibid., 250.
97. Kerrigan 2001, 6.
98. V&A Museum No. M.164–1925
99. London Museum 1975, 146.
100. Hume 1969, 249.
101. Streeter 1980, 126–7.
102. Hume 1969, 250.
103. Ibid., 251.
104. London Museum 1975, 146 citing Grieg, S (date not given) *Middelalderske Byfund fra Bergen og Oslo*, 89–90.
105. Reproduced in Kagané 1995, 122.
106. Reproduced in, Childs 2003, Title Page.
107. Hume 1969, 250.
108. Diderot 1966, plate XXIX.
109. Reproduced in Mandel 2001, 188.
110. See Inv.-Nr. A 2846, Germanischen Nationalmuseum, Nürnberg.
111. Hume 1969, 250.
112. There are two beautiful, but plain examples of these on display at Johann Keppler's house in Regensburg, Germany.
113. These include a picture by an unknown draughtsman of a door in the Nürnberg Rathaus, *c.* 1530, in Mende 1979, 155, a pewter tankard with a picture of one dated 1588, in Vogt 2003, 79, a 1607 engraving with a triangular padlock on a chest in the left-hand corner from Antwerp, reproduced in Bath 2003, 85 and a Nürnberg engraving by Paul Fürst from 1629, reproduced in Coupe 1967, 242 and plate 46. See also the undated plate 112 in Coupe 1967.
114. Hume 1969, 250.
115. Diderot 1966, plate XXIX.
116. Reproduced in Mandel 2001, 188.
117. Diderot 1966, plate XXIX.
118. *MWA* 1982, 202.
119. NMS MJ13.
120. Now displayed at Edinburgh Castle.
121. NMS.
122. Eras 1974, 51.
123. Diderot 1966, plate XXIX.
124. Eras 1974, 92.
125. Hume 1969, 250.
126. ECA ED008/1/4–8.
127. D'Allemagne 1968, 85.
128. *MWA* 1982, 290.
129. National Galleries of Scotland NG2464.
130. Edwards & Ramsey 1957, 110.
131. *MWA* 1957 & 1982 and *TA* 1877–1978.
132. In particular, there are two safe locks and on an iron door in the 'charter room' of Hopetoun House.
133. ECA ED008/1. Nor was he a burgess. *Edinburgh Burgesses* 1929.
134. *Edin Marriage Reg* 1905, 13.
135. Pride 1996, 72.
136. This is on the eighth floor, north side, east flat off the common stair. The north side of the Mylne's building might be earlier than 1690. Pinkerton & Windram 1983, 22.
137. Weatherill 1996, 9.
138. Monk 1994, 27.
139. Ibid., 28 and Eras 1974, 105.
140. Eras 1974, 104.
141. Monk 1994, 30.
142. Eras 1974, 107.
143. Monk 1994, 36.
144. Colston 1891, 25. The Reform Bill of 1832 is stated by Colston as being in 1833.
145. Several still survive today. The Incorporation of Hammermen has many lawyers, but most of the Skinners are actual practicing, or retir ed skinners.
146. *Post-Office Annual Directory* 1806, 29.
147. Ibid., 1811, 37.
148. Ibid., 1827, 25.
149. Ibid., 1832, 26.
150. Ibid., 1834, 13.
151. Ibid., 1852, 58.

Summary

In the fifteenth century Edinburgh's craftsmen shifted from the older guild structure to a new system which modern historians have labelled 'corporatism' through the institution of incorporation. The Incorporation of Hammermen was one of the larger and wealthier of Edinburgh's fourteen incorporated trades.[1] From 1578 to 1730 nineteen deacon conveners of trades were hammermen, making it the fifth largest contributor to that office,[2] which met in the hammermen's own meeting hall.[3] From 1406 to 1750, 134 hammermen became guild brethren, meaning that 16 per cent of the incorporation had the wealth required to join the guild.[4] The Incorporation of Hammermen was part of a craft aristocracy in early modern Edinburgh.

The hammermen also had an internal hierarchy of the various metalwork-crafts which were incorporated. The locksmiths were one of the largest[5] and most influential[6] of these crafts by the mid-eighteenth century. They were a part of the hammermen's contribution to the craft aristocracy. Many of the deacons and boxmasters of the hammermen were locksmiths. They were the fourth largest contributor of guild brethren in the incorporation, indicating that they were not a poor craft in terms of wealth and that their products were in considerable demand in Edinburgh's metalwares market. The locksmiths were, by any measure, an important craft.

They were also a highly skilled craft. The unofficial association of the gunsmiths, clockmakers and framesmiths with the locksmiths was due to the fact that they all shared skills which would eventually be utilized by mechanical engineers. The relationship of these trades appears to have been a common one, as similar groupings were found in other European towns.

While early modern locks could be easily picked, that is not to say that they were poorly made. The security technology available at the time was easily circumvented, but European society as a whole kept using warded technology up until the Industrial Revolution – a warded lock was better than no lock. The technology available was often supplemented by clever tricks of the smiths' own design. Hidden levers and buttons concealed parts to the locks. Ingenuity made up for some of the deficiencies in medieval technology and was every bit as important a skill as hammering or filing. The workplace, tools and techniques utilized by locksmiths seem to have been relatively common across Europe. A locksmith did not need a lot of space to ply his trade, provided he had a bench, forge and the appropriate tools.

One of the best sources for learning about the locksmith art is the surviving material culture, such as the collection of locks and keys in the National Museum of Scotland. This sample shows that several time periods are underrepresented by the surviving objects. There are many examples from the Georgian period, but the early modern era is not represented as well. This might indicate that survivability improved with time, or it might reflect changes in wealth as Scotland entered the 1707 Union of Parliaments and increased trade overseas. The heavy representation of low-cost, stock-lock related items might also be indicative of the Scottish economy. It is most likely that the large number of keys and padlocks is due to their size; these objects took up little space and were easy to store.

The data from Edinburgh sources has ramifications for the metalworkers as a whole. By the eighteenth century, certain products were fading in importance in Edinburgh's economy. Armour and weapons, which were no longer in private hands, were becoming less important compared to domestic items such as pewterware, horse tack, locks or clocks. The tradesmen who made these products therefore had different degrees of wealth. While saddlers were always in the aristocracy of the metalworkers, pewterers were not. This changed over the course of the early modern period, as the pewterers came to dominate the Incorporation of Hammermen. The locksmiths, who were not mentioned in the 1483 seal of cause,[7] were by 1750 one of the more important crafts.

There are also ramifications for the Edinburgh incorporations as a whole. After the 1583 decreet arbitral more craftsmen had the option to join the guild. While never as influential as the merchants, the crafts were far more important in the seventeenth century than they had been two centuries earlier. As Edinburgh's economy grew and diversified, the production sector followed suit.

Moreover, this study has ramifications for several aspects of European urban history. Edinburgh was of a comparable size to many cities on the continent, and the surviving records provide data on the growth and decline patterns of the metalworking trades in the early modern period. While growth was the dominant trend for the metalworkers' guild, certain times and certain trades experienced decline. Some trades faded away as consumer demand shifted towards other products; some experienced astounding growth; others were remarkably constant. In a European context, this information could shed a great deal of light on how close to European trends Edinburgh was. It was shown in chapter 3 that unofficial patterns of association between craftsmen who used similar techniques and materials were happening not only in Edinburgh, but also in Ulm, Germany. Edinburgh was unique in terms of Scottish burghs, but was it also unique in terms of European towns?

The research leading up to this book has highlighted several other areas which offer possibilities for future research. First there are the minute books of the other fourteen crafts, many of which survive, though not as completely as those of the hammermen. This study represents an underdeveloped aspect of urban history: the in-depth analyses of specific trades. While there were many books on craft guilds written in the later nineteenth century, there has been precious little new material on them since then. Colston's *The Incorporated Trades of Edinburgh* was published in 1891. Marwick's *Edinburgh Guilds and Crafts* was published in 1909. While these are still very good sources for the fourteen crafts, they are dated and in some instances inaccurate. A new book on the fourteen trades needs to be done, incorporating the recently done tax and demographic analysis for Edinburgh. The collections of the National Museum of Scotland should also be utilized for the new research. There are many objects of relevance in the Trades Maiden Hospital, where many of the remaining volumes of incorporation minute books reside. A history of the baxters along with charts of bread prices, or the masons and wrights with a survey of their surviving structures, is only a sample of the possibilities of combining sources to revamp Colston's and Marwick's books. Little work has been done recently on their meeting houses and the activities which took place there. Of interest are also the occupations which were not organized into craft guilds, such as the brewers, stablers and carters. Excavations have been done on property pertaining to the brewers, which would yield much useful information. The occupational structure of Scotland's urban areas could be studied in far greater detail.

Other work which could be done includes a survey of relations between merchants and craftsmen. While the stereotype is that the two groups were polar opposites, always at odds with each other, more recent work has challenged this view.[8] The 1483 seal of cause for the Incorporation of Hammermen,[9] as well as various comments in their minute books,[10] show that there was a degree of tension between the craftsmen and the merchants. With so many sources available for the Edinburgh crafts, this topic merits further attention. How deeply engrained was the merchant-craftsman rivalry in early modern Edinburgh? How did their relationship change with the 1583 decreet arbitral?

One last suggestion for future research would make use of material culture. A recent study of clocks done by the British Museum looked at the metallurgical aspects of their construction.[11] Metallurgists analysed the microstructures of clock springs and wheels from early modern clocks. It would be fascinating if a metallurgist were to look at locks using the same techniques. How fine was the steel used in Scottish lock springs? Was there variation in the quality? Was there any variation between Scottish microstructures and European? Many keys retain traces of finishes which prevented rust. Apparently, the common finish was tin.[12] Several objects in the National Museum of Scotland have copper alloy finishes, while others have a silver-coloured finish. What was the make up of the coatings on Scottish examples?

From 1450 to 1750 there were many changes in the religious, political and socio-economic structure of Edinburgh. The Reformation brought many changes, such as improvements to education and reform of religious practices. The minute books of the Incorporation of Hammermen show that while religion was still an integral part of everyday life, seen in the many prayers and oaths given by craftsmen, the overall tone of the post-Reformation meetings was increasingly centred on business.[13] The reform of religion in all its aspects was a slow process, not completed until the seventeenth century.[14] In the interim, the internal politics of the craft incorporations went through difficult changes reflecting how fundamental religion was to society.

Throughout the early modern period Scotland's government went through a series of events which consolidated and centralized political control. By the sixteenth century, government was physically located in Edinburgh and with the advent of central law courts and a standing army, violence was less often in the hands of individuals. With the introduction of corporatism in the fifteenth century through the institution of incorporation, crafts were legalized and increasingly politicized.[15]

The socio-economic changes after 1450 did not affect the methods of craft production; as Farr states, 'decentralized small commodity production was the norm from the Black Death to industrialization'.[16] The attitudes towards who could produce and how production was funded, however, were starting to change by the seventeenth century. As described in chapter 2, guild brethren could employ other craftsmen in their booths. While this is not quite the industrial factory of the nineteenth century, or a merchant-funded manufactory, it was more capitalistic than the single-craftsman booth which was still the norm throughout the early modern period. True to the concept of 'constant returns to scale', an idea whereby growing output has to be matched by growing input of labour and raw materials,[17] craft production was taking advantage of the labour surplus and growing wealth of the craft aristocracy. As can be seen in table 2.6, the number of hammermen becoming guild brethren increased dramatically after the 1583 decreet arbitral. The craftsmen could have continued small scale, private production, but many opted for larger-scale subcontracting. This indicates increasing decentralization before the Industrial Revolution.

Across Europe, the 'putting out system', whereby merchant capital funded larger-scale production, was becoming increasingly evident. Edinburgh had several examples of this type of production in its manufactories. It has been stated that the utilization of manufactories, such as ropeworks, glassworks, soapworks, iron forges, saltpans and coal-mining operations, confirms the presence of the spirit of modern capitalism, which took off as an ideology amongst businessmen in Scotland in the seventeenth century.[18] At the end of the sixteenth century, trade in Scotland was still based on the import of manufactured products and the export of raw materials.[19] Measures were taken to change this, especially in the reigns of James VI and Charles I. One of their more important economic policies was to encourage the establishment of manufactories.[20] Many of these were set up by peers and gentlemen. Lord Erskine had leather tanning, Sir George Bruce had coal mining and Sir George Hay had glassworks.[21] Whether merchant- or gentleman-funded, the new manufactories were a diverse and prolific sector of the early modern economy.[22]

In 1641 a more systematic industrial policy was introduced, oriented towards solving the lack of capital, high-quality domestic raw materials and skilled labour, as well as the competition of superior foreign goods.[23] The various acts about manufactories were designed not only to increase the wealth of Scotland, but also, like incorporations, to provide a measure of social control in that they were designed to employ the poor. One example of this is the cloth manufactory at St Paul's Work, in Canongate.[24] With the growing number of poor across Europe,[25] these workhouses became more common.

By the eighteenth century, there was significant expansion of industry backed by merchant capital and based on changing business practices of the seventeenth century.[26] The merchant community itself was changing. Growth of numbers became stagnant in the later seventeenth century and the actual body of merchants became more institutionalized by the 1681 formation of the Merchant Company.[27] As Helen Dingwall says, 'It attempted to centralize and incorporate trading activity as well as protect privileges of individual merchants'.[28]

The bonds of the older merchant guild were loosened by the growth of larger-scale corporate trading and previously held monopolies on craft-manufacture started to slacken, though corporate control of craftsmen remained intact.[29] Certain occupations, such as medicine and law, became professionalized,[30] markets were expanded, consumer demand increased and manufactured products became more diverse.[31] Luxury items were increasingly produced for the growing presence of wealthy gentlemen and nobility in towns[32] and cheaper versions of luxury products were consumed by the growing 'middling sort'.[33] The economy of the eighteenth century was more 'diverse, extensive, and segmented than ever before, but the outlines of, and the trajectory toward, such an economy are clearly discernable in preceding centuries'.[34]

By the nineteenth century, Edinburgh, Scottish and even European societies were starting to think of the economy in new, more liberal ways,[35] which would culminate in the abolition of guild privilege. In some areas this happened sooner than in others. London's companies started to lose power after the great fire of 1666, though their committees were often important lobbies for economic regulation.[36] By 1846 Edinburgh's incorporations were no longer allowed exclusive rights to manufacturing.[37] Dublin's guild system broke up in 1840.[38] This happened in Spain in 1812, in Sweden in 1847 and in Austria in 1859.[39] Europe's corporate regime, which was so fundamental to the religious, political and socio-economic status of early modern craftsmen, gave way to more modern and liberal ideas of business.[40]

The findings of this book, when applied to a wider history of Edinburgh in the early modern period, show an occupational group which was steadily growing, a consumer society whose tastes were becoming more refined and a stunted growth of lock technology which was a feature of much of urban Europe. It is important to note that Edinburgh was not alone; most of these changes were characteristic of a broader, European context, illustrating that Edinburgh was a thoroughly European town. 'Europeanness', however, is not easy to define. While similarities can be found in all urban centres, differences existed too. Many of the overall trends affecting Europe also touched Edinburgh. Corporatism is one of the most important in terms of the locksmiths. While it is true that not all of Europe's cities were affected by corporatism at the same time,[41] most of them accepted the corporate regime at some point between 1450 and 1750. Edinburgh's incorporations did have a lot in common with corporations in other towns. The groupings of certain occupations, the tools, techniques and workplaces, and the types of products made, were all similar to those of other towns of comparable size. Many of the approaches to exclusion, training and governing were also similar. While there were subtle differences, the overall experiences of urban craftsmen in the early modern period were strikingly similar. The 'European town' may not be an absolute, but Edinburgh had more in common with it than not. Edinburgh was a European capital and much of the security-related material culture used in Scotland was also used on the Continent. The locksmith craft emphasizes the fact that Edinburgh was a distinctively European town.

NOTES

[1] Lynch 1988, 274, 276 and Dingwall 1994, 77.
[2] ECA *An Historical Sketch of the Municipal Constitution of the City of Edinburgh* 1826, 75.
[3] Dingwall 1995, 36.
[4] See tables 2.6 and 2.7. *Edinburgh Burgesses* 1929
[5] See tables 1.4 and 2.0.
[6] See tables 2.8, 2.11 and 2.12.
[7] See appendix.
[8] Lynch 1981, 49.
[9] See appendix.
[10] ECA ED008/1/7, 76.
[11] Wayman 2000
[12] *MWA* 1982, 290.
[13] ECA ED008/1.
[14] Lynch 2000, 281.
[15] For example, there was an increase in craft councillors from two to six in 1583. Lynch 1981, 16–17.
[16] Farr 2000, 55.
[17] Ibid., 50.
[18] Marshall 1992, 129–30.
[19] Ibid., 130.
[20] Turnbull 2001, 25.
[21] Donaldson 1998, 258.
[22] Marshall 1992, 130.
[23] Ibid., 131.
[24] Harris 2002, 100, 508.
[25] Farr 2000, 15.
[26] Turnbull 2001, 38.
[27] Dingwall 1994, 274, 196 and 174, and Houston 1994, 358.
[28] Dingwall 1994, 274.
[29] Ibid., 174, 180–1, 274, and ECA ED008/1.
[30] Dingwall 1995, 9 and Dingwall 1994, 215
[31] Farr 2000, 49
[32] Ibid., 62. Edinburgh had more workers in luxury trades than other Scottish burghs. Whyte 1995, 206, and Whyte 1987.
[33] Lynch 1989, 88.
[34] Farr 2000, 53.
[35] Ibid., 276. This idea is today called 'liberalism'.
[36] Gadd & Wallis 2002, 163–4.
[37] Colston 1891, 25.
[38] Webb 1929, 241.
[39] Farr 2000, 282.
[40] This was not, of course, an overnight process, much of it started in the eighteenth century. Ibid., 278.
[41] Frankfurt on the Main did not experience corporatism until 1617. Soliday 1974, 142–3. Nürenberg's town council did not allow corporatism. Strauss 1966, 97.

Appendix: 1483 Seal of Cause

SEAL OF CAUSE FOR THE INCORPORATION OF HAMMERMEN OF EDINBURGH[1]

2ND MAY 1483

Till all and sindrie quhais knawledge thir present lettres salcum, Sir Patrik Baroun of Spittalfield knycht and provest of Edinburgh, Patrik Balbyrnie of that ilk, Dauid Craufuird of St Gely Grange, and Archibald Todrik, baillies of the said burgh, with the consent and advyse of the counsall of the samyn, greting, Forsamekill as the hedismen and maisteris of the Hammermen craft, bayth blaksmythis, goldsmythis, lorymeris, saidlaris, cutlaris, buclar makaris, armoreris, and all vtharis, within the said burgh of Edinburgh, the day of the daitt of thir present lettres, presentit thair bill of supplication till ws beseikand reformatioun and remeid of the greitt iniuris and skaythis done to thame, as was contenit in thair said bill, of the quilkis thair followis a pairt, that thairthrow the said iniuris and vtharis may be eschewit in tyme to cum, sen thay depend thairvpoun, and in lyikwis vpoun the honor and worschip of the said burgh, als weill as vpoun thair singular availl and proffit: In the first thair complaint buir and specifyit that thay war rycht havely hurt and put to greit poverty throw the doun cumming of the blak money, walking [and] warding, and in the payment of zeldis and extentis quhilkis thay war compellit to do be vse, and to be compellit thairto be our Lordis authoritie mandimentis and chargis, and in lyik wyis that thay wer havely hurt be the dayly mercat maid throu the hie streitt in cramis, and on the baksyde the toun in bachling of hammermenis werk pertening to thame of thair craft, in greit dishonour to the burgh, and inbraking of the auld gude rule and statutes of thair craft, and vpoun vther skathis that thay sustenit in defalt of reformation. We heirfoir, havand etc., till equitie and justice of remeid, considering weill thair supplicatioun and iust petition according to the gud reule of the burgh, haf statute and ordanit, and be thir oure letteris statutis and ordanis, that na hammerman, maister, feit man, servand nor vtharis, tak vpoun hand fra this tyme furth till exerce or vse ony ma craftis bot alanerly ane, and to live thairvpoun, sua that his vther brether and craftismen of the saidis craftis be not hurt throu his large exercitioun and exceeding of boundis. Item, that thair sall [be] na oppin mercat vsit ony of the saidis craftis, or werk pertening to thame of thair craft, vpoun the hie strettis, nor in crammis vpoun buirdes, nor bachlit nor schawn in handis, for to sell in na pairt foir nor baksyde within this burgh, bot alanerly on the mercat day. Item, that upoun ilk Settirday efternone tua or thre of the worthiest maisters and maist knawledge of the saidis craftis quhilk sall haif powar with ane officiar with thame to pas serch and se all mennis work of the said craftis, gif it be sufficient in stuff and workmanschip gude worth and hable work to serve the Kingis liegis with and quhair it beis fundin faltiue to forbid the samyn to be sauld vnder the pane of escheitt as oft as it happinis to be fundin faltiue. Item, that all vnfre hammermen baith buith-halderis and vtharis fra this tyme furth cum to the maisteris of the saidis craftis or he be maid maister, to be examinat gif he be worthy thairto, and than he to be maid freman gif he beis fundin sufficient, and do his dewty to the toun and craft and to the altar as vtharis dois, ans set up buith, and gif he beis sufficient in his craft, and not of powar to mak his expenssis hastely vpoun his fredome, he sall bruk the priuiledge of a stallanger for ane yeir and na langar, and all vtharis that ar vnfre, not examinit nor worthy to hald buiths, sall either be prentis to a maister for certain yeiris, or ellis, gif he be aigit, to be a feit man with a maister, and not to laubour his awn werk vnto the tyme that he be habill and worthie to be maister and do his dewtie thairfoir as said is. Item, it sall not be lauchfull to ony maister of the saidis crafts to ressett or resaif ane vthar mannis prentis as servand, nor gif him ony werk, sa lang as he is bunden to his maister at he cummis fra, and beis payit of his dewtie and fee. Item, that na commoun cramaris in the toun vse to sell or tapp ony hammermenis werk, nor regrat it agane till vthar mennis vse, and that all thir craftismen abouewritten sall convene quhen thame lykis, and to commoun vpoun the breking of thir statutes aboue exprimit, and to certifie the provest and baillies thairof that iustice and pwnitioun may be done thairvpoun quhen and how it requyris, and that every man brekar of thir forwrittin statutis pay for ilkane of thame, als aft as thay happin to be brokin, in his defalt pay viij s. to the reparatioun and habillimentis of thair altar, and specially that all men of the said craftis do and fulfil thair auld consuetude and vse to the vphald of devyne service at the said altar weikly and daly, and to the priest craft and altar as effeiris. And this till all quhom it efferis or may effer we mak knawin faythfully be thir our presentis, to the quhilkis in witnessing we haif gart hing our commoun seill of caus at Edinburgh, the secund day of May, the yeir of God a thousand four hundreth auchty and thre eiris.

NOTE

[1] Smith 1906, 181.

Glossary

backsprent Possibly the seventeenth-century term for the tumbler, which holds the bolt in either the locked or un-locked position. It could also be an internal part for setting the latch bolt continuously open; a snib?

baxter Baker

bow Part of a key that is left outside of a lock for applying pressure from the human hand to work the mechanism. There were many shapes and sizes throughout the centuries. Somewhat resembles a bow (as in bow and arrow), which probably gave rise to the name.

bolt Part of lock that is thrown from lock into door frame (jam) to prevent the door being opened. It is used as a bar to secure the lock and door to the keeper (jamband) and door frame.

bridge Possibly the term for warding inside the lock.

cordwainer Shoemaker. Also called 'cordiner'.

kist Scots word for chest, also called a 'chist'.

kist lock Lock used on a kist. Several different forms occurred throughout the centuries. Many involved some kind of bolt and sprent band mechanism.

pass key Key that opens more than one lock.

pass lock Any type of lock that is worked by the key of another lock. If a key for an outside door also opens the lock for a chamber door, then the two locks are pass locks.

pipe lock A lock which has a pipe key instead of a through key. The opposite of a through lock.

bhank Part of a key that goes inside the lock. Connected to the bit and part of the stem.

bhield Escutcheon, or key-hole cover.

bprent band Part of a lock – usually on a kist lock – that swings on a hinge or hinges into a position that would allow a shackle, attached to the back of said sprent band, to be engaged and held by the bolt of the lock. In this way, the sprent band, and whatever it is attached to, are held to the lock. For kists, the sprent band is usually fastened to the lid, while the lock is attached to the box front. When the bolt is thrown backward, it releases the sprent band, which swings up on its hinge and frees the lid.

standing vice Large vice attached to a bench with a long leg attached to the floor directly below. Also known as a post vice, or a leg vice.

stem Part of a key. Long and usually cylindrical; the main body of a key which connects the bow to the shank and bit.

study An anvil for working metal.

warding A series of obstacles inside the lock which 'ward' off false keys. They usually resemble 'C'-shaped fences, and come in a variety of shapes in cross section.

Bibliography

UNPUBLISHED PRIMARY SOURCES

EDINBURGH CITY ARCHIVES (ECA)

1826 *An Historical Sketch of the Municipal Constitution of the City of Edinburgh*. Edinburgh.

The Incorporation of Hammermen of Canongate. 'Hammermen Craft of the Canongate 1613–87', 69 SL.

The Incorporation of Hammermen of Edinburgh. 'Minute Books 1494–1937', ED008/1.

The Incorporation of Hammermen of Edinburgh. 'Sasines, Charters, Instruments, and other documents involving Hammermen and the Incorporation of Hammermen 1501–1686', ED008/2/26.

1558 Muster Roll, Burgh Records, Council Minutes, Vol. III, Folios 126v–137r.

NATIONAL MUSEUMS OF SCOTLAND (NMS)

Whitelaw, C. E. 'Transcripts of Edinburgh Hammermen Minute Books 1575–1556'.

PUBLISHED PRIMARY SOURCES

Amman, J. & Sachs, H. 1568 (1973 ed) *The Book of Trades (Ständebuch)*. New York.

APS 1814–75 *The Acts of the Parliaments of Scotland*, 12 Vols & Index. London.

Campbell, R. 1747 (1969 ed) *The London Tradesman*. Devon.

Chambers, E. 1728 (1752 ed) *Cyclopaedia*. London.

Commissioners of Excise 1890 *A List of Persons Concerned in the Rebellion*, SHS. Edinburgh.

Coupe, W. A. 1967 *The German Illustrated Broadsheet in the Seventeenth Century*, Vol. II. Baden-Baden.

Cranstoun, J. 1891 *Satirical Poems of the Time of the Reformation*, Vol. I, Scottish Text Society, Edinburgh.

Diderot, D. 1966 ed 'Serrurier', in *Encyclopédie ou Dictionnaire Raisonné des Sciences, des Arts et des Metiers, c. 1751–72*. Stuttgart-Bad Cannstatt.

Edgar, W. 1742 *The Plan of the City and Castle of Edinburgh*, as reprinted in Barrott, H. N. 2000 *Atlas of Old Edinburgh*. Edinburgh.

Edinburgh Apprentices 1906 *Register of Edinburgh Apprentices 1583–1666*, Grant, F. J. (ed) SRS. Edinburgh.

Edinburgh Apprentices 1929 *Register of Edinburgh Apprentices 1666–1700*, Watson, C. B. B. (ed) SRS. Edinburgh.

Edinburgh Burgesses 1929 *The Roll of Edinburgh Burgesses and Guild Brethren, 1406–1700*, Watson, C. B. B. (ed) SRS. Edinburgh.

Edinburgh Burgesses 1929 'The Roll of Edinburgh Burgesses and Guild Brethren, 1701–60', *in Register of Edinburgh Apprentices 1666–1700*, Watson, C. B. B. (ed) SRS. Edinburgh.

Edin Marriage Reg 1905–6 *Register of Marriages for the Parish of Edinburgh, 1595–1700*, Paton, H. (ed) SRS and 'Edinburgh Marriage Register, 1701–50', in *Register of Edinburgh Apprentices 1583–1666*, Grant, F. J. (ed) SRS. Edinburgh.

Edin Recs 1869–1976 *Extracts from the Records of the Burgh of Edinburgh 1403–1716*, 13 Vols, Marwick, J. D., Wood M. & Armet H. (eds) SBRS. Edinburgh.

Exchequer Rolls 1878–1908 *The Exchequer Rolls of Scotland*, Stuart, J. & Burnett, G. (eds). Edinburgh.

Gibson, A. & Smout, T. C. 2005 *Scottish Economic History Database, 1550–1780*, www.ex.ac.uk/~ajgibson/scotdata/scot_data base_home.html

Gordon of Rothemay, J. 1647 *Edinodunensis Tabulam*, Map of Edinburgh. Edinburgh. Online at www.nls.uk/maps

Jousse, M. 1627 *La Fidelle Ouverture de l'art de Serrurier*. La Fleche.

Luiken, J. 1694 (1704 ed) *Spiegel Van Het Menselyk Bedryf*. Amsterdam. Online at http://diglib.hab.de/drucke/lp-92/start.htm).

Moxon, J. 1703 (1989 ed) *Mechanick Excercises*. New Jersey.

MWA 1957 *Accounts of the Masters of Works, 1529–1615*, Vol. I, Paton, H. M. (ed). Edinburgh.

MWA 1982 *Accounts of the Masters of Works, 1616–49*, Vol. II, Imrie, J. & Dunbar, J. G, (eds). Edinburgh.

Neve, R. 1726 (1969 ed) *The City and Country Purchaser and Builder's* Dictionary. New York.

Paton, H. 1902 *Register of Interments in the Greyfriars Burying-Ground, Edinburgh 1658–1700*. Edinburgh.

Pennecuik, A. 1722 *An Historical Account of the Blue Blanket: or Crafts-Men's Banner*, reproduced in Colston, J 1891 *The Incorporated Trades of Edinburgh*. Edinburgh. *Post-Office Annual Directory*, 1806–53. Edinburgh.

'Rates of Customs' 1867 'The Book of the Rates of Customs and Valuation of Merchandises in Scotland AD 1612', in 1867 *Ledger of Andrew Halyburton*. Edinburgh.

Smith, D. 1996 *John Knox House*. Edinburgh.

Stow, J. 1994 *A Survey of London Written in the Year 1598*. Dover.

TA 1877–1978 *Accounts of the Lord High Treasurer of Scotland*, Vol. I–XIII, Dickson, T. (et al). Edinburgh.

Weigel, C. 1963 *Die Bauleuthe aus dem Ständebuch von Christoff Weigel, 1698*. München.

PUBLISHED SECONDARY SOURCES

Baillie, G. H. 2002 *Watchmakers and Clockmakers of the World*, Vol. 1. London.

Bain, E. 1887 *Merchant and Craft Guilds. A History of the Aberdeen Incorporated Trades*. Aberdeen.

Baker, P. H. J. & Law, R. J. 1999 *The English Watchmaker's Mandrel. Its Origins and Development*, reprinted from *Antiquarian Horology*, Vol. 24, Numbers 5 & 6. Ticehurst, East Sussex.

Bateson, D. 1987 *Scottish Coins*. Princes Risborough.

Bath, M. 2003 *Renaissance Decorative Painting in Scotland*. Edinburgh.

Ben-Amos, I. K. 1991 'Failure to Become Freemen: Urban Apprentices in Early Modern England', in *Social History*, Vol. 16. Cambridge.

Blair, C. 1995 *Scottish Firearms*. Bloomfield, Ontario.

Bray, S. 2001 *Making Clocks*. Swanley.

Bruton, E. 2000 *The History of Clocks & Watches*. London.

Caldwell, D. H. 1977 'A Wooden-stocked Fishtail Pistol', in *The Proceedings of the Society of Antiquaries of Scotland*, Vol. 108. Edinburgh.

Campbell, M. 2000 *Decorative Ironwork*. London.

Carr, H. 1954 *The Mason and the Burgh*. London.

Childs, J. 2003 *Warfare in the Seventeenth Century*. London.

Christianson, D. 2002 *Timepieces*. New York.

Clune, Revd G. 1943 *The Medieval Guild System*. Dublin.

Clutton, C., Baillie, G. H. & Ilbert, C. (eds) 1982 *Britten's Old Clocks and Watches and Their Makers*, Ninth Edition. London.

Colston, J. 1891 *The Incorporated Trades of Edinburgh*. Edinburgh.

Coutts, W. 1987 'Provincial Merchants and Society: A Study of Dumfries Based on the Registers of Testaments 1600–65', in Lynch, M. (ed) 1987 *The Early Modern Town in Scotland*. London.

Crossley, D. 1990 *Post-Medieval Archaeology in Britain*. London.

Cutmore, M. 1985 *The Pocket Watch Handbook*. London.

Dalgleish, G. & Maxwell, S. 1987 *The Lovable Craft 1687–1987*. Edinburgh.

D'Allemagne, H. R. 1968 *Decorative Antique Ironwork*. New York.

Dareau, M. J. 1997 *500 Years of Scottish Clockmaking*. Edinburgh.

Dennison, E. P. & Coleman, R. 1998 *Historic Dalkeith*. Edinburgh.

Dennison, P. 1998a 'Power to the People? The Myth of the Medieval Burgh Community', in Foster, S., Macinnes, A., & MacInnes, R. (eds) 1998 *Scottish Power Centres*. Glasgow.

Dingwall, H. M. 1994 *Late Seventeenth-Century Edinburgh: A Demographic Study*. Aldershot.

Dingwall, H. M. 1995 *Physicians, Surgeons and Apothecaries: Medical Practice in Seventeenth-Century Edinburgh*. East Linton.

Donaldson, G. 1998 *Scotland: James V – James VII*. Edinburgh.

Duley, A. J. 1997 *The Medieval Clock at Salisbury Cathedral*. Much Wenlock, Shropshire.

Edwards, P. 2000 *Dealing in Death: The Arms Trade and the British Civil Wars, 1638–52*. Stroud.

Edwards, R. & Ramsey, L. G. G. (eds) 1957 *The Early Georgian Period 1714–60*. London.

Eras, V. J. M. 1974 *Locks and Keys throughout the Ages*. Folkestone.

Farr, J. R. 2000 *Artisans in Europe, 1300–1914*. Cambridge.

Flett, I. & Cripps, J. 1988 'Documentary Sources', in Lynch, M. (et al) 1988 *The Scottish Medieval Town*. Edinburgh.

Foster, S, Macinnes, A., & MacInnes, R. (eds) 1998 *Scottish Power Centres*. Glasgow.

Friedrichs, C. R. 1979 *Urban Society in an Age of War: Nördlingen, 1580–1720*. Princeton.

Friedrichs, C. R. 2003 *The Early Modern City 1450–1750*. Harlow.

Gadd, I. A. & Wallis, P. (eds) 2002 *Guilds, Society & Economy in London 1450–1800*. London.

Gilbert, J. 1977 'The Usual Money of Scotland and Exchange Rates Against Foreign Coin', in Metcalf, D. M. (ed) 1977 *Coinage in Medieval Scotland*. Oxford.

Gilhooley, J, 1988 *A Directory of Edinburgh in 1752*. Edinburgh.

Greenlaw, J, 1999 *Longcase Clocks*. Princes Risborough.

Hallett, M. 2000 *Hogarth*. London.

Harris, S. 2002 *The Place Names of Edinburgh*. London.

Henson, G. 1831 (1970 ed) *Henson's History of the Framework Knitters*. Devon.

Hildebrand, K.-G. 1992 *Swedish Iron in the Seventeenth and Eighteenth Centuries*. Södertälje.

Holmes, N. 1998 *Scottish Coins: A History of Small Change in Scotland*. Edinburgh.

Houston, R. A. 1994 *Social Change in the Enlightenment: Edinburgh, 1660–1760*. Oxford.

Hume, I. N. 1969 *A Guide to Artifacts of Colonial America*. Philadelphia.

Joynson, P. 1996 *Local Past*. Aberfoyle.

Kagané, L. 1995 *Bartolomé Esteban Murillo: The 17th-Century Spanish Master*. Bournemouth.

Kauffman, H. J. 1995 *Metalworking Trades in Early America*. Mendham, NJ.

Kelvin, M. 1996 *The Scottish Pistol: Its History, Manufacture and Design*. London.

Kerrigan, M. 2001 *The Instruments of Torture*. Staplehurst.

London Museum 1975 *Medieval Catalogue*. London.

Loomes, B. 1998 *Brass Dial Clocks*. Woodbridge.

Lumsden, H. & Aitken, Revd P. H. 1912 *History of the Hammermen of Glasgow*. Paisley.

Lynch, M. 1981 *Edinburgh and the Reformation*. Edinburgh.

Lynch, M. (ed) 1987 *The Early Modern Town in Scotland*. London.

Lynch, M. (et al) 1988 *The Scottish Medieval Town*. Edinburgh.

Lynch, M. 1988 'Towns and Townspeople in Fifteenth-Century Scotland', in Thomson, J. A. F. 1988 *Towns and Townspeople in the Fifteenth Century*. Gloucester.

Lynch, M. 1989 'Continuity and Change in Urban Society 1500–1800', in Houston, R. A. & Whyte, I. D. (eds) 1989 *Scottish Society 1500–1800*. Cambridge.

Lynch, M. 2000 *Scotland: A New History*. London.

Mackenzie, W. M. 1949 *The Scottish Burghs*. Edinburgh.

Makey, W. 1987 'Edinburgh in Mid-Seventeenth Century', in Lynch, M. (ed) 1987 *The Early Modern Town in Scotland*. London.

Mandel, G. 2001 *Clefs*. Paris.

Marshall, G. 1992 *Presbyteries and Profits: Calvinism and the Development of Capitalism in Scotland, 1560–1707*. Edinburgh.

Martin, C. 1998 *Scotland's Historic Shipwrecks*. London.

Marwick, J. D. 1909 *Edinburgh Guilds and Crafts*. Edinburgh.

Maryon, H. 1971 *Metalwork & Enamelling*. New York.

Mason, S. A. 2000 *The History of the Worshipful Company of Framework Knitters*. Leicester.

McKean, C. 2000 *The Making of the Museum of Scotland*. Edinburgh.

Melling, J. K. 1988 *Discovering London's Guilds and Liveries*. Aylesbury.

Mende, M., *Das Alte Nürnberger Rathaus*, Band I., (Nürnberg, 1979).

Miller, G. (et al) 1991 *Approaches to Material Culture Research for Historical Archaeologists*. Pennsylvania.

Milton, G. 2002 *Samurai William*. London.

Molander, B. 1985 *Järn I Gamala Byggnader*. Stockholm.

Monk, E. 1994 *Keys: Their History & Collection*. Princes Risborough.

Mowat, S. 1994 *The Port of Leith*. Edinburgh.

National Museum of Antiquities of Scotland 1892 *Catalogue of the National Museum of Antiquities of Scotland*. Edinburgh.

Pfeiffer-Belli, E. 1979 *Schlüssel und Schloß*. München.

Pinkerton, R. M. & Windram, W. J. 1983 *Mylne's Court: Three Hundred Years of Lawnmarket Heritage*. Edinburgh.

Pride, G. L. 1996 *Dictionary of Scottish Building*. Edinburgh.

Reid, S. 1998 *All the King's Armies*. Staplehurst.

Ribbert, M. (et al) 1991 *Der Geshichte Treuer Hüter*. Ulm.

Ricketts, H. 1965 *Firearms*. London.

Robinson, M. (ed) 1992 *Concise Scots Dictionary*. Edinburgh.

Seaver, P. S. 1985 *Wallington's World: A Puritan Artisan in Seventeenth-Century London*. Stanford.

Sked, P. 1999 *Culross*. Edinburgh.

Smart Martin, A. 1991 'The Role of Pewter as Missing Artifact: Consumer Attitudes Toward Tablewares in Late 18th-Century Virginia', *in* Miller, G. (et al) 1991 *Approaches to Material Culture Research for Historical Archaeologists*. Pennsylvania.

Smith, D. R. 1985 'The Ironmill', *in* Smith, D. R. (ed) *Old Dalkeith*, Issue 2. Edinburgh.

Smith, J. 1903 *A Handbook and Directory of Old Scottish Clockmakers*. Edinburgh.

Smith, J. 1906 *The Hammermen of Edinburgh and Their Altar in St. Giles Church*. Edinburgh.

Smith, J. 1975 *Old Scottish Clockmakers from 1453 to 1850*. Wakefield.

Smout, T. C. 1985 *A History of the Scottish People 1560–1830*. London.

Soliday, G. L. 1974 *A Community in Conflict: Frankfurt Society in the 17th and Early 18th Centuries*. Hanover, NH.

Statistical Account 1845 *The Statistical Account of Edinburghshire by the Ministers of the Respective Parishes*. Edinburgh.

Stell, G. P. & Hay, G. D. 1995 *Bonawe Iron Furnace*. Edinburgh.

Stevenson, D. 1996 *King or Covenant? Voices from Civil War*. East Linton.

Stevenson, D. 1987 'The Burghs and the Scottish Revolution', *in* Lynch, M. (ed) 1987 *The Early Modern Town in Scotland*. London.

Strauss, G. 1966 *Nuremberg in the 16th Century*. New York.

Streeter, D. 1980 *Professional Smithing*. Mendham, NJ.

Swanson, H. 1999 *Medieval British Towns*. London.

Tabraham, C. (ed) 1999 *Edinburgh Castle*. Musselburgh.

Torrie, E. P. D. 1988 'The Guild in Fifteenth-Century Dunfermline', *in* Lynch, M. (et al) 1988 *The Scottish Medieval Town*. Edinburgh.

Turnbull, J. 2001 *The Scottish Glass Industry 1610–1750: 'To Serve the Whole Nation With Glass'*. Edinburgh.

Unwin, G. 1938 *The Guilds & Companies of London*. London.

Vaudour, C. 1980 *Clefs et Serrures*. Rouen.

Vogt, P. 2003 *Fayence und Steinzeug aus Vier Jahrhunderten*. München.

Wagner, M. 1980 *Das Alte Nürnberg*. Hürtgenwald.

Wagner, M. 1978 *Nürnberger Handwerker*. Wiesbaden.

Ward, J. P. 1997 *Metropolitan Communities: Trade Guilds, Identity and Change in Early Modern London*. Stanford.

Warden, A. J. 1872 *Burgh Laws of Dundee*. London.

Wayman, M. L. (ed) 2000 *The Ferrous Metallurgy of Early Clocks and Watches: Studies in Post Medieval Steel*. London.

Weatherill, L. 1996 *Consumer Behaviour & Material Culture in Britain 1660–1760*. London.

Webb, J. J. 1929 *The Guilds of Dublin*. London.

White, A. 1987 'The Impact of the Reformation on a Burgh Community: The Case of Aberdeen', *in* Lynch, M. (ed) 1987 *The Early Modern Town in Scotland*. London.

Whitelaw, C. E. 1923 'A Treatise on Scottish Hand Firearms of the XVIth, XVIIth, & XVIIIth Centuries', *in* Jackson, H. J. 1923 *European Hand Firearms of the Sixteenth, Seventeenth and Eighteenth Centuries*. London.

Whitelaw, C. E. 1977 *Scottish Arms Makers*. London.

Whyte, D. 2001 *Clock & Watch Makers of Edinburgh and the Lothians 1539–1900*. Edinburgh.

Whyte, I. D. 1987 'The Occupational Structure of Scottish Burghs in the Late Seventeenth Century', *in* Lynch, M. (ed) 1987 *The Early Modern Town in Scotland*. London.

Whyte, I. D. 1995 *Scotland Before the Industrial Revolution: An Economic and Social History c. 1050 – c. 1750*. London.

Wild, J. M. 2001 *Wheel and Pinion Cutting in Horology: A Historical and Practical Guide*. Marlborough.

Wood, L. I. 1905 *Scottish Pewter-ware and Pewter*. Edinburgh.

UNPUBLISHED SECONDARY SOURCES

Lindsay, J. S., unpublished scrapbook of photographs and drawings of wall anchors (Bayswater, *c.* 1945)

Lynch, M. 1998 unpublished paper on Edinburgh for Utrecht Conference. Edinburgh.

BIBLIOGRAPHY

UNPUBLISHED PHD THESES

Allen, A. M. 2005 *The Locksmith Craft in Early Modern Edinburgh*. (PhD thesis, University of Edinburgh).

Bennett, H. M. 1981 *The Origins and Development of the Scottish Hand-knitting Industry*. (PhD thesis, University of Edinburgh).

Caldwell, D. H. 1981 *Guns in Scotland: The Manufacture and Use of Guns and their Influence on Warfare from the Fourteenth Century to c. 1625*. (PhD thesis, University of Edinburgh).

McMillan, J. 1984 *A Study of the Edinburgh Burgess Community and its Economic Activities, 1600–80*. (PhD thesis, University of Edinburgh).

ARTEFACTS

National Museums of Scotland (NMS), Edinburgh, Collection of Locks and Keys, MJ, MK, K2002, L.

George Heriot's School, Edinburgh, Stonework Depicting a Goldsmith's Booth, above North Entrance.

Ulmer Museum, Ulm, Germany, Guild Boards, Inv. Nr.A.B.344.

Index

Aberdeen 2, 33, 62, 74, 79
Amsterdam 73
anchorsmiths 97
Angsberg 61
apothansherers 26
apprentices 6, 8–9, 10, 19–21, 29–37, 40, 42–4, 67, 73, 81–6, 91, 101, 103
armourers 6, 7, 9, 12, 14, 17, 24–6, 30, 41, 45, 47, 49, 52–6, 61–2

bailies 8, 10, 12, 17, 18, 41, 85–6, 90
bakers (*see also* baxters) 94
barbers (*see also* chirngeons) 7–8, 18, 57
baxters 1, 7–9, 11, 18, 57, 163
bell founders (*see also* founder) 14, 16–7, 26, 41, 45, 47, 49, 61, 65–7
bell hangers 136
beltmakers 14, 17, 25–6, 41, 45, 47, 49, 54–6, 61
Bennett, Dr 1
Berwick 5
Bishops Wars 21, 43–4
Blackfriars 6
blacksmiths 6, 7, 9, 12, 13, 16, 17, 24–7, 28, 41, 45, 46–9, 52–6, 61–3, 67, 73–4, 77, 97, 105, 107
Blois, France 49
bonnetmakers 1, 7–8, 11, 18, 57, 92–3
booths 31, 34, 36–9, 44, 48, 72–5, 90–6, 98–9, 101, 103–5, 107, 119, 164
bowers 8
boxmasters (*see also* treasurers) 12, 13, 26, 30, 33, 50–6, 61, 76, 107, 162
braziers (*see also* coppersmiths) 25–7, 49, 53, 56, 61
Bristo 32
buckler makers 6, 7, 9
builders 2, 113, 115
burgesses, burgess-ship 11, 19, 24–7, 29–34, 36–44, 46–8, 62–4, 67, 75, 77–9, 81–7, 90–2, 111
button-mould makers 14, 41, 45, 47

candlemakers 7–8, 121
Canongate 14, 16–17, 32, 68, 74–5, 90, 92, 164
cardmakers 17
Charles I 164
chirugeons (*see also* barbers) 7–8
Civil War 70
claspmakers 26
clerks 2, 13–14, 19, 27–8, 35–7, 42, 56, 67–8, 75, 78–9, 111
clockmakers 24, 30, 49, 54, 56, 61, 73–7, 80, 133, 162
coopers 6, 8
copper coinage 6
coppersmiths (*see also* braziers) 14, 24–6, 27, 30, 41, 45, 47–9, 53–6, 61
cordiners 10, 18, 57
cordwainers 7–8
corporatism 6, 22, 162, 164–5
councils 41–3, 56–7, 74, 90

Covenant, Wars of 21, 25, 44
craft riots 10
Cromwell, Oliver 79
cutlers 6, 7, 9, 12, 14, 24–7, 41, 45, 47–53, 55–6, 61, 90

dagmakers/pistolmakers 26, 31, 49, 52, 61, 65–9, 72–3, 87, 92
damaskers 14, 25, 41, 45, 47
Darien Scheme 20
David I 16, 120
Deacon Brodie 133, 142–3
deacons 6–7, 11–14, 18, 26, 28–30, 33, 36–7, 42, 50–7, 61, 68, 74, 76, 162
Dean of Guild 10, 29, 41, 44, 74
decreet arbitral of 1583 6, 38, 40, 43, 45–7, 56–7, 162–4
decreet arbitral of 1622 28
Diderot 77, 99–100, 110, 115, 129, 132
drapers 49
Dublin 165
dyers 8, 38

Edinburgh City Archives 1, 2, 19
Edinburgh Council 33
Elizabeth I 79
engravers 14, 26, 41, 45, 47
essays 2, 9, 13, 28–31, 35–7, 62, 67–8, 74–5, 80–7, 108–10, 120, 122, 132–4
Exeter 94

fairs 91
farriers 14, 25, 41, 45, 47, 61
fermorers 31
fishers 38
fishmongers 8
fleshers 7–8, 10–11, 18, 38
founders 8, 25, 27
framesmiths (*see also* stocking-frame makers) 61, 64, 78–80, 162
freemen 2, 9–10, 13–14, 19–21, 24–5, 27–30, 32–41, 46, 56, 64–5, 67–9, 75–6, 78–9, 81–7, 91, 109, 134
French Rage 40
furriers 8, 11, 18, 33, 57

Geneva 61
Glasgow 14, 33, 37, 70, 92, 127, 136
glaziers 8
glovers 8
goldsmiths 1, 6–8, 9–10, 18, 24, 49, 57, 61, 77, 92
gunlocks 69–72
gunsmiths 8, 14, 16, 17, 25, 28, 31–2, 41, 45, 47, 54, 56, 61, 64–5, 67–9, 73, 77, 80, 87, 162
gunstockers 68
guilds, guildry 1–2, 5–6, 9–10, 14, 18, 24, 29–30, 38–49, 56–7, 61–3, 67, 73–4, 85–6, 96, 113, 162–5

Hammermen of Aberdeen, Incorporation of 8, 33
Hammermen of Canongate, Incorporation of 17, 77

INDEX

Hammermen of Edinburgh, Incorporation of 1–2, 5, 7, 11, 13–14, 17–22, 24–5, 27, 29–30, 32–4, 36, 38, 40, 42, 44, 46–9, 56–7, 61–4, 66–8, 73–5, 78, 80, 90–1, 93, 101, 107, 110, 133–4, 136, 162–4, 166–7
Hammermen of Glasgow, Incorporation of 33
Hammermen, Societies of 16
hatmakers 7–8
Holyrood 16, 34
hookmakers 61
hourmakers (*see also* watchmakers and knockmakers) 31, 61, 75
Hume, Ivor Noël 2, 124, 127, 129

incorporated trades 12, 20, 38, 45, 107
   committees 13, 28
   freedom 9–10, 14–15, 21, 29–33, 35–8, 41–3, 74, 81–7, 91, 120
Incorporation of Mary's Chapel 6–7, 33
incorporation 6–11, 34, 57, 61, 81–7, 136, 162, 164–5

jackmakers 61
Jacobite Rebellion 1745 34
James II 14
James III 5, 90
James IV 65–6
James V 66
James VI 164
jewellers 8
journeymen 2, 6, 8–9, 19–21, 29–36, 38, 73

kirkmaster (*see* deacon)
knockmakers (*see also* watchmakers) 8, 26, 48–9, 56, 61, 64, 73–5, 77, 85–6

Law, Alexander, 37
Laws of the Four Burghs 5, 38
Leith 14, 16–17, 32
litsters 8
locksmiths 8, 12, 14, 16–7, 24–7, 28–9, 31–2, 41, 45, 47–56, 61–5, 67–9, 72–5, 78–84, 162
   history of craft 62–7
   joined trades 61, 64–80
   keys 119–22, 125–27, 133, 135–6, 157, 159, 162
   locks 109–16, 119–30
   materials 103–5, 163
   processes 116–18
   services 115–16
   tools and techniques 91–2, 95–103
   work produced 96–7, 107–13, 115, 119–20, 133
   workplace 90–8
London 20, 32, 49, 61, 91, 164
lorimers 6–7, 9, 12, 14, 17, 24–7, 30, 40–1, 45, 47–50, 52–4, 56, 61, 65, 67–8, 70, 73, 90, 115
Louis XIII 1
Lynch, Michael 6, 10–11, 14–15

Magdalene Chapel 6, 12–13, 16, 27–8, 35–6, 57, 127
markets 90–2
Marwick 5, 39, 163
Mary of Guise 10
masons 6–8, 10, 29, 33, 42, 57, 113, 115, 163
masters 6, 8–9, 12–14, 19–21, 24–6, 28–38, 40, 44, 46, 48, 54, 56–7, 61–2, 65, 68, 73–6, 91, 96, 109, 116, 122, 132–3

mathematical instrument-makers 41, 45, 47
melters (*see also* founders) 65, 67, 73
Merchant Company (1681) 44, 56, 164
merchants 5–6, 9–10, 14, 20–2, 29–31, 38, 43–4, 46, 49, 56–7, 91–3, 103, 162–4
militia 39, 43
ministers 31
Moxon, Joseph 2, 97–104, 116–8, 124

National Archives of Scotland 1
National Museum of Scotland 1–2, 74, 118–36, 137–159, 162–3
Neighbourhood Court 10
Nuremberg, Germany (*see* Nürnberg, Germany)
Nürnberg, Germany 1, 10, 33, 73, 77, 94–6, 98, 100, 125, 129

padlocksmiths 107
painters 8, 26
Paris 73
periwigmakers 30
pewterers 8, 12, 14, 24–6, 41, 45, 47–9, 51–6, 61–2, 162
pinmakers 14, 25, 41, 45, 47, 61
plumbers 8
portioners 31
Portsburgh 16–17, 32
Potterrow 16–17, 81
potters 16, 65
poulterers 8
provosts 10, 12, 41, 57, 122

Reformation 2, 10–11, 163
Restoration 21
Reval, Estonia 24, 61
Royal Society of London for Improving Knowledge 2
Rynd, Janet 6

saddlers 6–7, 9, 12, 14, 17, 24–7, 29, 41, 45–56, 61–2, 115, 162
sasines 10, 90
seals of cause 7–11, 22, 24, 27, 31, 56, 62–3, 90, 162–3, 166–7
servants 5, 7–9, 12, 19–21, 24, 29–34, 36, 38, 41, 65, 74, 78–9, 81–6, 91–2
shearsmiths 8, 12, 14, 25–6, 41, 45, 47, 49–50, 53, 56
sheathmakers 14, 25–7, 41, 45, 47
shoemakers 38
sievewrights 8
skinners 1, 7–8, 11, 18, 57, 90
slaters 8
smiths 16, 24–5, 48–9, 61–2, 90, 97, 113, 115
Smout, T.C. 37
spurriers 24, 41, 45, 47, 61, 92–3
St Eloi 2, 6
St Giles Kirk 2, 6, 10
St Leonards 6
Statuta Guilde 5
stocking-frame makers (*see also* framesmiths) 14, 25, 41, 45, 47
surgeons 1, 10, 43, 57
swordslippers 14, 24–5, 41, 45, 47

tailors 7–8, 11, 17–8, 31, 43, 57, 92–3
taxation 11
town council 10–11, 18, 75
Trades Maiden Hospital 1, 13, 28, 36–7, 163
treasurers (*see also* boxmasters) 10, 12

175

Ulm, Germany 61–2, 124, 163
unfreemen 11, 19, 21, 27, 30, 43–4, 91
Union of Crowns 20
Union of Parliaments 20–1, 57, 68, 134, 162
upholsterer 8

warding 1, 6, 29, 62, 109, 115, 117, 121, 124, 132, 134–6, 162
warehouses 92
watch/knockmakers 14, 16, 25, 28, 31–2, 41, 45, 47, 55–6, 61, 64, 68, 73–5, 76–7, 85–6, 97

waulkers 7–8, 11, 18, 57
Weatherkill, Lorna 48, 135
weavers (*see* websters)
websters (*see also* weavers) 7–8, 10, 18, 57
White, Ian D. 18
white-iron smith 8, 14, 25–7, 30, 41, 45, 47, 49, 55–6, 61
wholesalers 93
workmen 113
wrights 6–8, 10, 17, 29, 31, 33, 57, 68, 78, 113, 115, 163
writers 31

26.